Crime in the Digital Age

controlling telecommunications and cyberspace illegalities

PN Grabosky

Russell G Smith

with the assistance of

Paul Wright

Transaction Publishers • The Federation Press
1998

Published in North America by
    Transaction Publishers
    Rutgers University
    New Brunswick
    New Jersey 08903
    United States of America
    Ph: (732) 445 2280
    Fax: (732) 445 3138

Published in Australasia and the rest of
the world by
    The Federation Press
    71 John St, Leichhardt, NSW, 2040
    PO Box 45, Annandale, NSW, 2038
    Australia
    Ph: (02) 9552 2200
    Fax: (02) 9552 1681

National Library of Australia Cataloguing-in-Publication data:

Grabosky, Peter N (Peter Nils),
Crime in the digital age: controlling telecommunications and cyberspace illegalities

Bibliography.
Includes index.
ISBN 1 86287 269 4 (pbk)
ISBN 1 86287 270 8

1. Computer crimes - Australia. 2. Computer crimes - Australia - Prevention. 3.
Telecommunication - Law and legislation - Australia. 4. Telecommunication - Australia -
Corrupt practices. I. Smith, Russell G. II. Title.

364.1680994

Transaction Publishers: ISBN 1-56000-379-0 cloth
                         ISBN 0-7658-0458-1 paper

Typeset by The Federation Press, Leichhardt, NSW.
Printed by Ligare Pty Ltd, Riverwood, NSW.

Contents

Acknowledgments

This book could not have been written without the generous support and encouragement of many people. Adam Graycar suggested one day early in 1995 that we embark upon a new direction of inquiry, and seek assistance from the Telstra Fund for Social and Policy Research in Telecommunications. This we did, successfully. We are grateful to the Fund, and to its Administrator, Anita Hopkins, for their support.

We would like to express our special appreciation to our collaborator Paul Wright, for his technological insights generally, for sharing his knowledge of cryptography, as well as for his contributions to Chapters Two and Ten.

We were also fortunate to have received generous and valuable advice from Dennis Challinger, Ken Day, David Harris, Allan Kearney, John Langdale, Bruce Matthews, Phil Masters, Frank Nolan, John Pinnock, Greg Williams, and Mick Williams.

We thank staff of the JV Barry Library at the Australian Institute of Criminology for their exceptional support in suggesting and locating relevant material throughout the course of our project.

Bob Anderson, John Braithwaite, Simon Bronitt, Dorothy Denning, Richard Harding, Richard Hundley, Colin Scott, Haydn Strang and Glenn Wahlert read and commented on all or part of the manuscript, and we are particularly indebted to them for their guidance.

Finally, we were privileged to be able to share our findings with a variety of government agencies, colleagues and users of digital technologies as our work progressed. We hope they found them to be of some use. If, despite the best efforts of all of those named above, any errors or shortcomings remain, we assume full responsibility.

PN Grabosky
Russell G Smith
Australian Institute of Criminology
Canberra

Acronyms

ANI	Automatic Number Identification
ARPANET	Advanced Research Projects Agency Network
ATM	Automated/Automatic Teller Machine
BBS	Bulletin Board System
BITS	Bank Interchange and Transfer System
CADS	Computer Anomaly Detection System
CERT	Computer Emergency Response Team
CHAPS	Clearing House Automated Payments System (England)
CHIPS	Clearing House Interbank Payments System (US)
CND	Calling Number Display
CRT	Cathode-Ray Tube
DISA	Direct Inwards System Access
EDD	Electronic Data Delivery System
EFTPOS	Electronics Funds Transfer at Point of Sale
EMR	Electromagnetic Radiation
ESN	Electronic Serial Number
GSM	Groupe Speciale Mobile
HFC	hybrid coaxial cable
IDD	International Direct Dialling
IMEI	International Mobile Electronic Identity
MIN	Mobile Identification Number
PABX	Private Automatic Branch Exchange
PIN	Personal Identification Number
RITS	Reserve Bank Information and Transfer System
RTGS	Real Time Gross Settlement
SET	Secure Electronic Transactions
SHERIFF	Statistical Heuristic Engine to Reliably and Intelligently Fight Fraud
SIM	Subscriber Identification Module
STD	Subscriber Trunk Dialling
SWIFT	Society for Worldwide Interbank Financial Telecommunications (Belgium)
TEMPEST	Transient Electromagnetic Pulse Emanation Standard
UTP	unshielded twisted pair

Table of Cases

TABLE OF CASES

Table of Legislation

TABLE OF LEGISLATION

1

INTRODUCTION

Willie Sutton, a notorious American bank robber of fifty years ago, was once asked why he persisted in robbing banks. "Because that's where the money is", he is said to have replied.[1] The theory that crime follows opportunity has become established wisdom in criminology; opportunity reduction has become one of the fundamental principles of crime prevention.[2]

Perhaps the most significant development of our time, even more significant than the end of the cold war, is the revolution in information technology which we are currently experiencing. Recent and anticipated changes in telecommunications technology in light of the convergence of communications and computing are truly breathtaking, and have already had a significant impact on many aspects of life. Banking, stock exchanges, air traffic control, telephones, electric power, and a wide range of institutions of health, welfare, and education are largely dependent on information technology and telecommunications for their operation. We are moving rapidly to the point where it is possible to assert that "everything depends on software" (Edwards 1995). The exponential growth of this technology, the increase in its capacity and accessibility, and the decrease in its cost, has brought about revolutionary changes in commerce, communications, entertainment, and most other institutions. Along with this greater capacity, however, comes greater vulnerability. Telecommunications technology has begun to provide criminal opportunities of which Willie Sutton would never have dreamed.

The enormous benefits of telecommunications are not without cost. Since Wheatstone and Cooke first patented their system of communication by the means of electromagnetic impulses carried over wires in 1837, crimes have been committed either through the misuse of telecommunications equipment, or against telecommunications equipment. Every technological development has provided a new opportunity for criminality which has often been exploited. Unfortunately, as we move into the 21st century where broadband telecommunications services such as interactive video telephony will become widely available, the opportunities for criminality will be enhanced. Now is the time to raise awareness of the potential for the criminal abuse of telecommunications technology, and to develop strategic responses to the law enforcement and regulatory challenges which this new technology brings.

This volume provides an overview of telecommunications and crime. The overall objects of this work are to identify:

---

1   There remains considerable doubt whether the words were Sutton's (he denies ever having said them), or rather those of an imaginative journalist. See Keyes (1993: 16).
2   See Clarke (1992, 1995).

- current and emerging forms of criminality involving telecommunications systems as the instruments and/or the targets of criminal activity;
- organisational and regulatory shortcomings which facilitate the commission of the illegality in question;
- difficulties arising in the detection, investigation, sentencing, and other outcomes of the legal process;
- countermeasures to minimise future risk of telecommunications crime, without inflicting collateral harm or imposing excessive costs.

We will also discuss issues arising out of the global reach of telecommunications. It has become trite to describe the ways telecommunications systems have, figuratively speaking, made the world a smaller place. Few can now ignore the fact that financial decisions made in London or Tokyo quickly reverberate around the world, and have an impact locally. Celebrity images manufactured in Hollywood become the new icons in Russia; pornographic images crafted in Denmark are accessible to 15-year-olds in Australia. The corresponding potential for trans-jurisdictional offending will pose formidable challenges to the successful mobilisation of effective countermeasures.

This book will conclude with a discussion of the most appropriate regulatory configuration to address the various forms of telecommunications-related crime identified. The ideal configuration may be expected to differ, depending upon the activity in question, but is likely to entail a mix of law enforcement, technological and market solutions. Moreover, these configurations will continually evolve in line with inevitable technological developments.

Before we begin to explore specific forms of telecommunications-related illegality, a brief overview of telecommunications technology and its applications is appropriate.

The telecommunications environment

Electronic communications technology developed early in the nineteenth century, initially with telegraphs connected by wires and later with wireless telegraphy and telephony services (see generally, Durie 1988). Some of the more important telecommunications milestones for Australia include the use of the first telegraph service in Melbourne in 1854, the installation of a submarine telegraph link to Tasmania in 1859 and the connection of Australia with the rest of the world on 19 November 1871. In 1918, test radio signals were passed between Sydney and Britain and by 1922, a direct twenty-four hour wireless telegraphy service to Britain was established, with a radio telephone service being offered in 1930. A national Telex system began operation in 1954 which was shortly followed by the introduction of Subscriber Trunk Dialling (STD) in 1956. International Direct Dialling (IDD) began in the mid-1980s and in 1988, Integrated Digital Services Network commenced operation which enabled the transmission of combinations of voice, text, image and data. At present, Telstra alone has some 8.6 million customers who make around twenty-five million calls a day (Harris 1995), which enabled Telstra to return a A\$2.3 billion profit for the financial year 1995-96.

Over the same year, it has been estimated that the market for telephones in Australia grew in volume between 11 and 13 per cent (Ries 1996). A recent survey of 3258 Australian households revealed that 96.8 per cent of those surveyed had a telephone connected, 24.1 per cent had a mobile telephone, 13.4 per cent had a cordless telephone, while 4.3 per cent had a car phone (Australian Bureau of Statistics 1996).

Globally, the volume of international traffic on the public telephone network has grown considerably in recent years. With an annual growth rate of 12 per cent, it has been estimated that by the year 2000, 106 billion minutes of international traffic will be generated annually by 1.2 billion telephone sub-scribers (http://www.telegeography.com:80/Publications/tg96_intro.html).

The traditional system that enables telephone messages to be placed into a system and switched into a trunk is called switching. A loop which connects the subscriber to a telephone exchange provides a path for two-way speech signals as well as the signals used for ringing, switching, and supervisory functions. The telephone set on the customer's premises consists of a transmitter for converting voice energy into electrical energy, a receiver for performing the reverse process, and appropriate circuitry for carrying out the necessary additional functions.

The exchange to which a telephone is connected must make the connection between the telephone and an appropriate outgoing trunk. The connection is made by a switching system located at the exchange. Since the number of trunks is typically smaller than the number of subscriber lines, there is a great deal of line concentration, which in turn is possible because individual customers use their telephones only a small portion of the time.

The appropriate connection is obtained from the number dialled by the subscriber. As each number is dialled, a two-frequency tone is generated and sent to the exchange. The resultant train of tones is decoded at the exchange and used to switch the call to the appropriate destination.

The term "digital", as used in the title of this book, refers to the elements of information which are transmitted. Just as matter is comprised of atoms, so it is that sound frequencies and visual images can be "broken down" and reduced to a string of 1's and 0's.[3] Developments in information processing technology now enable the storage and transmission of sound and pictures with unprecedented speed and clarity. The use of the term "Digital Age" recognises that these developments are having profound effects on contemporary society.

By far the most important development in telephony in recent years has been the introduction of cellular mobile telephone services which were introduced in Sydney and Melbourne around 1987. There are now approximately three million mobile telephone subscribers in Australia who spend between A$10 and A$500 a month on their calls, thus creating a market estimated to be worth A$3.5 billion a year (Crowe 1996a). The analogue mobile telephone network in Australia is provided by Telstra at present with Optus selling services on that network. The digital networks are provided by three carriers (Telstra, Optus and Vodafone) and about twenty companies sell mobile telephone services on these networks. At present, Telstra has 1.77 million analogue and 230,000 digital

---

3   For a lucid exposition of digitisation and its implications, see Negroponte (1995).

subscribers, Optus has 750,000 analogue and 250,000 digital subscribers while Vodafone, which entered the mobile telephone market in 1993, has 150,000 digital subscribers (O'Neill 1996). As existing analogue services are phased out, the number of digital mobile telephone subscribers will increase. By the year 2000, the Bureau of Transport and Communications Economics has estimated that mobile telephone sales will have reached between five and seven million while Optus has forecast this to be closer to eight million (O'Neill 1996). The Cellular Telecommunications Industry Association estimates that there are 36 million cellular telephone subscribers at present in the United States (Cunningham 1996).

With mobile cellular telephones, a number of features permit billing of a subscriber who may be calling from anywhere in the world (see generally Brooks and Davis 1994, and Dancer 1996). Analogue telephones require two important pieces of data to be transmitted each time a call is placed. The first is the electronic serial number (ESN), which is similar to the vehicle identification number on a car. It identifies the manufacturer of the telephone as well as the serial number of the telephone. The second item is the mobile identification number (MIN). This is the ten-digit area code and telephone number that is assigned to the telephone. When a call is made or received, these two pieces of information are sent to the nearest cell site or base station. The cell site verifies that the user is a valid subscriber, and once the call is placed, the numbers inform the cell site operator whom to bill. Every few minutes while the mobile telephone is switched on but not being used for an actual call, both numbers are again transmitted so that the network is able to verify the location of the telephone.

Digital mobile telephones convert all signals and numbers into a digital data stream for transmission. This has a number of advantages, including the ability to encrypt signals for greater security and the ability to enter into agreements which enable calls to be made globally; in Australia using the GSM, a system named after a European organisation called the "Groupe Speciale Mobile" (Dancer 1996). Subscribers are identified to the network by a Subscriber Identification Module (SIM) which is registered with the network operator and enables calls to be billed to that number including calls made on overseas networks. Removing the SIM card enables the liability for calls to be transferred to another mobile telephone.

Networked, or "online" services are another area of rapid development. Such services have been defined as "a system of electronic information accessed through the use of a public telecommunications network which allows for the transfer in both directions of text, graphics, sound and video between a user, other users and the system" (Australian Broadcasting Authority 1995).

The Internet is the world's largest computer network. Extending across the globe, it was originally developed by the United States Defence Department in the late 1960s in order to protect military communications from interference from external sources. The original network was known as the Advanced Research Projects Agency Network (ARPANET) which circumvented the need for a centralised super-computer by interconnecting remote terminals, thus reducing vulnerability to military attack. The Internet of today allows direct and immediate communication between computer terminals anywhere in the world without mediation by a central computer (see Kassel and Kassel 1995 for a review of the development of the Internet).

A wide range of online services are provided both publicly through the Internet and privately through proprietary or closed networks which obtain access to the Internet via so-called gateways. Public online services include electronic mail, which enables users to send text messages and attached files to other specific users via personal computers; newsgroups, which operate on the public Usenet system and which enable information to be transmitted publicly between users; Internet relay chat which operates like newsgroups but in real time rather than subject to delayed transmission and the World Wide Web which permits publishers to present text, graphics, sound and video to users who are able to search for and to retrieve information using a variety of client systems or browsers. Online services also include such private networks as private automatic branch exchanges (PABX) and automated teller machines (ATM).

The Internet is an international environment in which individual nation states are interconnected. Data networks are connected with one another by a common set of protocols such that text and images can be sent and received within seconds throughout the world. Communications are able to be made between computers located in one building or organisation via a local area network, or over greater distances through metropolitan and wide area networks.

Four groups of participants are involved in providing online services. **Network infrastructure providers or licensed telecommunications carriers** such as Telstra, Optus, Sprint, MCI, and British Telecom, provide the technology necessary for electromagnetic impulses to be conveyed across existing telephone lines. **Online access providers** are organisations which enable users to gain access to networks while also providing support and other services for users. **Content providers** are those individuals who publish material, created either by themselves or by others, which is transmitted on networks. Finally, **users** are those consumers of online services who gain access to material on networks. There is considerable overlap between the activities of members of each of these groups as each may take on the roles of the other to a certain extent, although there are, in most nations, specific regulatory restrictions on who may be a carrier.

Recently, telecommunications systems have been used not only to communicate on a one-to-one basis but communally in the form of electronic discussion groups. Bulletin Board Systems (BBS), for example, use telecommunications networks to link individuals via their computers throughout the globe and provide the ability to send messages between users, to upload and download computer files and to communicate freely.

In 1992, there were between 30,000 and 40,000 Bulletin Boards in operation in Australia. This was the second largest number following the United States (Wallman 1994). Throughout the world there are estimated to be between 60,000 and 100,000 Bulletin Board operators in business (United States, Information Infrastructure Task Force 1995).

The Commonwealth *Report of the Computer Bulletin Board Systems Task Force* explains Bulletin Board Systems as follows:

The primary function of a Bulletin Board System is a source of shareware software (generally obtained via links to other computer systems in Australia and overseas). They provide the ability to send messages between users of the BBS, and or the ability to upload and download computer files (for example games, computer applications, shareware software, images or text files). They also provide a communication service for users, often in the form of electronic discussion groups or forums. Some BBS are currently connected to worldwide messaging networks which facilitate global messages or software transfers (Commonwealth of Australia, Attorney-General's Department and Department of Communication and the Arts 1994a).

Bulletin Boards have a number of functions some of which are legal, for example those operated by commercial organisations such as software companies to assist licensees with software applications, or organisations which provide information regarding conferences or events, and others which are illegal and provide pirated copies of software and other material. Finally, there are those Bulletin Boards for which a registration fee is required which provide services such as online searching facilities and the dissemination of adult material.

Many Bulletin Board users are able to gain access from home via modems and the public telephone network. Users simply dial the number of the Board through their personal computer in order to gain access to a central or "host" computer system. They generally register their name and other details to gain access rights and are then given a password and often charged annual access fees.

Generally, those who use online services include private individuals as well as business organisations. Access to many sites is free of charge while other services are subscription-based with access dependent upon payment of a fee for a given period of time.

One of the most recent developments in telecommunications is the so-called "smart phone", a telephone with a small display panel which enables simple online activities to be carried out including access to the Internet and electronic mail. In 1995, 250,000 smart phones were sold in the United States, although it is thought that the market may not be as great as initially anticipated (Shiver 1996).

Around 600,000 Australians are already connected to the Internet, some through educational and business enterprises and others privately at home through the use of modems connected to personal computers. A recent survey of Australian households estimated that 262,000 individuals use the Internet from home (Australian Bureau of Statistics 1996). Globally, the Internet consists of more than 9.4 million server computers linked to over 120 million users. At the end of 1993, the Internet was already carrying approximately 45 billion packets of information a month (Kassel and Kassel 1995). Some 95 million electronic mail messages were sent worldwide in 1995 (Meredith 1996). In January 1996, it was estimated that there were over 170,000 commercial organisations making use of the Internet, while a survey conducted by Mastercard and Visa in September 1995, found that 32 per cent of Internet users had purchased goods over the Internet (Watson 1997).

It has been estimated that by the year 1999, there will be some 200 million Internet users (*Janet Reno v American Civil Liberties Union*, 26 June

1997, Supreme Court of the United States, No. 96-511). In the near future, broadband services will be made available such as those which enable interactive video images to be transmitted and received across fibre optic cables using digital technology which will make services provided on the Internet more attractive to users.

In the field of television broadcasting, the development of cable technology has taken on considerable importance in the United States and Britain. It has recently been estimated that the cable industry in the United States is worth the equivalent of A$25 billion with more than 11,000 cable operators servicing over 57 million paying customers (Schieck 1995).

By most indications, the 21st century will be the century of electronic commerce, and the basic medium of this commerce will be electronic funds transfer. Electronic funds transactions are carried out via computer networks connected over telecommunications systems. Telstra, the principal telecommunications carrier in Australia, originally developed an overlay network for banks called "Transend" which used a conventional packet switch network for information transport and specially provided front-end access and additional management and control so as to match the ability of the more advanced privately developed transaction networks. There is currently debate about whether the banks will continue to use Transend or will utilise the Internet instead (Amos 1995).

Banks use a variety of computer systems with which to convey electronic signals along telephone wires. Westpac, for example, uses a system called "Handyway" which connects branch computers and Automated Teller Machines (ATMs) to the bank's "host computer" at head office via Telstra's Austpac network (Tyree 1990).

Data passing through such a network are protected using a publicly available algorithm which encodes messages and an electronic key known to the sender and the recipient. Personal Identification Numbers (PINs), for example, travel in encrypted form from a terminal to the host computer where authorisation occurs. The major security risk associated with such a system lies in the possibility of the encryption keys being ascertained, in which case data within the system can be revealed or manipulated (Sullivan 1987; see also the discussion of cryptography, below).

Data travelling through banking networks are required to comply with specified security standards. In Australia, compliance with Australian Standard AS2805 is required, although not all financial institutions are achieving this standard at present (Sneddon 1995).

Systems may also be operated either "online", in which case there is direct real-time communication between the customer and the host computer, or "off-line", in which case the transaction is recorded on a computer for later transmission to the host computer at the bank's head office (Meijboom and Stuurman 1988). This provides another source of security risk as an off-line transaction may be carried out without immediate verification of the amount held in credit on behalf of the customer at head office, thus enabling the customer to overdraw an account.

The enforcement challenge

The size of the problem

It is understandably common for one concerned about a given social problem to seek some indication of its incidence, prevalence, cost, or some other measure of magnitude. Unfortunately, telecommunications-related crimes, unlike bank robberies or fatal motor vehicle accidents, tend to defy quantification. Some of the most deftly perpetrated offences with or against telecommunications systems are never detected, not even by their victims; of those which are, some are concealed from authorities because disclosure could prove embarrassing or commercially inconvenient to victims.

Quantification can also be deceptive. Throughout this discussion we provide estimates of the financial losses suffered by the victims of telecommunications crime. Often these amount to billions of dollars lost by organisations such as large telecommunications carriers and financial institutions. Although the magnitude of such losses may be difficult to grasp, the telecommunications and computer industries are of such size that figures of this nature are readily understandable. Some estimates need to be treated with caution, however, as they are based on figures extrapolated from relatively small surveys to represent losses suffered by industries which have an enormous customer base and deal daily in turnovers amounting to vast sums of money. In assessing the global impact of such crime, however, it is important to consider the losses which have clearly been documented, and there are abundant examples of substantial and quantifiable sums being stolen throughout the world.

There are other instances in which relatively small sums may be involved, but these, too, may be important to consider. What appears to be a trivial matter may in fact be the tip of a very big iceberg indeed. A classic illustration has been provided by Stoll (1991) whose pursuit of a US$0.75 accounting error in a computer account led to an international espionage ring.

Even qualitative descriptions can be illusory. Many people, regardless of their calling, are inclined to accentuate their accomplishments. Telecommunications criminals are no exception. While some thrive on anonymity, others seek notoriety. This latter group often embroider their activities. There may be significant gaps between what they do, what they say they do, and what they think they do. Law enforcement agencies, on the other hand, have been known to overstate the magnitude of a problem in order to justify maintaining or enhancing their resource base. Other actors who arguably have commercial incentives to accentuate the gravity of a problem include the security industry and the news media.

Beyond the reluctance of victims to report, the technologies of secrecy and anonymity noted above often make detection of the offender extremely difficult. Those who seek to mask their identity on computer networks are often able to do so, by means of "looping", or "weaving" through multiple sites in a variety of nations. Anonymous remailers and encryption devices can shield one from the scrutiny of all but the most determined and technologically sophisticated regulatory and enforcement agencies. Some crimes do not result in detection or loss until some time after the event. Considerable time may elapse before the activation of a computer virus, or between the insertion of a "logic bomb" and its detonation.

Extraterritorial issues

One of the more significant aspects of telecommunications-related crime is its global reach. While international offending is by no means a uniquely modern phenomenon, the globalisation of telecommunications significantly enhances the ability of offenders to commit crimes in one country which will affect individuals in a variety of other countries. This has profound implications for detection, investigation and prosecution of offenders.

Two problems arise in relation to the prosecution of telecommunications offences which have an international aspect: first, the determination of where the offence occurred in order to decide which law to apply and, secondly, obtaining evidence and ensuring that the offender can be located and tried before a court. Both these questions raise complex legal problems of jurisdiction and extradition (see Commonwealth of Australia 1996, Chapter 4; Lanham, Weinberg, Brown and Ryan 1987).

Even if one is able to decide which law is applicable, further difficulties may arise in applying that law. In a unitary jurisdiction, such as New Zealand, where there is one law and one law enforcement agency, determining and applying the appropriate law is difficult enough. In federal systems, such as Australia and the United States, however, extraterritorial law enforcement becomes more difficult. The principal difficulty concerns the wide variety of laws which exist in different jurisdictions.[4] In Australia, this problem is being addressed at present by the Model Criminal Code Officers Committee of the Standing Committee of Attorneys-General which is drafting uniform criminal legislation for introduction in each Australian jurisdiction.

Because each of the offences considered in this book takes place with the use of computer networks linked via telephone connections, many of the offences involved come within the federal jurisdiction of the Commonwealth of Australia. The enforcement of federal offences, such as those to do with telecommunications, federal government computers or facilities, and banking, is the responsibility of federal law enforcement agencies which are usually best equipped to carry out such investigations, and trained in the investigation of crimes which happen to involve an extraterritorial element.

Criminal activities committed from across the globe, however, pose even greater problems. Sovereign governments are finding it difficult to exercise control over online behaviour at home, not to mention abroad. As a result, regulation by territorially-based rules may prove to be inappropriate for these types of offences (Post 1995).

Extraterritorial law enforcement costs are also often prohibitive. Moreover, the cooperation across international boundaries in furtherance of such enforcement usually requires a congruence of values and priorities which, despite prevailing trends towards globalisation, exists only infrequently.

---

4   In other federal systems, such as Canada and Germany, relevant law is a responsibility of national government. For the German example, see Martin (1996).

Images, ideas, and practices regarded as perfectly acceptable in one place may be regarded as heinous in another. The authorities in one jurisdiction who are untroubled by electronic depictions of nudity, the works of Salman Rushdie, or the virtues of Tibetan independence, are unlikely to expend much time and effort in assisting the authorities in those jurisdictions who are offended by such content.

It has, for example, taken decades to achieve a modest consensus about the merits of international mutual assistance in furtherance of combating drug traffic and money laundering. Even in those nations characterised by agreement in principle, the actual implementation can be difficult (Nadelmann 1993). Similar problems exist in relation to international copyright regulation and banking arrangements.

Other issues which may complicate investigation entail the logistics of search and seizure during real time, the sheer volume of material within which incriminating evidence may be contained, and the encryption of information, which may render it entirely inaccessible, or accessible only after a massive application of decryption technology (see below).

Additional problems are reflected in the difficulty of exercising national sovereignty over capital and information flows. Jurisdictional issues may arise from transborder online transmission. If an online financial newsletter originating in Albania contains fraudulent speculation about the prospects of a company whose shares are traded on the Australian Stock Exchange, where has the offence occurred?

One of the main concerns involving the prosecution of individuals who steal telecommunication services is the wide variety in legislative provisions which operate in different jurisdictions (see, for example, the enormous range of offences which exist in OECD countries relating to theft of telecommunications services: OECD 1986). Some of the more technical legal problems associated with the prosecution of frauds involving an interjurisdictional element are discussed by Lanham, Weinberg, Brown and Ryan's *Criminal Fraud* (1987).

In Australia, the *Crimes Act* 1914 (Cth) expressly applies throughout the whole of the Commonwealth as well as beyond the states and territories (s 3A) and this provision has been used to permit the prosecution of a computer crime involving telecommunications services which took place in the State of Victoria but which involved a number of overseas jurisdictions (*R v* Jones, 3 June 1993, County Court of Victoria). Offences committed against the *Crimes Act* 1914 (Cth) which involve the use of telecommunications equipment or services will be within the jurisdiction of the Commonwealth as they relate to the constitutional power of the Federal Parliament to make laws with respect to postal, telegraphic, telephonic and like services (Commonwealth Constitution s 51(v)). It has also been decided that Commonwealth telecommunications offences take priority over State offences where an inconsistency exists (*Kelly v Shanahan*; *Ex parte Shanahan* [1975] Qd R 215). In addition, it has been held that where conduct involves the commission of both State and Federal offences, offenders should only be prosecuted and sentenced in respect of those offences which most appropriately reflect the gravamen of their conduct (*R v Liang and Li* (1995) 82 A Crim R 39). Finally, s 76F of the *Crimes Act* 1914 (Cth) specifically provides that the offences specified in s 76D (unlawful access to data in Commonwealth and other computers) and s 76E (damaging data in Commonwealth and other computers) are not intended to exclude or limit the concurrent operation of any law of a State or Territory.

Thus, although it may be legally possible to prosecute offenders who make illegal use of services between various jurisdictions, even internationally, significant problems may arise in detecting such illegality and in proving allegations successfully. As an OECD paper said in 1986 when discussing the problems of prosecuting international computer crime:

> For international cooperation to be effective there must be agreement as to what is criminal at the national level and what sanctions should attach to a given offence. Extradition treaties need to be adequate to deal with offences committed in various jurisdictions. There are also problems of differing laws as to search and seizure, service of documents and the taking of testimony or statements of persons (OECD 1986: 68).

The legal challenges lie not so much in attempting to create uniform legislation internationally, which is unlikely ever to occur, but rather in ensuring that individual countries are able to prosecute those offenders within their own borders who infringe local laws.

In discussing the jurisdictional problems associated with prosecuting computer offences generally, the English Law Commission in its Working Paper, *Computer Misuse* (Law Commission 1988) referred to the distinction between "result crimes" and "conduct crimes". In result crimes, which require that a particular result occurs, jurisdiction is determined according to where the consequence of the accused's physical acts occurred, not where the acts took place. For conduct crimes, in which the offence is constituted by the act itself, jurisdiction is determined by the location of the accused's actions which constitute the offence. The Law Commission recommended amending the law to permit courts to deal with cases where "any act or omission forming part of any offence or any event necessary to the completion of any offence" occurs within the jurisdiction. Similarly, courts would be empowered to deal with cases in which machinery involved in the commission of the crime, such as a computer, is located within a particular jurisdiction.

As in other areas of telecommunications crime, jurisdictional problems sometimes create difficulties for law enforcement agencies attempting successfully to prosecute offenders who commit crimes which concern a number of countries.

The case of *R v Thompson* [1984] 1 WLR 962 (see also [1984] *Criminal Law Review* 427) discussed in the chapter below on electronic funds transfer crime, raises just such problems, although in that case the criminal transaction was found to have been committed within the jurisdiction of the English court and the offender convicted. The court held that Thompson's deception occurred in England when he requested that the funds in question be transferred from the Kuwaiti bank to the English bank.

Jurisdictions in Australia have enacted a number of reforms recently to facilitate the prosecution of crimes occurring internationally and to ensure that profits made out of such illegality are able to be confiscated. In addition, the

Australian Law Reform Commission's work on cross border civil remedies deals with the law relating to claims arising out of civil or commercial transactions that involve or require enforcement in other countries (Australian Law Reform Commission 1996).

As will become apparent below in Chapter 8, the difficulty with electronic funds transfer fraud lies in the need to have international cooperation in making laws which are consistent throughout the world. Partially, this is being resolved by the introduction of uniform codes of conduct which govern the use of such technologies as ATM and Electronic Funds Transfer at Point of Sale (EFTPOS).

Because telecommunications crimes may be committed in concert by a number of individuals each of whom resides in a different jurisdiction and each of whom contributes differently to the joint criminal enterprise, the possibility exists that no single individual may be able to be prosecuted or, alternatively, each individual may have committed a variety of offences in different jurisdictions and be subject to multiple punishment.

Cryptography

Although cryptography has an ancient heritage, stretching back to Egypt more than 3500 years ago (Kahn 1967), its widespread application to telecommunications has only occurred recently. Modern cryptography entails the mathematical transformation of communications to protect against unauthorised access to content, and to ensure its authenticity (see Tyree 1996a).

A cryptographic system consists of an encrypt function, which scrambles (encrypts) data, and an inverse decrypt function, which restores data to its original form. Encryption conceals data from anyone who does not know the secret key needed for decryption.

Two types of cryptography are in common use (see Case 1995). In secret key, or symmetric cryptography, a single random number is generated which becomes the key used by a mathematical algorithm to scramble and unscramble data. The number acts like a temporary password which allows access to the data. The problem which is created with secret key cryptography is that the key needs to be sent to those who need to use it to decrypt messages, and such transfer may risk compromising the security of the key.

Public key or asymmetric cryptography splits the key into two parts, a public key and a private key. The private key is held by the user and is never released. The public key may, however, be freely disseminated. Data secured by a public key can only be read with the corresponding private key. Messages may also be digitally signed by someone who uses his or her private key to encrypt a set of characters. Anyone could then use the corresponding public key to decode those characters, proving that only the person with the private key could have sent the message.

Public and private keys may be kept on either computer software or on hardware tokens. Software encryption keys are usually kept in a computer's hard drive which presents problems if a personal computer is stolen or malfunctions. Alternatively, encryption keys may be embedded in smart cards (computer chip plastic cards) which can be kept separately from the computer and used by a special reader attached to the computer. Smart card tokens cannot be compromised unless they are stolen and the thief is able to break the card's password (Case 1995).

Encryption is an important factor in several of the information security functions that facilitate the conduct of modern business. In 1994 the US Fedwire and Clearing House Interbank Payment Systems alone daily handled about 350,000 transmitted transactions worth up to US$2,000,000,000,000,000 of business across the global telecommunications networks. The benefits of effective encryption applied to interbank transfers are obvious. As we will see, however, cryptography is a double-edged sword, as it can also be used to conceal illegal activities from lawful investigation (Denning 1995).

Despite the challenges which exist in cyberspace, the information superhighway does have benefits for law enforcement agencies. Although its potential has yet to be realised, the use of technology for general public relations, for the communication of basic information for crime prevention, and for the exchange of information in furtherance of criminal investigation may be expected to increase dramatically in years ahead. Already photographs displayed on the Internet have led to the arrest of persons on the FBI's most wanted list. The activities of pornographers and software pirates may also be traced effectively using information available on the Internet.

Of course, a great deal of information which may be used in furtherance of criminal activity is also available on the Internet. An abundance of free software to facilitate electronic intrusion, information regarding the vulnerability of sites and systems, and other helpful information relating to modus operandi are accessible with little difficulty.

In relation to cryptography, the potential threat which this technology has for concealing communications from lawful interception for law enforcement and national security purposes, has led governments to propose a variety of solutions, some of which may have the effect of infringing individual privacy. One of the most recent international attempts to balance privacy rights with law enforcement needs, is the OECD's *Guidelines for Cryptography Policy* of 27 March 1997 (OECD 1997). These guidelines affirm the need for security and confidentiality of communications while not jeopardising public safety, law enforcement and national security interests. They stress that government controls on cryptographic methods should be no more than are essential to the discharge of government responsibilities but leave open the question of whether governments should or should not create legislation which allows lawful access to encrypted communications. Where national legislation is enacted which permits lawful access to encrypted data, various guidelines are stated which seek to ensure that individual privacy is safeguarded.

These guidelines are an example of many which are being created by governments throughout the world which seek to ensure that all telecommunications services develop fully while at the same time protecting individuals' rights.

At present, many of the laws which apply to the provision of telecommunications services were designed to regulate less sophisticated technologies such as simple telephone services. The task for policy makers is to ensure that new regulatory strategies operate effectively so as to govern but not stifle acceptable conduct. The challenge which confronts these policy makers resides in the fact that developments in telecommunications technology occur at a pace which is beyond the capacity of policy processes to keep abreast of. We turn now to a brief overview of the various forms of illegality involving telecommunications systems and services as instruments and/or as targets.

Varieties of telecommunications-related crime

The variety of criminal activity which can be committed with or against telecommunications systems is surprisingly diverse. Some of these are not really new in substance; only the medium is new. Others represent new forms of illegality altogether.

The following generic forms of illegality represent the most significant forms of telecommunications-related illegality facing society today. The list is, however, not exhaustive and new forms of illegality are no doubt emerging as we write. Online gambling is a case in point. Nor are the following categories mutually exclusive. Indeed, some activities may entail a number of forms of illegality. Scanning a digital communication in order to obtain proprietary information, a technique of industrial espionage, may entail elements of interception, hacking, vandalism, fraud, piracy, and criminal conspiracy, to take but one example.

Illegal interception of telecommunications

Developments in telecommunications provide new opportunities for electronic eavesdropping. From activities as time-honoured as surveillance of an unfaithful spouse, to the newest forms of political and industrial espionage, telecommunications interception has increasing applications. Here again, technological developments create new vulnerabilities. In New York, for example, two individuals recently used a sophisticated scanning device to pick up some 80,000 cellular telephone numbers from motorists who drove past their Brooklyn apartment. Had the two not been arrested, they could have used the information to create cloned mobile telephones which could have resulted in up to A$100 million in illegal calls being made (Anonymous 1996a). The electromagnetic signals emitted by a computer may themselves be intercepted. Cables may act as broadcast antennas. Existing law does not prevent the remote monitoring of computer radiation.

Electronic vandalism and terrorism

As never before, western industrial society is dependent upon complex data processing and telecommunications systems. Damage to, or interference with, any of these systems can lead to catastrophic consequences. A recent United States government study estimated that some 250,000 separate attempts to penetrate United States defence installations had occurred during the previous year (United States, General Accounting Office 1996a). Not all of these are attributable to harmless curiosity. Defence planners around the world are investing substantially in information warfare — means of disrupting the information technology infrastructure of defence systems (Stix 1995).[5] Whether motivated by curiosity, vindictiveness or greed, electronic intruders cause inconvenience at best, and have the potential for inflicting massive harm (Hundley and Anderson 1995).

Stealing telecommunications services

Ever since the original "phreakers" of twenty-five years ago attacked telecommunications systems out of curiosity, telecommunications services have been vulnerable to theft (see Clough and Mungo 1992). From those whose motives were confined to simple mischief making, to those who have made theft of services a way of life and a major criminal industry, those who steal services pose a significant challenge to telecommunications carriers, service providers, and to the general public, who often bear the financial burden of fraud.

The market for stolen telecommunications services is large indeed (Smith 1996). There are those who simply seek to avoid or to obtain a discount on the cost of a telephone call. There are others, such as illegal immigrants in some nations, who may find it difficult to acquire legitimate telecommunications services without disclosing their identity and their status. There are others still who appropriate telecommunications services to conduct illicit business with less risk of detection.

Telecommunications services may also be stolen by manipulating the operation of mobile telephones. In the United States, it has been estimated that mobile telephone fraud is costing the industry a million dollars a day (Brooks and Davis 1994), while all forms of telephone fraud in the United States result in losses of A$5.3 billion annually (Schieck 1995).

Telecommunications piracy

Each year, it has been estimated that losses of between US$15 billion and US$17 billion are sustained by industry by reason of copyright infringement (United States, Information Infrastructure Task Force 1995). Arguably, the speed and accuracy with which copies of works may now be made has been dramatically enhanced by such modern technology as online telecommunications networks. Copyright infringement may occur quickly and without difficulty, and may be carried out by anyone capable of using the Internet. The Software Publishers Association has estimated that US$7.4 billion worth of software was lost to piracy in 1993 with US$2 billion of that being stolen from the Internet (Meyer and Underwood 1994).

As broadband services continue to become available with text, graphics, sound and video information being freely accessible via cable modems, the potential for copyright infringement involving such works will be enhanced enormously. It is already possible to download compact disks and feature films from the Internet (Fox 1995).

---

5   See also the website of the Institute for the Advanced Study of Information Warfare (IASIW) http://www.psycom.net/iwar.1.html.

Pornography and other offensive content

Content considered by some to be objectionable exists in abundance in cyberspace. This includes, among much else, sexually explicit material, racist propaganda, and instructions for the fabrication of incendiary and explosive devices. Telecommunications systems can also be used for harassing, threatening or intrusive communications, from the traditional obscene telephone call to its contemporary manifestation in "cyber-stalking", in which persistent messages are sent to an unwilling recipient. In one recent case, a student composed a sadistic fantasy and sent it out over the Internet. He used the name of a fellow student as the story's victim, and was initially charged with communicating a threat, although this was later withdrawn (Platt 1996).

The rich diversity in thresholds of tolerance around the world, combined with the global reach of telecommunications, make this a particularly difficult regulatory challenge. What is offensive to authorities in the People's Republic of China might be welcome in overseas Tibetan communities. Materials offensive to religious leaders in Iran may fail to raise an eyebrow elsewhere.

Telemarketing fraud

The use of the telephone for fraudulent sales pitches, deceptive charitable solicitations, or bogus investment overtures is a large industry in the United States. The intensification of commercial activity in the United States and globally, combined with emerging communications technologies, would seem to heighten the risk of sales fraud. Already, evidence is emerging of fraudulent sales and investment offers having been communicated over computer networks and bulletin boards. Further developments in electronic marketing will provide new opportunities for the unscrupulous, and new risks for the unwitting.

Electronic funds transfer crime

The proliferation of electronic funds transfer systems will enhance the risk that such transactions may be intercepted and diverted. Existing systems such as ATM, and EFTPOS technologies have already been the targets of fraudulent activity and the development of stored value cards or smart cards, super smart cards and optical memory cards will no doubt invite some individuals to apply their talents to the challenge of electronic counterfeiting and overcoming security access systems. Just as the simple telephone card can be reprogrammed, smart cards are vulnerable to re-engineering. The transfer of funds from home between accounts and in payment of transactions will also create vulnerabilities in terms of theft and fraud, and the widescale development of electronic money for use on the Internet will lead to further opportunities for crime. What for the past quarter-century has been loosely described as "computer fraud" will have numerous new manifestations.

Electronic money laundering

For some time now, electronic funds transfers have assisted in concealing and in moving the proceeds of crime. Emerging technologies will greatly assist in

16

concealing the origin of ill-gotten gains as well as hiding legitimately derived income from taxation authorities. Large financial institutions will no longer be the only ones with the ability to achieve electronic funds transfers transiting numerous jurisdictions at the speed of light. The development of informal banking institutions and parallel banking systems may permit central bank supervision to be bypassed, but can also facilitate the evasion of cash transaction reporting requirements in those nations which have them. Traditional underground banks, which have flourished in Asian countries for centuries, will enjoy even greater capacity through the use of telecommunications.

With the emergence and proliferation of various technologies of electronic commerce, one can easily envisage how traditional countermeasures against money laundering may soon be of limited value. I may soon be able to sell you a quantity of heroin, in return for an untraceable transfer of stored value to my "smart-card", which I then download anonymously to my account in a financial institution situated in an overseas jurisdiction whose laws protect the privacy of banking clients. I can discreetly draw upon these funds as and when I may require, downloading them back to my stored value card.

Telecommunications in furtherance of criminal conspiracies

The essential element of a criminal conspiracy consists of one or more individuals entering into an agreement to commit a criminal offence. Modern telecommunications facilities clearly provide an effective means by which such agreements may be reached. The emergence of networks which are inaccessible to law enforcement agencies through the use of private key encryption and the technology of high speed data transfer can greatly enhance the capacity of sophisticated criminal organisations to engage in their preferred activities. There is evidence of telecommunications equipment being used to facilitate organised drug trafficking, gambling, prostitution, and trade in weapons (in those jurisdictions where such activities are illegal). Although the use of telecommunications facilities does not cause this illegal conduct to occur, it certainly enhances the speed and ease with which individuals may act together to plan and to execute such activity.

Common themes

The above forms of illegality need not occur in isolation. Just as an armed robber might steal an automobile to facilitate a quick getaway, so too can one steal telecommunications services and use them for purposes of vandalism, fraud, or in furtherance of a criminal conspiracy.[6] Electronic vandalism may have elements of obscenity, as was the case when the web page of the United States Department of Justice was vandalised in August 1996.

Communication of some forms of prohibited material (such as that relating to the manufacture of drugs or explosive devices) may itself entail criminal conspiracy in some jurisdictions. Even legitimate telemarketing may be

---

6   For a discussion of a notoriously versatile offender, Kevin Mitnick, see Hafner and Markoff (1991).

regarded as intrusive and offensive to some recipients. Intrusions and interceptions for purposes of industrial espionage may also be accompanied by theft of intellectual property.

In addition, a number of themes run through each of the forms of illegality described above. Foremost of these are the technologies for concealing the content of communications. Technologies of encryption can limit access by law enforcement agents to communications carried out in furtherance of a conspiracy, or to the dissemination of objectionable materials between consenting parties.

Also important are technologies for concealing a communicator's identity. Electronic impersonation, colloquially termed "spoofing", can be used in furtherance of a variety of criminal activities, including fraud, criminal conspiracy, harassment, and vandalism. Technologies of anonymity further complicate the task of identifying a suspect.

Let us now embark upon our journey to some of the darker reaches of cyberspace. We begin by exploring the illegal interception of telecommunications, past present and future.

2

ILLEGAL INTERCEPTION OF TELECOMMUNICATIONS

The ability to communicate freely, and with some measure of privacy, is arguably one of the fundamental tenets of democracy. Throughout history, however, attempts have been made to obtain information covertly using a variety of surveillance techniques. These extend from the simple act of intercepting and reading another person's mail, through physical surveillance such as by the use of informants, to the use of electronic listening devices, optical methods of recording information such as video cameras, location positioning systems such as those used for vehicle tracking, and the interception of electromagnetic impulses as they travel across telecommunications systems. In order to safeguard individual privacy, various legal restrictions have been imposed on the extent to which certain forms of surveillance may be carried out.

The legal regulation of the interception of communications for security and law enforcement purposes has a lengthy history in the common law world, extending back to Oliver Cromwell's law of 1657. This established the state's monopoly with respect to postal deliveries, thus enabling the interception of letters considered to be a threat to certain state interests (Fitzgerald and Leopold 1987).

In Britain, since 1663, it has been necessary to obtain authorisation to intercept letters from the Secretary of State. In the case of telephone interception, formal authorisation was not required until 1937 (Fitzgerald and Leopold 1987). Comprehensive legislation regulating the interception of telephone communications was not, however, introduced in Britain until 1985 (*Interception of Communications Act* 1985). Until then, there was no law which made the interception of communications illegal, apart from the common law offence of eavesdropping which was punishable as a common nuisance and was abolished in Britain by sub-s (1)(a) of s 13 of the *Criminal Law Act* 1967 (Eng).[1]

In Australia, as we shall see in Chapter 10, legislative controls on the interception of communications were not introduced until 1960 (*Telephonic Communications (Interception) Act* 1960 (Cth)), while in the United States, the first comprehensive legislation to regulate interception appeared with the *Omnibus Crime Control and Safe Streets Act* 1968 (18 USC §§ 2510-20), although earlier legislation in 1934 was interpreted to restrict the use to which intercepted communications could be put (*Federal Communications Act* 1934 § § 605).

---

1   See Blackstone's Commentaries (1809) 15th edn, vol iv, p 168 and *Malone v Metropolitan Police Commissioner* [1979] Ch 344 at 355-6 per Sir Robert Megarry VC for a comprehensive history of the law of interception.

Developments in telecommunications technology have greatly enhanced the ability to obtain reliable information through electronic means, and such technology is being used in a wide variety of contexts, from conducting surveillance of an unfaithful spouse, through to the newest forms of political and industrial espionage. Law enforcement and national security agencies also make use of surveillance technology, not always with legal authorisation.

The information which passes over telecommunications systems comes in a variety of forms. In prohibiting the interception of communications which pass over telecommunications systems in Australia, s 5 of the *Telecommunications (Interception) Act* 1979 (Cth) defines a communication as including "a conversation and a message . . . whether in the form of speech, music or other sounds; data; text; visual images, whether or not animated; or signals".

In addition to information in the form of communications, telecommunications carriers and service providers possess other information which arises out of the use of a system. Information, or "traffic data", exists which identifies the locations from which calls are made and received as well as the duration, frequency and patterns of calls. The strategic use which can be made of such information is discussed by Fitzgerald and Leopold (1987).

Security codes such as personal identification numbers and credit card identifying information are also transmitted across the systems and these have considerable value in the criminal world for gaining access to computer systems as well as for fabricating false identities and producing counterfeit plastic cards. With the advent of digitised online services such as the Internet, much more personal information is transmitted which has crucial strategic importance for national, commercial and private interests as well as the illegitimate interests of organised crime (see Chapter 10). It is little wonder, therefore, that the interception of telecommunications has become a primary focus of the modern sophisticated offender.

This chapter examines the various ways in which criminal offences may be committed through the illegal interception of telecommunications and the ways in which criminals have made use of interception to further their activities.

Electromagnetic impulses may be intercepted at any point in the telecommunications system. The present discussion will examine all forms of illegal entry other than those which are dealt with specifically in other chapters, which concern unauthorised access for the purposes of stealing telephone services, committing acts of computer vandalism, theft of funds and intellectual property, and other organised acts of unauthorised access to systems through computer hacking.

Audio and video surveillance using listening devices and cameras but which do not involve the interception of communications passing over telecommunications systems will also not be examined to any great extent (see *R v McNamara* [1995] 1 VR 263 and Bronitt 1996).

A wider discussion of the use of telecommunications in furtherance of organised crime and lesser criminal conspiracies, and the nature and extent to which interception of communications takes place for legitimate law enforcement and security purposes, appears in Chapter 10.

The nature and extent of illegal interception

Sources of information

Evidence of unauthorised or illegal interception of communications is scant, since victims of such activities are often unaware that interception of their communications has taken place, and offenders, including at times, law enforcement and particularly national security agencies, are generally unwilling to publicise their improprieties.

The principal source of information on the extent to which illegal interception of communications takes place comes from judicial proceedings, either before courts or tribunals, in which attempts have been made to rely upon evidence obtained in this way. In addition, there are the rare instances in which individuals have been prosecuted for infringing relevant legislation. The 1993-94 Annual Report of the Commonwealth Director of Public Prosecutions reports only one summary prosecution for an offence against the *Telecommunications (Interception) Act* 1979 and no offenders were dealt with on indictment.

There are also the many instances of telephone tapping which make their way into the popular media. In Britain, the most famous in recent times is that involving the Prince and the late Princess of Wales in which interceptions were alleged to have been conducted by, or released to the media by MI5, the British Government security service (see Morton 1994). In the United States recently, a transcript of an illegally intercepted conference telephone conversation has been used in support of allegations that the Speaker of the House of Representatives, Newt Gingrich, breached an undertaking given to the House Ethics Committee on 21 December 1996 in respect of an inquiry into an alleged violation of taxation laws (see Pianin and Merida 1997).

Finally in Australia, various government inquiries and Royal Commissions into police and other forms of corruption and illegal activities, as well as the use of interception itself, have documented instances in which illegal interception has taken place. The Stewart Royal Commission of Inquiry into Alleged Telephone Interceptions (1986), in particular, provided evidence of widespread unlawful interception of communications by various law enforcement agencies throughout Australia.

The techniques of interception

Until the 1980s, all consumer telephone services involved the transmission of a signal analogue of the microphone input along a pair of wires to the telephone exchange. The signal was easily shared, simply by connecting a telephone or similar device across the two wires at any point between the normal handset and the exchange. Party lines were often arranged this way, to contain costs when carriers provided services to remote subscribers.

Early forms of devices for intercepting fixed-wire analogue transmissions included high impedance headphones with a capacitor and alligator clips which were simply attached to wires; inductive devices which had a rubber sucker with an induction microphone containing a coil and a transmitter; taps connected in series or in parallel with the wires on an extension or switchboard;

"drop in" microphones which were placed in a telephone handset; telephone socket taps which were concealed in the wall socket of telephones; and surveillance systems which contained both tapping and bugging devices (Farr 1975; Fitzgerald and Leopold 1987).

The Stewart Royal Commission of Inquiry into Alleged Telephone Interceptions (1986) examined the extent to which interception devices are available in the community and estimated that approximately 30,000 devices had been sold in Australia in the twelve-month period preceding the inquiry (Stewart 1986). These devices varied greatly in price from as little as a few dollars to substantially larger sums and were readily available for sale to the public. Although it is now illegal to manufacture, advertise, display, offer for sale, sell, or possess interception devices (s 85KZB of the *Crimes Act* 1914 (Cth)), such devices are still freely available throughout the world (see Beaumont 1994 and Brookes 1996). One of the most notorious companies to deal in interception devices in the United States, the Spy Factory Inc., has, however, recently been wound up following a prosecution involving sixty-nine counts alleging money laundering, smuggling, conspiracy, possession and sale of interception devices (Anonymous 1997a).

The technological developments taking place in the world of telecommunications including digitisation and the convergence of telecommunications and information technology, mean that interception is now a highly technical procedure which requires considerable expertise. Although digitisation has the security advantage of enabling transmissions to be encrypted (see below), the interception of a digitised transmission may now be carried out without the previous hallmarks associated with fixed-wire interception such as crackles and clicks audible to the caller.

Authorised law enforcement and security agencies are maintaining their levels of expertise in the modern world of telecommunications (Australian Federal Police 1995), although with the move towards privatisation of telecommunications and the loss of jobs in public telecommunications organisations throughout the world, there now exists a considerable body of trained individuals who may be tempted to use their expertise for unlawful purposes.

In the United States, for example, since 1978, the National Intelligence Academy (NIA) at Fort Lauderdale, Florida, has been the leading private sector "bug school" which trains police officers from across the United States in techniques of interception and surveillance. The NIA also has links with an organisation, Audio Intelligence Devices (AID), a company which manufactures bugging equipment (O'Toole 1978). The NIA does not, however, always adhere to strict entry criteria when selecting trainees, and inevitably through retirements, resignations, or layoffs, many NIA graduates are able to migrate to the private sector taking their training and expertise with them. Schweizer (1993), for example, describes the ease with which it is possible to find private investigators willing to engage in both legal and illegal interceptions for a fee.

Both NIA and AID are mentioned in the Report of the Stewart Royal Commission as interception training and equipment resources which were used by an Australian company, Pacific Communications Pty Ltd. An AID telephone interception device, for example, with unique Australian law enforcement technical characteristics, but not part of the registered inventory of authorised lawful interception agency devices, was discovered in the field in Australia in 1983. All factors pointed to the device being used for illegal interception by an unauthorised person or persons. The Stewart Royal Commission concluded that illegal interceptions of telephone conversations were being carried out by persons, other than police, on a large scale throughout Australia and locally-based training of unauthorised persons in the skills of illegal interception seemed most probable.

Illegal interception by law enforcement agencies

Chapter 10 discusses the extent to which lawful interception of communications takes place for law enforcement and national security purposes. Where warrants have not been lawfully obtained or where they are defective for some reason, an otherwise lawfully undertaken interception will be against the law, and those involved may be prosecuted.

In the United States throughout the twentieth century, both Federal and State law enforcement agencies have, on occasions, carried out telephone interceptions without lawful authority and these have sometimes resulted in officers being convicted of infringing the so-called wiretapping laws (see Dash 1959, Donner 1980, Marx 1988, Lieberman 1973, O'Toole 1978, Charns 1992, and Kessler 1993). Although wiretapping was initially found not to be in breach of the Fourth Amendment to the United States Constitution as a form of unreasonable search and seizure (*Olmstead v United States* 277 US 438 (1928), see Adler 1996), subsequent legislation made the practice illegal. A number of illegal interception operations were conducted with the knowledge and authority of heads of government and law enforcement agencies and were invariably rationalised on the basis that extreme measures were needed to combat serious crime. Occasionally, however, the information collected was barely relevant to suspected criminal operations. O'Toole (1978), for example, recounts the example of a campaign of illegal interceptions conducted in Texas in the early 1970s in which more than one thousand illegal interceptions were carried out over a seven-year period:

> The Criminal Intelligence Division had compiled thousands of dossiers on citizens having no criminal records or associates. Most of the individuals spied upon were political activists of one coloration or another. The spy files were full of personal information, often including sexual gossip, and much of the data could only have been acquired through wiretapping.

Until the enactment of the *Omnibus Crime Control and Safe Streets Act* 1968 (18 USC §§ 2510-20), the Department of Justice was said to have carried on a twenty-five year program which flagrantly violated the previous legal prohibitions against wiretapping. J. Edgar Hoover estimated that before interception became legally regulated, the Federal Government was conducting between fifty and one hundred wiretaps at any one time, all of them illegal. Even after the enactment of the 1968 legislation, illegal wiretapping continued to be practised by the United States Government. In 1972, for example, it was revealed that more than 300 wiretaps had been improperly authorised in contravention of the provisions of the Act (see Lieberman 1973 for an account of the development of wiretapping controls in the United States, and examples of unlawful interceptions).

Fitzgerald and Leopold (1987), in their review of the history of telephone tapping in the United Kingdom, note the large number of interceptions carried out without warrants by both law enforcement agencies and security services over the years. It should be recalled, however, that legislation was only introduced in 1985 regulating in a formal way the interception of telecommunications in Britain. Prior to this, although authorisation was required for such interception, authorities were not, strictly speaking, acting unlawfully in conducting interceptions if a warrant had not been obtained.

In Australia, the Stewart Royal Commission (1986) into the so-called "Age Tapes" specifically examined allegations of illegal telephone interceptions which were said to have been conducted by various law enforcement agencies throughout Australia. Mr Justice Stewart was commissioned to examine, amongst other things, whether the tapes disclosed criminal offences and whether changes to law enforcement procedures were necessary. The Report concluded that "from 1967 or 1968, over a period of some fifteen or sixteen years, a sophisticated system for the illegal interception of telephone conversations was developed within the New South Wales Police, introduced at the direction of the Commissioner of that police force. . . . Over 200 interception operations actually were conducted and some of them continued for a considerable time" (Stewart 1986: 338, see also Grabosky 1989 for an examination of the background to the Royal Commission).

More recently, the Review of the Long-Term Cost Effectiveness of Telecommunications Interception (Barrett 1994), found that interceptions carried out for law enforcement and security reasons almost always complied with the *Telecommunications (Interception) Act* 1979. Barrett noted that such breaches which have taken place have generally occurred at the operational level, and involved failures adequately to record the uses and communication of intercepted information. No evidence was found of any intention deliberately to subvert or to circumvent the Act and breaches were attributable to inexperience, shortcomings in training, and so on.

The cases of *R v Padman* (1979) 25 ALR 36, in which the police had recorded a conversation between the accused (who was allegedly involved in the importation of cannabis resin) and his brother, then resident in London; *R v Migliorini* (1981) 38 ALR 356, in which the police had recorded a telephone conversation in order to obtain evidence of blackmail; and *R v Campbell* (1994) 78 A Crim R 1, in which telephone conversations were intercepted by the police who were investigating allegations of taxation fraud, all involved unlawful interceptions of communications without warrants. In each case, however, the evidence was admitted in the discretion of the court (see below for a discussion of the admissibility of intercepted material). One of the most recent examples of alleged illegal interception by police in Australia was provided in evidence given to the Wood Royal Commission into the New South Wales Police Service, in which a former Senior Constable of Police, codenamed FT3, alleged that police in New South Wales had illegally intercepted the telephones of various SP bookmakers (Anonymous 1996b). Subsequent evidence to the Royal Commission indicated that a former police commissioner was aware that illegal telephone interceptions were taking place but accepted a police report denying it (Brown 1996).

Illegal interception by private individuals

One of the earliest instances of telegraphic interception occurred in 1867, when a Wall Street stockbroker collaborated with Western Union telegraph operators to intercept telegraph dispatches sent to Eastern newspapers by their correspondents in the West. The intercepted messages were then replaced by counterfeit ones which reported bankruptcies and other financial disasters supposedly befalling companies whose stock was traded on the New York Stock Exchange. When the share prices were driven down, the wiretappers then purchased their victims' stock (O'Toole 1978).

In Britain, the first successful prosecution of a private individual for telephone interception occurred in 1974 in the case of *R v Graham Blackburn* (*Times* (London) 6 June 1974, Leeds Crown Court). In that case a private detective had tapped the telephone of a client's wife during a divorce case by hardwiring a link from the distribution cabinet outside the wife's house. Blackburn pleaded guilty to conspiracy to effect a public mischief and was fined £500 (Fitzgerald and Leopold 1987). A few months later, however, the House of Lords in *Director of Public Prosecutions v Withers* [1975] AC 842, held that there was no such offence as conspiracy to effect a public mischief. In that case, the defendants had obtained information as to the financial standing of certain individuals by making telephone inquiries of government agencies and banks pretending that the information was required for official purposes.

In Australia, the Stewart Royal Commission (1986) had no doubt that illegal interceptions of telephone conversations were conducted by persons other than police on quite a large scale, and concluded that this was a more serious invasion of privacy than interceptions undertaken by the police. The Commission was unable to establish, however, any case where an interception had been effected for some purpose other than the investigation of crime.

An instance of interception by a private individual is reported in the case of *R v Smith and Martin* (1991) 52 A Crim R 447. Martin had commissioned Smith, an inquiry agent, to intercept certain communications by installing an interception device on the telephone line of one of Martin's former employees who was to give evidence against Martin and Smith in a criminal trial on charges of corruption and forging and uttering. It was planned to use the material obtained through the interception to discredit the evidence of the Crown witness in the trial. Smith and Martin were charged with having conspired with various individuals to commit an offence against the *Telecommunications (Interception) Act* 1979. They were sentenced to three years' imprisonment which was reduced to two years on appeal.

The case is interesting in that the offenders were able to obtain the interception equipment without difficulty from a supplier in Queensland and install it, albeit with the somewhat reluctant help of a Telecom employee who was an acquaintance of one of the offenders. Thirty-three tapes were used in the recording of the conversations but none was actually used in the trial as intended.

Interception is also said to have been used for industrial espionage purposes. In 1990, for example, the Australian Federal Police were reported to have found interception devices on the telephones of Perth entrepreneur Robert Holmes à Court, Sydney stockbroker Peter Burrows, and Melbourne financial journalist Terry McCrann. It was alleged that an executive of Bond Corporation had arranged the interceptions, which were carried out by a Sydney consultant to discover if information was being leaked to the discredit of Bond Corporation. The allegations were denied by Alan Bond although an employee of Bond Corporation, who had dealings with the security consultant, was said to have had his employment terminated (Gawenda 1990; Wilkinson and McClymont 1990).

Large corporations in the United States have also been the targets of various forms of interception by foreign competitors seeking to discover sensitive, commercially valuable design and product information. Examples described by Schweizer (1993) include companies such as IBM, Boeing and General Electric who have had communications intercepted by competitors in countries as diverse as Japan, Germany and France.

Business executives in the United States who similarly wish to engage in illegal interception of their competitors' communications, should find no difficulty carrying out such activities. One study, for example, describes how Federal law enforcement agents posing as business executives approached 115 private detectives to see whether they would be willing to tap the telephone line of a business competitor. One in three agreed to do so, while 40 per cent of the others offered to train someone else to do it, or suggested do-it-yourself phone taps and explained how to install them (Schweizer 1993).

Evidence obtained through the interception of telephone conversations has frequently been used in the investigation of allegations of unprofessional conduct brought against registered medical practitioners by medical registration bodies. In Britain, the General Medical Council is charged with investigating the professional conduct of doctors and a number of inquiries have relied heavily on the use of interception evidence. Such inquiries are judicial in nature and the admissibility of such evidence is governed by the same considerations as apply in the criminal courts (see Smith 1994).

Evidence relating to charges of sexual misconduct between doctors and their patients (*Fox v General Medical Council* [1960] 3 All ER 225 (JC); *Libman v General Medical Council* [1972] AC 217 (JC); Mary Valvis (1969) *British Medical Journal* Supplement 1: 101) and unprofessional canvassing for patients who were seeking termination of pregnancies (Derek Segall (1971) *British Medical Journal* Supplement 2: 5; Sisir Datta (1972) *British Medical Journal* Supplement 4: 108) has been obtained in this way. On each occasion the doctor in question was unaware that the conversation was being intercepted and that transcripts of the conversations would be tendered in evidence in subsequent disciplinary inquiries. In each case reliance on this evidence contributed to the doctor being found guilty of serious professional misconduct.

These cases are examples of instances in which both legal interceptions conducted by the police (in the above cases of sexual misconduct), and illegal interceptions carried out by media representatives (in the above cases of canvassing for abortion patients), were both used as evidence in disciplinary proceedings unrelated to the purposes for which the interceptions were originally carried out. Where the interceptions took place illegally without a warrant, the evidence was admitted in the discretion of the committee hearing the charges of misconduct.

In Australia, evidence obtained through the interception of telephone conversations has also been tendered in disciplinary inquiries conducted by medical registration boards.

The proceedings involving Geoffrey Edelsten arose out of his conviction on 27 July 1990 of soliciting one Christopher Dale Flannery to assault one Evans and of perverting the course of justice by obtaining an adjournment of Flannery's murder trial fixed for 31 January 1984 by certifying that Flannery was unfit for trial in order that he would not be tried by a particular judge.

Part of the evidence used against Edelsten consisted of transcripts of two mobile car telephone conversations which had been scanned and recorded by an amateur without Edelsten's knowledge. Mr Justice Lee held that the communications which had been scanned and recorded had been intercepted in breach of the *Telecommunications (Interception) Act* 1979 but that they were nonetheless admissible in evidence. It was further held that the *Listening Devices Act* 1984 (NSW) was inapplicable to the interception of communications passing over a telecommunications system (*Edelsten v Investigating Committee* (NSW) (1986) 7 NSWLR 222; see also *R v Edelsten* (1990) 21 NSWLR 542).

In the case of *T v Medical Board of South Australia* (1992) 58 SASR 382 an obstetrician and gynaecologist, Dr T, had been charged with unprofessional conduct comprising three counts of sexual misconduct with a patient, and found guilty of two of them.

Part of the evidence against him consisted of a transcript of a telephone conversation between the doctor and the patient which the patient recorded by holding a tape recorder to the handset of a telephone. The majority of the Full Court of the Supreme Court of South Australia (Olsson J dissenting) held that this was not a prescribed interception. The court held unanimously, however, that the recording infringed s 4 of the *Listening Devices Act* 1972 (SA) and so was inadmissible. The court ordered that the erasure of Dr T's name from the Medical Register be set aside and that his registration be reinstated.

The dilemma created by interception technology

The technological ability to intercept, listen to, and record communications as they pass over a telecommunications system has created a dilemma for society which has been framed in the following way by Lord Mustill in the decision of the House of Lords in *R v Preston* [1993] 4 All ER 638 at 648e:

> In the first place there is the tension within the organs of state, between those which look for the maximum use of intercepts for the common good, to forestall treason, spying and crime, and those whose functions and culture incline

towards protection of the individual, and specifically to the protection of the individual's right of privacy.

The requirements of law enforcement and security agencies

The benefits of interception for law enforcement are varied and often difficult to measure quantitatively (Barrett 1994). Information obtained through interception may, on the one hand, directly result in the conviction of an offender. Alternatively it may prevent a crime from being committed. Information may also result in a suspect pleading guilty to an offence. Law enforcement personnel may also be saved from personal danger during undercover operations where interception evidence is used in preference to personal surveillance observations.

In a number of countries, legislation requires telecommunications service providers to assist law enforcement and national security agencies in gaining access to communications for authorised purposes through interception. The various rules which apply in Australia and the United States, along with a discussion of the impact which encryption technology is having on such capabilities, are described in Chapter 10.

Privacy concerns

For decades, it has been accepted that, in order to maintain the technical quality of the telephone system, technicians may listen to telephone conversations from time to time. Generally, such intrusions are tolerated as they are expected to be rare, of very brief duration and the technical staff neither record nor use the private content of the communications other than for legitimate maintenance purposes.[2] The overall quality of contemporary telecommunications services is such that customers rarely come into contact with these restoration and repair activities. Reliance is also placed on the integrity of telecommunications employees to adhere to the legal requirements which permit such intrusions to occur.

In other situations, however, there is a general reluctance on the part of the public to permit their communications to be intercepted, although this may be decreasing in recent times to some extent, in view of the need for interception to combat telecommunications and computer-related crime. In the United States, for instance, between 1974 and 1994 there has been a gradual increase in the extent to which wiretapping is approved from 16 per cent in 1974 to 18 per cent in 1994, with a corresponding decrease in the percentage of people who disapprove of wiretapping from 80 per cent in 1974 to 76 per cent in 1994 (United States, Bureau of Justice Statistics 1994: Table 2.41).

The Australian Commonwealth Privacy Commissioner (1992: paras 4.8-11) describes the privacy concerns relating to interception as follows:

Perhaps the most obvious privacy issue associated with telecommunications in the public mind is the degree of confidentiality callers should enjoy when

---

2   Recent exceptions to customer tolerance are the Casualties of Telecom (COT) cases which involved longstanding disputes between customers and Telecom, now Telstra, in Australia. See Telecommunications Industry Ombudsman 1994: 9.

making a telephone call or sending data over a telecommunications network . . . Whilst [the *Telecommunications (Interception) Act* 1979] imposes very strict controls over the physical interception of telephone lines (wire-tapping); it arguably does not deal comprehensively with related intrusions such as: participatory monitoring (including recording of conversations by one party); interception by electronic means (listening devices or bugs); interception of exclusively radio-communications (including mobile phones); or interception of traffic information as opposed to traffic content. Some of these issues are addressed to varying degrees in State laws on listening devices and interception, but there is no national framework or minimum standard.

In a subsequently published information paper entitled *Privacy Implications of New Communications Networks and Services* (1994), the Privacy Commissioner noted that the existing legal protections against eavesdropping "do not sit easily with individuals' reasonable expectations of confidentiality" and that "in the context of predicted growth of wireless-based communications networks, the issue of interception is likely to become more prominent". Further concerns related to the expected growth of wireless-based telecommunications services, such as wireless-based business telephone systems and computer local area networks, which may exacerbate the privacy concerns associated with interception. The Privacy Commissioner considered that traffic data should be regulated under the *Telecommunications (Interception) Act* 1979 and that the existing protections governing radio communications be strengthened to cover all messages or conversations transmitted by radio communications.

The Australian Law Reform Commission Report on Privacy (1983, vol i, 30, para 1094) noted the need for privacy to be respected in the following terms:

> Similarly, an individual's claim to personal autonomy involves a claim to have some control over the way in which he interacts with others. This implies the ability to exclude others from conversations or communications into which he enters and the ability to prevent, within limits to be discussed below, other people spying on his activities. Were he unable to do this, his ability to regulate for himself his interaction with others would be compromised.

Balancing competing interests

Respect for an individual's privacy is not, however, an absolute interest but is subject to other interests in society which may be seen as being of competing importance. One of these is the need for crime to be prevented, investigated and prosecuted. The European Court of Human Rights in the case of *Klass v Federal Republic of Germany* [1979] 2 EHRR 214 at 231 in its judgment stated that "powers of secret surveillance of citizens, characterising as they do the police state, are tolerable under the Convention only in so far as strictly necessary for safeguarding the democratic institutions". The Australian Law Reform Commission has also acknowledged this competing interest by observing that "in some instances, the social benefits that flow from police use of interception and monitoring techniques (in the form of more effective and efficient law enforcement) outweigh the cost, in privacy terms, to individuals of the use of those techniques" (Australian Law Reform Commission 1983).

In deciding the case of *Malone v Metropolitan Police Commissioner* [1979] Ch 344 at 377D, Sir Robert Megarry VC explained the problem succinctly:

> I think that one has to approach these matters with some measure of balance and common sense. The rights and liberties of a telephone subscriber are indeed important; but so also are the desires of the great bulk of the population not to be the victims of assault, theft or other crimes. The detection and prosecution of criminals, and the discovery of projected crimes, are important weapons in protecting the public. . . . The question is not whether there is certainty that the conversation tapped will be iniquitous, but whether there is just cause or excuse for the tapping and for the use made of the material obtained by the tapping.

The regulatory framework

In describing the regulatory framework which governs the interception of communications, it is helpful to distinguish six forms of activity, sometimes popularly described as tapping, bugging, tracking, spying, hacking, and scanning. The object of each of these is to gain information in a covert way without the permission or knowledge of those who create or control that information.

Tapping Communications (Interception). Tapping, or interception of telecommunications systems, involves the connection of some device to a system in order to enable communications in the form of electromagnetic impulses to be recorded as they pass along the system. Both fixed-wire telephones and mobile telephones which use part of a telecommunications system, are subject to interception controls. Interception may also take place with the use of radio scanning devices.

Bugging Private Conversations. Bugging, or the surveillance of sounds as they are made, involves listening to and recording sounds as electromagnetic impulses either before they enter a telecommunications system or after they leave a system, or independently of such a system.

Tracking Locations. Tracking involves the use of listening devices to track an individual's whereabouts

Spying. Spying is the monitoring and recording of both visual and sound information through the use of video surveillance devices.

Hacking into Computer Networks. Hacking, or obtaining unauthorised access to a computer network, involves the use of a computer to obtain access to a computer system by means of keying in access codes and passwords without permission.

Scanning Electromagnetic Radiation. The final way in which information may be obtained involves what has been described as computer eavesdropping or scanning. This involves the use of devices which are able to scan electromagnetic radiation which is emitted from computers and convert this into visual images.

In Australia, various Federal and State laws apply to each of these forms of activity and it is important to realise that the *Telecommunications (Interception) Act* 1979 which is a Commonwealth Act of Parliament, was intended to cover the field of telecommunications interception and thus, to the extent of any inconsistency, applies in priority to State or Territory laws which seek to regulate the same subject matter (*Miller v Miller* (1978) 141 CLR 269; *Edelsten v Investigating Committee of New South Wales* (1986) 7 NSWLR 222).

The legislation governing the interception of communications is not, however, entirely satisfactory, with the Act being described by one commentator as "a model of legislative obscurity, being confusing, circular, and verbose" (Re 1995).

Tapping fixed-wire communications

The starting point in examining the law of interception of fixed-wire communications as it applies within Australia is the *Telecommunications (Interception) Act* 1979 (Cth) which defines "interception" in sub-s (1) of s 6 as follows:

> . . . interception of a communication passing over a telecommunications system consists of listening to or recording, by any means, such communication in its passage over that telecommunications system without the knowledge of the person making the communication.

The 1979 Act applies only to communications which pass over a system or series of systems for carrying communications by means of guided or unguided electromagnetic energy or both, and includes equipment, a line or other facility that is connected to such a network that is within Australia, but does not include a system or series of systems for carrying communications solely by means of radio communications.

The recording of speech or sounds, before being converted into electro-magnetic impulses, or which have been converted from electromagnetic impulses, are not interceptions within the meaning of the 1979 Act. The recording of words spoken as part of a conversation external to a telecommunications system, however, is governed by the listening devices legislation in each State or Territory. This is the view taken in the case of *R v Oliver* (1985) 57 ALR 543 (see also Collier 1994: 59, n. 10).

In *R v Oliver*, tape recordings of telephone conversations were made by the use of a microphone held externally to the telephone. The conversations contained evidence of Oliver's involvement in a conspiracy to import cocaine from Peru to Australia. The court held that the tape recordings were admissible in evidence because there had been no interception of a telecommunications system as the recording was made by a mechanism external to the telephone.

The contrary view, that speech may be intercepted after it has passed through the system and is recorded by the use of a tape recorder held to the handset, is found in *R v Curran and Torney* [1983] 2 VR 133, although this was based on earlier legislation.

In *R v Migliorini* (1981) 38 ALR 356, it was held that recording a telephone conversation by means of a suction cup affixed to a telephone receiver and connected to a tape recorder was an illegal interception as it involved picking up the signal in its transmission over the telecommunications system within the meaning of s 6 of the 1979 Act. The device had been affixed to the telephone by the police without a warrant in order to obtain evidence of conversations in which

A\$20,000 had been demanded and which led to the accused being charged with blackmail. The court allowed the evidence to be admitted pursuant to sub-s (6) of s 7 of the 1979 Act. The court noted, however, that in future, the police would be required to obtain a warrant prior to such interceptions taking place.

Section 7(1) of the *Telecommunications (Interception) Act* 1979 prohibits the interception of communications passing over the telecommunications system in the following circumstances:

> s 7(1)   A person shall not—
> (a) intercept;
> (b) authorize, suffer or permit another person to intercept; or
> (c) do any act or thing that will enable him or another person to intercept,
> a communication passing over a telecommunications system.

These prohibitions are subject to certain exceptions which are set out in sub-ss (2) to (5) of s 7 of the Act. They allow for interceptions to be made in connection with the installation and maintenance of telecommunications systems, discovering and locating listening devices, where warrants have been issued to law enforcement and security agencies, and in various other circumstances of urgency and in emergency situations where it is not reasonably practicable to obtain a warrant.

The issue of interception warrants to the Australian Security Intelligence Organization (s 9) and to law enforcement agencies is subject to specific and detailed regulations. In the case of law enforcement agencies, warrants may be issued to assist in the investigation of Class 1 or Class 2 offences pursuant to ss 45 and 46 of the Act respectively.

Class 1 offences include various serious crimes including murder, kidnapping, narcotics offences, offences being investigated by the National Crime Authority and various ancillary offences such as aiding, abetting, and conspiracy (s. 5). Class 2 offences include offences punishable by imprisonment for 7 years or more and various other serious crimes involving serious personal injury or property damage, drug trafficking, serious fraud, and certain other offences such as taxation and computer crimes and other forms of organised crime (s. 5D).

Warrants are issued by the Telecommunications Interception Division of the Australian Federal Police and other agencies who now use the Telecommunications Interception Remote Authority Connection system introduced in February 1994.

Certain communications may, however, be listened to and recorded without infringing the provisions of the *Telecommunications (Interception) Act* 1979 (Cth). These are described in sub-s (2) of s 6 of the Act:

> s 6(2)   Where a person lawfully on the premises to which a telecommunications service is provided by a carrier, by means of any apparatus or equipment that is part of that service:
> (a) listens to or records a communication passing over the telecommunications system of which the service forms a part, being a communication that is made to or from that service;
> (b) listens to or records a communication passing over the telecommunications system of which the service forms a part, being a

communication that is being received at that service in the ordinary course of operation of that telecommunications system; or

(c) listens to or records a communication passing over the telecommunications system of which the service forms a part as a result of a technical defect of that system or the mistake of an officer of the carrier; the listening or recording does not for the purposes of this Act, constitute the interception of the communication.

In the case of *R v McHardie and Danielson* (1983) 2 NSWLR 733, tape recordings of telephone conversations made on a tape recorder attached to a telephone by Telecom were admitted in evidence because the person recording the communication was lawfully on premises and the device had been provided by Telecom pursuant to sub-s (2)(a) of s 6 of the Act. The case arose out of events known at the time as the "Woolworths Bombing Extortion Case" and related to a series of bombings in December 1981 of three Woolworths stores in Sydney. An extortion demand threatening further bombings was made, demanding payment of a ransom of gold, diamonds and cash amounting to A$1 million. McHardie was arrested at night in a diving suit, under Taronga Park wharf, when he was endeavouring to remove the ransom suspended in the water beneath the wharf.

Intercepting radio communications

The *Telecommunications (Interception) Act* 1979 applies only to communications which pass over a telecommunications network which excludes services for carrying communications solely by means of radio communications (s 5). Thus, if a communication is made solely by means of radio communication its interception will not infringe the 1979 Act.

Most existing cellular telephone services make use of both radio and wirebased systems, thus making the communication not one which is made solely by radio communications. Accordingly, such communications may not be intercepted other than in accordance with the provisions of the 1979 Act (Collier 1994: 61). In *Edelsten v Investigating Committee of New South Wales* (1986) 7 NSWLR 222 the court held that a communication from a mobile car phone which was intercepted by the use of a radio scanning device was an unlawful interception in breach of the 1979 Act but that evidence of the communications could nonetheless be admitted in evidence (see also *R v Edelsten* (1990) 21 NSWLR 542).

Collier (1994: 61) argues that when mobile communications are made solely through satellite with only switching and control being ground-based, the provisions of the *Telecommunications (Interception) Act* 1979 will no longer apply.

Law enforcement agencies need to be able to intercept communications for legitimate purposes whether they take place over fixed-wire or radio systems. It has been estimated that by the year 2000, mobile communications will be an element in one half of the world's telecommunications connections (Barrett 1994). It will, therefore, be necessary for law enforcement and security agencies to have the capability to intercept communications which extend beyond national boundaries through the use of GSM and satellite communications (Thorogood

1996). The expansion of interception capabilities in this way may, however, create significant privacy and human rights concerns.

In Britain, it has recently been held by the House of Lords that the *Interception of Communications Act* 1985 (UK) does not apply to the interception of communications carried across the airwaves between the handset of a cordless telephone and the base station connected to the public telecommunications system (*R v Effik* [1994] 3 All ER 458). The police in England had used a radio receiver and tape recorder to record telephone conversations made between the appellant and another person using a cordless remote telephone. When the cordless telephone was being used, the police used their radio receiver in an adjoining flat to overhear and record the conversations. The material thus obtained provided evidence which led to the appellant being convicted of four counts of conspiracy to supply heroin and cocaine.

Because the police had not obtained a warrant for such interception, it was argued that the evidence should be disallowed. The House of Lords decided, however, that a warrant was unnecessary since the communications which were intercepted were not passing through the public telecommunications system but rather a private system operated through the use of the cordless telephone. Thus, the evidence obtained was admissible in the trial.

Recent amending legislation in the United States (18 USC §§ 2510(1) and (12)) now provides that the radio portion of a cordless telephone communication falls within the interception legislation thus requiring police to obtain a warrant prior to intercepting such transmissions (Schwartz 1995).

Bugging private conversations

Listening to or recording a conversation which does not involve a communication passing over a telecommunications system, is governed by various Listening Devices Acts in each State and Territory throughout Australia: *Invasion of Privacy Act* 1971 (Qld); *Listening Devices Act* 1969 (Vic); *Listening Devices Act* 1972 (SA); *Listening Devices Act* 1984 (NSW); *Listening Devices Act* 1979 (WA); *Listening Devices Act* 1990 (NT); *Listening Devices Act* 1991 (Tas); *Listening Devices Act* 1992 (ACT); see also *Australian Federal Police Act* 1979 (Cth) and *Australian Security Intelligence Organization Act* 1979 (Cth).

The manner in which listening devices may be used varies greatly between different jurisdictions, some permitting recording of private conversations by a party to the conversation, while others require legal authorisation in the form of a warrant before recording may take place. In Victoria, for example, the law prohibits the use of any listening device to overhear, record, monitor, or listen to any private conversation to which the person is not a party without the consent, express or implied, of the parties to the private conversation (for example *Listening Devices Act* 1969 (Vic) s 4(1)). The Victorian legislation also prohibits the communication or publication of private conversations overheard, recorded, monitored or listened to whether or not the person was a party to the conversation except in certain prescribed circumstances, such as in the course of legal proceedings, or in the public interest or in the course of the duty of the person publishing the communication or for the protection of that person's lawful interests (*Listening Devices Act* 1969 (Vic) s 4(2)).

In Britain, publishing a communication made in breach of similar such legislation may give rise to an action for breach of confidence.[3]

Various individuals are exempted from compliance with these prohibitions where the conduct relates to specified law enforcement and national security activities and where lawful authorisation is first obtained. Whether or not it is unfair for suspects to have their conversations recorded through the use of listening devices employed by law enforcement agencies is a matter of some controversy, particularly where a suspect's right to silence and privacy may have been infringed.[4]

Legislation such as that which operates in Victoria is framed in such a way as, in all probability, to exclude from its application communications carried out on computer networks such as online Bulletin Boards. Although the position may be less certain where "talking" computer software is used, it is unlikely in view of the objective circumstances of the conduct that communications carried on between parties at remote computer terminals would fall within the definition of "private conversations" for the purposes of the legislation (see *R v Storey* [1995] ACL Rep (Iss 3) 130 VIC 35).

On occasions, it may be difficult to distinguish between an act of tapping and one of bugging. As we have already seen, in the case of *T v Medical Board of South Australia* (1992) 58 SASR 382, in which a telephone conversation was recorded by holding a tape recorder to the handset of a telephone, the court unanimously held this to be an act of bugging which infringed s 4 of the *Listening Devices Act* 1972 (SA). The majority of the court (Olsson J dissenting), found that the conduct did not entail a proscribed interception within the meaning of sub-ss (1)(a) of s 7 of the *Telecommunications (Interception) Act* 1979.

This decision follows a decision of the Court of Criminal Appeal of New South Wales in *R v Oliver* (1985) 57 ALR 543, 548 in which the majority of the court (Roden J not deciding this issue) held that recording a communication by holding a microphone near a telephone handset did not breach the 1979 Act as the passage of the communication over the system was complete before the recording was made. The court did not, however, deal with the question of whether such a recording infringed the listening devices legislation of New South Wales.

Tracking Locations

Listening devices may also be used to track an individual's whereabouts, although tracking devices alone do not fall within the existing legislative framework. Installing a tracking and listening device, would invariably require physical

---

3   *Francombe v Mirror Group Newspapers Limited* [1984] 2 All ER 408 relating to the illegal recording of conversations under the *Wireless Telegraphy Act* 1949 (Eng). See also *John Fairfax Publications Pty Ltd. v Doe* (1995) 37 NSWLR 81 in which the restrictions on publishing material intercepted by telephone tapping are discussed.

4   See Bronitt 1996 discussing the case of *R v O'Neill* (1995) 81 A Crim R 458; see also *Barker v The Queen* (1994) 127 ALR 280 and *R v Truong,* unreported decision of the Supreme Court of the Australian Capital Territory, 19 March 1996.

access to premises, which may involve illegal activity unless a search warrant were first obtained.

The Wood *Royal Commission into the New South Wales Police Service* recently recommended that a warrant system be created to authorise the installation and use of both tracking and video surveillance devices for law enforcement purposes (Wood 1997: 458-9).

Spying

Spying involves the monitoring and recording of both visual and sound information through the use of video surveillance devices. Currently, there is no specific legislation which regulates such activity in Australia apart from the ordinary rules which govern the use of search warrants to permit entry to private premises. It has been held that it is legal to use a video camera to record the activities of people in public places (*Bathurst City Council v Saban* (1985) 2 NSWLR 704), and that video cameras do not fall within the definition of listening devices for the purposes of listening devices legislation (see *R v McNamara* [1995] 1 VR 263 in relation to s 3 of the *Listening Devices Act* 1969 (Vic)). It has been argued that provided entry to private premises has been gained lawfully, there will be no illegality if that opportunity is used to install a video surveillance device (Wood 1997: 457).

The Wood *Royal Commission into the New South Wales Police Service* recommended that a warrant system, similar to that which regulates listening devices, be created to permit video surveillance devices to be installed and used in private premises. It was not, however, thought necessary to regulate the use of such devices in public places (Wood 1997: 458).

Hacking into computer networks

The question arises as to whether hacking into a computer network amounts to interception of communications passing over a telecommunications system.

It will be recalled that the definition of interception in s 5 of the *Telecommunications (Interception) Act* 1979 (Cth) includes "a conversation and a message . . . whether in the form of speech, music or other sounds; data; text; visual images, whether or not animated; or signals". Arguably, computer-generated digital information would fall within the definition of "messages" in the form of "data" bringing all forms of interception of computer transmissions which pass over a telecommunications system within the scope of the legislation. Whether the mere act of "viewing" messages as they pass over a system as opposed to "recording" or "downloading" messages would amount to interception is conjectural (see Hughes 1991).[5]

Faris and Andrews (1995) discuss the use by the police of data taps which entail the use of software to record the transmission of computer data. The purpose of the tap is to show that a suspect either gained access to particular data, information or the computer system itself. There are difficulties, however, in

---

5   We are grateful to Simon Bronitt of the Australian National University for drawing this distinction to our attention.

presenting the result of such interception to a court, as print-outs will not necessarily record data which were seen by a suspect at any given time and will not truly represent what appeared on the suspect's screen (*R v Maynard* (1993) 70 A Crim R 133).

An alternative approach which is being trialed at present entails the insertion of a miniature video camera in the suspect's computer which enables images which actually appear on the suspect's screen to be recorded. Law enforcement agencies may not, however, be able to make use of such devices since video cameras have been held not to be listening devices within the meaning of s 3 of the *Listening Devices Act* 1969 (Vic) (*R v McNamara* [1995] 1 VR 263).

Wasik (1991), in discussing this issue in the context of the *Interception of Communications Act* 1985 (Eng), which raises essentially similar issues to the Australian legislation on this point, identifies a number of difficulties in establishing that hacking constitutes unlawful interception.

First, communication is unlikely to include the transmission of information between computers, as computer networks are data processing facilities rather than telecommunications facilities (see *R v McLaughlin* (1980) 53 CCC (2d) 417). In Australia, however, communication expressly includes data messages (s 5 of the *Telecommunications (Interception) Act* 1979) and online facilities such as Bulletin Board Systems specifically contemplate the use of computer terminals as a way of holding a textual conversation, occasionally conducted in real time. In New Jersey in 1993, the electronic surveillance legislation was amended in various ways, one of which extended the laws to cover computer-to-computer communications (Delaney, Denning, Kaye and McDonald 1993).

The second difficulty relates to the concept of interception. Gaining access to a computer network is said to involve the initiation of a communication, rather than its interception. This point was stressed by the English Law Commission which concluded that the offence of illegal interception of a communication would seldom be appropriate to computer hacking (Law Commission 1988). Greenleaf (1996a) has also raised the problem of applying the defence of consent where access is gained to a computer network. Interception is only an offence where it is made without the knowledge of the person making the communication. With many Internet users, however, it is difficult to specify which person is making the communication and thus it would be difficult to determine who is required to consent. Thirdly, most instances of unauthorised access to computers would involve gaining access to Local Area Networked terminals. There is some debate as to whether such networks form part of a telecommunications system, particularly where they are not connected to a carrier's network (Greenleaf 1996). These last two issues would most probably exclude the concept of hacking from that of interception. The issue is of some importance where law enforcement or security agencies need to obtain access to computer networks outside the scope of the interception legislation. In addition, Internet service providers could be held liable for illegal interception in carrying out certain acts in relation to digital messages which pass over their systems. For a more general discussion of computer hacking in relation to interception of communications in Britain, see Fitzgerald and Leopold (1987) and in the United States, Adler (1996).

As we will see in the next chapter, computer hacking is, of course, an offence against both Commonwealth and State laws. Section 76B of the *Crimes Act* 1914 (Cth) creates various offences involving unauthorised access to data stored on Commonwealth computers, while s 76D creates offences of unauthorised access to data through the use of Australian facilities or facilities provided by telecommunications carriers. Whether an act of intercepting data while being transmitted across a computer network involves unauthorised access to data is unclear.

A number of States and Territories also have laws which prohibit, to varying degrees, unauthorised access to computers or computer systems: s 309(1) *Crimes Act* 1900 (NSW); s 9A *Summary Offences Act* 1966 (Vic); s 44 *Summary Offences Act* 1953 (SA); s 440A Criminal Code (WA); s 257D Criminal Code (Tas); s 175 Criminal Code (Qld); s 222 Criminal Code (NT); s 135J *Crimes Act* 1900 (ACT). It is by no means certain, however, whether these laws would proscribe the unauthorised interception of digital data passing over a networked telecommunications system.

In proposing amendments to these various laws, consideration might be given to the question of whether computer hacking should be included within the definition of interception in order to regulate access to computer systems by law enforcement and security agencies, or whether it is sufficient to proscribe hacking in existing computer criminal laws, with an exemption being given to various law enforcement and security agencies.

Scanning electromagnetic radiation

Electromagnetic radiation (EMR) is emitted from the circuit boards, visual display units, keyboards, cables, printers, and modems of most personal and laptop computers. Touch-sensitive screens are generally excellent EMR sources. Telex and facsimile machines are similarly vulnerable to scanning. EMR can be readily converted back to its original information (Wasik 1991). Since the early 1980s, it has been possible to discover the content of information being carried electronically through computer networks by externally scanning EMR (see Van Eck 1985). The principles of such scanning have been described as follows:

> All electronic devices emit some low level electromagnetic radiation. Whenever an electric current changes in voltage level it generates electromagnetic pulses that radiate invisible radio waves. . . . Associated unshielded cabling can act as an antenna and increase interception range. Computers attached to unshielded telephone lines are easy prey as the telephone line acts as an excellent antenna. . . . Average scanning range is approximately 30 yards (Jones 1996).

Weak radiations can couple into metallic conducting materials about the house, such as unshielded telephone cables, mains' power cables, or even water piping, thereby increasing the distance at which they may be scanned to a kilometre or more. It is also known that a clear text signal from a radiating part of the computer, such as the screen or keyboard, can become superimposed on top of the encrypted signal of data file transmission. Even a very weak signal may then be detected and recovered using commercially available hardware and software. It has been estimated that a device which would enable signals to be scanned from a kilometre away can be purchased in the United States for around US$4000 (Wolfe 1995). A less sophisticated device can be constructed by modifying the components of some older television sets (Seline 1990).

In the United States, the National Communications Security Information Memorandum (5100A) specifies levels of EMR which equipment may emit without compromising the information contained in the system. Equipment which is so-called "TEMPEST certified" (Transient Electro-Magnetic Pulse Emanation Standard) is thus secure for confidential government work (Seline 1990).

The question arises, however, as to whether scanning infringes interception, listening devices or computer hacking legislation. The consensus of opinion seems to be that computer eavesdropping is not illegal in the United Kingdom (see, for example, Law Commission 1988), and the United States (Seline 1990). In Canada, the Criminal Code creates an offence of obtaining indirect access to a computer service (s. 301.2(1)) which arguably includes electromagnetic scanning, although this is restricted to "computer services" only. It has been argued that electromagnetic scanning ought not be criminalised as it would be too difficult to police such a covert activity (Seline 1990). It has also been argued that observing people and objects even with the use of devices such as powerful binoculars is not illegal and undertaking essentially the same activity through the airwaves similarly should not be made illegal (Wasik 1991). In Britain, as long ago as 1972, a new offence was contemplated of "surreptitious surveillance by means of a technical device", although not in the context of computer eavesdropping, but this was never enacted (United Kingdom 1972, Younger Committee).

Scanning of this nature is reported on occasions such as the English case of an eavesdropper who scanned electronic transaction information transmitted by a bank in the United Kingdom. Despite the fact that the information was encrypted, the code was defeated and the individual successfully obtained £350,000 by blackmailing the bank and several customers by threatening to reveal certain information to the Inland Revenue. No prosecution was mounted for either interception or computer hacking although proceedings could have been taken for other offences (Nicholson 1989).

Where law enforcement and security agencies engage in such activities there is arguably a need for some legal authorisation and this may best be provided through the mechanism of an interception warrant. In Australia, this would require the amendment of the existing definition of interception in the *Telecommunications (Interception) Act* 1979.

Interference with networks

In addition to the rules set out in the *Telecommunications (Interception) Act* 1979 a variety of other Commonwealth laws regulate conduct which involves the interception of communications.

These include a variety of offences under the *Crimes Act* 1914 (Cth) such as causing a communication to be received by a person other than the person to whom it is directed (s 85ZD — 1 year's imprisonment); interfering with, or using devices to interfere with, facilities in such a way as to hinder the normal operation of the service (s 85ZG — 2 years' imprisonment); tampering or interfering with a facility belonging to a carrier (s 85ZJ — 1 year's imprisonment); and connecting equipment to a network for use in the commission of an offence (s 85ZK — 5 years' imprisonment).

In addition, s 253 of the *Telecommunications Act* 1991 (Cth) creates an offence of knowingly or recklessly connecting to a telecommunications network customer equipment in respect of which a permit for connection to a telecommunications network is not in force. This offence carries a maximum penalty of A\$12,000.

The prohibition of interception devices

The Younger Committee on Privacy in England (United Kingdom 1972: para 570) argued against the enactment of laws which would prohibit the manufacture, importation, sale, advertising and use of interception devices arguing that such laws would be unduly cumbersome and ineffective and would place an unjustified burden on industries which manufactured such devices for legitimate purposes, such as highly-powered cameras.

In Australia, a different approach was taken and in an endeavour to deter illegal interception, the manufacture, advertising and trade of interception devices was prohibited by s 85KZB of the *Crimes Act* 1914. This provision creates an offence of manufacturing, advertising, displaying or offering for sale, selling or possessing an apparatus or device of a kind capable of being used to intercept communications in contravention of s 7 of the *Telecommunications (Interception) Act* 1979. A penalty of 5 years' imprisonment is provided for non-compliance.

It has also been held that supplying and installing devices capable of intercepting communications infringes sub-s (1)(c) of s 7 of the *Telecommunications (Interception) Act* 1979 as being an act that will enable another person to intercept a communication passing over a telecommunications system (*R v Duncan* (1991) 56 A Crim R 460). In the United States it is also illegal to manufacture, distribute, possess, or advertise interception devices (18 USC § 2512).

Admissibility of interception evidence

Although information obtained through interception often has considerable strategic importance for tactical intelligence purposes by both law enforcement and security agencies, its principal use is in the detection of crime and its prosecution.

The *Telecommunications (Interception) Act* 1979 expressly provides, however, that evidence obtained through both lawful and unlawful interceptions is inadmissible in court proceedings other than in the circumstances set out in the Act (s 77(1)(a)). The effect of ss 63A, 74, 75, 76 and 76A is that lawfully obtained interception evidence can be given in a wide range of proceedings relating to various serious crimes including Class 1 or Class 2 offences. It has recently been held, however, that the record of a lawfully undertaken telephone interception is inadmissible in a bail application as this is not an exempt proceeding within the meaning of the Act (*Director of Public Prosecutions v Serratore*, unreported, 11 October 1995, New South Wales Court of Appeal).

The court has a discretion to exclude evidence which has been unlawfully or improperly obtained on public policy grounds where the public interest in securing a conviction is outweighed by the unfairness to the accused by reason of the unlawful circumstances in which the evidence was obtained (see *Bunning v Cross* (1978) 141 CLR 54 at 65 per Barwick CJ and at 74 per Stephen and Aickin JJ, following *R v Ireland* (1970) 126 CLR 321 at 334-5 per Barwick CJ).

The High Court in *Ridgeway v The Queen* (1995) 69 ALJR 484 discussed the rules which apply to the exercise of the court's discretion to exclude evidence which has been unlawfully or improperly obtained by law enforcement agencies and outlined the various factors which are to be taken into consideration in exercising the discretion. *Barker v The Queen* (1994) 127 ALR 280 discusses the admissibility, in Australia, of evidence obtained unlawfully through the use of listening devices and recording telephone conversations in the United Kingdom.

Since the commencement of the *Evidence Act* 1995 (Cth) and the *Evidence Act* 1995 (NSW) in 1995, federal courts and courts in the Australian Capital Territory and New South Wales in criminal proceedings are required to refuse to admit evidence if its probative value is outweighed by the danger of unfair prejudice to the accused (s 137 of both Acts). Section 138 of both Acts sets out the circumstances in which a court should exercise its discretion to refuse to admit evidence which has been improperly or illegally obtained. In *R v Truong* Supreme Court of the Australian Capital Territory, 19 March 1996 evidence of an illegally recorded conversation was admitted pursuant to s 138.

In the case of unlawful telecommunications interceptions, the courts have, on a number of occasions, allowed evidence of interceptions to be admitted despite the fact that warrants have not been obtained or defective warrants have been used. In *R v Padman* (1979) 25 ALR 36 illegal recording was made of a conversation between the accused (who was allegedly involved in the importation of cannabis resin) and his brother, then resident in London; in *R v Oliver* (1985) 57 ALR 543 illegal recording was made of telephone conversations implicating the accused in a conspiracy to import cocaine from Peru to Australia; in *R v Campbell* (1994) 78 A Crim R 1 illegal recording was made of conversations relating to allegations of taxation fraud against the accused; in addition, Bronitt (1996) discusses *R v O'Neill* (1995) 81 A Crim R 458 in which covert recordings were made of the accused admitting to having attempted to kill her husband by administering a potentially life-threatening dose of insulin while he was asleep.

Sweeney and Williams (1990) discuss generally the rules which govern the admissibility of intercepted telephone conversations and transcripts of conversations and note that for recordings to be admissible, the voices on the tapes need to be identified, the circumstances of the conversation established and the continuity of the recording proved (*Butera v Director of Public Prosecutions (Vic)* (1987) 164 CLR 180).

The rules relating to the admissibility of interception evidence are such that the question of striking a balance between the interests of law enforcement and the protection of individual liberty is left to the judiciary to assess. As will be discussed below, the sanction available to the judiciary of disallowing the reception of unlawfully or improperly obtained evidence is a powerful weapon in controlling both law enforcement and security agencies in relation to the manner in which they carry out their activities.

Jurisdiction

The *Telecommunications (Interception) Act* 1979 (Cth) applies to communications which pass over a telecommunications system that is within Australia (s 5). It is not, however, necessary for both parties to the communication to be located within Australia at the time when the communication passes over the system. In *R v Padman* (1979) 25 ALR 36 (in relation to the *Telephonic Communications (Interception) Act* 1960) one of the parties to the intercepted communication was resident in London. Accordingly, the interception of communications which may involve parties calling from or being called in other countries falls clearly within the jurisdiction of the 1979 Act as long as the communication passes over an Australian telecommunications network at some point.

Control strategies

As in other areas of telecommunications and crime, the interception of communications may be regulated either through the use of the law or through reliance upon market-based technology. Governments throughout the world have, in relatively recent times, preferred to adopt the legal regulatory model in which interception has been prohibited other than in specific situations relating to the investigation of criminal and national security matters. Comprehensive reporting and accountability mechanisms have been introduced to ensure that interception is used only for legitimate purposes and under official scrutiny. Nonetheless, law enforcement agencies in various jurisdictions throughout the world continue to conduct interceptions outside the current legal regulatory framework. Interception devices have also been banned but they continue to be available on the black market and frequently used by private individuals.

The question which arises, therefore, is whether reliance upon the law in this area is the most effective way of controlling telecommunications interception.

The legal response

Maintaining a legislative regulatory framework with respect to the interception of telecommunications will offer some general and specific deterrent effects which will, hopefully, ensure that serious infringements of privacy will be kept to a minimum and that official bodies will resort to the use of interception only in prescribed circumstances. The recent legislative extensions to the ability of law enforcement agencies to undertake interception have resulted in increased numbers of warrants being applied for in Australia. Presumably, the perceived need to engage in unauthorised acts of interception has thus been reduced. Applications for official interceptions are thus open to scrutiny by the courts and, on rare occasions,[6] rejected where the circumstances do not warrant the infringement of privacy which the proposed interception would entail.

Members of the public, other than law enforcement and national security personnel, are also presented with a clear indication that the private use of interception is considered to be contrary to the best interests of the community. Achieving this aim requires, however, that the laws be framed in a clear, simple, and intelligible form which can hardly be said of the existing legislation.

In order for a legal regulatory framework to be justifiable, it is necessary for infringements to be investigated and prosecuted, which seems not to take place at present. There are almost no reported cases in which illegal interception has been prosecuted despite the fact that reports occasionally appear in which evidence obtained unlawfully through interception of communications has been tendered in criminal proceedings.

Finally, the existing legislative framework fails adequately to deal with some of the more recent technological developments such as screening electromagnetic radiation from computers and the vastly increased use of radio communications which in the future may exist outside current legislative controls. The question of whether hacking into a computer network amounts to illegal interception also requires clarification. Amending legislation should also aim to be consistent across jurisdictions and, hopefully, across national boundaries as well (Bronitt 1996). The Council of Europe Recommendation, R(95)13, for example, supports the harmonisation of laws relating to the interception of telecommunications in order to ensure faster and more effective international cooperation to deal with cross-border crime (Csonka 1996).

The technological response

In addition to relying on the law to protect the privacy of one's communications, individuals use a variety of technological means to ensure that communications remain private, or, at least, if they are intercepted, their content will be indecipherable or the fact of interception made apparent.

Unfortunately, the use of such technology not only protects private citizens from having their communications intercepted by others for illegitimate reasons, but also protects criminals from having their illegitimate communications intercepted by government agencies.

Encryption. Since 1881, when the first patent of a telephone scrambler was approved, attempts have been made to ensure that confidential communications may not be heard or read by unauthorised persons. The mere fact that a communication may be intercepted does not guarantee that the information it contains will be able to be understood by those conducting the interception, be they lawfully authorised or not.

Encryption devices, which convert data transmitted electronically into coded form, have principally been used in recent times to protect the confidentiality of digital computer data. In the past, however, the encryption and

---

6   In the year 1994-95, of 698 interception warrant applications made in Australia, only 6 were refused or withdrawn: *Telecommunications (Interception) Act* 1979 Report for the Year Ending 30 June 1995: 15.

decryption of telex and telephone messages was a central part of military intelligence activities. Now that cellular telephone communications are digitally based, the possibility of protecting their content through encryption is available (see La-Vey 1996), although because of the costs associated with this, at present, encryption is largely confined to the protection of data transmission (Barrett 1994).

In Australia, and indeed in many other countries throughout the world, there is no legislative regulation of the manufacture, sale, or use of encryption devices and accordingly this technology is freely available both to legitimate law enforcement and security agencies as well as criminals. In view of the costs associated with the use of encryption, the use of such devices by offenders is said not to be a major concern in Australia at present.

In the United States, however, where organised crime involves considerably larger sums of money, the government is keenly aware of the threat which encryption technology poses to the legitimate use of interception by government agencies. As a result, the government has proposed that the use of encryption devices should be tightly controlled and that if private individuals encrypt messages, law enforcement and security agencies should always have the ability to decrypt such messages for legitimate law enforcement and security purposes authorised under warrant (Denning 1995).

There are two ways of addressing the encryption problem. First, the government may proscribe the use of all encryption systems to which the government does not hold a key. This is the approach taken in France. An alternative approach utilises the so-called "clipper" system developed in the United States in April 1993 in which properly authorised third parties are able readily to decrypt intercepted messages for law enforcement or national security purposes (Barrett 1994).

The Council of Europe has recently proposed that consideration be given to placing restrictions on the possession, distribution, or use of cryptography. A Committee of Ministers of the Council took the view that "irrespective of the legitimate interests of the users of cryptography, its use should not create insurmountable obstacles for the investigating authorities to uncover the content of data during the lawful execution of a legal order to intercept a communication or seize data" (Csonka 1996).

The OECD, however, has recommended that individuals should be free to make use of cryptography in order to enhance the security and confidentiality of communications. In its Guidelines for Cryptography Policy (OECD 1997), the needs of law enforcement and national security are acknowledged, but these should be restricted as much as possible in order to protect individual privacy.

Interception detection and prevention devices. Various devices are commercially available to detect and prevent interception of telecommunications (Beaumont 1994; Stewart 1986). These include simple meters which are able to detect fixed-wire taps and a range of filtering devices which are able to detect radio frequency interception and prevent it being effective through the transmission of electronic interference. One countermeasure claims to remove taps by exposing them to very high voltage which may inadvertently cause damage to exchanges as well as risk injury to telecommunications personnel. Obviously, the use of such dangerous devices should be proscribed.

Various commercial products are also available to prevent computer eavesdropping including the use of computers which limit the amount of EMR which is emitted, and shields which prevent emissions from extending beyond certain areas or the external walls of buildings. TEMPEST insulated covers/ containers, for example, may be used on each micro-computer. It is also possible to produce electronic interference (noise) which will prevent EMR from being scanned, although some scanning devices are able to filter out such noise. By using micro-computers which do not use cathode-ray tubes (CRTs) for video display the amount of emanation is reduced although it may still be intercepted (Wasik 1991, Wolfe 1995, Jones 1996).

Emission screening tends to be expensive, however, making its use beyond the budget of all but those organisations which deal in high-level security information. Individual micro-computer shields, for example, are said to cost between US$2000 and US$4000 per micro-computer (Wolfe 1996).

Conclusions

Until relatively recent times, the use of interception was unregulated with law enforcement and security agencies being largely able to employ interception whenever it was needed. This resulted in considerable abuse of the practice and led to the enactment of legislation prohibiting the use of interception except in certain closely controlled circumstances.

Advances in technology, however, have now made it possible to conduct surveillance with very little chance of being detected. In the future, when considerably greater amounts of digital data will be transmitted across telecommunications systems, the potential for extensive infringement of privacy from both official and unofficial sources is substantial. Fitzgerald and Leopold (1987: 236), for example, describe the likely use of interception in the world of the future where fibreoptic cables transmit much more information governing every aspect of people's lives and make the comment that "unless society has evolved ways of controlling covert surveillance by the state, we will run the risk of becoming a society with no private space, anywhere".

There is, of course, the view that it may be impossible to analyse all of the data which can possibly be collected in the future and that the sheer quantity of information may be a factor in safeguarding people's privacy. Modern computing technology, however, is capable of scanning many millions of characters a second thus making such an argument of little consequence.

As the telecommunications industry becomes deregulated, and as the number of carriers, service providers, and re-sellers of services increases, the difficulties of coordinating the interception of communications will increase greatly. In addition, existing interception legislation applies only to communications which pass over a public telecommunications network, thus excluding private networked systems of the future.

Digital data transmission will, on the one hand, make interception much easier to carry out covertly, while, on the other hand, permit the encryption of messages making them difficult if not impossible to decipher.

Mobile communications of the future may also take place solely via radio and satellite systems thus taking them outside the jurisdiction of existing legislative interception controls (Collier 1994).

The costs associated with legal interception are also likely to increase greatly and consideration will need to be given to the most appropriate means of ensuring that official interception is appropriately funded. In addressing this issue, Barrett (1994) has suggested that carriers should pay for the cost of official interception and then recover these costs from law enforcement and security agencies, rather than recovering costs from telecommunications subscribers or the government generally. Barrett (1994) also noted the need for international agreement on the funding and technology to enable international telecommunications interception for law enforcement and security purposes to occur.

Finally, the question remains as to how best to ensure that members of the community as well as official bodies comply with the law of interception. In addition to the possibility of prosecuting those breaches which do come to light, it may be preferable for the law to be changed to ensure that evidence illegally obtained is inadmissible in judicial proceedings. This may well be a more effective way of ensuring that government agencies comply with the law than through the use of traditional sanctions (Bronitt 1996).

3

ELECTRONIC VANDALISM AND TERRORISM

Many forms of telecommunications-related crime are simply traditional crimes committed with modern tools. Despite use of the term "vandalism" in the title, which is common enough, and also evokes images of the sacking of Rome by the original Vandals in the 5th Century AD, the activities which are the subject of this chapter are distinctly modern.

In the present context, we use the term "hacking" to refer to unauthorised access to computer systems, and "vandalism" to refer specifically to intrusion for the primary purpose of hindering a system's operation or functioning, or inflicting damage on the system or its contents.[1] The concern here is with destructiveness. Subsequent chapters will address issues of intrusion for the purpose of financial gain, theft of intellectual property, or as instrumental to other forms of criminal activity.

As never before, western industrial society is dependent upon complex telecommunications systems. Destruction of or damage to any of these systems can have horrific results. The loss of one scientist's research data, serious as it may be for the individual in question, might not appear to have much wider impact. But trust and confidence in the systems that support commerce, communications, air traffic control, electric power generation, and other major modern institutions are at the very core of our society. Thus, even the mere potential for disruption and harm is cause for concern. In the realm of national defence, complex weapons systems are vulnerable to intrusion, so much so that techniques of interference with telecommunications systems as a military tactic have been accorded considerable recent attention (Stix 1995; Waller 1995).[2] Indeed, it has even been suggested that the applications of telecommunications to terrorism may one day rival the more traditional techniques of bombing and hostage taking. The technologies with which to engage in such interference are inexpensive and easily available (Defense Science Board 1996).

As with many other forms of crime, sophisticated or more conventional, the number of intrusions coming to official attention, whatever their motive, represents the tip of an iceberg.[3] So much so that we regard it for the time being as futile to speculate on quantifying the incidence and prevalence of electronic

---

1   The term "hacker" was originally used to refer to those who applied their ingenuity to refine existing computer programs. The term "cracker" was reserved for those who intruded upon computer systems for whatever reason. Over the past two decades, the term "hacker" has become synonymous with intruder.

2   See also the website of the Institute for the Advanced Study of Information Warfare (IASIW) http://www.psycom.net/iwar.1.html

3   By way of illustration, the US Defense Information Systems Agency attempted nearly ten thousand intrusions on information technology facilities of the US Department of Defense. Of these, approximately 88 per cent were successful. Only 4 per cent of these were detected, however, and of those detecting an intrusion, only 5 per cent reacted. See Crowell (1995).

vandalism. We are, however, willing to speculate that the growth and pervasiveness, indeed the globalisation of information technology mean that all else being equal, the number of potential victims and of potential offenders are increasing exponentially. Where opportunity exists, there is likely to be no dearth of those willing to try their hand.[4]

It should be borne in mind that not all damage to computer systems results from foul play. Accidents happen, such as power failures and fires. Software may be poorly designed and tested; the resulting "bugs" can bring a system down. By way of illustration, on one occasion in May 1991, a farmer accidentally cut a fibre-optic cable while burying a dead cow. As a result, four major air-traffic control centres were closed for over five hours. In 1992, a software error caused a major breakdown in AT&T long distance services (Neumann 1995).

Unskilled users can cause themselves and their colleagues no end of frustration because of inadvertent mistakes. But the annals of information technology are bulging with examples of electronic vandalism.[5]

At the outset, it is important to recognise that the world of hacking is renowned for its myth and hyperbole. Journalists specialising in information technology may be tempted to add a touch of excitement to a subject which might otherwise be inaccessible to the computer non-literate reader. As we will note, the desire for recognition, indeed, for notoriety, is characteristic of a number of hackers.[6] We describe the following forms of electronic vandalism in a manner consciously designed neither to glamorise the practice, nor to invite emulation.

In the first weeks of 1990, a 20-year-old Australian man, using a personal computer from his home in Melbourne, gained unauthorised access to computers at the University of Melbourne, CSIRO in Victoria, universities in Finland and the United States, the Lawrence Livermore Laboratory in California, and the National Aeronautics and Space Administration. The NASA computer was shut down for 24 hours as a result.

In November 1988, a computer program was introduced into the Internet which quickly impeded the operation of an estimated 6000 computers across the United States. Costs of subsequent diagnoses and system maintenance were substantial.

Denning (1995) relates how in one case, a nurse gained unauthorised access to a hospital's information system and modified patient records, including those relating to prescriptions, x-ray scheduling and recommendation for discharge.

United States defence installations have been popular targets (United States GAO 1996). So too have university computing systems, by virtue of their accessibility to inquisitive and technically competent young people.

---

4   Given the rapid move to electronic finance, commerce, and even to electronic money, one might expect an even greater number of intruders who will be motivated by financial gain. This will be the subject of later chapters.

5   For an introductory overview, see Stoll (1991); Hafner and Markoff (1991) and Sterling (1993).

6   Thus the adoption of the name "Legion of Doom" by one group of enthusiasts in the United States. See generally Sterling (1993).

Varieties of electronic vandalism

Electronic vandalism may take three basic forms. The first entails erasure of data files, or indeed system files, to destroy them altogether. The second involves encryption of files to impede their accessibility. Without the encryption key, the data still exist, but are not readable. The third form entails overloading a system so that its processes either slow down significantly or grind to a halt, thereby significantly impairing the system's capability or disabling it entirely. No data are destroyed, but the system is to a certain extent immobilised.

Beyond these three major kinds of vandalism, there exist a variety of lesser forms, such as leaving messages of one kind or another — the electronic equivalent of graffiti. Even in the absence of damage to data or to a system, the mere indication of unauthorised access will require the time and attention of system administrators. For example, the vandalism of the Web page of the United States Department of Justice in August, 1996 and the Central Intelligence Agency and US Air Force later in that year, entailed punctuating the standard content of the page with offensive phrases and pictures. Departmental and Agency IT personnel had to restore the pages and secure them from further intrusion.[7]

\ The potential harm which can flow from the above activities should not be trivialised. It ranges from minor annoyance to the disruption or destruction of computer systems on which essential services depend.\ Security measures to reduce the risk of intrusion are very costly (Denning 1996a). Beyond the costs of defending one's system, it has been estimated that a 48-hour network failure would have catastrophic effects for 20 per cent of *Fortune* 500 businesses (Higgins 1996). Disruption of services such as electricity generation and air traffic control can lead to substantial loss of human life.

The manner in which electronic vandalism may occur depends upon access to a network of computer systems, usually gained through a telephone connection and the use of a user name, followed by a password. Access may be gained from one's home by using a personal computer connected via a modem to a network. After gaining access to a system, the intruder may interfere directly with files, erasing them or altering them in some form. Alternatively, he or she may act indirectly, by introducing a new software program into the system, which affects the system and its files in some manner.

\Alternatively, intrusion may be less direct. A floppy disk may contain contaminated program elements. Files attached to electronic mail messages may themselves be corrupt. Some of the more sophisticated forms of intrusion are achieved by means of an intentionally contaminated computer chip contained within a peripheral device such as a printer. \

The most familiar of these introduced programs is commonly referred to as a "virus", a software program which is attached to a larger program, and which replicates itself by attaching to other programs and files when the host program

---

7   While popular, US agencies are not exclusive targets. A South Korean hacker broke into the home page of the Japanese Foreign Ministry early in 1996 (personal communication, R Anderson and R Hundley, 1996), and in May 1997 a hacker in England substituted a recorded message placed by a recruitment agency for prospective applicants for positions in MI5, with information indicating that MI5 had been taken over by the KGB (Bradley 1997).

begins to run. Depending upon their structure, viruses can inflict catastrophic damage on a system or may be relatively harmless, such as those which may be limited to presenting a simple message while inflicting no loss or damage to data.

The characteristic of a computer virus which gives rise to its name is contagion. That is, viruses can be transmitted within and between systems, unknowingly and unintentionally by various media. It is often very difficult to identify the origin of a virus, as it can be transmitted to a number of hosts serially or simultaneously. Its very existence may not become apparent for some time after its original transmission.

"Worms", like viruses, can copy themselves rapidly from one system to another. Worms differ from viruses in that rather than attach themselves to another program, they are independent pieces of software. They are also distinctive in that unlike some viruses, they do not destroy data; they are, however, capable of consuming network resources and ultimately shutting the system down.

Literally thousands of different worms and viruses have been identified around the world since the mid-1980s. Over 2000 had been documented by 1992 (Cavazos and Morin 1994). Australia has been a major resource for the creation and dissemination of worms and viruses. The creators of viruses and worms often take pride in the sophisticated nature of their product and its properties. These may include the exceptional virulence of a virus, or a process of mutation which makes identification difficult, or a growth pattern of such a nature that the virus goes undetected for a prolonged period.

The low visibility of electronic vandalism renders futile any attempt to estimate its cost. As noted above, potential costs are catastrophic. Short of actual death and destruction, merely a simple virus may cost thousands of dollars in system repair or remedy. One can appreciate that the necessity of checking every file on each of one thousand computers in a medium-size organisation is not a trivial matter. The mere presence of an intruder motivated solely by curiosity whose activities are limited to exploration without harm can entail significant costs and system "down time". Even without any actual damage, the costs in time, human resources, and productivity foregone can be very significant.

Delivery media

The introduction of harmful computer programs into a system can be accomplished in a number of ways. "Bombs" are programmed to remain dormant, then to "explode", triggering some action at a predetermined time or upon the occurrence of a particular condition. "Time bombs" are designed to activate at a particular time, such as Friday the 13th. "Logic bombs", on the other hand, detonate when a particular event occurs, such as when a specified file is opened or copied.[8]

"Trojan horses" are software programs which are concealed within a program ostensibly performing a legitimate function. When this program is run, it

---

8   In addition to their antisocial applications, logic bombs can be used to protect intellectual property. Software manufacturers have the capacity to build a logic bomb into a product so that it detonates when an illicit copy is made (see Chapter 5).

activates the Trojan horse and performs the unauthorised operation. This could entail the release of a virus or worm, or the copying and forwarding of an identifier and password.

How intrusions happen

The first computer networks established in the 1960s were developed to facilitate communications within a relatively small community of scientists. As such, they were designed to be open and freely accessible. Indeed, they invited experimentation. Much as in a small country town, people left their doors unlocked, figuratively speaking. In the early days, basic information required to gain access to a computer system, such as an identifier and password could often be obtained by inference. The most relaxed computer security regimes provided a figurative open door by using such terms as "visitor" and "guest". Neighbours would wander in for a brief chat, and perhaps leave a note if no-one were home at the time. But the *gemeinschaft* of the early networks gave way in the face of exponential growth. The diversity of motives and increasing anonymity which accompanied this growth was not matched by commensurate developments in system security. The accessibility to intruders of computer systems at US defence installations such as those described by Stoll (1991), while almost unthinkable today,[9] reflected the practices which prevailed early in the computer era.

As computer security procedures have become more sophisticated, so too have the means of breaching them. Requisite information for system access was at times obtainable from data discarded with an organisation's waste paper — thereby inviting a practice known as "dumpster diving". Otherwise, collusion with an employee of a target organisation could facilitate access to that organisation's system. Another means of obtaining access to computer systems is through what is called "social engineering", an umbrella term which embraces a variety of persuasive and/or fraudulent methods of obtaining access codes and passwords (Knightmare 1994, Chapter 5).

These could entail, inter alia, impersonating a manufacturer's technical representative, pretending to be an authorised user, or even seducing a systems administrator (Hafner and Markoff 1991, part 1). Intrusions may also occur through collusion with an "insider", a current user of the system who reveals access details to an outside intruder. If the captured passwords are those belonging to system administrators, the intruder can take control of the "root" of the system and program it to enable easier access with less risk of detection at some future time. This can facilitate a wide range of illegal acts from fraud to vandalism.[10]

An even more sophisticated means of access is through electronic impersonation or "spoofing". This entails the disguising of one's computer to electronically appear like another computer in order to gain access to a system that would normally be restricted (Icove, Seger and VonStorch 1995).

---

9   In 1996 a person was found to have gained access to US defence installations from Argentina through computers at Harvard University.

10   Disgruntled insiders can use their position to engage in extortion against employers. See Wilding 1997.

Alternatively, gaining access to one system can open doors to other systems. In one case, intruders obtained access to a system at the Boeing Company. Through this system, they established trusted network connections with other systems both within Boeing and outside the company (MacLean 1994).

Motives

Motives for hindering or damaging telecommunications-dependent systems are numerous and varied (Anderson 1994). These motives are not necessarily mutually exclusive. One should be wary of accepting the hackers' own vocabulary of extenuation, especially those who have been charged in relation to their intrusion. Here the excuse may be devised in order to bolster a criminal defence or as evidence in mitigation.

Perhaps the most common is the sheer intellectual challenge of penetrating a system. It is no small feat (one should refrain from describing it as an achievement) to gain unauthorised access to and inflict damage upon a large computer system. There are those astute intruders for whom such an undertaking, particularly in today's environment of enhanced computer security, is analogous to a chess game with a grand master. In the words of one convicted offender:

> I mean basically with him it's a hot challenge thing trying to do things that other people are also trying to do but cannot. So I mean, I guess, it's the sort of ego thing. It's saying, I mean, knowing that you can do stuff that other people cannot, and I mean that's basically it. The challenge and the ego-boost you get from doing something like that, whereas other people try and fail (*R v Jones* 3 June 1993, County Court of Victoria).

The sensation of power which some derive from access to electronic "forbidden fruit" can be quite attractive.

Complementing this motive is the desire for self-expression and for peer recognition. Some intruders tend to be rather boastful, so much so that their "exploits" are often pure myth. Even those with a grain of truth are often considerably embellished. Prestige targets such as government installations and defence establishments are often favoured.

Given the relative youth of many intruders to date, it is not surprising that frivolity and mischief underlie a great deal of intrusion. Other hackers may simply be motivated by curiosity. For example, repeated unauthorised attempts to access former President Reagan's credit records have been reported (Clough and Mungo 1992). Curiosity can also underlie some of the more destructive practices. Hackers interested in observing the behaviour and impact of viruses and worms may be more concerned with process than with outcome.

On the darker side, the vengeful or vindictive hacker may harbour a grudge against a particular target, such as a former employer, a foreign state, or against society in general. Large systems, be they identified with government agencies, large companies, or telecommunications carriers, are often perceived as symbols of society at large — what young people of twenty-five years ago referred to as "The System". Attacking a computer system remains one way of attacking The System, or at least, of "making a statement".

At the extreme, it may not be long before intrusions are undertaken for the most sinister of motives — as instruments of terrorism. While contemporary terrorists seem to prefer explosives, the possibility of disabling entire communications networks or other major systems would seem to provide a wide variety of attractive targets.

Other intruders may suggest that their basic motive was pure curiosity, and that any inconvenience or damage resulting was essentially accidental. The Morris worm, which partially incapacitated the Internet in 1988 (Hafner and Markoff 1991) has been described as such.[11]

Hackers often seek to rationalise their deeds by downplaying the harm which they inflict. If systems are temporarily immobilised, with no destruction of data, the intruder may cling to the argument that no actual damage was done. This does, however, ignore the reality of cost and inconvenience, in addition to collateral damage which may be occasioned by the intrusion.[12] Coping with intruders requires human resources which could otherwise be devoted to enhancing system capabilities.

Alternatively, hackers may seek to excuse themselves by suggesting that by testing the vulnerability of systems to intrusion, they are actually making a contribution to computer security. Aside from those activities arising in part from social engineering, intrusions and any associated antisocial conduct are facilitated by the distance, both physical and personal, between intruder and target. Detection of an intrusion and identification of the perpetrator are often more difficult when achieved exclusively by electronic means; whatever inhibitions an intruder might have against the infliction of harm are lessened by the lack of personal contact with the target system and those dependent upon it. Unlike direct physical intrusion of a building, an office, or a filing cabinet, the experience of long range damage somehow seems less real to the perpetrator.

The capability of intruders has increased markedly over the past decade. Stoll's (1991) description of the manual trial-and-error methods employed by the German intruders he pursued in the mid-1980s seem quaintly archaic in today's context of automated attack applications, "sniffer" programs which capture system account and password information, and the sophisticated use of software vendor diagnostics to identify system vulnerabilities (Icove, Seger and VonStorch 1995). Much of this technology is available commercially, or even publicly accessible online. Indeed, a proliferation of electronic discussion groups and bulletin boards exist for the discussion of intrusion techniques and opportunities.[13]

Mobilisation of law

The reasons for the existence and magnitude of a dark figure are not unique to telecommunications-related crime. Skilful intrusions may go undetected.

---

11 The defendant, for obvious reasons, steadfastly maintained that he has no intention of inflicting damage.
12 For an excellent review and critique of the hacker's vocabulary of extenuation, see Spafford (1992).
13 References withheld.

Computer systems often "crash" because of internal hardware or software inadequacies, and it may be difficult to distinguish spontaneous malfunctions, and those caused by the incompetence of legitimate users, from those occasioned by intrusion. The most accomplished intruders will endeavour to cover their tracks. Hackers may achieve anonymity by intruding upon one system and using it to access another. Indeed, "looping" through various systems may make the intrusion even more difficult to trace. The practice of electronic impersonation or "spoofing" was noted above; anonymous re-mailers, essentially free email forwarding sites, can convert return addresses to pseudonyms and render email untraceable. |

Many intrusions are not perceived as serious enough to warrant calling them to the attention of law enforcement authorities, who may not always have the capacity or the inclination to deal with them.[14] Others are sufficiently serious to be potentially embarrassing. Institutional victims, in particular, may have a strong interest in preserving an image of inviolability, and are thereby disinclined to disclose their vulnerability by calling it to the attention of public authorities.

Otherwise, administrators of a system which has been attacked or damaged may often be more concerned with restoring their system than with pursuing the intruder. In some circumstances, system restoration can only be accomplished through procedures which destroy evidence essential to a criminal prosecution. Here we see a situation analogous to that faced by a victim of personal crime, where having to cooperate with a criminal investigation and subsequent prosecution may be counter-therapeutic, actually impeding recovery from the experience of victimisation.

Criminal investigation of intrusion may not be automatic. Not all law enforcement agencies are endowed with the technical expertise necessary to investigate computer crime. Scarce investigative resources are less likely to be devoted to an intrusion resulting in minor loss or damage, much less to a simple electronic trespass.[15]

But even when authorities seek to respond to intrusion with the full force of the law, challenges are formidable. Successful prosecution will require identification of the perpetrator (or someone vicariously liable such as a BBS operator), evidence of an offence, and intent on the part of the perpetrator to commit the offence in question.

These challenges are compounded when the offender operates across national boundaries. Successful prosecution of an offender situated in another country who introduces a virus into an Australian system requires an Australian complaint, proof of the perpetrator's identity, evidence of intent on the part of the perpetrator, and the perpetrator's presence in Australia or in a location from which he or she is extraditable for the alleged offence. The cost of producing the requisite evidence, and steering it through courts of law can be formidable, and may well exceed the capacity of enforcement and prosecutorial authorities. The

---

14   Stoll (1991) provides a classic account of how an apparently minor intrusion entailed matters much more complex and sinister. However, law enforcement agencies were generally disinclined to become involved with the case until its full ramifications became apparent.

15   One exception would entail intrusions in defence-related systems.

difficulty of prosecuting across State and Territory jurisdictions in a federal system is somewhat less, but remains quite burdensome.

Legal framework

Criminal laws have generally proven adequate to deal with electronic vandalism, at least in substantive terms, in western industrial societies. Traditional law such as that relating to malicious damage can fit the facts in many instances. Otherwise, many jurisdictions have enacted laws to criminalise unauthorised access to systems, and destruction, or modification of files and/or data. A useful review is provided by Icove, Seger and VonStorch (1995). In Australia, amendments to the *Crimes Act* 1914 (Cth) were enacted in 1989 to create a range of offences, including unauthorised access to data stored in Commonwealth computers, damaging, interfering with or destroying data in a Commonwealth computer, or obtaining unauthorised access to data stored in a Commonwealth computer.

These offences require proof of intent as well as lack of authority, lest one be liable for stumbling accidentally into a system, no matter how remote the possibility. In the United States, however, offences of strict liability exist for which proof of damage occurring will be sufficient; it is not necessary to prove intent to damage.[16]

Investigation/response

If they have not already done so, most large law enforcement agencies are now recruiting personnel experienced in the investigation of computer crime, or are training existing personnel in the techniques of forensic computing. There is, moreover, a growing information security industry which commands substantial expertise in the investigation of telecommunications-based crime, and which can be engaged on an occasional basis to assist with investigations. Telecommunications carriers also have extensive expertise in preventing the use of their facilities for criminal purposes, and in investigating those cases of misuse which do occur.

Identification of intruders can be extremely difficult, particularly when the most skilled are able to mask their identities. Even when an intrusion is detected in progress, it may be difficult to trace its origin. The law may not permit an interception of the intruder's line; in Australia, legal interception requires a warrant, which may only be obtained in relation to specified offences (see Chapters 2 and 10). Nor would the law in many jurisdictions permit a counter-attack — an intrusion of the intruder's own system by agents of law enforcement. Moreover, any incriminating evidence which an intruder may have on her computer may be quickly deleted or encrypted. Other impediments to successful prosecution arise from the requirement of proving that the accused was the actual perpetrator of the offence in question. Rarely, if ever do such offences have eye-witnesses. Offenders leave no physical evidence, such as fingerprints or voice recording. The advent of automated intrusion techniques reduces the likelihood

---

16   *United States v Morris* 928 F 2d 504, 505 (2d Cir) *cert denied*, 112 SCt 72 (1991).

that the intruder will leave a characteristic "signature", that is a repeated spelling error or other distinctive keystroke pattern. The mere fact that an offence was committed through a particular account does not necessarily imply that the holder of the account committed the offence, as passwords can be stolen or shared.

Governmental response to computer intruders has been uneven. Apparent increases in hacker activity in the mid-1980s moved the United States Government to bring exemplary prosecutions against a number of intruders. Of those which succeeded, most resulted in non-custodial penalties (Sterling 1993).

Since that time, investigative methods, particularly in the United States, have become more aggressive. In late 1995, the US Justice Department began intercepting computer lines at Harvard University, in an effort to identify a person who was using Harvard facilities to access computer systems at US defence installations. It is no secret that law enforcement agencies maintain a watching brief over hacker bulletin boards; as is the case with other areas of criminal investigation, former intruders are sometimes engaged by law enforcement authorities as undercover informants. In return for immunity from prosecution one hacker continued to operate his bulletin board on behalf of the United States Secret Service (Clough & Mungo 1992).

One would imagine that the future of computer crime investigation will entail the continuation, if not the intensification of such investigatory methods.

Outcomes

One of the most noteworthy aspects of computer crime to date is the relative leniency with which sentencing authorities respond in the aftermath of a conviction. Custodial sentences are unusual, especially so in the absence of significant financial loss. This is despite the fact that the penalties set out, for example, in the *Crimes Act* 1914 (Cth) are substantial, for some offences attracting a maximum term of ten years' imprisonment. The Australian case arising from the shutdown of the NASA computer, noted above, resulted in a community-based order and a suspended sentence.[17] The Internet worm case resulted in 3 years' probation, 400 hours of community service, and a fine of A$10,000. In the absence of major financial catastrophe or bloodshed, sentencing authorities, like members of the general public, perceive electronic vandalism as considerably less heinous than drug trafficking or bank robbery. They respond accordingly.

Long-term issues: security

One cannot expect dramatic short-term change in the quantity and quality of law enforcement resources devoted to the investigation of electronic vandalism, or in changes in public and judicial perceptions of the seriousness of the illegality in question. Thus, to an even greater extent than in many diverse areas of crime and public policy, prevention will remain the first line of defence against hacking. One expects that computer security will be among the fastest growing industries of the early 21st century. The Computer Security Institute, an industry group, has estimated that sales of computer security software will grow from US $1.1 billion

---

17   *R v Jones*, 3 June 1993, County Court of Victoria 1993.

in 1995 to US$16.2 billion in the year 2000. Security seems destined to play a more central role in the culture of organisations generally.

It might be appropriate to begin to think about countermeasures against intrusion as one would think about the prevention of household burglary. Self-help comes first. Law enforcement agencies lack the capacity to prevent burglary; their capacity to prevent electronic intrusion is even less. Just as a quarter-century ago one could leave one's house unlocked, one could a decade ago confidently leave one's computer system with little in the way of security in place. Those days are gone. Just as a significant proportion of residential burglaries in western societies today are facilitated by unlocked doors and windows, so too, figuratively speaking, are electronic intrusions.

The first line of defence is access control. The more accessible and user-friendly a system, the more vulnerable it is to attack. Systems can be designed and managed in a manner which will significantly reduce their vulnerability to unauthorised access. Fundamental principles of computer security should be instilled in all new users (Russell and Gangemi 1991). These include such basics as the safeguarding of passwords, and procedures for the screening of exogenous materials such as floppy disks and software.

The human factor must also be recognised as essential to information security. The integrity of systems personnel, indeed, of one's entire workforce, is an essential element of computer security. Information to facilitate an intrusion may slip from within the walls of an organisation by design or by accident. Careful recruitment, training and supervision of personnel can reduce the risk of loss at some future date.

An important defence against intrusion is simply good housekeeping. This will include attentive system administration, maintaining an up-to-date list of valid account holders, terminating dormant accounts, and limiting the number of users with special access privileges. In the absence of security which attends to such matters automatically, a security-conscious systems administrator will review patterns of system activity and be on the alert for any anomalies in use or timing.

The burgeoning information security industry has developed a range of very sophisticated technologies for the prevention of unauthorised access. Among the techniques available are automated intrusion detection systems, designed to identify anomalies in patterns of use. In addition, recent technological advances have led to the development of biometric devices which recognise certain physiological characteristics such as voice, fingerprint, or retinal image, and location based authentication systems which can identify the geographical location of a user (Denning and MacDoran 1996). Such a system would, for example, record each user's characteristics of access and use, such as time of login and typical keystroke pattern. Any variation from the established pattern can trigger an automatic request for authentication or notification of the system administrator. Sophisticated authentication techniques have also been developed, such as those where a server sends an unpredictable challenge to the user, who computes a response using some form of authentication token.

One means of constructively channelling inquisitive inclinations of potential intruders is to enlist their energies in furtherance of telecommunications security. Levy (1996) describes how Netscape offers a "Bugs Bounty" entailing cash prizes to individuals who succeed in identifying security weaknesses. While one might think twice about the wisdom of employing hackers as systems administrators (an electronic equivalent of entrusting the henhouse to the fox) strategies for safely capitalising on public expertise may have some merits.

But some threats may be too great to be left to the vagaries of markets and to the vigilance of prospective victims alone. In the United States, a President's Commission on Critical Infrastructure Protection was established on 15 July 1996 by Executive Order 13010, with a view towards developing policy for the protection of essential services such as water supply, electrical power, transportation, and banking from threats both physical and digital.

There are those organisations whose security considerations are such that there is no external connectivity, and others whose internal systems are complemented by a single dedicated computer linked to the outside world. In effect, those in the latter category have two separate systems, one for internal and one for external communications. More sophisticated systems are designed to achieve this without actually creating two separate systems, by building what are colloquially termed "firewalls" (Cheswick and Bellovin 1994).

Firewalls are arrangements designed to protect against illicit access from external sources. The more sophisticated firewalls screen traffic originating from outside sources, while still allowing internal users to communicate freely with the world. Firewalls are necessary, but not sufficient, to protect a system from viruses. As noted above, many viruses are introduced not through the Internet, but also from floppy disks.

Anti-viral software exists which recognises specific characteristics of known viruses. Virus scanning software has been developed which runs whenever a computer is booted. "Electronic immune systems" will soon be able to detect invaders and mobilise against them (*Wall Street Journal* 6 January 1997, B2). Indeed, one may safely predict that careers and fortunes will be made in developing technologies of computer security in years ahead.

The future of computer security will be analogous to a game of leapfrog. Emerging intrusion methodologies will be met with new security measures, which will in turn challenge the resourcefulness and adaptability of intruders. They in turn will develop new techniques (Whalley 1996).

Reducing the risk of repeat victimisation

Systems which have suffered intrusion may be particularly vulnerable to repeat attacks.[18] The intruder, and those with whom he or she may be in contact, may be

---

18   The phenomenon of repeat victimisation is by no means unique to telecommunications systems. Victims of residential burglary are significantly more likely to suffer repeat victimisation. Reasons for this greater risk may include the offender's particular knowledge of the premises and its points of access; the fact that the offender may share this information with peers, who in turn may be attracted to the target; or because of the target's location this may render it especially vulnerable. These factors appear to be as applicable to attacks on computer systems as they are to residential burglary. Analogies with residential property crime can be further instructive. Just as immediate attention to enhance the security of burglary victims in the immediate aftermath of an offence can significantly reduce the risk of revictimisation, so too can the mobilisation of security measures in the aftermath of a computer intrusion.

aware of intrusion pathways. Methods of intrusion, and the identity of vulnerable targets, are freely communicated on electronic bulletin boards.

Emergency response can shore up vulnerability and reduce the likelihood of repeat victimisation. Just as it is wise for the victim of household burglary to change the locks and enhance the security of the home, so too is it appropriate for system administrators to attend to security following an intrusion. To this end, Computer Emergency Response Teams (CERTs) have come into existence around the world to assist systems administrators in the aftermath of major difficulties, whether or not they were intentionally caused. CERT personnel assist in maintaining or restoring system integrity and data recovery where possible.

Ethics

There exists at present a diversity of views about computer intrusion. There are, at one extreme, those of libertarian inclination who regard all information as free, and all systems public. On the other hand, there are those who place paramount importance on the privacy of individuals and information. There are those who would favour intrusions in legitimate defence of national security, or perhaps in furtherance of criminal investigation (subject to appropriate safeguards). There may be other life-threatening circumstances in which intrusion could be justified (Spafford 1992).

While it may be difficult to change the values of those individuals who are immersed in the culture of electronic libertarianism, the possibility of developing values in the wider public which discourage electronic trespassing and vandalism is worth some consideration. Until recently, the general public has been arguably nonchalant about system security and ignorant about the potential harms which intrusions may occasion. Widespread death or injury has yet to occur as a result of hacking; until such harm does occur, it may be difficult to overcome community tolerance. Society in general must recognise the importance of maintaining the integrity of telecommunications systems and the very real harm which can arise from violations of that integrity.

At one level, basic principles of computer ethics can be instilled in children (and adults) from the time of their initial introduction to information technology. A greater emphasis on computer ethics in school curricula might also contribute to heightened ethical awareness over time. Training in computing should be accompanied by an ethical component; information making it clear that intrusion and destruction is costly and harmful to individual human beings, and to society in general, not merely to amorphous organisations.

The threat of intrusion, not to mention destruction, can have a chilling effect on commerce and on the use of information technology generally. It should always be borne in mind that any message designed to discourage antisocial applications of information technology should be structured and presented in such a manner as not to inspire the very activity it is intended to prevent. But even the best efforts at raising ethical sensitivity will be insufficient to dissuade the mischievous and the malevolent. Authorities in the United States have sought to remedy this in part by mobilising very significant investigative resources against computer intruders (see Sterling 1993; Hafner and Markoff 1991).

The lack of a credible deterrent from the criminal law may be compensated for in part by the availability of civil remedies for victims of intrusion (Lyman 1992). This is by no means a panacea, however. The cost of civil litigation can be substantial, and the outcome, by no means certain. Statutes conferring standing to sue may require a criminal conviction. If a criminal conviction is not required in order to recover costs from the perpetrator, the victim is then required to prove the requisite elements, albeit on the balance of probabilities rather than beyond reasonable doubt. There remains the fact that defendants (especially those working alone) may be judgment-proof.

Law enforcement

Law enforcement agencies will continue to be confronted with cases of computer crime, and may be expected to improve their in-house skills quite significantly in the years ahead. Even so, given the rapid pace of technological change, there may well be occasions when they will require outside expertise. One expects law enforcement agencies increasingly to harness resources outside their ranks in furtherance of their mission; they may also be expected to exploit new developments in technology for use in detection and investigation.[19]

The trans-jurisdictional nature of much computer vandalism suggests the growing necessity of cooperation *between* law enforcement agencies. Given the global nature of telecommunications, this cooperation will not be limited to agencies from contiguous jurisdictions, but will be required of organisations from vastly different cultures, and located on opposite sides of the planet. To this end, steps to improve international cooperation in response to electronic vandalism, such as those taken by the United Nations, the European Union, and the OECD, will become increasingly prominent (United Nations 1994). These will include such issues as investigation across jurisdictional boundaries, not to mention search and seizure of evidence, and extradition.[20] Given the privatisation of telecommunications around the world, international private sector cooperation may be expected to play an important role as well.

Developments in electronic vandalism may well create demands for changes in the law. There are those who would favour making it a crime merely to write a computer virus, or to release a virus inadvertently. Persons who discuss intrusion techniques on computer bulletin boards could find themselves accused

---

19   Securities industry regulators and cash transactions reporting authorities use sophisticated information technologies to detect anomalous dealings.

20   Extradition to the United States of the Argentine hacker mentioned above (fn 9) appears to have been precluded by the absence of a comparable offence under Argentine law.

of aiding and abetting a criminal act, as could those who operate BBSs. Such questions are not likely to remain exclusively in the realm of the hypothetical; a significant incident might be sufficient to elevate them to the policy agenda. The day may come when national laws and international agreements may well permit "electronic hot pursuit" and aggressive "counter-hacking" in response to intrusions.

Civil liability too may be affected by developments in hacking. Issues relating to the duty of care owed by systems administrators, indeed, by managers generally, have just begun to be canvassed. Finally, there is the need for any legislation which is enacted to be uniform in order to facilitate the prosecution of offences which involve various jurisdictions ↑

Conclusion

Tremendous advances in information security have been achieved since the early days of the Internet. It may be that security consciousness (and practice) have progressed to a degree sufficient to exclude most amateur opportunists. The future threat of intrusion would appear to come not from the merely inquisitive, but from the very purposeful. Techniques of "information warfare" may be employed by terrorist organisations with no less effect than the traditional bomb. The exploitation of communications technology by sophisticated criminal organisations may well facilitate more efficient criminal conspiracies generally, as well as very complex financial crimes. Both of these issues are addressed in later chapters. Beyond this, criminal organisations may also be in a position to practise their own form of information warfare, for purposes of extortion, to weaken targets generally, or to impede law enforcement. The skills developed by intruders will not be reserved for pranks. On the other hand, not only will they be accessible to extortionists, and money launderers, but they may also be available to law enforcement.

Suffice it to say that the term "computer literacy" is already becoming a bit quaint. While it may be premature to speculate on the long-term future of the information technology industry, observers have already begun to speculate on the potential risks posed by the possible downsizing and automation which could produce legions of unemployed, dispossessed, and angry programmers and computer security specialists. Their very considerable skills would still be available to the highest bidder, which in future may be a criminal organisation. At the very least, the potential for individual vandalism would be greater than ever (Edwards 1995). As such, information security seems destined to become one of the growth industries of the early 21st century.

There seems little doubt that industrial society will become even more dependent upon information technology than it is today. As a matter of public policy therefore, it seems appropriate that enhanced access to and fluency with information technology, will be important goals of any society. How to encourage widespread exploration and innovation while discouraging antisocial behaviour will be one of the great challenges of the years ahead.

4

STEALING TELECOMMUNICATIONS SERVICES

This chapter will consider how best to devise and regulate the provision of telecommunications services so as to minimise the opportunities for theft while at the same time deterring potential offenders from embarking upon acts which use telecommunications equipment for personal gain. Theft of intellectual property raises other specific questions which will be canvassed in the following chapter on telecommunications piracy. Similarly, theft of funds using telecommunications systems will be dealt with in Chapter 8 on crimes involving electronic funds transfer.

The history and extent of telecommunications theft

Early cases

Clough and Mungo (1992) review the history of telecommunications crime throughout the world. They describe its commencement almost thirty years ago when telephone operators were replaced by computers. Ironically, it was telecommunications personnel themselves who were implicated in the early cases of theft of services. The Bell Telephone Company believes that the first case of theft of a long-distance telephone service occurred in 1961 when a local office manager discovered some inordinately lengthy calls to an out-of-area directory information number. A multi-frequency transmitter (Blue Box) was discovered connected to the telephone which enabled free calls to be made from the telephone. This operated in the United States as follows:

> When the Blue Box is properly activated, it is possible to dial area code '800', a toll-free number, and then by generating a 2600-cycle tone, disconnect the '800' number while still giving the Blue Box operator access to the long-distance network. By then generating the appropriate sequence of multifrequency tones, any other number may be reached, without the call being reflected on the caller's telephone bill (Annotation 1977: 450).

The technology to enable the Blue Box to be made was derived from information published in a 1954 *Bell System Technical Journal* article, "In-band signal frequency signalling", and a subsequent article published in November 1960 which disclosed the details of Bell's tone system. This fact is important for policy makers to consider when devising crime prevention strategies, for often in the history of telecommunications crime, information or access has been provided which inadvertently facilitates theft by telecommunications employees themselves.

If one examines the history of theft of telecommunications services one important factor emerges which distinguishes these crimes from traditional property offences. This is the purpose for which the illegal conduct is carried out. The very early cases of improper use of services were often undertaken not for

63

profit but out of curiosity. Sheer interest in how systems work and the challenge of defeating security measures provides a powerful incentive which drove many individuals to commit offences against telecommunications systems.

For example, in 1969, John Draper, aged 26, used a children's toy whistle which produced a 2600-cycle tone to obtain free calls. He experimented with various other devices to obtain free international calls and was finally apprehended by the FBI making unauthorised calls between San Jose and Sydney in order to listen to the Australian Top Ten. His explanation was as follows: "I learned about a system. The telephone company is a system. A computer is a system. . . Computers. Systems. That's my bag. The telephone company is nothing but a computer". He was convicted on a number of occasions and in 1976 sent to Lompoc Federal Prison in California for two months (Clough and Mungo 1992; Parker 1983).

Similarly, Joe Engressia from Memphis, found that he could obtain telephone services free by whistling into the mouthpiece at the appropriate time. Prior to being convicted for malicious mischief, he said: "I don't hate Ma Bell the way some phone phreaks do. I don't want to screw Ma Bell. With me its the pleasure of pure knowledge" (Clough and Mungo 1992).

The use of traditional sanctions such as imprisonment may be quite inappropriate to regulate such conduct as is evidenced by the fact that a number of these early telecommunications offenders were recidivist offenders who continued to engage in their illegal conduct regardless of the legal consequences. Leslie Lynne Doucette, for example, was convicted in Canada in 1987 of telecommunications fraud involving organised criminality and was sentenced to ninety days' imprisonment with two years' probation. Upon her release from prison, she moved to the United States where she continued to operate a nationwide voice-mail computer fraud scheme, finally resulting in her receiving a twenty-seven month sentence of imprisonment in Chicago; at the time, one of the most severe sentences for computer crime ever handed down (Cook 1991a and 1991b; Clough and Mungo 1992).

Current estimates

Statistical information on theft of telecommunications services is scant, and that which does exist is plagued by the traditional problems associated with some crime statistics of incompleteness, inconsistency, imprecision and inability to address the "dark figure" of unreported crime. A number of anecdotal estimates do, however, exist.

In Australia, the Australian Federal Police have uncovered a number of telecommunications frauds in recent years, some of which have resulted in prosecutions being conducted and terms of imprisonment being imposed.

In 1992, for example, two individuals were prosecuted for manu-facturing devices designed to intercept public telephone lines enabling calls to be made without charges being incurred (Australian Federal Police 1993). Later, in February 1993, a man was sentenced to eight years' imprisonment for his part in a fraud involving more than A$400,000 in which he operated an international switchboard providing cheap calls between the Middle East, Australia and elsewhere (ibid 16). 1994 saw a large increase in reports of stolen telephone services including one case involving six individuals who used a company's telephone system to make international calls resulting in the company losing approximately A$50,000 (Australian Federal Police 1994).

Internationally, the losses sustained through theft of telephone services are even more substantial than in Australia. Recent British Telecom statistics cited by Schieck (1995) suggest that in 1990, security failures at BT cost approximately the equivalent of A$595 million of which A$58 million related to four main types of billing fraud (see below). In Germany, annual losses are estimated to amount to the equivalent of A$350 million (Peachey and Blau 1995). Telephone fraud in the United States is estimated to amount to the equivalent of A$5.3 billion annually while in 1993, the cable television industry in the United States lost nearly A$6.6 billion from theft of premium and basic services (ibid 2-5). Olson (1994) cites some recent examples of telecommunications fraud in which an American chemical company lost the equivalent of A$900,000 in three weeks while an Ohio manufacturer lost A$400,000 over one weekend.

Mobile telephone fraud is a recent area of particular concern. In the United States, Brooks and Davis (1994) estimate that cellular telephone fraud is costing a million dollars a day to the industry with the equivalent of A$900 million a year lost on illegal calls actually detected. The Federation of Communication Services, a European mobile communications trade organisation, estimates that the equivalent of A$200 million is lost through mobile telephone fraud in Europe annually (Wong 1995a).

In Britain, the Parliamentary Office of Science and Technology (1995) estimates that between 12,000 and 15,000 analogue and up to 1000 digital mobile telephones are stolen each month and that up to 40 per cent of car break-ins in London are for the purpose of stealing a mobile telephone. The British Industry and Government Study Group on Mobile Phone Fraud has also estimated that the total quantifiable direct costs to the mobile telephone industry and its customers of mobile telephone fraud is in excess of the equivalent of A$250 million. Mobile telephone subscription fraud, alone, is estimated to amount to the equivalent of A$144 million per annum or 1 per cent of network turnover (United Kingdom, Industry and Government Study Group on Mobile Phone Fraud 1995). One company, Vodafone, estimated in its 1994 Annual Report that it had lost the equivalent of A$26 million in profit through fraud and loss of equipment (Wong 1995a).

In Victoria, there has been a 294 per cent increase in the number of mobile telephones stolen from 4183 in the year 1994-95 to 12,293 in the year 1995-96. The value of stolen telephones is now over A$8.8 million with over 1000 telephones being stolen each month, 66 per cent of which were stolen from motor vehicles (Victoria Police, Statistical Services Division 1996). Over the same period in Victoria, mobile telephone subscriptions increased just over 200 per cent to 1.17 million. In one recent case in Victoria, an offender received an eight-month term of imprisonment, four months of which were suspended, for stealing 100 mobile telephones from motor cars in the inner city region of East Melbourne (Adams 1996).

In New South Wales, similarly large increases have been reported with 11,361 mobile telephones reported stolen in 1995 or 1739 per month, considerably more than in previous years (New South Wales Police Service 1996).

A recent instance of unauthorised use of a mobile telephone involved offenders in Perth, Western Australia, who unlawfully obtained access to an Adelaide subscriber's telephone and made more than A$15,000 worth of calls to an adult telephone service over a six-week period (Anonymous 1996a).

One of the largest telecommunications frauds ever discovered involved a group of Palestinians in the occupied territories of Israel who made long-distance calls to other Middle-Eastern countries while having the calls charged to cellular telephone subscribers in Arizona. This arose out of an Israeli law which prohibited calls being made to nearby countries due to security risks, thus forcing the Palestinians to adopt alternative means to make calls to their friends and relations. One United States Secret Service operation which took place in Phoenix, Arizona in January 1992 resulted in the recovery of thirty-five cellular telephones and ten thousand microchips and notebooks filled with electronic codes. In nineteen days it was estimated that 57,000 calls had been diverted through Arizona with United States telecommunications companies losing the equivalent of up to A$1.3 million in long-distance charges and air time (Ramirez 1992). Once again, the deterrent effects of conventional sanctioning may have proved ineffective in dealing with the motivations of such individuals.

The legal background

Theft and dishonesty

At common law, larceny could only be committed in respect of something capable of being removed and a telephone service clearly was an intangible item outside this requirement. In *Low v Blease* (1975) 119 Sol J 695; [1975] Crim LR 513, for example, the English Queen's Bench Divisional Court held that electricity is not property within the meaning of s 4 of the *Theft Act* 1968 (Eng) and that it is not appropriated by switching on the current.

This definitional problem has largely been resolved in Australia by the introduction of various statutory definitions of theft which include intangible items of property such as electricity, thus bringing the unauthorised use of a telephone service within the definition of theft, at least of the electricity consumed.[1] The value of the electricity used in a telephone call is, however, not representative of the value of the service being provided and accordingly more specific criminal regulation is required.

The Australian Capital Territory and Victoria have various statutory property offences modelled on the provisions of the *Theft Act* 1968 (Eng), while the other States and the Northern Territory have their own legislative enactments

---

1   *Crimes Act* 1900 (NSW) s 154C; *Criminal Law Consolidation Act* 1935 (SA) s 154; *Queensland Criminal Code* s 408; *Western Australia Criminal Code* s 390; *Tasmanian Criminal Code* s 233.

governing property crime. Applying these laws to the theft of telecommunications services creates a number of difficulties.

Telecommunications offences

Illegal use of telecommunications services may fall within a variety of federal Australian legislative provisions as well as the various state property crimes referred to above.

Sections 76A to 76F of the *Crimes Act* 1914 (Cth) create various offences to do with computers, such as unauthorised use and damage and these may be relevant where telecommunications equipment is used to facilitate the commission of the offence, such as where unauthorised access is gained to computers connected via networks. In addition, interference with the components of a telephone (especially a mobile telephone) may infringe some of these provisions.

The more specific offences relating to the improper use of telecommunications services are created by ss 85ZB to 85ZKB of the *Crimes Act* 1914 (Cth) which, with appropriate maximum penalties, are as follows.

s 85ZD — Wrongful delivery of communications — causing a communication to be received by a person other than the person to whom it is directed (1 year's imprisonment).

s 85ZE — Improper use of telecommunications services — using services to menace or harass or using services in an offensive way (1 year's imprisonment).

s 85ZF — Fraudulent representations and devices — defrauding a carrier of any rental, fee or charge or causing a service to be supplied to another person without payment of the proper rental, fee or charge (5 years' imprisonment).

s 85ZG — Interference with telecommunications services — interfering with, or using devices to interfere with, facilities in such a way as to hinder the normal operation of the service (2 years' imprisonment).

s 85ZH — Sending signals to a satellite operated by a carrier without authority (A$12,000).

s 85ZJ — Interfering with carrier facilities — tampering or interfering with a facility belonging to a carrier (1 year's imprisonment).

s 85ZK — Connecting equipment to a network for use in the commission of an offence (5 years' imprisonment).

s 85ZKA — Manufacturing, advertising, selling, using or possessing unauthorised call-switching devices other than for bona fide purposes (5 years' imprisonment).

s 85ZKB — Manufacturing, advertising, selling or possessing devices to intercept communications in contravention of the *Telecommunications (Interception) Act* 1979 (5 years' imprisonment).

In addition, s 253 of the *Telecommunications Act* 1991 (Cth) creates an offence of knowingly or recklessly connecting unauthorised equipment to a network and s 7 of the *Telecommunications (Interception) Act* 1979 (Cth) creates an offence of improperly intercepting a communication passing over a telecommunications system.

Applying these various provisions to offences committed in respect of mobile telephones creates various problems in view of the many novel ways in which such frauds may be perpetrated. For example, the act of cloning a mobile telephone (see below) may involve crimes of theft, various computer crimes as well as a number of telecommunications offences.

Thus, although this legislative armory is extensive, it is not by any means certain that future offences involving theft of telecommunications services will be covered.

How, then, are telecommunications services stolen?

The ways in which services are stolen

Table 1 (appended to this chapter) summarises the principal ways in which telecommunications services have been stolen throughout the world over the last thirty years. This information has been compiled from a number of sources including Clough and Mungo (1992), Delaney (1993), Brooks and Davis (1994), Sulc (1994) and Denning (1995). A number of the types of theft referred to in Table 1 relate only to services available in the United States and some have been effectively prevented by technological and other solutions.

Offending has been directed against various targets within the telecommunications system which, for the sake of convenience, have been grouped in nine categories. In relation to each of these target groups a range of illegal activities have been devised by individuals to obtain services without cost to the user and these are described in the method column along with their designation in the offence type column. Finally, control and preventive strategies are identified in the final column.

Metering system fraud

Metering system fraud, or what is known as "boxing", entails the use of electronic devices to by-pass systems which are used to establish metering of calls and the subsequent billing of services. This was the earliest fraud to appear in connection with telephone services and was often carried out through curiosity rather than as an attempt to obtain services for financial gain although, clearly, it was necessary to act illegally in order to carry out the activities in question. Most of this kind of fraud involved the use of devices (in boxes of different colours and about the size of a pocket calculator) which generate signalling and dialling tones. The operation of the original Blue Box in the United States has been described above. The construction and use of these devices required some technical knowledge concerning the operation of switching in telephone systems, although often the desired result was achieved by trial and error. Carriers have, on the whole, dealt with these offences through the means of technological countermeasures.

Billing system fraud

Billing system fraud is directed at the provision of services without cost by means of deception and deceit, in which false or misleading information is given regarding the identity of the subscriber or the party to be billed. For example, an offender may ask an exchange operator to charge a call to his or her home account, which in fact is an account belonging to an unknown third party, and if the operator fails adequately to verify this fact with the third party, the call may be improperly billed to the third party rather than the offender (Delaney 1993).

In Chapter 7 below, we review a number of instances of telemarketing fraud which involve the manipulation of telephone billing systems. These so-called premium service frauds entail offenders deceiving their victims into dialling long-distance or pay-per-call numbers without realising the extent of their liability. Various strategies are used to keep callers on the line for lengthy periods in order that they incur substantial fees, a proportion of which are then paid to the fraudster.

In Victoria, two students were convicted of defrauding Telecom of approximately A$24,000. In 1992 they illegally connected an electronic device to wires within Telecom "pits" adjacent to public telephone booths which caused nine separate 0055 information numbers repeatedly to ring. For every call made, Telecom received 35 per cent of the call charge while the service provider received the remaining 65 per cent, of which a proportion was paid to the offenders as information providers. By causing a constant stream of calls to be made to the numbers, the offenders were able to deflect some A$167,000 of Telecom's money to the service providers who then paid part of this into various bank accounts opened by the offenders in false names (*R v Liang and Li* (1995) 82 A Crim R 39).

Occasionally, technological flaws in systems may be exploited in order to obtain services without effective contractual arrangements being established. Customer-owned coin-operated telephones, for example, may be used by offenders to gain access to unrestricted dial tones by overcoming in-built security measures or simply by connecting their own handset to the line provided.

Charging calls to subscribers' accounts using stolen, unallocated, expired or bogus telecommunications credit cards has also been used. A number of techniques have been employed to obtain account and security numbers for use in such frauds. *Shoulder surfing* is the technique of spying on people when they enter their account and security numbers in public places, either through the use of cameras or simply by looking over their shoulders. *Cracking* or *scanning* entails the use of a computer and a sequential number dial-out programme to obtain the four-digit Personal Identification Number (PIN) which follows an area code and telephone number. Finally, traditional criminal techniques of *social engineering* have been used to trick gullible people into revealing their account and security numbers in the belief that they are required for legitimate purposes (Delaney 1993). Such techniques have become rife in connection with mobile telephone crimes, discussed below.

Action taken to prevent such abuses has generally been directed at establishing subscribers' identities with certainty and authenticating evidence provided at the time contracts for the provision of telephone services are entered into. In addition, telecommunications carriers and service providers have also devised a variety of technological means to detect and prevent such activities such as the use of standard prefix numbers which indicate charging rates for premium calls and the use of carrier calling cards which have enabled fraudulent billing of services to be avoided (Olson 1994). Finally, and most importantly, customers have been alerted to the problem and asked to be more careful when using account and security numbers.

Exchange fraud

A wide variety of offences have been directed at services offered through telephone exchanges, and again use is made of systemic defects in order to obtain services in the name of fictitious or anonymous subscribers or by employing deceit to obtain fees for services provided to non-existent entities. Call diversion facilities have been used on a number of occasions.

One of the largest areas of exchange fraud involves the use of Private Automatic Branch Exchanges (PABX) which are customer-operated computerised telephone switching systems. As well as providing internal telephone communications within an organisation, a PABX may be linked with other public or private networks. A PABX which is equipped with a Direct Inwards System Access (DISA) service allows remote callers to make long-distance calls through the PABX at the expense of the company operating the PABX. Using various devices, offenders are able to re-route STD calls through the PABX without cost to the caller (Cook 1991b, Steffens 1993, Olson 1994, Thrasher 1994). In Britain it was reported that five companies lost the equivalent of A$150,000 in two weeks due to PABX fraud, one victim recording 19,000 unauthorised calls in one night (Peachey and Blau 1995). In another recent case, illegal access was gained to Scotland Yard's PABX DISA system by individuals in the United States who incurred calls to the value of A$1.29 million for which Scotland Yard was liable. It is said to be taking civil action against the company which installed the system (Tendler and Nuttall 1996).

Network "Looping" or "Weaving" involves making calls via various computer networks in order to obtain toll-free calls and is elegantly described in Clifford Stoll's *The Cuckoo's Egg* (1991).

A mixture of technological countermeasures and enhanced identification checks have been successfully employed to counter such schemes.

Line interception

Line interception or "Teeing-In" has been used by offenders throughout the history of the telecommunications industry to make use of services which are lawfully provided to other subscribers. Originally, wires were attached to existing private or public lines to obtain free calls, although in recent years the use of devices to overcome line access controls, such as for cable television services, has been used to obtain free services. For example, in the case of *United States v Neplokh* (1993, United States District Court, Northern District of California) various individual and corporate defendants were convicted of selling cable television equipment designed to intercept television programming without

70

authorisation.[2] In Britain, following the decision of the House of Lords in *BBC Enterprises v Hi-Tech Xtravision* [1993] 3 All ER 257, the *Broadcasting Act 1990* (Eng) was amended to create an offence of making, importing, selling or letting for hire any unauthorised decoder for encrypted television broadcasts (see Long 1995). In Australia, recently proposed amendments to the *Copyright Act 1968* (Cth) would make the fraudulent reception of encoded television broadcasts and the commercial dealing in unauthorised decoding devices illegal attracting both civil and criminal sanctions.[3]

Countermeasures in this area have generally been directed at auditing of billing and physical line surveillance to detect illegal points of entry.

Mobile telephone fraud

Mobile telephony has provided significant opportunities for offenders to obtain services without any or with only minimal cost. Offenders have employed both traditional techniques which were used to obtain fixed wire services free, such as the use of false identities when engaging services, as well as novel approaches which make use of technological flaws in security procedures. Some of the many strategies employed to obtain services improperly include the following.

Stolen mobile telephones. Because mobile telephones are, indeed, mobile, they may be stolen and immediately used by offenders to obtain calls unless access to calling is protected by a PIN. Such unauthorised calls will be charged to the legitimate subscriber until such time as the theft is reported and the service withdrawn. As we have seen, there has been a substantial increase in the number of mobile telephones stolen throughout the world and many of these thefts are associated with violence. In London, for example, a taxi driver was reported to have died after having his mobile telephone stolen in circumstances of violence (Wong 1995a).

Subscription fraud. As with fixed wire services, offenders have taken out mobile telephone subscriptions using false identification details and incurred fees until such time as the service is cancelled for non-payment of fees. Occasionally, offenders may conspire with dishonest telecommunications staff in order to circumvent identity and credit-rating checks (Wong 1995b).

Obtaining network access. We have seen in the Introduction how billing of analogue mobile telephone services is achieved through the transmission of security identification information through the airwaves in the

---

2   See also the cases of *United States v Hux, dba Fireball Electronics* 26 July 1991, United States Court of Appeals, 8th Cir No. 90-2914 and *United States v Suppenbach aka Decoder Bob* 26 July 1993, United States Court of Appeals, 8th Cir No 92-3698.

3   In the United States, the *Report of the Working Group on Intellectual Property Rights* (United States, Information Infrastructure Task Force 1995: 230) recommended the creation of new offences in relation to devices which are used to infringe copyright in the following terms: "The Copyright Act should be amended to prohibit the importation, manufacture or distribution of any device, product or component incorporated into a device or product, or the provision of any service, the primary purpose or effect of which is to avoid, bypass, remove, deactivate, or otherwise circumvent, without lawful authority of the copyright owner or the law, any process, treatment, mechanism or system which prevents or inhibits the violation of copyright". In Britain, s 297A of the *Copyright Designs and Patents Act 1988* creates a criminal offence of making, importing, selling, or hiring unauthorised satellite decoding devices.

form of the telephone's electronic serial number (ESN) and its mobile identification number (MIN). Unauthorised access to the network is gained initially by ascertaining the ESN/MIN combination. The techniques of shoulder surfing, scanning and social engineering, referred to above, have been used to obtain mobile telephone security numbers. For example, ESN/MIN combinations have been obtained by individuals claiming to be engineers who request details of the numbers ostensibly to check the network, or by garage mechanics who note the numbers on mobile telephones of cars being repaired. Electronic scanners have also been developed which are capable of reading these numbers while they are being transmitted through the airwaves. Such devices store the numbers obtained and then load them into computer software ready for programming into another telephone (Brooks and Davis 1994). Alternatively, security numbers can be obtained directly from manufacturers and retailers who have less than adequate security procedures in their offices (Sulc 1994), or even some dishonest subscribers may pass on their own security numbers to others who use them to make counterfeit telephones (Wong 1995b).

In the United States, specific legislation now makes illegal the possession, trafficking, or use of scanning devices used in mobile telephone fraud. There exist as well various other provisions which prohibit the possession of instruments used for the purpose of obtaining unauthorised telecommunications services (*United States Code*, Title 18, § 1029). The penalties provided for infringement are substantial: a maximum fine of US$50,000 or imprisonment for up to fifteen years for a first offence; and a maximum fine of US$100,000 or imprisonment for up to twenty years for subsequent offences (see Schwartz 1995 and Cunningham 1996).

Counterfeit telephones. Having obtained an ESN/MIN combination, offenders then seek to produce a counterfeit copy or clone of the mobile telephone, thus enabling calls to be billed to the legitimate subscriber without his or her knowledge until such time as an account arrives. The fraud is carried out by writing a computer program containing an algorithm that allows the ESN to be changed. This is burned into an EPROM (microchip) and inserted into the cellular telephone replacing the original EPROM. The program can tell the telephone to send out a different ESN on each dial-out, and it may give the owner the ability to re-program the telephone's ESN from the keypad whenever he or she wants (Delaney 1993). In the United States, software which enables the cloning of mobile telephones is freely available through mail order services or electronics flea markets for less than A$65, although, again, possession of such material has recently been made illegal (Walters and Wilkinson 1994, Schwartz 1995).

Although a number of instances of cloning have occurred in Australia, the problem is largely confined to the United States and Britain at present. In Britain, for example, cloning is said to have increased by 500 per cent during the period August 1994 to August 1995 with over 4000 incidents per month (United Kingdom, Industry and Government Study Group on Mobile Phone Fraud 1995). The Cellular Telecommunications Industry Association estimates that 60,000 cellular telephones are cloned each day in the United States and Canada (Cunningham 1996), while in the United States, organised criminals make widespread use of counterfeit telephones which are often disposed of after only one call is made, thus avoiding detection (Ramo 1996).

Roaming fraud. Where calls are made in a so-called "roaming" environment, out of reach of the subscriber's normal cell site, offenders in the United States and Europe, where a number of mobile telephone carriers are licensed to operate, have discovered that it is possible to change a mobile telephone's ESN/MIN combination randomly or sequentially every one or two calls. This can confuse the cellular switch for a sufficiently long period to enable a call to be made without incurring a charge (Sulc 1994, Brooks and Davis 1994). Obviously, lengthy calls cannot be made using such an approach. This method of fraud began in California in 1988 and reached New York in 1989. During 1990, the United States Secret Service provided an algorithm to cellular carriers which would prevent mobile telephones from being used in this way (Delaney 1993). In addition, recent pre-call validation technology has limited the extent to which such frauds may occur.

"Lifetime phones". Some illegal mobile telephones were developed in the early 1990s in the United States. These "Lifetime Phones" which had the ability to store as many as ninety-nine valid ESN/MIN pairs, were completely programmable through the keypad. They were capable of being used as clones; manually programming another legitimate subscriber's ESN/MIN pair into these telephones made them look like legitimate telephones. The Lifetime Phone was available throughout the United States and Canada for the equivalent of around A$2000 (Cunningham 1996).

Illegal sale of services. In the United States, the proliferation of illegal mobile telephones was such that organised groups of criminals became involved in selling telephone services to those who were unable to obtain legitimate access to services such as the indigent and illegal immigrants. In New York City, one such group, the "Orchard Street Finger-Hackers" became notorious. This group of offenders, who came out of the cocaine-dealing sub-culture, sold stolen long-distance telephone services in various unsavoury neighbourhoods to a captive clientele of illegal immigrants who were desperate to call home (see Sterling 1993 and Ramo 1996).

Countermeasures. Traditional countermeasures, such as enhanced subscriber identification checks and early invoicing, have been employed to thwart the efforts of mobile telephone service offenders, while new technological solutions have been devised to reduce the opportunities for offending. In such a field of rapid technological change, however, offenders keep close pace with any technological countermeasures designed to stop their activities.

Employee fraud

The final type of offending relies upon the knowledge and contacts which employees of telecommunications organisations have regarding the operation of systems and security procedures. Often, offences are committed by staff themselves, although occasionally staff provide others with access to services through weak links in security procedures. Examples of such fraud include the improper use of line testing facilities to connect the offender or third parties to

IDD calls at a reduced cost or for free, or the direct theft of telecommunications equipment for personal use or resale.

In the *Review of Matters Affecting the Australian Telecommunications Commission* conducted by Mr Frank Vincent QC (as he then was), details were given of a range of criminal activities engaged in by Telecom staff which were dealt with pursuant to the disciplinary provisions of the *Telecommunications Act 1975* (Cth), the current legislation at the time. Although Telecom employees were disciplined for a range of acts of misappropriation of equipment and other fraudulent conduct, the scale of such illegality was not large (Vincent 1984). In 1992, the New South Wales Independent Commission Against Corruption found that a number of Telecom employees had sold confidential Telecom information to certain private investigators (ICAC 1992).

More recently, in Western Australia, a number of employees of Telstra were allegedly involved in fraudulent attempts to win radio competitions through the manipulation of exchanges to enable their calls to be selected as the winning call. One employee was alleged to have won A$50,000 in a competition requiring his to be the 10th call, while another employee allegedly arranged for his to be the 92nd call, enabling him to receive A$10,000 (Morfesse 1996).

Another example of fraud which may be committed by employees involves the redirection or misappropriation of telephone numbers themselves. In the case of *Bowden v Boucher* (1996) 70 ALJ 612, a woman employed by a telephone fantasy business improperly told customers who had called for sexually explicit conversation, that the telephone number of the service was to be changed and then provided them with an alternative number. This number directed callers to another similar business which she established in competition with that of her former employer. Approximately A$40,000 in goodwill was lost by the original business by reason of the redirection of customers for which the court awarded equitable compensation.

In the United States in 1994, an employee of MCI Telecommunications Corporation, was charged with stealing more than 100,000 telephone calling cards that were used to make US$50 million worth of long-distance calls. The fraud was perpetrated by the employee who was a switch engineer, using computer software to divert and hold calling card numbers from a variety of carriers that ran through MCI's switching equipment. The numbers were then purchased by hackers in the United States and Europe who sold them to Europeans to be used to make calls to the United States which were billed to legitimate subscribers (Anonymous 1994).

Personnel screening and operational controls have generally been successful in dealing with such problems (see Sims and Sims 1995).

Policies for the 21st century

Areas of emerging crime

The Commonwealth Bureau of Transport and Communications Economics Final Report, *Communications Futures* (1995) identified the technological developments which are likely to influence residential markets in the period 1995 to 2005, noting particularly the importance of mobile communications, the Internet, private data networks and the growing convergence of computing and communications technologies and products. The emergence of pay television and the subsequent evolution over the next decade into other broadband products such as video-on-demand and switched broadband services including video telephony were also mentioned as likely developments. One of the latest examples of convergence of data processing and communications technology is the so-called "smart phone" which has a small display panel and can be used for simple online computing including access to the Internet (Shiver 1996).

If such developments take place on a wide scale it seems that new social divisions could emerge based upon access to and familiarity with the new technologies. (See the Australian Bureau of Statistics (1996) figures on ownership of mobile, cordless and car telephones referred to in Chapter 1). People without access to these products may feel isolated and deprived and a new environment conducive to criminality may be created in which theft of telecommunications equipment and services will become a major social problem. Alternatively, it has been argued that once the market for telecommunications equipment has been saturated, the desire to obtain telephones and services illegally may decline (Wong 1995b). In a recent study by Coutorie (1995), however, in which the opinions of various experts were canvassed in order to predict the types of crimes which would be prevalent in the future, both traditional and non-traditional experts agreed that computer system attacks via telecommunications systems would be a high-technology area of concern (1995).

The financial implications could be ominous for business. New telecommunications services, initially, will be much more expensive than standard telephony services which, even at present, can lead to substantial losses for those in the industry. The motivation to steal services will be greater for those who feel isolated and unable to participate in the highly-publicised global telecommunications community. Unless adequate precautions are taken, organised crime may emerge as a significant threat to further business and technological developments. Put simply, customers may be reluctant to take up the new technologies through fear of falling prey to telecommunications fraudsters, while organisations may be reluctant to invest in enterprises if substantial crime-related losses are thought to be a real possibility.

Detection and reporting

A number of problems have been encountered by law enforcement agencies in detecting theft of telecommunications services. At the outset is the difficulty of persuading individuals to report illegal conduct. Often, subscribers are simply unaware that they have been victimised. When they do discover the problem they may be reluctant to report the matter. As an OECD report noted:

> The victim may be no clearer than the offender of his rights and obligations and may not be prepared to divulge information if the consequence could be to threaten a market position or commercial credibility (OECD 1986).

Carriers who may become aware of illegal activities may also be unable to draw these to the attention of subscribers due to concerns over confidentiality and privacy. They may also feel reluctant to notify customers in a fiercely competitive marketplace through fear of losing customer confidence in their security measures.

Turning to some specific areas of illegality, Delaney (1993) describes a number of practical problems for law enforcement agencies in investigating PABX frauds, such as gaining information and time delays in obtaining warrants, while Sterling provides an account of some of the problems encountered in various FBI operations conducted against adult telecommunications career criminals (Sterling 1993).

The Cellular Telephone Industry Association in the United States has adopted a number of strategies to deal with cellular fraud including close liaison with law enforcement agencies and the use of joint training sessions to help law enforcement officials understand what cellular fraud is and how they can fight it (Sulc 1994). In late 1992, for example, a joint operation involving the cellular telephone industry and law enforcement forces, called "L.A. Blitz" was conducted in Los Angeles which resulted in the arrest of twenty-two people, the confiscation of sixty-six "no-bill" telephones, 3000 chips, twelve computers, and new software. More recently, in 1995, state and local police in the United States arrested more than 3000 individuals for telecommunications offences while in the first six months of 1996, the United States Secret Service arrested 259 individuals for telecommunications fraud (Cunningham 1996). Police in the United States are also starting to employ so-called "sting" operations. In one case in 1995, for example, United States agents apprehended three alleged offenders who had been selling cloned mobile telephones and using the international operation to launder the proceeds of drug trafficking. The agents had placed an advertisement on the Internet seeking to purchase cloned telephones, and, using a lawfully-obtained interception warrant, located the offenders by tapping their e-mail replies (Morrison 1995).

Since 1984, in Britain, New Scotland Yard has had a specialist computer crime unit with national responsibilities for liaison with telecommunications organisations, training of law enforcement personnel, and coordination of investigations (Austen 1996). On 13 June 1995, the Industry and Government Study Group on Mobile Phone Fraud was established, which has recommended the introduction of additional specialist law enforcement units to deal with mobile telephone fraud and the establishment of specific points of contact within each police force area to complement the initiatives being taken by the industry to reduce the opportunity for the commission of mobile telephone fraud (United Kingdom, Industry and Government Study Group on Mobile Phone Fraud 1995). Interpol also has a computer crime committee which coordinates cross-border investigations and conducts law enforcement training courses (Austen 1996).

In Australia in 1990, the Australian Telecommunications Authority established a Law Enforcement Advisory Committee (1995) to assist law enforcement and government security agencies in enforcing laws throughout the country. Both Federal and state law enforcement agencies are thus provided with a source of current information on the operation of telecommunications networks and new technological developments.

Clearly, law enforcement agencies need staff who are trained to the same or higher levels of expertise than the offenders, and this may best be achieved by utilising the services of telecommunications personnel on a consultancy basis. Specific law enforcement units could also be established to investigate telecommunications crime, which may help to legitimise this area of offending as worthy of attention in the eyes of law enforcement and other government agencies.

Regulatory reform

In deciding how best to approach the problem of telecommunications crime and particularly the theft of services, policy makers may choose to proceed down a variety of paths. One is to take legislative and administrative action to deal with the problem before it becomes unmanageable. Coutorie (1995) states this position well.

> High technology crime has not yet directly affected many individuals in society and law enforcement administrators have been reluctant to dedicate much of their limited resources to this arena of crime. If nothing is done until it becomes politically important enough to target, law enforcement will be hopelessly behind the learning and technology curves to address the problem. Enormous resources, at enormous expense, and the use of outside law enforcement will have to be brought to bear to control it.

Already some of these fears have been realised in relation to the theft of mobile telephone services and some argue that it is already too late to introduce regulatory reforms. An alternative path requires policy makers to take a more cautious approach such as that described in relation to the regulation of online intellectual property.

> Australian governments should not succumb to the temptation to over-regulate and too quickly move to mandate severe civil and criminal [offences] before electronic commerce matures and becomes embedded in our daily lives. Rather the response should be one of rapid response to problems as they arise, informed by acute sensitivity to the need to protect the interests of both individual citizens and firms (Buckeridge and Cutler 1995).

In the sensitive commercial marketplace at a time when communities are attempting to realise the potential of new technological developments, a cautious approach to regulation may be preferable. Arguably, this could best be achieved by self-regulation in the industries concerned and by a realisation that both the providers and users of services have a role to play in protecting their own interests and in preventing illegality for the benefit of all concerned. This point was emphasised recently in relation to the regulation of computer bulletin boards in the *Report of the Computer Bulletin Board Systems Task Force*. This Task Force did, however, oppose the option of taking no action at present and waiting until the extent of the illegality became significant. This position was explained as follows.

> Although the problem is statistically small at present, the issues raised by it will continue to grow in significance as the technology develops. If an attempt is not made to come to grips with it at this point, the difficulty of doing so at a later date can only be expected to increase. Further, to do nothing at all at this time may be interpreted by the segment of the community which abuses, or may

abuse, the technology as an admission of impotence by government (Commonwealth of Australia, Attorney-General's Department and Department of Communication and the Arts 1994: 9).

Other regulatory strategies may also have something to offer. Employment law, for example, may have an important role to play in regulating unauthorised access to facilities and improper use of services by providing for employment-related sanctions for those who engage in theft of services. Clear guidelines on what is and what is not acceptable in the workplace would need to be provided in advance to employees with the consequences of non-compliance explicitly stated in contracts of employment.

Although registration and licensing of traders has been suggested for mobile telephones, caution may well be called for in introducing extensive bureaucratic systems of this nature. The United Kingdom Parliamentary Office of Science and Technology (1995), for example, considered that such schemes may inhibit trade and reduce competition in the mobile telephone industry. As an alternative, the Office recommended more advanced property marking schemes such as the use of identity numbers on printed circuit boards.

The technical and practical difficulties associated with implementing reforms also need to be considered, for as the OECD noted, technical legal problems of prosecution and proof may mean that it is difficult to achieve convictions and to enforce sanctions, thereby adding to the enforcement challenge.

> One of the factors inherent in information and telecommunications technologies is that their misuse can leave no trace; but law is traditionally based on texts and material evidence of acts which, for computer-related crime, are often unavailable. This makes it difficult to assess the scale of and to detect and prosecute computer-related crime (OECD 1986: 24).

This problem of the ephemeral nature of telecommunications could present insurmountable difficulties for those, like Fisse (1990), who suggest that the use of civil remedies may be preferable to the continued expansion of the criminalisation of certain property offences. In the realm of theft of telecommunications services, for example, it may well be impossible to prove the loss and damage necessary to succeed in civil proceedings.

Criminalisation

While many illegal activities relating to telecommunications services are covered by the existing law, the further criminalisation of such conduct has a number of dangers. First, is the difficulty, noted by Dunning (1982), of over-codifying behaviour:

> one does not want to enact a new provision every time a new permutation of criminal behaviour arises. Ideally, the elasticity of a common law system will supply the omissions of the legislature but there are limits to which our judiciary will, and indeed can, go.

As we have already seen, there is a wide array of criminal offences which govern the use of telecommunications systems and although these have not been rigorously interpreted as yet, it is likely that they will be effective in dealing with most situations in which services are stolen. Where omissions exist, parliament could enact specific laws with limited effect. In relation to mobile telephone crime, the United Kingdom Parliamentary Office of Science and Technology (1995) suggested that the following be made illegal: re-chipping of telephones except under licence; possession of re-chipping equipment; the interception of network security data (ESN and International Mobile Electronic Identity (IMEI) numbers) and the possession of radio scanners. In 1997, in Britain, legislation was enacted which created new offences of possessing or supplying anything which may be used for fraudulently obtaining a telecommunications service (*Telecommunications (Fraud) Act* 1997 (Eng)). The maximum penalty for the fraudulent use of a telecommunications system is now five years' imprisonment.

In order to prevent any negative effects of such laws on the industry, it may be preferable to focus new laws on those who manufacture and distribute goods used in carrying out illegal activities rather than enacting strict liability offences relating to the possession of illegal equipment by consumers.

The role of crime prevention

The area of telecommunications crime provides some excellent examples of what might be described as "counterproductive crime prevention", namely, the negative and unintended consequences of some crime prevention strategies (Grabosky 1996). Some examples include the escalation of offending due to frustration which technological barriers impose, the forbidden fruit phenomenon of activities being criminalised and creative technological adaptation to telecommunications crime prevention strategies.

An examination of the motivations behind the theft of telecommunications services is a good starting point.

Greed and profit-making are the traditionally-recognised reasons for stealing telecommunications services and it has been argued that some offenders have established lucrative businesses of dealing in stolen equipment and services (Delaney 1993). Providing services to facilitate other illegal activity is also common such as the use of stolen mobile telephones in drug importation and distribution where anonymity of both the caller and receiver is critical (see Natarajan, Clarke and Belanger 1996). Take, for example, the case of Pablo Escobar, one of the world's most notorious cocaine traffickers, whose location was ascertained by law enforcement agencies tracing his cellular telephone activity. In July 1992, a small fleet of aircraft equipped with scanning devices and onboard computers with voice recognition programs, flew over Medellin while monitoring thousands of calls, some of which matched samples of Escobar's voice, thus facilitating the identification of his location (Thompson 1996). Young (1995) and Kearney and Papadopoulos (1997) provide other examples of tracing the whereabouts of offenders through their mobile telephone activity).

Hacking into telecommunications systems may, as we saw in Chapter 3, be carried out for reasons of curiosity, intrigue and entertainment, rather than profit-making (Hiber and Christy 1994).

Traditional crime prevention strategies will continue to offer many opportunities for combating the activities of offenders who operate in the high-technology world of telecommunications and who are motivated by greed and a desire for personal gain. Applying Clarke's (1992 and 1995) categories of situational crime prevention to the present context yields the following techniques which may be used to prevent theft of telecommunications services.

Increasing the effort

Target hardening:	Tamper-proof telephones and lines
Access control:	Passwords, PINs, tokens, biometrics and encryption
Deflecting offenders:	Use of computer games and the Internet
Controlling facilitators:	Registration of telephones and service users, caller identification

Increasing the risks

Entry/exit screening:	Checks on use of passwords and PINs
Formal surveillance:	Computerised auditing of use of services and billing
Surveillance by employees:	Public telephone location, carrier audits
Natural surveillance:	Carrier employee reporting of colleagues

Reducing the rewards

Target removal:	Government or industry funded services, phonecards
Identifying property:	Registration of telephones and equipment
Removing inducements:	Restricted publicity of crimes
Rule setting:	Clarification of telephone billing procedures

While these traditional responses may be appropriate to deal with some forms of theft of telecommunications services, policy makers may need to be more imaginative and look to various alternative controls. Some of these are as follows.

Opportunity reduction by telecommunications organisations

The *Telecommunications Act* 1991 (Cth) contains a number of provisions which require carriers and service providers to take steps to ensure that their facilities are not used for illegal purposes. Sub-section (1) of s 47 of the *Telecommunications Act* 1991 (Cth), for example, requires carriers "to do their best to prevent telecommunication networks and facilities . . . from being used in, or in relation to, the commission of offences against the laws of the Commonwealth and of the States and Territories" (see also ss 53 and 88). Although s 47 does not permit a carrier to disconnect a service to a subscriber in breach of the rules of procedural fairness (see *Telstra Corporation Limited v Kendall* (1994) 55 FCR 221, discussed by Watts 1995), organisations are obliged to take obvious precautions such as conducting reasonable identification checks on new subscribers by requiring readily verifiable information to be provided.

Telecommunications organisations should also take care to ensure that their technological equipment cannot be used to perpetrate illegal acts. In *Kennison v Daire* (1986) 160 CLR 129, for example, an individual was convicted of obtaining A$200 from his bank account, which had previously been closed, from an automatic teller machine. In discussing this case, Fisse (1990) argues that the law of theft should not be used to protect organisations such as banks against errors which expose consumers to high temptation and which can readily be avoided by technological means.

In the United States, where obvious fraud prevention steps have not been taken by carriers, some subscribers have argued in civil proceedings that they should not be held personally liable for fees incurred by reason of telecommunications fraud where the carrier has acted negligently in failing to ensure that systems operate securely. In one case in 1990, a company refused to pay an account totalling the equivalent of A$551,000 which had been improperly incurred. It counterclaimed against the carrier in the sum of A$13 million for loss suffered as a result of the carrier's neglect in failing adequately to warn it of vulnerabilities in its PABX system which had enabled 30,000 unauthorised calls to be made (*Mitsubishi v AT&T Communications*. See Cook 1991b; Flanagan and McMenamin 1992).

In relation to mobile telephone offences, some carriers have refused to permit subscribers to use subscriber identification module (SIM) cards on other countries' networks without first having undergone special credit checks. In Europe, some service providers have even considered the withdrawal of roaming capabilities entirely in order to reduce losses (Blau 1994). In the United States, carriers initially dealt with roaming frauds by blocking calls made to those countries most frequently called by offenders such as Colombia and the Dominican Republic. In France, network operators only permit international use of mobile telephones at the specific request of a subscriber, while in the United Kingdom, Cellnet only allows international use of mobile telephones to specified customers. In order to guard against the payment of accounts with bad cheques, some carriers only allow customers to have network access after cheques have cleared (Wong 1995b).

Vodafone has a fraud prevention strategy of automatically routing high-cost international calls via operators who check upon the identity and credit rating of the caller, while Vodac, the service provider owned by Vodafone, has introduced a system whereby the SIM card can only be used with the mobile telephone it was purchased with. Some have also argued that the SIM card system should be abolished and that all SIM data should be anchored in the circuit boards of mobile telephones (Purton 1994). In Australia, one company has produced software for an international database of stolen mobile telephones. The IMEI numbers of stolen telephones as well as unsold telephones are recorded on the database and when one of these handsets is used to make a call, the relevant authorities are automatically notified. Once a telephone is reported as stolen, it will not be able to be used and the caller can then be traced by the police (B. D. Software 1997; see also Anonymous 1996c). AUSTEL's Law Enforcement Advisory Committee 1995 is also considering the use of such databases for all carriers.

Most recently, British Telecom and MCI in the United States have collaborated on a project called SHERIFF (Statistical Heuristic Engine to Reliably and Intelligently Fight Fraud). This is a network-embedded global fraud detection and management system which is able to scan networks to detect a wide range of products (McIntosh 1997).

All of these strategies are aimed at carriers and service providers taking decisive action to protect themselves as well as their subscribers.

Technological countermeasures

The primary strategy adopted by the telecommunications industry to deal with theft of services has been the adoption of technological means to prevent continuing abuse of systems. The case of cellular mobile telephones is a good example of how continual technological improvement has been used to combat the ingenuity of criminals in obtaining services for free. In the words of Albanese (1988):

> Rapid changes in technology generate opportunities for theft that can be exploited by criminals for financial gain. Only after thieves experience some success does the government, or private industry, take steps to reduce the opportunities for theft. This improvement in detection and/or prevention technology must then be matched, or surpassed, by criminals if they are to avoid apprehension.

Some of the target-hardening strategies which manufacturers, carriers and providers have adopted to control mobile telephone fraud include the use of software to detect calls being transmitted from a counterfeit telephone at the same time as another legitimate source (call collisions), to block the receipt of calls from cloned telephones altogether, velocity checks which are able to determine whether a telephone has moved too fast between serving areas to be legitimate, toll access restrictions to prevent unauthorised access to international dialling, unusual activity analysis to detect unusual usage patterns such as lengthy international calls as an indication of fraud, dialled-number analysis which allows the carrier to block out high-risk countries or individual numbers, analysis of time of day, minutes of usage or credit activity for abnormal patterns of usage, radio frequency fingerprinting which measures the characteristics in a telephone's signal, and voice print matching which compares the subscriber's voice print with that recorded at the cell site (Sulc 1994; Walters and Wilkinson 1994; Wong 1995a; Young 1995). In the United Kingdom, however, the Parliamentary Office of Science and Technology (1995) has observed that the use of some of these strategies may be difficult to implement with nearly two million telephones on each analogue network and the fact that service providers need access to network operators' billing data in real time rather than with the current twelve-hour delay.

Elsewhere, it has been reported that mobile telephone security numbers are being protected by devising viruses which will infect systems which gain unauthorised entry into a chip (Anonymous 1993). New digital telephones which adopt the Cellular Industry Standard IS-54 will also be much more difficult, but not impossible, to clone (Walters and Wilkinson 1994; Markoff 1997). Systems are also in place which enable cellular telephones to be locked by the use of a

PIN when the telephone is not in use allowing incoming calls still to be received but if the telephone is stolen outgoing calls will not be able to be made (Cellular One 1994). Finally, various systems are being trialed to identify mobile telephone transmissions by the use of digital signatures (Brooks and Davis 1994). Each of these technological strategies carries with it further costs which, inevitably, will be passed on to customers. Because it is the customers who suffer losses arising out of fraudulent activities, manufacturers, carriers and service providers may be reluctant to incur costs themselves in devising such crime prevention strategies.

Human resource industry controls

Although accounting for only a relatively small proportion of illegal activities, conduct committed through internal security breaches or by the conduct of industry personnel may be prevented by ensuring that reliable and trustworthy staff are employed and that staff are adequately remunerated and have good working conditions, thus reducing the relative attractiveness of illegal conduct (see Sims and Sims 1995 for a review of the effectiveness of human resource management strategies for countering corporate misconduct generally). Internal organisational controls such as separation of responsibilities and rotation of duties should enable misconduct by employees to be more easily identified. Specific training and ethical education of staff may also alert employees to the fact that security arrangements are in place within organisations (see Sumner 1996 and Kling 1996 for discussions of ethical behaviour in the digital age).

Self-help and user education

Education has long been considered as one of the most effective ways of reducing the threat of criminality. Both children and adults need constructive training in the ethics of high technology and the undesirability of manipulation of technological systems for entertainment or financial gain (see, for example, Bequai 1987; Kling 1996; and Sumner 1996). Walters and Wilkinson (1994) similarly stress the importance of training and awareness of employees in fraud prevention strategies. They argue that there is a need for employee screening processes and fraud awareness training and that support vendors, sales agents and retailers need to be held accountable for fraud which results from their negligence.

In addition, users are able to take many steps to detect illegality before it becomes a major problem or to avoid victimisation completely. Companies such as Bell Atlantic (1996), Pacific Bell (1996) and Cellular One (1994), for example, offer advice to customers as to how telephone fraud may be prevented.[4] Some recommended practices include noting the presence of frequent wrong numbers or hang-up calls, observing difficulties in placing outgoing calls, difficulties in retrieving voice mail messages and having incoming callers constantly receiving busy signals or wrong numbers. Some fraud prevention strategies which are recommended for customers to adopt include checking bills for unusual calls, particularly those involving high charges such as ISD numbers,

---

4   See also Royal Canadian Mounted Police "Economic Crime Prevention Web Page", http://www.rcmp-grc.gc.ca/html/ecbweb.htm.

keeping ESN and MIN numbers secure, locking telephones with a PIN when not in use, not leaving telephones unattended in cars, using only authorised technicians and eliminating international dialling capabilities of telephones when not being used.

Delaney (1993) discusses various other strategies for preventing PABX fraud including making the person responsible for the system look for early warning signs, such as rapidly increased use, system slowdown due to excessive use, outgoing calls to foreign countries or unusual areas, and high off-hour use. Similarly, Cook (1991b) suggests assigning one person to oversee the PABX system, daily monitoring of the system, limiting the number of people with access to the PABX long-distance code, changing the code frequently and checking for multiple failed attempts to gain access to the system.

In relation to cable television, Schieck (1995) suggests that subscribers check billing records to ensure that they are being billed correctly, protect passwords and have different passwords for different levels of access, periodically change passwords, remove people from access to systems when they leave employment, conduct regular audits of services and educate suppliers, cable operators and the public as to the laws which apply and the problems of theft of cable services.

In the event that these fraud prevention strategies prove not to be successful, various companies now offer insurance against telecommunications fraud. Tele-Fraud Insurance, offered by Kemper National Insurance Company in the United States, for example, provides insurance cover in respect of damage to telecommunications equipment, loss of business income, and the cost of calls fraudulently made (McKenzie 1995). One would hope that they require a variety of preventive measures to be taken as a condition of their cover.

Conclusions

Theft of telecommunications services has been one of the most enduring types of telecommunications crime which has been evident since the beginning of telephone systems. It provides one of the clearest examples of the synergy which exists between crime prevention and the innovative skills of individuals to overcome security measures to commit further crime. Each technological development designed to thwart criminal endeavours has been quickly followed by the creation of a new form of crime designed to exploit a new security loophole. These few directions for future policy may assist in ensuring that the full potential of global telecommunications developments will be realised while at the same time providing both service providers and users with some expectation that their property rights will be respected.

In order to achieve effective crime prevention in this area, close cooperation is needed between those who manufacture and design telecommunications systems, those who provide and operate those systems, and those of us who make daily use of telephones. Only where such cooperative efforts fail, will law enforcement be needed to investigate the activities of offenders and to alert security technicians to flaws which exist in systems. Arguably, much more may be achieved in reducing theft of telecommunications services by directing resources into crime prevention than by attempting to prosecute those who choose to overcome the skills of telecommunications security technologists.

Table 1
Theft of Telecommunications Services

TARGET	OFFENCE TYPE	METHOD	CONTROL STRATEGY
Metering System	Switching System By-Pass ("Blue Box")	Device which generates tones to by-pass switching systems	Technological countermeasures
	Meter Inhibition ("Black Box")	Device which prevents metering from being initiated	Technological countermeasures
	Coin Drop Simulation ("Red Box")	Device which emits tones which simulate the sound of coins dropping	Technological countermeasures
	Bent Wire	Defeats call charging equipment on public telephones	Technological countermeasures
	Interference with External Software	Interfering with public telephone software to obtain international calls at local rates	Software improvement
	Free Lines	The provision of non-metering exchange lines to subscribers	Operational contro
	C5 Fraud	Use of tone simulators on 0800 IDD services to obtain the destination country's network free	Operational contro
	Counterfeit Debit Cards	Use of unauthorised debit cards in public telephones to obtain free calls	Technological countermeasures
Billing System	Free COCOT Services	Using customer operated coin telephones to obtain access to free dial tones	Technological countermeasures
	Third Party Billing	Charging calls to home accounts without authorisation	Subscriber identification and authentication
	Telephone Calling Cards	Charging calls to accounts using stolen, unallocated, expired or bogus telephone calling cards	Account and card authentication
	Non-Existent Account Billing	Charging calls to non-existent accounts or third party accounts	Account authentication
	Telex Answer-Back	Using telex answer-back codes to pass on charges to third parties	Subscriber identification and authentication
	Telex Handling Charges	Defaulting on the payment of telex handling charges	Subscriber identification and authentication
	0055 Premium Services	Establishing multiple 0055 services to receive profits and defaulting on payment of service fees	Subscriber identification and authentication

Table 1 (cont.)
Theft of Telecommunications Services

TARGET	OFFENCE TYPE	METHOD	CONTROL STRATEGY
Billing System	Mass Pager Billing of High-Cost Calls	Engaging a high-cost-to-caller line and sending mass messages for pagers to call this number	User risk awareness education
Telephone Exchange	Small Exchange IDD Access	Obtaining access through small exchanges for IDD services	Exchange personnel screening
	IDD Call Diversion	Use of exchange-based call diversion services to obtain IDD calls for free	Technological countermeasures
	Public Telephone Reverse Charge Schemes	Using automatic calling number identifiers to obtain reverse charge calls to public telephones for free	Technological countermeasures
	Meter Registration	Causing exchange-based meters to register lower usages than actually incurred	Technological countermeasures
Private Automatic Branch Exchange	PABX Dial-Out Billing	Improperly using a PABX dial-out code to bill outside calls to the owner of the PABX	PABX code security enhancement
	Direct Inwards System Access (DISA)	Charging STD calls to PABX without authorisation	PABX user identification and authentication
	Network Looping (Weaving)	Using PABXs to gain improper access to networks and defaulting on payment of network access fees	PABX user identification and authentication
Telephone Lines	Unauthorised Teeing-In to Public Telephones	Interception of cables serving public telephones to obtain free international calls	Line surveillance and protection
	Unauthorised Teeing-In to Private Subscribers' Services	Unauthorised connections to subscribers' lines to bill calls without their knowledge of permission	Line surveillance and protection
	Hacking into Unallocated Lines	Obtaining access to unallocated lines to obtain calls without paying	Line information controls
	Unauthorised Re-Connection	Unauthorised activation of disconnected services	Technological countermeasures
CableTV Lines	Unauthorised Teeing-In to Cable TV Lines	Obtaining Cable TV services without being a subscriber	Line surveillance and protection
	Unauthorised Cable TV De-Coding	Obtaining Cable TV services without the use of subscriber decoding devices	Subscriber identification and authentication

Table 1 (cont.)
Theft of Telecommunications Services

TARGET	OFFENCE TYPE	METHOD	CONTROL STRATEGY
Telecommunications Equipment	Theft of Telecommunications Equipment	Stealing any telecommunications equipment	Traditional theft prevention strategies
Telephone Numbers	Theft of Telephone Numbers	Diverting calls to other numbers or misappropriating numbers	Personnel screening and operational controls
Mobile Telephones	False Subscriptions	Taking out a subscription using false identification details and failing to pay fees incurred	Subscriber identification and authentication
	Counterfeiting (Cloning)	Identifying an analogue telephone ESN/MIN combination and reproducing this in another telephone to bill calls to another subscriber	Security of numbers software analysis of call patterns and usage, making scanners illegal
	Roaming Fraud	Frequently changing analogue telephone ESN/MIN combination to obtain calls prior to billing (not in Australia)	IS-41 and IS-54 call validation technology
	Network and Billing Weaknesses	Utilising similar network weaknesses as with wired telephones.	Technological countermeasures
	Non-Payment of International Accounts	Subscribing in one country and making calls in another without settling account in home country	Subscriber identification and authentication
	Theft of Mobile Telephones	Using a stolen mobile telephone until the owner reports it stolen	Restricted access using PINs and early reporting
Employees	Test Desks	Improper use of test desk facilities to connect third party IDD calls for profit	Personnel screening and operational controls
	Exchange Test Line Interception	Obtaining access to test lines in exchanges to permit IDD calls to be made at a local rate or for free	Personnel screening and operational controls
	Exchange Trunk Test Line Interception	Using exchange-based trunk line testing facilities to connect third party IDD calls at a local rate or for free	Personnel screening and operational controls
	Faultman's Ring-Back System	Using automatic test equipment to gain improper access to trunk networks for free	Personnel screening and operational controls
	Improper Operator Connections	Operators improperly connecting third-parties for profit without charging or allowing extended time calls	Personnel screening and operational controls

5

TELECOMMUNICATIONS PIRACY

The industrialised world in the 1990s is undergoing what could be described as a techno-legal revolution, and the area of greatest activity is occurring in the legal changes proposed to deal with new communications and information technology. This chapter focuses on one of the most complex and intractable areas, namely the application of intellectual property laws in the world of telecommunications. Specifically, it considers how best to regulate offences of piracy committed through the use of telecommunications services and equipment.

Invoking the concept of piracy in the present context is apposite, as the offence is one committed against those who conduct their affairs internationally. William Hawkins (1824) defined a pirate in 1716 as "one who, to enrich himself, either by surprise or open force, sets upon merchants or others trading by sea, to spoil them of their goods or treasure". Some 300 years later, digital treasure in the form of information is carried internationally via fibre-optic cables and satellites and is being set upon by pirates who, again for self-enrichment, make copies of works belonging to others in order that they may use the information contained in the works free of charge or pass them off as their own intellectual creations.

Intellectual property

The nature and purpose of copyright protection

Intellectual property rights encompass copyright, patents, trademarks, designs and certain other specific rights such as plant breeders' rights and rights in respect of circuit layouts and confidential information. Both civil remedies, such as damages and injunctive relief, as well as criminal sanctions such as fines and imprisonment, may be imposed where intellectual property rights have been breached. Intellectual property rights which are most likely to be infringed on the Internet are those relating to copyright and such infringements are generally remedied through the use of the civil law. The present paper, however, focuses on the criminal offence provisions which apply to copyright infringement in the online environment.

Copyright laws provide a restricted form of protection for works by giving creators exclusive control over various acts in relation to their works including the reproduction, publication, performance in public, broadcast, adaptation and transmission of literary, dramatic and musical works. The creators of artistic works have other rights in relation to these works. Only those intellectual productions which are original are protected, and protection is extended only to the form in which an idea is expressed rather than the idea itself. It has been held that computer software, for example, is protected under copyright laws as this is an expression of a set of instructions to the computer (*Autodesk Inc v Dyason* (1992) 66 ALJR 233; *Autodesk Inc v Dyason (No 2)* (1993) 67 ALJR 270).

The manner in which copyright infringements may occur in the online environment has been the subject of considerable debate in recent years. The first question which arises concerns the identification of the creators of works. Blakeney (1995) describes this problem as follows.

> Digital technology blurs the distinction between authors and users. The combination of manipulation and networking leads to a situation where a new work may be created by a multiplicity of contributors raising the problem of who is in a position to complain about the theft of such works.

The next issue relates to the type of work protected by copyright. Traditionally, works the subject of copyright protection were literary, dramatic, musical or artistic works although this has since been extended to sound recordings, films and sound and television broadcasts (Ricketson 1984). The advent of digitisation now permits all such works to be converted into the same type of format capable of being transmitted electronically. Questions have arisen as to the extent to which copyright protection should apply in respect of digitised versions of works wherever and whenever they may be used.

This issue has particular relevance in determining whether copyright has been infringed when works are dealt with on the Internet (Fielding 1993; Blakeney 1995). The United States *Report of the Working Group on Intellectual Property Rights*, for example, identifies various ways in which copyright infringement may occur on the Internet (United States, Information Infrastructure Task Force 1995):

> Placing a work into a computer, whether on a disk, diskette, ROM, or other storage device or in Random Access Memory for more than a very brief period.
>
> Scanning a work into a digital file.
>
> Digitising any works such as photographs or sound recordings.
>
> Uploading a digitised file from a user's computer to a Bulletin Board System (BBS) or other server.
>
> Downloading a digitised file from a BBS or server.
>
> Transferring a file from one computer to another.
>
> Transferring any file where a screen display is made.

Whether or not such acts constitute unauthorised reproduction, publication, performance in public, broadcast, transmission to subscribers to a diffusion service, or adaptation of the work is subject to debate.

Not every use of a work will infringe copyright, however. Although everyone is at liberty to borrow and read a book without breaching copyright, the question arises as to whether an Internet user is able to peruse the contents of a file when displayed on a computer screen without infringing copyright.

The doctrine of fair dealing also allows works to be used under certain conditions relating to content and dissemination. The application of fair dealing defences to copyright infringement involving digital communications has recently been examined by the Australian Copyright Council, and various reforms have been suggested (Australian Copyright Council 1996). Published works created by authors who died fifty years ago or more are also not protected.

Ideas and facts not protected

The question of whether information should be treated as a proprietary commodity has particular relevance to the Internet. The law of theft has traditionally not been available to deal with situations in which information has been taken without the authority of the owner (*Oxford v Moss* (1978) 68 Cr App Rep 183), as information is regarded as being too valuable a public commodity to have its ownership vested in any particular individual (Law Reform Commission of Tasmania 1986).

Where information is made available on the Internet, owners may simply not wish to place restrictions on the manner in which it is used and may not seek any financial reward from those who make copies of works in the public domain. Indeed, it may be impossible to know who has had access to a work on the Internet and how it has been used as information may be copied and presented on a screen without in any way interfering with the owner's original work.

Other copyright owners, however, particularly commercial enterprises, may see it as financially essential to have their works, such as computer software, protected by copyright as the viability of their business may depend upon fees being paid each time the work is reproduced. For example, Ling Yan of the Beijing company Sun Tendy who created the first Chinese language word processing program, "Chinese Star", lost ten pirated copies of his program for every one sold, thus substantially reducing the success of his business (Forney 1996).

Similarly, creators of works may not be at all happy for their works to be altered by others on the Internet and republished under their own name or subjected to derogatory treatment. The manner in which such moral rights are protected will be considered below.

If protections are not made available to the creators of works, the Internet may not flourish, particularly as an international marketplace, owing to creators being unwilling to place their work in an unprotected environment. Creativity, which is one of the main objects which copyright law seeks to encourage, may be stifled, with the community suffering a loss in the production of new intellectual works. As van Caenegem (1995) has recently observed:

> The benefits of [the Information Superhighway] are clear: savings in cost of production, speed and ease of access, flexibility and enhanced research capacity. However, if uncompensated, this form of access would leave a copyright owner with possibly inadequate rewards, and the balance between risk and incentive will be disturbed to a degree which will result in less than optimal production of copyright works.

The argument that information on the Internet should be free

The contrary argument favoured by some such as Barlow (1994) and Samuelson (1996), is that the Internet should be free of intellectual property law restrictions with all information being accessible and unencumbered. This, it is argued, is because "cyberspace" is sovereign unto itself and should be self-governed by its inhabitants — or "netizens" — individuals who will rely on their own ethics — or "netiquette" — to determine what uses of works, if any, are improper. This argument was rejected by the United States Working Group on Intellectual Property Rights in 1995 because activity on the Internet takes place neither in outer space nor in parallel, virtual locations.

> Computer network transmissions have no distinguishing characteristics warranting such other-world treatment. Further, such a legal free-for-all would transform the [Global Information Infrastructure] into a veritable Dodge City. As enticing as this concept may seem to some users, it would hardly encourage creators to enter its confines (United States, Information Infrastructure Task Force 1995: 14-15).

Freedom for one person may, however, entail oppression for another. The benefits of having free access to information on the Internet and the ability to download or alter any files without restriction may result in creators of works suffering substantial damage both to their economic position and to their intellectual reputation. This, in turn, may result in creators of works simply not using the online environment fully. In the words of Simpson (1995): "the freedom of cyberspace may prove to be a transitory and illusory one . . . The friendly anarchy of its early days may not provide a forum where either education or commerce can flourish".

Copyright law is "intended definitely to grant valuable, enforceable rights to authors . . . to afford greater encouragement to the production of literary works of lasting benefit to the world" (United States, Information Infrastructure Task Force 1995). The aim is not to reward the author although this occurs incidentally in the law's attempt to achieve its ultimate purpose, namely to release the products of creative endeavour to the public.

A delicate balance exists in copyright law between, on the one hand, the private interests of encouraging creativity and protecting the rights of creators of works, and, on the other hand, securing the public interest of gaining access to information. Wodetzki sounds a note of warning for regulators in the following terms:

> Simply charging down the path of stronger protection without giving due consideration to the need for a continued balance between ownership and access would be a mistake . . . If our copyright laws are made too "strong", we run the risk of entering the information age with an impoverished public domain. If students and researchers are not free to make fair use of digital works, then Australia's hope of becoming a clever country will surely suffer (1996: 12-13).

The current climate of reform

Throughout the world there has been a recognition that existing laws are incapable of effectively regulating activities on the Internet. The United States *Report of the Working Group on Intellectual Property Rights*, for example, explains the reason why the National Information Infrastructure is creating such a problem for copyright regulation in the following terms:

The establishment of high-speed, high-capacity electronic information systems makes it possible for one individual, with a few key strokes, to deliver perfect copies of digitised works to scores of other individuals — or to upload a copy of a bulletin board or other service where thousands of individuals can download it or print unlimited "hard" copies (United States, Information Infrastructure Task Force 1995: 12).

At the G-7 Ministerial Meeting on the Global Information Infrastructure in February 1995, Ministers noted that unless rules for the effective protection of intellectual property are taken into account from the outset, the development of the information superhighway will be severely hindered (ibid 130).

More recently, at the Diplomatic Conference on Certain Copyright and Neighboring Rights Questions conducted by the World Intellectual Property Organisation in Geneva in December 1996, an amended Copyright Treaty was agreed upon which will form the basis for copyright reforms in the digital age (World Intellectual Property Organisation 1996). The Copyright Treaty deals specifically with the question of copyright on the Internet by providing that the authors of literary and artistic works have the exclusive right to authorise any communication of their works to the public by wire or wireless means, including making available to the public works in such a way that members of the public may have access to them from a place and at a time individually chosen by them (article 8).

Thus, online interactive transmissions on the Internet are covered by copyright, although merely providing facilities for enabling or making a communication does not. The Treaty also contains provisions concerning technological measures for protection and electronic rights management information (article 11). Specific provisions were not included to deal with certain temporary, transient and incidental reproductions of works, as the Conference agreed that these were already protected. The Treaty also contains provisions on the copyright protection of computer programs and original databases and on the right of rental for works.

In Australia, the process of copyright reform has been under way for some time now. Ricketson (1996), for example, cites the National Information Services Council *Agenda Papers for the First Meeting of the Council* (10 August 1995) as indicating that the current review of copyright law by the Copyright Law Review Committee should consider the question of the detection and enforcement of copyright infringements on the information superhighway and the way in which the moral rights of authors are to be accommodated within this new environment. Ricketson (1996) argues strongly for the protection of moral rights in the digitised environment where works may be electronically manipulated and where it is necessary to ensure that works are authentic.

Similarly, the Copyright Convergence Group in its Report, *Highways to Change: Copyright in the New Communications Environment* explained the problem as follows:

The arrival of satellite, [Multipoint Distribution Services] and cable subscription television is imminent. Australia has a plethora of other new information and entertainment services and the prospect of broadband digital delivery systems ... These developments have resulted in a considerable level of consternation on the part of copyright owners and users . . . In the newly digitised communications environment, traditional modes of exploitation of copyright material are universally acknowledged as becoming marginalised, or in some cases, irrelevant (Commonwealth of Australia, Copyright Convergence Group 1994).

At the time of writing, the government in Australia is carrying out an extensive process of reform directed at the telecommunications industry as well as the law of copyright in so far as it relates to the digital transmission of information. The primary telecommunications carrier in Australia, the Telstra Corporation, has been partially privatised and the industry opened to increased competition on 1 July 1997 (see Ferguson 1996 and Brown 1996).

The Copyright Law Review Committee is also working on a major reference to reform and to simplify the existing *Copyright Act* 1968 (Attorney-General's Department, Copyright Law Review Committee 1996).

Under the existing 1968 Act, copyright owners' exclusive rights in relation to the electronic transmission of literary, dramatic or musical works to the public are currently limited to the right to broadcast the work (s 31(1)(a)(iv) — which means the right to transmit it by wireless telegraphy under s 10(1)) and the right to cause the work to be transmitted to subscribers to a diffusion service (s 31(1)(v)), which again is limited to transmission over wires. These rights are, however, limited and do not provide adequate protection for the transmission of copyright works on the Internet (see van Caenegem 1995).

To enhance the range of protections, particularly in respect of digital works, schedule 5 to the Copyright Amendment Bill 1996, proposes the creation of a new, broadly based, technology-neutral right of transmission to the public to replace the existing communications rights. Even this approach has been criticised in view of the fact that it may not extend to all forms of activity on the Internet and does not resolve the question of whether transmission over the Internet involves transmission of works to the public (Thomas 1995). Van Caenegem (1995) also argues that such a right would alter considerably the scope of copyright protections which exist at present and by controlling access to copyright works the proposed law may tend to inhibit rather than encourage the wide dissemination of facts and ideas, thus restricting one of the main policy aims underlying copyright.

Finally, the Copyright Amendment Bill 1996 included amendments to introduce comprehensive moral rights protections for creators of copyright works and films. The introduction of three rights was proposed: the right of attribution (the right to be identified as the creator of a work), the right against false attribution (the right to take action against false attribution) and the right of integrity (the right to object to derogatory treatment of a work which prejudicially affects a creator's honour and reputation). These protections would extend to creators of computer programs.

These reforms seek to ensure that Australian copyright law will be able to accommodate the changes which are to be introduced if the reforms to the telecommunications industry occur and broadband technological services become widely available. Hopefully, the new legislative controls will enable the full potential of the Internet to be realised by ensuring that authors will not withhold their works from this environment through fear of becoming the victims of Internet piracy. The concern, however, is that expanding copyright protections such as by granting a broadly based transmission right may inhibit free communication of knowledge and ideas through fear of infringing copyright.

The nature and extent of the problem

General estimates

Globally, trade in intellectual property represents a substantial component in national economies. The Australian Department of Foreign Affairs and Trade estimates that intellectual property trade accounts for A$740 billion or 20 per cent of all trade. In Australia, copyright works account for 2.9 per cent of Gross Domestic Product or approximately A$15 million (Burton 1996). Considerable sums are collected each year on behalf of copyright owners by the collecting societies. The Copyright Agency Limited, for example, had a gross income of A$10.9 million in 1994 while the Audio Visual Copyright Society's gross income for 1994 was almost A$5.4 million. The Australian Performing Rights Association, which licenses the public performance and broadcast of musical works had a gross income in 1993 of approximately A$47 million. Clearly, such an industry provides great opportunities for illegality (Australian Copyright Council 1996).

There are, however, few estimates of the extent to which copyright is infringed by Internet users and those which do exist suffer from problems of extrapolation of data and under-reporting. The problem is, however, thought to be widespread.

There is some evidence that intellectual property infringements generally are being reported more often than in the past. For example, *Annual Reports* of the Australian Federal Police over the last four years (see Table 2) provide data on copyright and patent offences reported and cleared since the year 1992-93.

Table 2
Australian Federal Police Copyright and Patent Offences

Year	Reported No.	Cleared No.	%*	Male No.	Female No.	Value Stolen (A$)
1992-93	763	519	68	15	4	17,840
1993-94	597	247	41	12	2	410,061
1994-95	1,924	303	16	24	5	838,310
1995-96	486	42	9	5	1	630,500

* Offences cleared as a percentage of those reported
Source: Australian Federal Police *Annual Reports.*

In the United States, the latest *Intellectual Property Loss Survey* conducted every three years by the American Society for Industrial Security (ASIS), found a 323 per cent increase in intellectual property loss incidents from 9.9 incidents reported per month in 1992 to an average of 32 incidents per month in 1995. Intellectual property losses of US$440 million were reported, principally in high-technology businesses, with overall losses relating to all types of misappropriated information amounted to US$5.1 billion (Heffernan and Swartwood 1996).

The *Report of the Working Group on Intellectual Property Rights* (United States, Information Infrastructure Task Force 1995) also estimated that losses sustained by industry arising out of copyright infringement are between US$15 billion and US$17 billion annually.

In a recent survey of computer crimes experienced by a sample of corporate security directors in the United States, it was found that intellectual property was the most common target for theft. This was in part due to the wide use which is made of digital technologies for business. One major corporate research laboratory, for example, indicated that information about new generation products which had not yet received patents was communicated over the Internet, thus creating a major security threat (Carter and Katz 1996).

Others engaged in business are keenly aware of the growing threat of computer-based economic and industrial espionage (see Venzke 1996). Those industries which maintain confidential and sensitive information on computer networks seem to be the most vulnerable, although as we have seen in Chapter 2 on illegal interception, spying on companies may take place using a wide variety of surveillance devices.

Developments in computer technology are frequent targets for industrial espionage. In the 1980s, it has been argued that industrial espionage conducted by Japanese companies nearly devastated the United States computer industry based in Silicon Valley in California. IBM, for example, was the victim of a number of instances of piracy (Schweizer 1993; see also Marx 1987).

Assuming that the increase in reports of copyright infringement accurately reflects an increase in the number of incidents which are taking place, this may be partly due to the ease with which accurate copies of works may be made using modern technology, such as computer networks. Acts of copyright infringement may occur quickly and without difficulty and may be carried out by anyone capable of using the Internet. Infringements of copyright also relate to each of the forms of protected works as illustrated in the following examples.

Audiovisual material

Copyright infringements relating to audiovisual material, such as information stored on audio cassettes, videotapes and compact disks, are extensive in the un-networked community at present, and as digital versions of such material begin to appear on the Internet, it is likely that they, too, may be the subject of piracy.

In Europe, the International Federation of the Phonographic Industry (IFPI) estimates that pirate sales of records and audio cassettes were worth US$2.25 billion dollars in 1994, representing 10 per cent of the world market, while pirate sales of compact discs (CDs) increased ten times in the space of five years, from 9 million in 1990 to 90 million in 1994. ALPA, the French anti-piracy association, estimates the annual sale of pirated videos to be US$125 billion, again 10 per cent of the market. According to IFPI, 45.5 million pirate CDs were sold in Poland in 1993, while only 22.5 million were legal (Reilhac 1995). In China, the problem is much more extensive. The International Intellectual Property Alliance, for example, estimates that China produces 100 million pirated CDs a year, while its annual domestic market is only between five and seven million. It is also estimated that the illegal reproduction of film, music, computer software and CDs in China cost companies in the United States A$2.3 billion in 1995 (Erickson 1996). Such estimates are, however, based on figures provided by those from within the industries concerned and hence their objectivity may be questionable.

Even the use of existing telecommunications technology has given rise to proceedings for copyright infringement. In the case of *Telstra Corporation Limited v Australasian Performing Right Association Limited*[1] Telstra was held liable for breach of copyright for permitting music to be played to the recipients of telephone services while "on hold" by reason of transmitting the works to subscribers of a diffusion service and broadcasting the works.

The decision of the High Court appears to impose strict liability on telecommunications carriers for the transmission of copyright material over their networks as part of a service, regardless of whether the carrier actually supplies, operates or consents to the use of the equipment, from which the material originates, such as an Internet Bulletin Board or Web site. Thus, Telstra was held liable not only for its own transmission of music but for the use of copyright material by third parties, despite the fact that it had no control over such use (see Watts and Gilchrist 1996; Leonard 1995).

As broadband services continue to become available with text, graphics, sound and video information being freely accessible via cable modems, the potential for copyright infringement involving such works will be enhanced enormously. Already in the United States it is possible to download compact disks and feature films from the Internet and this development has led to the establishment of an international group called Imprimateur to devise strategies to prevent copyright infringement of audiovisual material on the Internet (Fox 1995).

Computer software and bulletin boards

At present, however, the area of greatest concern relates to computer program and software piracy committed on Internet Bulletin Board Systems (BBSs) which were described in Chapter 1. We have also seen, the substantial number of BBSs which now operate throughout the world.

The Copyright Law Review Committee explains the potential which Bulletin Board Systems have for copyright infringement as follows:

> It is the ability to copy information, such as computer programs and other copyright materials, by downloading them from the BBS that is a concern for copyright owners. The anonymity with which users can access BBS and post messages makes detection of such practices extremely difficult (Commonwealth of Australia, Attorney-General's Department, Copyright Law Review Committee 1995: 309).

---

1   High Court of Australia (14 August 1997, No S 89/1996); [1997] ACL Rep (Iss 9) 240 HC 1.

Unfortunately, this potential for misuse has been realised in Australia, Britain and the United States.

Australia. In the un-networked environment, Australia has the unenviable reputation of having the highest incidence of software piracy in the developed world with personal computer users and educational institutions being the prime offenders (Chester 1996). The Software Publishers Association has identified 1600 Bulletin Board Systems which carry illegal software, and has estimated that A$7.4 billion worth of software was lost to piracy in 1993. By some industry estimates, A$2 billion of that amount was stolen over the Internet (Meyer and Underwood 1994).

In a survey commissioned by the Business Software Association of Australia in 1992, it was found that 2.2 million units of software had been sold in Australia but that 6.5 million units had actually been installed on personal computers. In addition, it was estimated that 4.3 million units of software had been stolen resulting in losses to the national software industry of A$260 million (McIntosh 1996b and Neiger 1996). Already, there have been a number of criminal and civil actions taken in respect of infringements committed on the Internet or through the use of telecommunications networks.

In Australia, since the decision of the High Court of Australia in *Autodesk Inc v Dyason* (1992) 66 ALJR 233 and *Autodesk Inc v Dyason (No 2)* (1993) 67 ALJR 270, the unauthorised copying of computer software may amount to a breach of copyright (see Argy 1993). Sub-section (5A) of s 132 of the *Copyright Act* 1968 (Cth) now specifically provides that transmission of a computer program which results in the creation of an infringing copy shall be deemed to be an illegal distribution of the program.

In July 1994, the Australian Federal Police investigated a former employee of a Sydney-based international company who had copied program source codes and files and then electronically mailed these to his personal computer. The value of material taken was conservatively valued at A$300,000 and the offender was found guilty and sentenced to 200 hours community service with his computer equipment being forfeit to the AFP (Australian Federal Police 1995).

In Victoria, proceedings have been taken against four computer organisations in respect of allegations of software piracy. One case was settled for an undisclosed sum in October 1996 (Anonymous 1996d). Recently, the Australian Visual Software Distributors Association has estimated that 15 per cent of computer video games infringe copyright which costs distributors approximately A$20 million each year (Crowe 1996b).

One of the most recent instances in which legal proceedings have successfully been taken in respect of computer software downloaded from the Internet is the case of *Trumpet Software Pty Ltd v Ozemail Pty Ltd* (1996) 34 IPR 481 (10 July 1996, Federal Court of Australia). In that case, Ozemail Pty Ltd was found to have infringed copyright which subsisted in shareware software called "Trumpet Winsock", which was used to interface between an Internet user and the Internet protocol. Ozemail Pty Ltd had downloaded a version of the software from an Internet site and had distributed an altered form of this in a promotional free package attached to a computer magazine. The object was to attract customers to Ozemail as an Internet Service Provider by enabling them to connect through the use of the software. No fees were, however, paid to Trumpet Software.

The case is important in that it confirms that in Australia copyright exists in shareware software on the Internet and that unauthorised copying may result in liability (see de Zwart 1996).

Britain. Computer software piracy in Britain is also being carried out on a wide scale and has led to the creation of an organisation, FAST (the Federation Against Software Theft) to investigate and prosecute offenders. Early in 1996, for example, FAST seized over £7 million worth of illegal software following a nine-month investigation into offenders said to be earning up to £1000 per week in piracy. FAST estimates that approximately £400 million has been lost due to software piracy in Britain (Netlaw 1996).

The United States. There have been a number of reports of computer software being pirated in the United States since the late 1980s (eg Bequai 1987). Recently, the problem of commercial software being uploaded onto Bulletin Boards and made available for free downloading in violation of copyright and software licensing agreements has become a particular concern (Denning 1995).

In 1990, the Software Publishers Association estimated that the software industry in the United States alone lost US$2.4 billion to domestic piracy while worldwide, piracy losses were between US$10 billion and US$12 billion (Walker 1994). The Association now conducts a vigorous campaign to prosecute copyright infringements relating to computer software (see Cheng 1995).

There have been numerous criminal prosecutions and civil actions involving copyright infringements of software. In November 1995, a Los Angeles software pirate, Thomas Nick Alefantes, known as "Captain Blood", was arrested and charged with two counts of fraud and trademark infringement relating to software piracy. An estimated US$1 million in illegally copied software, high speed duplicating equipment and US$15,000 cash was seized at the time of his arrest. The allegations relate to a software counterfeiting operation in which illegal software was sold and rented through advertisements placed in trade magazines. The mail order operation was conducted over a period of five years and involved the distribution of millions of dollars worth of illegally copied software (Anonymous 1995a).

In 1993, *Playboy Enterprises Inc v George Frena dba Techs Warehouse BBS Systems and Consulting, and Mark Dyess* 839 F Supp 1552 (MD Fla 1993), Playboy Enterprises won a suit against the operator of a Bulletin Board for allowing copyrighted images taken from *Playboy* magazine to be posted on the Board. Judge Schlesinger of the Florida District Court held that two copyrights of Playboy Enterprises had been infringed, the right to distribute copies of a work to the public and the right to display pictorial works publicly. The court held the Bulletin Board operator strictly liable for the display and distribution of unauthorised copies even though the operator may have been unaware of the infringement.

In *Sega Enterprises Limited and Sega of America Limited v Maphia* 857 F Supp 679 (1994), Judge Wilken of the District Court of California issued a preliminary injunction on 28 March 1994 against the operator of the Bulletin

Board, "Maphia", for uploading and downloading unauthorised copies of Sega's video games. The court found that a *prima facie* case had been established for both *direct* infringement, based on the BBS operator's having permitted the uploading of copyright games onto the BBS, and *contributory* infringement, based on the operator's role in copying the games including the provision of facilities, direction, knowledge and encouragement. The court said:

> Based on defendants' own statement that 45,000 bulletin boards like MAPHIA operate in this country, it is obvious that should the unauthorised copying of Sega's video games by defendants and others become widespread, there would be a substantial and immeasurable adverse effect on the market for Sega's copyrighted video game programs (at 688).

> Even if defendants do not know exactly when games will be uploaded to or downloaded from the MAPHIA bulletin board, their role in the copying, including provision of facilities, direction, knowledge and encouragement, amounts to contributory copyright infringement (at 686-7).

Perhaps the most celebrated case in recent years is that which involved David LaMacchia who was prosecuted for making US$1 million worth of computer software available on the Internet over a period of approximately six weeks.

LaMacchia, a 21-year-old student at the Massachusetts Institute of Technology, provided clandestine BBS locations on the Internet for the receipt and distribution of unauthorised copies of commercially published, copyrighted software. Because he sought no profit from his actions — actions that caused substantial economic harm to copyright owners — he could not be charged under the current criminal provisions of the copyright law, and the United States District Court dismissed an indictment charging him with wire fraud, on the ground that his acts did not violate the wire fraud statute (*United States v LaMacchia* 871 F Supp 535 871 F Supp 535 (1994)).

It was reported that:

> ... using pseudonyms and an encrypted address, LaMacchia set up an electronic bulletin board which he named Cynosure. He encouraged his correspondents to upload popular software applications (Excel 5.0 and Wordperfect 6.0) and computer games (Sim City 2000). These he transferred to a second encrypted address (Cynosure II) where they could be downloaded by other users with access to the Cynosure password. Although LaMacchia was at pains to impress the need for circumspection on the part of his subscribers, the worldwide traffic generated by the offer of free software attracted the notice of university and federal authorities ... (at 536). The Indictment alleges that LaMacchia's scheme caused losses of more than one million dollars to software copyright holders. The indictment does not allege that LaMacchia sought or derived any personal benefit from the scheme to defraud (at 536-7).

LaMacchia's acquittal was affirmed on appeal and the United States Attorney's office in Boston announced on Friday 27 January 1995 that it would not appeal the decision (http://www-swiss.ai.mit.edu/dldf/us-pr-jen-27.text).

One of the most recent instances in which court proceedings have been taken in respect of alleged copyright infringement on the Internet involves the Church of Scientology (The Religious Technology Centre). In a series of actions, the Religious Technology Centre has sought interim orders restraining the publication of materials on the Internet which are said to infringe its copyright. Some of the applications have been refused on the grounds that the Church's works are already widely known[2] while in other cases, liability has been established.[3]

Databases

A further issue concerns the role which copyright law plays in the protection of compilations of information such as digitised databases. In Australia, under the provisions of the *Copyright Act* 1968, compilations of words, figures or symbols are protected as literary works (s 10(1)(a)). The copyright in a compilation relates to the selection and arrangement of material in works such as lists, directories and anthologies. Although the individual items which make up the compilation may not be protected, the selection and arrangement in a directory may be protected (Australian Copyright Council 1996).

Applying these rules to different forms of computer databases raises difficulties, however. In the decision of the United States Supreme Court in *Feist Publications Inc v Rural Telephone Service Company Inc* (111 SCt 1282; 11 L Ed 2d 358 (1991)), United States copyright law was found to preclude an author from claiming copyright protection in a telephone directory as there was insufficient originality involved in the compilation of information to warrant protection (see Cross 1994).

The recent World Intellectual Property Organisation Copyright Treaty of Geneva on 23 December 1996, states in article 5 that "compilations of data or other material, in any form, which by reason of the selection or arrangement of their contents constitute intellectual creations, are protected as such. This protection does not extend to the data or the material itself and is without prejudice to any copyright subsisting in the data or material contained in the compilation" (World Intellectual Property Organisation 1996).

At present in Australia, computer databases will only be protected where their creation has entailed a sufficient degree of labour and skill in the selection and arrangement of material to enable it to be considered as an original work. The Copyright Law Review Committee recently considered whether the legislation in Australia should be amended to clarify the protection of computer databases, but decided against introducing reforms as it took the view that the existing provisions provided adequate protection (Australia, Copyright Law Review Committee 1995).

---

2   *Religious Technology Centre v FACTNET Inc* 901 F Supp 1519, 1528, (1995).
3   *Religious Technology Centre v Netcom On-Line Communication Services Inc* 907 F Supp 1361 (1995); *Religious Technology Centre v Ward* unreported No 96-20207, 21 March 1996, United States District Court, Northern District of California, Whyte J; *Religious Technology Centre v Henson* unreported No C-96-20271, 5 April 1996, United States District Court, Northern District of California, Whyte J).

Legal issues

As with other areas of telecommunications and computer law, a wide range of legislative and common law rules bear upon offences when committed on the Internet.

Jurisdictional issues

There is no single copyright law which operates throughout the globe, but instead, there is an international system of principles to which individual nation states have regard when devising their own laws. Several international treaties, for example, set minimum standards for copyright protection throughout the world (United States, Information Infrastructure Task Force 1995).

Differences between the laws which apply in different international jurisdictions sometimes create problems for the effective prosecution of offenders who reside in different geographical regions from those in which they commit their offences or in which their victims reside. Such problems are, however, well known in international fraud litigation and it has generally been the case that few offenders have escaped liability only because their criminal enterprises have touched various jurisdictions. The criminal offence provisions of the *Copyright Act* 1968 (Cth), discussed below, apply only in respect of "acts done in Australia" (s 132(6)). Where an offender downloads a work in breach of copyright from an Internet site to a computer located within Australia, this would be sufficient to give an Australian court jurisdiction.

Other jurisdictional problems arise, however, in seeking to prosecute offences of copyright piracy under other pieces of legislation such as those considered below in relation to telecommunications and computers.

Evidentiary and procedural issues

In order to establish breach of copyright, there must be evidence of the existence of a valid copyright in the work in question and infringement such as through unauthorised copying or distribution. It is possible to prove infringement circumstantially such as by the offender having access to the work and two copies being present, both with common errors. To assist in proving infringement, publishers occasionally place deliberate errors in works which may then be used to verify the fact that the work has been reproduced (United States, Information Infrastructure Task Force 1995; Walker 1994). More recently, digital labelling systems have been developed which enable pirated copies of digital works to be identified and prevented from use (see Fox 1995).

As in other areas of the criminal law, the offender must "know or ought reasonably to have known" that the act complained of constituted an infringement and this may be difficult to prove where the work appears on the Internet, some of which is known to be in the public domain (see, generally, on proving intent through reasonable knowledge: *Pontello v Giannotis* (1989) 16 IPR 174).

Further, where hard copies of documents are not kept but material remains solely in a digital form, law enforcement agencies may encounter difficulties in producing evidence in court or even in gaining access to data protected by encryption devices.

Law enforcement issues

The *Copyright Act* 1968 (Cth) is silent as to which law enforcement agency has responsibility for investigating criminal breaches of copyright. Because Commonwealth legislation is involved, it is expected that the Australian Federal Police will have primary responsibility although State and Territory police services may also investigate infringements which involve this legislation. In addition, by virtue of s 13 of the *Crimes Act* 1914 (Cth), any other person may institute proceedings in respect of offences against Commonwealth laws.

Most law enforcement agencies are not, however, sufficiently well equipped in terms of technological expertise and resources to conduct investigations into copyright infringements, especially those which involve the transmission of works on the Internet. Often, law enforcement agencies see copyright infringement as an exclusively civil matter and demonstrate a reluctance to take action in the absence of substantial financial losses or other issues which take the offence into the realm of organised crime or major fraud. The Australian Federal Police, for example, has the following policy on copyright prosecutions:

> In reflection of our overall organisational priorities, the AFP is generally only in a position to consider allocating resources to investigation of those copyright or trademark matters which involve a significant breach of the relevant Commonwealth legislation, or where the activity is or may be linked to other serious offences within AFP jurisdiction (Kelcey 1995).

Similarly, the Victoria Police view copyright infringements as, prima facie, civil in nature with prosecutions being restricted to cases of large-scale activities or where offenders have insufficient means to meet civil judgments (Kelcey 1995).

Such priorities, arguably, reflect the view that notwithstanding the importance which copyright infringements have for business and the community generally, primary responsibility for the enforcement of copyright rests with the copyright owner.

In the United States, a number of law enforcement agencies are now making the investigation and prosecution of copyright infringements a priority. The Federal Bureau of Investigation, the United States Customs Service, the Secret Service and the Department of Justice's Computer Crime Unit are all involved in conducting high technology investigations of copyright offences (Walker 1994). In the Northern District of California which includes Silicon Valley, the United States Attorney's Office has announced a high-technology crime initiative to prosecute theft of copyright and other offences involving computers (Walker 1994).

Property offences

In order to establish that the property offence of theft has occurred, most jurisdictions require the deprivation of "property" belonging to some other person accompanied by an intention permanently to deprive the owner of it (Dunning 1982; Hughes 1990: 154; eg s 72(1) *Crimes Act* 1958 (Vic)[4]).

The question which arises in the present context is whether an offender could be prosecuted under such legislation for copying material belonging to another which appears on the Internet. The common law traditionally took the view that information did not amount to intangible property for the purposes of the law of theft.[5]

Williams (1983) argues that the infringement of copyright is not theft but a statutory copyright offence and that pirating a copy of a cassette would mean that one would be convicted of theft of the receipts which would be held as a constructive trustee for the copyright owner of the cassette. Similarly, Wasik (1991) notes that theft of copyright itself would only rarely arise, such as where a trustee wrongfully sold a beneficiary's copyright in a book for his or her own benefit. Copying another's work will infringe copyright rather than constitute theft of the copyright.

Most authorities take the view that copying information from a computer does not constitute the crime of theft as it is doubtful if "property" has been taken and if there is an intention permanently to deprive the owner of data which is merely displayed on another computer screen or held in a computer's memory for a short period (Hughes 1990; OECD 1986; Law Reform Commission of Tasmania 1986; Law Commission 1988; Wasik 1991).

An analogous non-digital situation arose in the case of *R v Lloyd* [1985] 1 QB 829, where the defendant, a cinema projectionist, clandestinely removed feature films due to be shown in the cinema at which he was employed in order that accomplices could make pirate copies. The English Court of Appeal quashed convictions for theft and conspiracy to steal the films because there was only a temporary borrowing of the films and they were returned intact. Such a borrowing, it was held, would only amount to a permanent deprivation if it could be established that there was an intention to return the item taken in such a changed state that all its goodness, virtue or practical value had been removed from the article (ibid 836-7 *per* Lord Lane CJ). Because the films in question could still be projected at the cinema, they had not had their value diminished.

In the case of computer data or software which has been downloaded from a Bulletin Board, this would be unlikely to amount to theft as the information would be retained without alteration on the site from which it was copied. Unless the offender flooded the market with so many copies that it would no longer be possible to sell the software or data in question at all, it cannot be

---

4   Sub-s (1) of s 71 of the *Crimes Act* 1958 (Vic) defines property as follows: "Property" includes money and all other property real or personal including things in action and other intangible property.

5   In *Oxford v Moss* (1978) 68 Cr App Rep 183, for example, a civil engineering undergraduate who dishonestly obtained the proof of an examination paper and returned the proof after reading its contents was found not guilty of theft of confidential information from the university at which he was enrolled.

said that there has been an intention permanently to deprive the copyright owner of the entirety of the data in question.

Copyright offences

In Australia, Division 5 of the *Copyright Act* 1968 (Cth) creates various criminal offences relating to infringement of copyright. The criminal sanctions apply in respect of infringements of copyright subsisting in any subject matter covered by the provisions set out in the civil parts of the Act and thus, in order to prosecute an infringement successfully, it is necessary to establish that the work in question is covered by a valid copyright. The criminal sanctions are thus said to be parasitic upon the ambit of the civil law (Wasik 1991).

Kelcey (1995), although critical of the legislation for creating offences in respect of conduct which is also subject to civil remedies, believes that the offence provisions should be retained but prosecutions should be mounted only in appropriate cases where civil remedies are inadequate.

The criminal provisions of the Act, are, however, subject to a number of restrictions. Some of the offences set out in s 132 require that the infringement be carried out for a commercial purpose such as by making copies for sale or distributing copies for the purpose of trade. Individuals who copy software from the Internet for their own personal or domestic use would, most likely, be subject to civil rather than criminal penalties (see Wasik 1991).

Other provisions require that the infringement affect prejudicially the owner of the copyright in the work and that the offender knew or ought reasonably to have known that the infringement would have that consequence. Establishing these requirements in respect of works copied from the Internet may present difficult problems of proof, particularly where the material has been placed on the Internet anonymously or in a restricted form.

Difficulties may also arise by reason of the way in which works are transmitted via computer networks. This question was addressed by the Copyright Law Review Committee in its Final Report, *Computer Software Protection* (Commonwealth of Australia, Attorney-General's Department, Copyright Law Review Committee 1995) which took the view that the existing provisions were inadequate in that s 132 of the Act would not apply where electronic reproductions of works were made because s 132 speaks only of dealing in "articles" which mean a physical or tangible article and not an electronically made copy.

Computer programs are included in the definition of literary works in sub-s (1) of s 10 of the Act and sub-s (5A) of s 132 specifically provides that "a transmission of a computer program that is received and recorded so as to result in the creation of an infringing copy . . . shall be deemed to be a distribution of that infringing copy". Whether these provisions are sufficient to cover the downloading of computer programs from Bulletin Boards is conjectural. The definition of distribution is also restricted by the above-mentioned limitations of commercial purpose and knowledge set out in sub-s (2) of s 132.

Sub-sections (5) and (5AA) of s 132 also create offences of causing works to be performed in public at a place of public entertainment. Because the definition of "place of public entertainment" refers to "premises" it would be unlikely that this provision would apply in respect of the Internet, even though members of the public have free access to certain sites on the Internet.

Accordingly, it is by no means certain that acts of copyright infringement which take place on the Internet are covered by the existing criminal provisions of the legislation in Australia. These problems may be addressed in the amendments proposed in the *Copyright Amendment Act* 1996 and through adoption of the World Intellectual Property Organisation's Copyright Treaty of Geneva 1996.

Turning to the question of the sanctions which are available, the existing penalties for infringements are set out in s 133 of the Act and range from fines of up to A$500 for individuals to fines of up to A$250,000 for companies and terms of imprisonment of up to five years.

In making a submission to the Copyright Law Review Committee, the Business Software Association of Australia argued that the penalties for software piracy should be increased but that this would be effective only if the resources of the Australian Federal Police were also increased to permit prosecutions to take place and if the courts actually imposed more severe penalties for software copyright infringement (Commonwealth of Australia, Attorney-General's Department, Copyright Law Review Committee 1995). As we have seen, there has, in recent years, been an increase in the number of prosecutions brought by the Australian Federal Police in respect of all intellectual property matters.

Sub-section (4) of s 133 of the Act also enables courts to order that infringing copies, and equipment used in their production be destroyed or delivered up to the copyright owner. Where offences are perpetrated on computer networks, this may have a substantial deterrent effect. In the case of *Irvine v Carson* (1991) 22 IPR 107, for example, the defendant pleaded guilty to six counts of possessing 101 infringing computer programs for the purpose of distribution (s 132(2A)(b) *Copyright Act* 1968 (Cth)) and the court ordered the forfeiture of 2000 infringing copies of the computer programs and operating manuals as well as two computers used by the defendant to copy the programs. The losses which the destruction and forfeiture orders would mean to the defendant were taken into account in determining the penalty of 120 hours' community service and A$500 costs which was imposed. Similarly, in making an order under comparable provisions of United States law (17 USC § 506(b) (1993)), a photocopier used illegally to duplicate a software operations manual accompanying copyrighted computer software was forfeited in the case of *United States v One Sharp Photocopier* 771 F Supp 980 (1991).

Telecommunications offences

In Australia, Part VIIB *Crimes Act* 1914 (Cth) creates various offences relating to telecommunications services and arguably some of these provisions could be used to prosecute acts of copyright infringement which occur on the Internet or which are otherwise facilitated through telecommunications services. Section 85ZK, for example, creates an offence of connecting or using equipment connected to a telecommunications network in relation to the commission of an offence against the law of the Commonwealth carrying a maximum penalty of five years' imprisonment. Where the Internet has been used to commit a copyright offence against s 132 of the *Copyright Act* 1968 (Cth), an offence against s 85ZK of the *Crimes Act* 1914 (Cth) may also be involved.

In the United States, laws relating to Mail Fraud (18 USC § 1341 (1988)) and Wire Fraud (18 USC § 1343 (1988)) have been used to prosecute copyright infringements which have taken place using telecommunications networks (Cream 1994).

In *Cooper v United States* 639 F Supp 176 (1986), for example, five defendants were convicted under the United States wire fraud statute of using telephone networks to distribute thousands of pirated sound recordings, whilst in the case of *United States v Shultz* 482 F 2d 1179, 1182, (1973) the defendant was convicted of using the mails in a scheme to sell counterfeit sound recordings.

Arguably, similar such prosecutions could be instituted in appropriate circumstances in Australia.

Computer offences

Sections 76A to 76F of the *Crimes Act* 1914 (Cth) also create various offences to do with computers, such as unauthorised use and damage and these may be relevant where telecommunications equipment has been used to facilitate the commission of an offence, such as where copyright infringements take place through the use of computers connected via telecommunications networks.

Although these provisions do not include an offence of unlawful copying of data on networks, sub-s (2) of s 76B does prohibit individuals from obtaining access to data stored in a Commonwealth computer with intent to defraud any person. Arguably, copyright infringements could fall within such a provision if the necessary intent were present and if Commonwealth data or computers were involved. As acts of Internet piracy would invariably be carried out using facilities or services belonging to a telecommunications carrier, this would provide the necessary connection sufficient to bring the matter within the provisions of the *Crimes Act* 1914 (Cth).[6]

Illegal importation

Various laws permit action to be taken with respect to material which infringes copyright being imported into Australia (see Sharpe 1989 and Kelcey 1995). Because infringing material produced from outside Australia may be transmitted into Australia via the Internet, the question arises as to whether such acts amount to illegal importation.

Paragraph (d) of sub-s (1) of s 32 of the *Copyright Act* 1968 (Cth) creates the criminal offence of importing an article into Australia for various commercial purposes when the person who carries out the act of importation knows or ought reasonably to know that the article infringes copyright. In the case of *Computermate Products (Aust) Pty Ltd v OziSoft Pty Ltd* (1988) 20 FCR 46,

---

6   The National Crime Authority in a recent unpublished paper (1995: 10) discussed the application of these provisions to unlawful copying of data on computers and recommended that unauthorised copying of data utilising Commonwealth computers should be an offence where fraudulent intent is involved.

the Full Court of the Federal Court of Australia held that the civil importation provisions of the *Copyright Act* 1968 applied in respect of the importation into Australia of computer game diskettes embodying computer programs for the purposes of resale in the course of trade.

If the amendments embodied in the Copyright Amendment Bill 1996 are enacted such that a technology-neutral broadly based right of transmission is introduced, downloading pirated computer programs or software from the Internet would, arguably, amount to illegal importation which if carried out for the requisite commercial purpose would attract civil and criminal sanctions (see generally, Commonwealth of Australia, Attorney-General's Department, Copyright Law Review Committee 1995).

In addition, sub-s (2) of s 135 of the *Copyright Act* 1968 (Cth) permits a copyright owner upon payment of a fee to give notice requesting the Comptroller-General of Customs to prevent the importation of goods named in the notice.[7] Although such a notice may be given in respect of all works which, by virtue of sub-s (1) of s 10 of the Act includes computer programs, it is unclear whether or not the notice provisions would apply to digital material imported via the Internet. There is also the practical difficulty of the Comptroller-General of Customs being unable to identify infringing works which are being imported electronically via the Internet.

In the United States, it is a felony to import, receive or transport goods "knowing the same to have been imported into the United States contrary to law" (18 USC § 545 (1988 & Supp IV 1992), see Walker 1994). Commercial importation of unauthorised copies of copyright works constitutes an act of copyright infringement and violates the law (17 USC § 501(a) (Supp IV 1992); 17 USC § 602 (1988 & Supp IV 1992). Would such a law apply to infringing copies imported via the Internet? Again, extending the law to this mode of transmission may be problematic owing to the fact that the Code refers to "goods".

The United States *National Stolen Property Act* 18 USC § 2314 (1993) provides for criminal sanctions to be imposed in respect of any person who "transports, transmits, or transfers in interstate or foreign commerce any goods, wares, merchandise, securities or money, of the value of US$5000 or more, knowing the same to have been stolen, converted or taken by fraud". The maximum penalty is a US$10 000 fine or ten years' imprisonment or both. Federal courts, however, have held that the Act applies to the theft of trade secrets but not to copyright or patents because there is no physical removal or theft of property (Cream 1994; *Dowling v United States* 473 US 207 (1985)).

Walker (1994) argues that recent cases may enable this law to be used to prosecute the interstate transmission of digital material which infringes copyright. There is, however, debate as to whether interstate transfer of digital material infringes the relevant laws.[8] The resolution of this question awaits a definitive determination by the courts in the United States.

---

7   Sub-s (7)(c) of s 135 of the Act restricts the operation of the notice provisions to works imported for a variety of commercial purposes rather than for private or domestic use.

8   In *United States v Riggs* 739 F Supp 414, 418-23 (1990), for example, it was held that the interstate electronic transfer of stolen computer data fell within the provisions of 18 USC § 2314 although in *United States v Brown* (925 F. 2d 1801 (10th Cir 1991)) it was held that the interstate transfer of a stolen computer code was not covered by 18 USC § 2314.

Advertising infringing copies of computer programs

Section 133A *Copyright Act* 1968 (Cth) creates an offence of advertising copies of computer programs which are known, or ought reasonably to be known, to infringe copyright. Arguably this section could apply to infringing copies which have been downloaded from Internet sites as well as to advertisements placed on the Internet where the advertisement is placed in Australia and the infringing copies may be downloaded to computers in Australia, even though the infringing copies may emanate from overseas Internet sites.

Civil proceedings

Given the finite nature of current law enforcement resources, it is appropriate to emphasise that the principal avenue for relief which the owners of copyright seek to exercise against those who infringe their exclusive rights, is through the civil courts in an action for damages and various other forms of relief provided for by s 115 *Copyright Act* 1968 (Cth) (see Kelcey 1995). The present chapter is not, however, concerned with the use of civil remedies other than in so far as it is necessary to establish breach of copyright in order to pursue a criminal prosecution.[9]

Regulatory issues

The development of the Internet and the digitisation of information has created a dilemma for those seeking to prevent intellectual property infringements. On the one hand, they may apply and extend copyright laws in order to ensure that individuals do not infringe the rights of creators who place their works on the Internet, or, on the other hand, they may retain the existing level of regulation or even restrict laws in the hope that other means will become available to protect works from Internet piracy.

Extending copyright laws may, however, restrict greatly the availability of information on the Internet, and indeed in the community generally, as users may fear that merely by obtaining access to material they will infringe the law. Restrictive copyright laws, however, may defeat the primary aims of the copyright system, namely, the encouragement of intellectual creativity and the production of new works.

In arriving at a workable solution, the policy aims underlying copyright laws need to be considered along with an appreciation of the way in which the Internet is used. In short, the rights of copyright owners need to be balanced with the rights of those in the community who seek access to information on the Internet. Many copyright owners, however, are also Internet users and in the future they may rely upon the Internet as a means of conducting research for the production of new works.

---

9   An important qualification of the right to recover damages which may be of importance if Internet service providers are to be held liable for infringing material which is found on their sites, is that damages are not to be recoverable where it is established that the defendant was not aware and had no reasonable grounds for suspecting, that an infringement had taken place (s 115(3)). In such cases, the plaintiff would be entitled to an account of profits only.

Internet ethics

One of the strategies which has been suggested by a number of writers is to change the behaviour of users through education in the ethics of using the Internet (see Sims and Sims 1995). The Copyright Law Review Committee (1996), for example, has argued that "in the long term, it may be possible to reduce inappropriate uses of others' intellectual creations by promoting respect for the intellectual property of others via public education". A similar view was expressed in the United States *Report of the Working Group on Intellectual Property Rights* in which it was argued that "public awareness of the importance of intellectual property in the information age is essential to the successful implementation and growth of the [National Information Infrastructure]" (United States, Information Infrastructure Task Force 1995).

Unfortunately, as has already been demonstrated, substantial sums of money can be gained through Internet piracy, particularly of computer software and other commercial works, and ethical codes of conduct may simply be ignored by offenders.

An alternative approach would be to devise ethical codes of conduct which, if breached, would result in users being denied access to further use of specific sites on the Internet or the Internet in full. The technological and administrative infrastructure necessary to operate such a registration scheme may, however, prove too difficult and costly to implement and may detract from the very freedom which some who use the Internet seek to affirm.

Alternatively, inducements could be given to Internet users to report unethical behaviour and copyright infringements to the authorities. In Australia, for example, the Business Software Association of Australia offers a A$2500 reward to individuals who telephone the Piracy Hotline to report illegal copying of software. The problem of software piracy in Beijing has been partially addressed by legislation which enables consumers to return counterfeit products for a full refund plus 100 per cent compensation (Forney 1996).

Marketplace regulation

Rather than attempt to regulate activity on the Internet through the use of copyright law, some have argued that it may be preferable for commercial enterprises to change the way in which they market their products and conduct their enterprises such that copyright infringement does not result in any meaningful loss.

It has been argued, for example, that creators should place material on the Internet without any expectation that their rights as authors will be respected, but rather in the hope that the material transmitted will advertise other works which are available commercially but not on the Internet (see Ricketson 1996). For example, summary papers or extracts from larger works may be placed on the Internet in the expectation that those interested in obtaining the complete work will obtain it for a fee elsewhere.

Other strategies which organisations are adopting were identified in the *Report of the Working Group on Intellectual Property Rights* in the United States:

> Some software companies are making their "client" software freely available for individual use in an effort to increase the market share of their "server" software. Some hypermedia magazine publishers on the World Wide Web are choosing to give away their product but charge sponsors for advertising space. A number of information service providers are charging for the use of search engines that add value to freely available public domain content (United States, Information Infrastructure Task Force 1995: 15-16).

In Australia, the Copyright Law Review Committee (1996) has raised for consideration a number of marketplace solutions to copyright protection. These include the use of frequent updates of material currently provided by looseleaf services and databases, thus enabling the freshness of the data to control its marketability. Alternatively, low initial price levels may be set for works with financial recompense being obtained by charging for additional services or enhancements of the works in question.

The problem with such strategies lies in the fact that they rely upon the continued existence of the dissemination of works in a non-digital form other than on the Internet. This detracts greatly from the development of the Internet into the sole or at least the principal means of communicating information in the future. If the Internet is regarded as a means of transmission which fails to protect the rights of creators of works it may be relegated to a system of advertising or a means of transmitting government public domain works only which would obviously reduce its attraction considerably.

Contractual arrangements

A more closely regulated system may seek to protect the rights of copyright owners by restricting access to material transmitted on the Internet to those who pay a fee and agree to abide by certain terms and conditions of use. Such a system operates to a limited extent now in respect of those Internet sites to which limited access is provided on a subscription basis and the Copyright Law Review Committee (1996) is considering extending use of contract as one alternative way in which intellectual property rights may be protected.

A number of suggestions have been advanced to extend this idea to specific uses of material. The *Report of the Working Group on Intellectual Property Rights* (United States, Information Infrastructure Task Force 1995), for example, discussed the question of "metering" each use of a copyright work on the National Information Infrastructure and charging each user a fee each time the work is used. This is now technically feasible but would require a considerable bureaucracy for its effective administration.

When electronic cash becomes more widely available, those wishing to download protected copyright works from the Internet may be required to pay a fee directly to the copyright owner or to a copyright collecting society. Such a possibility is already being canvassed as an alternative system for protecting and rewarding copyright creators (McIntosh 1996a).

The question also arises as to whether such arrangements should be framed in terms of individual contracts or by way of licenses to use copyright works (United States, Information Infrastructure Task Force 1995). Fielding (1993), for example, has raised the possibility of introducing a statutory licensing system in which users are permitted to copy works subject to an obligation to inform a collection agency and pay a fee.

Some of the difficulties with such arrangements are that those who are unable to afford the specified connection or licence fees may be denied access to the information being sought unless the fees are waived by individual copyright owners. In addition, such contractual arrangements will create private rights which may be impossible to enforce internationally where the identities of the contracting parties may be difficult to ascertain and their assets difficult to seize.

Technological solutions

A wide range of technological solutions have been suggested to deal with copyright infringement on the Internet. These involve restricting access to Internet sites or specific works, restricting use of works on the Internet, and introducing some form of electronic surveillance of activities on the Internet. Such approaches suffer from the problems of restricting freedom of Internet usage and may also involve the possible infringement of privacy. They do, however, facilitate the management of copyright licensing and collection schemes (see Australian Copyright Council 1996).

Restricting Access. In Australia, the Copyright Law Review Committee (1996) has raised the possibility of protecting copyright on the Internet by restricting access to works through the use of encryption or electronic locks which only allow authorised individuals to obtain access to specific works. The problem with such an approach is the risk that access keys, no matter how sophisticated, may be circumvented technologically.

The United States *Report of the Working Group on Intellectual Property Rights* describes four types of access control: server control, encryption, digital signatures and steganography.

Server control involves controlling access to the source of copies of works — information or data servers:

> . . . Access control is effected through user identification and authentication procedures that deny access to unauthorised users to a server or to particular information on a server. A second level for controlling access to and use of protected works can be exerted through control measures tied to the electronic file containing the work — e.g. by the use of "rendering software" (United States, Information Infrastructure Task Force 1995).

Encryption, or coding works in such a way that only specified users have access to the decoding key, may also be used to restrict access (Case 1995). Although criticised because of its ability to impede effective law enforcement, encryption is able to provide varying degrees of security depending upon the importance of the works to be protected.

Digital signatures can also be used to authenticate works and to secure works from reproduction (ibid 188-9), while steganography or digital fingerprinting may be used to identify illegally made copies of works (Kaneshige 1996). The Imprimateur study group established by the European Commission to regulate audiovisual piracy, for example, is examining the use of digital labelling of works which will identify them as they are being transmitted on the Internet. Software can then be used to identify the digitally-labelled works and to prevent unauthorised individuals from gaining access to them or from making copies without permission (Fox 1995).

Use Controls. Various technological devices have been designed to restrict the use to which copyright works may be put. For example, software can restrict further copying, limit usage to view or listen only, and restrict the number of times a work can be retrieved, opened, duplicated or printed (United States, Information Infrastructure Task Force 1995; see also Commonwealth of Australia, Attorney General's Department, Copyright Law Review Committee 1996).

A more radical approach is to make use of so-called Logic Bombs which are installed into programs. When activated through an act of unauthorised copying, they would destroy the copied data and even damage other software or hardware belonging to the offender (see Clough and Mungo 1992). The potential for such devices to result in liability for criminal damage, however, makes their use problematic.

Surveillance. Finally, devices might also be used which permit the electronic surveillance of networks or even private domestic computer and audiovisual systems in order to identify users who obtain access to or make use of copyright works in breach of owners' rights. Such an approach obviously raises significant privacy concerns (Commonwealth of Australia, Attorney-General's Department, Copyright Law Review Committee 1996).

One example involved the software company Cadsoft which was concerned at increasing piracy of its products. It offered a free demonstration program which unobtrusively searched the user's hard disk for illegal copies of Cadsoft software. Whenever the program found a pirated copy, it invited the user to print out and return a voucher for a free handbook. About 400 users responded including employees of IBM, Philips and various German Federal offices. In return the users received a letter from the company's lawyers seeking to collect 6000 Deutschmarks from each with a threat of civil action if they refused (cited by Neumann 1995).

The Prohibition of Security-Defeating Devices. If such technological solutions to copyright piracy are adopted, measures need to be taken to ensure that their effectiveness is not defeated through the use of technological means (see Australian Copyright Council 1996). One possibility is to prohibit the possession, manufacture or use of security-defeating devices in terms similar to the prohibitions which exist in various jurisdictions against decoding satellite transmissions (see Chapter 4).

Imposing liability on carriers and service providers

One regulatory strategy which is being subjected to fierce debate throughout the world at present is the imposition of liability for copyright infringement on telecommunications carriers and network service providers. Because such entities provide the facilities necessary to enable copyright infringements to take place, it has been suggested that they are best placed to detect and prevent infringements from occurring. Carriers and service providers have an interest in ensuring that networks are fully utilised and, as such, should be obliged to offer a secure environment in which works may be carried and transmitted.

The *Report of the Working Group on Intellectual Property* presents the argument that online service providers are in the best position to regulate the nature of material which appears on networks as they have a contractual relationship with users and have the ability to check any material which is distributed. Although it may be impossible to check everything which appears on the network, service providers have the ability to identify who is using their network and to investigate cases of infringement which are brought to their attention. At present there are more than 60,000 Bulletin Board operators and so there is a substantial number of individuals to conduct such surveillance. The Report further argues that service providers expect compensation for the use of their facilities and have the ability to disconnect subscribers if they fail to pay subscriptions. Accordingly, it would be feasible for them also to be able to disconnect subscribers who infringe copyright. Finally, service providers have the ability to take out insurance to protect themselves against claims for infringement of copyright being levelled against them.

In addition, it is argued that service providers have the ability to make their subscribers more aware of copyright law and to react promptly and appropriately to notice by copyright owners that infringing material is available on their systems. Service providers should make clear that infringing activity is not tolerated on the system and reserve the right to remove infringing material or disconnect the subscriber who participated in the placement of it on the system (United States, Information Infrastructure Task Force 1995).

There are, however, a number of legal and practical difficulties associated with the imposition of liability on carriers and service providers. The principal problem is whether or not such individuals can be said to authorise the placement of infringing material on their networks.

In view of the decision in *Telstra Corporation Limited v Australasian Performing Right Association Limited* referred to above, in which the High Court found Telstra liable for breach of copyright in respect not only of its own transmission of music on its network but also for the use of copyright material by third parties over which it had no control, carriers and service providers may now be liable for copyright infringement on the Internet in Australia (Watts and Gilchrist 1996; Leonard 1995).

The contrary argument is that carriers and service providers such as Bulletin Board Systems operators should not be held liable for material which infringes copyright which is placed on their networks. It has been argued, for example, that in order for carriers to be liable they would need to have knowledge of factual matters not generally known to a network operator and would be required continuously to apply legal skills in determining whether material infringes the rights of others (Watts and Gilchrist 1996). Elsewhere it has been argued that if Bulletin Board Systems operators exercise a reasonable level of care in monitoring and censoring their Bulletin Boards, then they should not be held liable for illegal acts which take place there. The standard of care, it is argued, should be higher for commercial operators but not so high as to discourage them from operating Bulletin Boards altogether (Wallman 1994).

In the United States, it has been argued that liability should attach only if the infringement is wilful and repeated or where the service provider has actual knowledge of the infringement and allows it to occur (United States, Information Infrastructure Task Force 1995). The problems which arise, however, are that it may well be impossible for operators to monitor the large amounts of information which are placed on their networks, it would be too difficult to identify infringing material, liability would impair communication and the availability of information and service providers would be driven out of business (see Hardy 1994 and Samuelson 1996).

A possible compromise would be to impose liability only in respect of those situations in which operators have actual knowledge of infringing material being present on their networks or should be expected to have such knowledge in view of the circumstances. A similar such restriction applies at present with respect of civil liability by virtue of sub-s (3) of s 115 of the *Copyright Act* 1968 (Cth), referred to above.

Where carriers or operators have been advised that infringing material is present on their networks, it would be reasonable for them to take steps to have the material removed and further infringements by the same offending individual prevented. Failure to take reasonable action in such circumstances would result in criminal and civil liability.

Interestingly, the World Intellectual Property Organisation's Geneva Copyright Treaty of 23 December 1996 provides that the provision of facilities for enabling or making a communication will not in itself amount to a communication within the meaning of the Treaty, thus restricting the potential liability of service providers in certain situations where infringing material has been passed across the Internet (see http://www.wipo.org/eng/diplconf/distrib/94dc.htm).

In devising appropriate legislation, it would be preferable for there to be uniformity with other legislative attempts to regulate the activities of online service providers. The recently proposed Bills in relation to the regulation of offensive material on the Internet in some states of Australia could serve as models for similar legislation which will impose liability on service providers who knowingly allow their networks to be used to transmit works which infringe copyright (see Greenleaf 1996b on the offensive material Bills. See also *Cubby, Inc v Compuserve Inc* 776 F Supp 135 (1991), discussed in Chapter 6 at n 11).

Alternatively, it has been suggested that online service providers should seek to comply voluntarily with a code of conduct rather than be subject to criminal sanctions.[10] Although Codes of Conduct are useful in establishing

---

10   A Code published by the Western Australian Internet Association requires service providers to adhere to the following requirement: "I, as an online service provider shall not: (a) Knowingly permit those parts of my system under my control to have publicly available for downloading files which infringe copyright or contain unlawful material, provided that the provision of cache, mailbox or directory usage to users shall not constitute permission to misuse such facilities; (b) Knowingly permit a user to engage in criminal activity using access to my system, provided that such activity is identified as criminal by competent law enforcement authorities . . . (Jones 1995: 22).

guidelines for acceptable practice, they have limited enforceability in an unregulated system.

Moral rights protections

Because copyright material placed on the Internet may be copied, manipulated and re-transmitted easily and quickly without apparent trace, the need arises for comprehensive protections to be enacted to guard against conduct which infringes so called moral rights.

Moral rights derive from the European doctrine of "droit moral" by which an author's intellectual and creative rights are recognised in addition to purely economic rights which are traditionally protected by Anglo-Australian copyright law.

Two moral rights are of primary importance in respect of works placed on the Internet: the right of attribution and the right of integrity. The right of attribution is a positive right to be made known to the public as the creator of a work where reasonable in all the circumstances. A subsidiary right against false attribution is the right to prevent others from wrongfully claiming authorship of a work and the right to prevent others from wrongfully attributing works to a creator. The right of integrity is the right to object to any material alteration, distortion or other derogatory treatment of a work where this prejudicially affects the author's honour or reputation.

Although Australian law at present provides some indirect protection of moral rights, the proposed amendments to the *Copyright Act* 1968 would ensure comprehensive protection for the owners of copyright works and films (see Commonwealth of Australia, Attorney-General's Department and Department of Communication and the Arts 1994).

Such reforms, if they extend to works placed on the Internet, will hopefully answer those critics of the present copyright protections who have argued that the creation of enforceable moral rights provisions is essential in the digital environment where works may be electronically manipulated with ease and where it is necessary to ensure that works are authentic (Ricketson 1996).

Criminalisation

The focus of the present chapter has been on the use of the criminal law to prosecute copyright infringements on the Internet. At present, as we have seen, there are a variety of criminal offence provisions which could be used to prosecute copyright infringements which occur on the Internet, although some, such as traditional property offences, would require some ingenuity in order to achieve a conviction. Others, which seem to be more appropriate to infringements which take place on the Internet, seem to be rarely used. Instead, prosecutors and law enforcement agencies seem to regard the use of the criminal law as inappropriate for the regulation of copyright which is seen as being predominantly a civil jurisdiction. In what circumstances, then, is a criminal prosecution appropriate and necessary in respect of copyright infringement on the Internet?

The first aspect to consider concerns the degree of harm involved in the copyright infringement. Clearly some infringements on the Internet may be trivial, difficult to isolate and may not warrant the substantial time and cost involved in detection and prosecution. In the United States, for example, the *Report of the Working Group on Intellectual Property Rights*, recommended that it should be a criminal offence wilfully to infringe copyright by reproducing or distributing copies with a retail value of US$5000 or more. By setting a monetary threshold and requiring wilfulness, it was intended that merely casual or careless conduct resulting in distribution of only a few copies would not be subject to criminal prosecution and that criminal charges would not be brought unless there is a significant level of harm to the copyright owner's rights (United States, Information Infrastructure Task Force 1995).

Where substantial sums of money are involved, or where organised infringements take place for commercial advantage, criminal prosecution may be justified, although arguably only after the victim of infringement has attempted to recover damages in civil proceedings.

The range of sanctions available to the criminal law may provide some justification for prosecution. Cream (1994), for example, notes that civil actions for damages for breach of copyright may be ineffective to prevent further infringements and be seen by offenders as "just another cost of doing business", even where substantial sums may be involved.[11] Criminal sanctions such as community service or imprisonment may, if appropriately used, provide more substantial deterrent effects.

In addition, the publicity which criminal proceedings attract may provide a strong deterrent to copyright infringement as may the use of new sanctions such as adverse publicity orders or orders which require offenders to refrain from using the Internet for specified periods of time, or completely. Existing confiscation of computer equipment sanctions may also, as previously mentioned, provide a powerful deterrent to offending.

Although the use of criminal proceedings has been rare in the past in respect of intellectual property infringements, it is likely that the future will see an expanded use of such an approach. Already, in Beijing, for example, the use of the criminal law against software piracy offenders has been extensive, with US$5 million in fines having been levied and 180 infringement cases sent to the courts in the last three months of 1995 (Forney 1996). In Australia, the Australian Visual Software Distributors Association has launched a campaign which will involve the criminal prosecution of individuals who infringe copyright in computer video games for profit. Those targeted include computer game retailers, importers of infringing works and organised groups who deal in infringing copies of the games. This has been considered necessary as civil proceedings have been found to be inadequate in terms of deterring future infringements. In the case of

---

11 Such as the famous case involving the Ford Pinto in the early 1980s (eg *Grimshaw v Ford Motor Co* 119 Cal App 3d 757, 791-2 (1981)) in which internal Ford engineering studies concluded that the cost of paying victims for injuries and death would be less expensive than installing a device that could prevent petrol from escaping from vehicles in collisions. US$127 million punitive damages were, however, awarded.

the video cassette industry, a policy of prosecuting offenders for breach of copyright resulted in 300 convictions which reduced the percentage of infringing video cassettes from twenty-five in 1986 to two in 1996 (Crowe 1996).

Conclusions

This chapter has highlighted the shortcomings of the current regulatory regime as it relates to infringement of copyright works transmitted digitally. In determining an appropriate regulatory response, a balance must be struck between the protection of various public and private interests. With respect to the Internet, the public interests include the right to obtain information and the right to free speech coupled with the need for efficiency in communication. Private interests relate to the need to protect authors' works from unauthorised reproduction or manipulation of a derogatory nature. An effective balance will enable Internet users to benefit from the wide range of facilities and services available on the Internet whilst ensuring that those who create material are adequately encouraged to continue the production of valuable works in the digital environment.

The solutions which do emerge should arguably achieve an optimal balance between freedom of information, and the incentives to create that information. Overly restrictive copyright laws may be beneficial to some copyright owners but may unnecessarily extend the monopoly which creators of works have over access to their works.

Unfortunately, the number and complexity of the legal and social issues in the debate over digital piracy are such that it is unlikely that all interests will be accommodated prior to reforms taking place. We can only hope that those regulatory responses which are adopted will be closely monitored and evaluated in order than any adverse consequences can be addressed prior to the global community suffering irremediable harm.

6

PORNOGRAPHY AND
OTHER OFFENSIVE CONTENT

One of the more contentious issues accompanying the recent rapid growth of telecommunications technology is the use of telecommunications systems for the transmission of objectionable or offensive material. The issue is contentious on two dimensions: first, there are, within and between nations, substantial differences of opinion as to what is offensive and what is not. Secondly, there are in some places equally strong differences of opinion relating to the balance between the rights of the individual and those of the state (the First Amendment to the Constitution of the United States protects material that many US citizens, not to mention those from less tolerant cultures, would find totally abhorrent). Today, both the issue of perceived offensiveness and that regarding individual rights and the legitimate power of the state are vigorously contested areas, at least in industrial societies.[1] In this chapter, we cannot hope to resolve these struggles, which are currently being fought out with considerable political ferocity around the world. Rather than taking "sides" in any debate, we shall seek to point in the general direction of policy solutions which seem feasible, within the constraints posed by commonsense, human nature, and available technology.

Notwithstanding the wide variation in communications content which someone, somewhere, might find objectionable, it would seem useful to attempt a broad categorisation of what this might include. In English-speaking democracies, at least, the subject matter which appears to generate most conflict is sex. Commercial telephone sex discussions, where an individual may receive content or engage in two-way communication on a pay-per-call basis, have been the subject of some concern, primarily because of their accessibility to children. But at present, the most energetic debate surrounds the availability of sexually explicit material on the Internet. Rather than indulge the reader's prurient interest, let us simply suggest that there is plenty of it out there.[2] Sexually explicit material, in written and pictorial form, exists in rich diversity on the Internet and the World Wide Web. That which seems to cause the greatest consternation (in rough descending order of concern) is sex involving children; sex between humans and animals; non-consensual sex; homoerotic activity; and depictions of consensual

---

1   There are, of course those nations whose telecommunications infrastructure is insufficient to support electronic depictions of erotica or other activities which might conceivably be deemed as unacceptable, and those dictatorships which seek to control communications of all kinds, for reasons of state.

2   In the words of the US District Court which heard an early challenge to attempts at censoring the Internet, it is "no exaggeration to conclude that the content on the Internet is as diverse as human thought" (*ACLU v Reno* 929 F Supp at 842 (1996)). For more detailed descriptions, see Whittle 1995; Platt 1996; and the controversial survey by Rimm (1995). It should be noted that access to such material by accident is most unlikely; a conscious, deliberate choice, and some degree of intended effort is usually necessary.

sexual activity between adult males and females. Pictorial depictions seem to attract more concern than mere verbal description.

There is an extensive literature addressing the question of the harm which may be occasioned during the production of sexually explicit material,[3] as well as the possibly adverse impact which exposure to such material might have on an individual. It should be noted, however, that the effects on individuals involved in the production and consumption of sexually explicit materials are varied and complex.[4] At the risk of oversimplification, one might suggest that exposure to some of the more extreme forms of content may cause considerable affront to many individuals, and perhaps lasting disturbance to some. Of perhaps equal concern is the fact that such exposure may enhance the risk that some individuals in some circumstances will engage in behaviour defined as inappropriate, if not illegal (Paik and Comstock 1994).

Another subject of communication which some regard as inherently objectionable is that which depicts or describes illegal practices, such as the manufacture and use of explosives or drugs, or techniques of sabotage and terrorism. Notwithstanding the fact that much of this material is readily available in public libraries and bookstores, its ease of access by electronic means appears to have made it more threatening. One hears anecdotal evidence about individuals being injured while attempting to assemble explosive or incendiary devices in accordance with instructions obtained through the Internet.[5] The Australian Federal Police have attributed an increase in Australian bomb incidents to the greater accessibility on the Internet of information relating to explosives.[6]

In addition to the above, another form of communications content which has been the subject of concern is that which entails vilification of a particular class or group of persons. Most common among these, at least in western industrial societies, are anti-semitic or racist propaganda. Communications which adherents of some religious faiths might regard as blasphemous or otherwise grossly offensive might also be grouped in this category, as might homophobic material. The boundary between political expression which may reflect adversely upon a class of people, and vilification of a more serious nature is not demarcated by a bright line. The possibility that racist propaganda can facilitate genocide, or forceful retaliation by the target group, has encouraged its prohibition in some societies.

Still other forms of communications content may be regarded as objectionable because they are perceived as instruments of cultural imperialism. Their combined availability and attractions are such that they tend to overshadow local content, and thereby thwart the development — indeed, threaten the

---

3   Concerns over the well-being of the subjects of pornographic depictions (especially children) are understandable. Emerging digital technology now permits depictions of children involved in sexual activity which are virtual fabrications, with absolutely no involvement of children in their manufacture. Nevertheless, the subject matter is regarded as so abhorrent, and the risk that exposure to it might inspire or possibly be construed so as to legitimate the activity in question, that few would advocate that its dissemination be made legal.

4   See, in relation to pornography and child protection, Hawkins and Zimring (1988).

5   Methods of computer intrusion, the construction of viruses, and stolen credit card numbers may also be made available on the Internet; these issues are the subject of other chapters.

6   *Sydney Morning Herald*, 8 August 1996, p 3.

preservation, of indigenous art, expression and values. There are understandable concerns in many nations that the telecommunications revolution will produce even more threatening outcomes than the total ascendancy of Hollywood and the "Coca-Colanisation" of humankind.

With regard to communications which are directed more or less personally, there are those which, intentionally or otherwise, harass or annoy the recipient. Perhaps the most familiar of these, which long predates the current revolution in information technology, is the obscene or threatening telephone call. Although regarded as trivial by some, the obscene telephone call is usually regarded by the recipient as not only offensive, but also quite intimidating, particularly when it occurs repeatedly.[7] There is some suggestion that it produces genuine and enduring anxiety in some recipients (Grabosky 1995a).

With the current proliferation of telecommunications technologies, new forms of objectionable personal communications exist, such as offensive electronic mail. We noted earlier that in one recent case, a student composed a sadistic fantasy and sent it out over the Internet. He used the name of a fellow student as the story's victim, and was charged with communicating a threat.[8] Obscene or offensive communications may be made through email, as over the telephone. The practice of sending foul and abusive electronic mail is referred to as "flaming". The practice of "Mail-Bombing" where a sender bombards the recipient with many messages, or a very long file, is another manifestation of this. In some cases, mail-bombing can be coordinated, as was the case in 1995 when, in protest against French nuclear testing in the Pacific, President Chirac's mailbox was targeted. The Prime Minister of Vietnam has suffered a similar fate (Shenon 1995a).

Perhaps of greater concern is the use of telecommunications in furtherance of extortion. Telecommunications systems have always been used to communicate threats; today, to a greater extent than ever before, they can serve both as the instrument and as the target of extortion (Froomkin 1995; Neumann 1995).

Libellous or defamatory information about an individual can be published digitally, as it can through print or broadcast media. Individuals can be subject to severe embarrassment and their personal or professional reputations seriously damaged by defamatory statements disseminated electronically. Recently a university lecturer in Western Australia was awarded substantial damages after having been the subject of unflattering, defamatory comment on the Internet (*Rindos v Hardwick*, Supreme Court of Western Australia, unreported, 31 March 1994).

Finally, there are unwanted communications of a commercial nature. The use of telecommunications in furtherance of marketing fraud is discussed below in Chapter 8; for present purposes, it is important to recognise that there are those

---

7   Repeated harassment by means of telecommunications becomes the electronic manifestation of stalking (Goode 1995).

8   Charges were later dropped *United States v Baker* WL 388472 (E D Mich) No CR 95-80106 (1995) http://www.law.vill.edu/chron/news/jakebake.htm. For a discussion of the Jake Baker case, see Platt (1996). A student was also convicted for threatening the President of the United States and his family via email. See: "In Jail for E-Mail", *Wired*, 2.10, October 1994, p 33.

individuals who find it a violation of their privacy to be contacted by telephone to receive an unsolicited commercial message, even if that commercial overture is entirely legitimate. Advances in telecommunications have brought the "junk fax" which can waste paper as well as tie up a telephone connection; and "junk email" of a commercial nature, which can take up the user's time and the computer's memory.[9]

The basic challenge facing those who would regulate harmful or offensive telecommunications is that of balancing a set of competing interests. First of these, is that of minimising harm, especially to the more vulnerable members of society such as children. Next is that of protecting individual privacy, freedom of expression, and freedom of association. Third is allowing telecommunications technology to develop in a manner which facilitates its entrepreneurial application, and its exploitation in furtherance of creativity and economic development. The importance attached to each of these criteria by individuals and by governments, will vary: privacy is less important to authorities in the People's Republic of China than to those in Australia. Freedom of expression is valued more highly in the United States than in Iran. Perceptions and concerns about potential harm arising from erotic depictions are greater in Singapore than in the Netherlands. This lack of value consensus will pose formidable challenges for international cooperation in furtherance of telecommunications content regulation.

The relevant regulatory and law enforcement questions which must be addressed in a given jurisdiction pertain first to defining precisely what content is objectionable, and second, to designing systems for its regulation. The diversity of potentially objectionable material and the proliferation of telecommunications media through which it may be disseminated make this a daunting task, especially in democratic societies.

One might begin by asking:

- what content is of sufficient intrinsic harm that its communication should be forbidden altogether (the communication of child pornography, through any means, is already defined as criminal by most nations);
- what content should be made inaccessible to some classes of people (ie children), but should otherwise be available on demand to consenting adults;
- what content is of such a nature that a given individual should be able to avoid exposure to it if he or she wishes.

Unfortunately, a great deal of discourse on objectionable material in cyberspace tends to treat cyberspace as a monolithic phenomenon. This is not at present the case, and the pace of technological change will make it even less so. Some new forms of telecommunications defy traditional regulatory models. In a very real sense, the distinction between public and private is blurred.

---

9   Recent disputes between Internet service providers and certain Internet advertisers have resulted in agreements to restrict advertising content to domains where such content can be blocked by filtering software (*Computer Underground Digest No 9.09,* 16 January 1997).

The number of different types of site one can presently visit through one's telephone connection is quite varied. The development of new technologies based on cable, satellite, and other media will open still newer horizons.

Those individuals who advocate the censorship of telecommunications media often fail to distinguish between telecommunications and broadcasting, and indeed to recognise that there are a number of different forms of telecommunications media. It is necessary to differentiate between telecommunications services which essentially provide access to public fora; those which exist to support communications which take place on a restricted basis; and those which support communications that are private. And these may exist under the same umbrella: some online services provide a variety of bulletin boards, electronic mail, and a chat feature, and may also make available electronic periodicals from their own file system. It is important to differentiate between content which can only be accessed deliberately, and that with which one is confronted passively. Means of access also vary; some bulletin boards are available only by direct dial, others may be reached through a network. Godwin (1996) has observed that the Internet is essentially a choice-driven medium, requiring deliberate, proactive conduct on the part of the individual recipient. Under the circumstances, the likelihood of having offensive content thrust upon one is unrealistic. This was acknowledged by the US Supreme Court in its 1997 decision striking down the *Communications Decency Act* 1996 (Title V of the *Telecommunications Act* 1996 Pub L 104-104, 110 Stat 56).[10]

Those forms of telecommunications which are to varying degrees public entail what might perhaps be regarded as the equivalent of attending a public meeting, perusing a public bulletin board, or browsing in a bookstore. Still others may be likened to activities of a less public, more restricted nature. A "members-only" computer bulletin board, accessible only after initial screening or subscription, is more like a regular conference call between members of an organisation, or like occasional closed meetings of a private club.

Then, there are those forms of telecommunications which are essentially private: a telephone conversation between two individuals, and interpersonal electronic mail are two examples. Others may be regarded as the functional equivalent of postal systems.

These degrees of "publicness" in telecommunications pose significant challenges to prospective regulators, for what is tolerable or entirely appropriate in private discourse may be entirely inappropriate in a public forum. In democratic societies, where the privacy of the individual tends to be accorded some value, surveillance and intrusion upon private telecommunications is justified only in matters of national security or serious criminal activity, and then subject to strict judicial safeguards. (The use of telecommunications in further-ance of criminal conspiracies is addressed in Chapter 10.)

Such analogies are a bit simplistic, however, for on the Internet, what is intended to be private may easily be transformed by design or by accident into something public. One occasionally sees email messages, which were obviously

---

10   *Reno et al v American Civil Liberties Union et al* (26 June 1997, Supreme Court of the United States, No 96-511) 96-511.

intended for a single recipient, inadvertently sent to an entire list of subscribers to a bulletin board or forum. Simple procedures for forwarding electronic mail can be used intentionally to disseminate very widely what was originally a one-to-one communication. The author of a collection of offensive stories intended for a small circle of like-minded friends was severely embarrassed when one recipient shared them more widely, causing affront to some of the secondary recipients.[11].

Beyond the problems posed by the vulnerability of some telecommunications technologies to unauthorised interception, means exist to "overhear" that which may not be intended for wider consumption. Software tools, colloquially referred to as "spiders", "wanderers" or "search engines" can identify references and quickly retrieve them. Comments made in what was assumed to be a restricted forum, such as a newsgroup, can thus be relocated to another context.

The global, non-hierarchical nature of telecommunications is such that anyone can now become a publisher. The sheer volume of content in cyberspace defies comprehension, much less centralised control.

Mobilisation of law in response to objectionable telecommunications

The prohibition of certain communications content raises the issue of who if anyone, should be the target of enforcement, and who should be liable for the offending material. Between the mind of the creator and the consciousness of the recipient there may be many institutions involved. These may include:

- the producer or manufacturer of the content in question;
- the originator of the transmission;
- the carrier such as MCA, Sprint, Telstra or Optus;
- the service provider, such as America OnLine;
- the recipient of the content.

Given the number of hands involved in the process, the globalisation of telecommunications can pose perplexing jurisdictional and other legal issues for authorities who seek to identify and sanction wrongdoing. The content in question may be entirely within the law of the jurisdiction in which it is created, and its originating transmission entirely legal.

The issue of extraterritorial application of a nation's law is a vexed one.[12] Difficulties in the identification, investigation, and prosecution of one who disseminates objectionable material are compounded when that person is physically situated in another jurisdiction, especially in a jurisdiction where the material in question is legal. Nevertheless, there are examples where persons have

---

11   Risks of wider dissemination of ostensibly private content are by no means unique to telecommunications. Private letters can be photocopied and published. As past and present members of the British Royal Family can attest, photographs and videos, not to mention recorded telephone conversations, can be broadcast (see Chapter 2 above).

12   In *Reno v ACLU*, the US Supreme Court noted in passing the "difficult issues regarding the intended, as well as the permissible scope of, extraterritorial application of the CDA", but disposed of the case on the other grounds (*Reno v ACLU* op cit, note 10).

been prosecuted in restrictive jurisdictions for activities which were entirely legal when and where they were undertaken.[13]

Because of the sheer volume of the traffic which they bear, not to mention considerations of privacy, scrutiny of content may lie beyond the capacity of the carrier and service provider. Carriers and service providers are not the functional equivalent of publishers. One would not consider penalising a telephone company for the use of obscenity in a telephone conversation; it would seem equally unrealistic to hold a carrier liable for obscene imagery among the billions of items of information which they transmit. On the other hand, large commercial systems are able to exclude offending newsgroups from their service when objectionable content is called to their attention.[14]

In those jurisdictions where relevant law exists, liability does not attach to one who does not exercise editorial control.[15] The university lecturer in Western Australia who was the subject of unflattering comment on an electronic bulletin board successfully sued the originator of the message for defamation. Damages lay against the originator, not the carrier or the organisation which provided access to the Internet.[16]

Total prohibition

In a number of nations, the perceived risk of harm arising from unregulated telecommunications is such that some fairly intrusive methods of control have been introduced. In 1996, for example, the People's Republic of China required its Internet users to register at local police stations. In Vietnam, Internet access is restricted to institutions such as university research centres and government

---

13   A favourite example, albeit one which predates the digital age, involves the prosecution of the male lead in the pornographic film *Deep Throat*. The film was made in Florida. Charges were laid in Memphis, Tennessee, a place the accused had never visited. See Dershowitz 1982, Ch 4. More recently, a postal inspector in Tennessee joined an adult-oriented bulletin board originating in California. After subscribing, he downloaded allegedly pornographic images, arranged for the delivery of a videotape, and sent an unsolicited video containing child pornography to the targets of the investigation, who were subsequently convicted on a number of federal obscenity charges. The appeals court ruled against the defendants on all counts (*United States v Thomas*, US District Court, Western District of Tennessee, 1994; US Court of Appeals for the Sixth Circuit, 1996; 1996 FED App 0032P (6th Cir) No 94-6648 and 94-6649).

14   Service providers are, for example, in a position to control "junk email" A recent court decision held that America OnLine could prevent an online advertising agency from sending mass unsolicited e-mail advertisements over the Internet *Cyber Promotions, Inc v America Online, Inc* United States District Court, Eastern District of Pennsylvania, CA NO 96-2486 November 1996.

15   In *Cubby Inc v Compuserve Inc* 776 F Supp 587 (1991), it was found that the service provider did not exercise editorial control, and was therefor not liable. In *Stratton Oakmont v Prodigy Services Co*, No 31063/94, NY Sup Ct, 24 May 1995, Prodigy was found to be a "publisher" of libellous statements made on one of its online bulletin boards. The service provider portrayed itself as suitable for family access, thereby implying a degree of editorial control. One may ask whether such exposure to liability constitutes a significant disincentive to the development of online services suitable for children.

16   The plaintiff might have chosen to sue the service provider.

agencies. Access in Saudi Arabia would be limited to companies, hospitals and universities.[17]

Depending upon the telecommunications technology in question, total prohibition may be an elusive goal. Detection may be difficult, particularly when the communication is essentially private and consensual, and the parties motivated to avoid public or official attention. Suffice it to say that those who use the Internet for illicit or illegal activities of the more serious kind (such as the communication of child pornography[18]) often employ the tightest security measures in order to prevent identification and access by authorities. While this poses a significant law enforcement challenge, it significantly reduces the risk of access by either unintending adults or children.

Total prohibition can be partially successful. It would seem that despite criticisms of its overbreadth and predictions of its unenforceability, the controversial Communications Decency Act[19] succeeded for a time in reducing the accessibility of some sexually explicit materials in the United States.[20] Immediately after the Act was signed, and despite the court injunctions which deferred its implementation pending determination of its constitutionality, some web sites proclaimed that they were closing in order to avoid non-compliance with CDA, and others began to include explicit warnings and disclaimers. By the mid-1990s a number of lists had closed down because of the risk of prosecution, and universities in the United States blocked access to some sites because of possible criminal liability (Fabrizius 1995).

Criminal prosecution

Prosecution for the production, transmission, receipt or possession of objectionable materials occurs occasionally. Official awareness of the illegality in question would appear to arise not from electronic surveillance, but rather from more traditional investigative practices.

The use of telecommunications to harass or threaten is prohibited under the criminal law of most jurisdictions (Cooper 1995; Butcher 1996). Difficulties in prosecution may arise, however, over questions of intent. Recently, as already mentioned, a student in the United States composed and transmitted a sadistic fantasy story over the Internet, and used the name of a fellow student as the name of the victim. The fellow student was sufficiently concerned to have notified the

---

17   Reuters News Service 6 April 1996.
18   Because of widespread prohibitions on child pornography, sexually explicit depictions of children are almost always communicated privately. As such, they are discussed below in our chapter on criminal conspiracies (Chapter Ten). Extensive materials relating to the interdiction of child pornography are available at Akdeniz, Yaman (1996) Regulation of Child Pornography on the Internet. http://www. leeds.ac.uk/law /pgs/yaman/child.htm
19   The Communications Decency Act was signed into law by President Clinton on 8 February, 1996. The Act makes it a crime, punishable by a maximum of two years imprisonment and/or a fine of up to $250,000, to transmit material on computer networks that is "indecent" or "patently offensive" if the speech can be viewed by a minor. The Act was challenged immediately, and, in 1997, was ruled unconstitutional by the US Supreme Court in *Reno v ACLU*, op cit.
20   For a discussion of initial attempts an online censorship in Australia, see Butler (1996).

authorities, who charged the author with threatening conduct. Charges were eventually dropped.[21]

Many jurisdictions have laws which prohibit harassment and stalking (Goode 1995). Stalking statutes generally make it an offence intentionally or knowingly to engage in a regular course of conduct designed to alarm or seriously annoy another individual. In addition to what was once termed "watching and besetting" (physical surveillance), this can include a variety of forms of communications, including the use of the telephone or sending electronic mail. Harassment can be classified as a form of stalking, and may entail the wilful, malicious, and repeated disturbing of another. It may also include the intentional communication of a credible threat which produces fear of physical harm. Many jurisdictions prohibit harassment by telephone, including:

- the making of obscene or lewd proposals;
- threatening to inflict injury; or
- calling repeatedly, whether or not conversation ensues.

Regulation

In Chapter 7, we will note how intrusive telephone calls of a commercial nature can be minimised by regulatory requirements in the telemarketing industry. Industry associations or individual companies can be required to maintain a register of individuals who have indicated a preference not to receive unsolicited commercial communications. Regulations may require that this "don't call list" be updated regularly and distributed to industry members.

Self-regulation

As noted above, individuals who wish to communicate privately, or within a close circle, can do so with little difficulty. A private bulletin board or news group can operate in such a manner that no-one would be exposed to its content except the users.

While it can hardly be regarded as a panacea, some form of self-regulation is an important safeguard against objectionable telecommunications. The Australian Broadcasting Authority (1996) sees a self-regulatory regime based on codes of practice and voluntary labelling by content providers as most appropriate for the online services industry in Australia. This would be complemented by user education about classification systems and available filtering options. Offence provisions would be reserved for only the most egregious violations.

Originators of communications of whatever nature are often able to take steps to ensure that recipients are not exposed to them unwillingly. The first step in such a process is disclosure. The principle of disclosure in advance is apposite to commercial content no less than to content of a more controversial nature.

By alerting the prospective recipient in advance to the nature of the content, one enables the intended recipient to exercise a degree of choice. Some

---

21 See above n 8.

individuals who make controversial material available online include a warning message or disclaimer such as the following:

> Warning!!! The material contained on this page deals with sexually explicit matter . . . If you are offended by material containing naked pictures of women, men or a combination of the two, do not look at this page. If you are under 18, you should not be looking at our pages in the first place.

Some sites limit public access to individuals who are able to provide verification of age. The Australian Broadcasting Authority (1996) suggests that Internet service providers limit accounts to subscribers who are 18 years of age or older. Presumably, responsibility for managing children's access to the Internet will then reside with parents or educational authorities.

Indeed, the growing commercialisation of the Internet is such that a credit card number is now required in order to access many "adult" sites. For the time being, this will inhibit access by those too young to acquire credit cards.[22] It would not, however, limit access to non-commercial sites of whatever flavour.

Compliance guidelines exist for industries as diverse as adult entertainment and telemarketing. Telemarketing codes of practice may include limitations on the times of day during which calls can be made, requirements for an explicit statement of the nature of the call, the use of basic telephone etiquette and the avoidance of recorded messages. They may also embrace such methods as "don't call" lists, and limitations on the frequency of calls to a given number (Australian Telecommunications Authority 1995).

A current regulatory trend is to encourage service providers to develop codes of practice.[23] This can be done by individual service providers or collectively, by an industry association. Although service providers cannot be expected to be intimately familiar with all of the content which they deliver, they are in a position to specify detailed terms of service. America OnLine (AOL), for example, reserves the right to suspend or terminate the account of any member engaging in any number of prohibited activities, including harassment in any form, impersonation, or unsolicited advertising. Users are prohibited from transmitting through AOL any material which encourages conduct that would constitute a criminal offence, give rise to civil liability, or otherwise violate any applicable law. The provider reserves the right to remove any content which it deems to be a violation of its terms of service, or to terminate any subscriber failing to abide by these conditions. In 1997, new contracts with its subscribers in the UK gave AOL wide latitude to disclose subscribers' private email and online activities to law enforcement and security agencies (Johnston 1997).

---

22 There are, of course, those who are able to use their parents' credit cards, but usually not without subsequent detection.

23 For example, a report produced under the auspices of the European Commission recommends a Code of Conduct for Internet service providers; a hotline for public complaints; and an independent self-regulatory body including industry representatives and users. The report also recommends the establishment of a website on illegal and harmful content to include information for parents, links to blocking and filtering software; and links to hotlines on which to lodge complaints. See European Commission (1996).

Exclusion/protection of children

Parental stewardship is one means of reducing the harm to children occasioned by undesirable content. Just as good parents are able to shield children from much of the unpleasantries of life, so too can they educate their children to evaluate advertising claims. They can, up to a point, exercise a degree of supervision over television viewing. So too can they instruct their children in the proper use of telecommunications. Parents can and should educate children in ways of safely negotiating cyberspace: for example, in not divulging one's street address or telephone number to strangers, and in not responding to suggestive or abusive messages.

Major commercial online services offer advice to parents, and guidance for limiting access to certain areas. Some service providers provide free blocking software to subscribers. Public interest groups can also provide constructive guidance to parents: in the United States, the Interactive Services Association and the National Center for Missing and Exploited Children have produced a pamphlet for parents entitled "Child Safety on the Information Highway".

Civil remedies may also be available for those who suffer loss or damage as a result of intrusive telecommunications. The university lecturer who was the subject of unflattering commentary over the Internet was awarded monetary damages; persons who become the target of harassing or threatening calls may seek injunctions or restraining orders.

Technological solutions

Protection from intrusive and objectionable telecommunications may also be facilitated by developments in telecommunications technology. Caller ID technology, which enables one to identify the originating number of an incoming telephone call, has been credited with reducing the number of harassing and obscene telephone calls in the United States (Clarke 1990). Combined with voice recording devices, Caller ID technology can significantly enhance the risk that the originator of an objectionable call will be identified (Center for Public Interest Law 1994).

Other telephone technology exists which can block calls originating at a particular number, record the originating number of all incoming calls, or emit a distinctive ring for calls originating from a particular number or set of numbers. Telephones can also be programmed to block outbound calls to particular numbers or types of location (for example STD or pay per call services).

Technologies also exist with which to filter electronic mail. These can block out messages sent by particular individuals, or from specified sites. Filter options exist for the "elm" email program on Unix systems; mail filtering programs such as "procmail" are available on many FTP sites. "Kill-file" options exist which allow users automatically to delete messages based on origin, subject, or words contained in the message.

Filtering and blocking technologies have also been developed to control access to questionable material on the Internet. Commercially available software programs such as "Surfwatch", "Cyber Patrol" and "Net Nanny" can be used to block access to certain Internet sites (Venditto 1996).

Such filtering software can be automatically updated: as new sites are discovered, access to them can be blocked. In addition to the blocking of particular sites, words, or terms, or limiting access to certain times of day, software is being developed which will permit the identification and blocking of naked human images. Some programs offer additional features such as logging of all online activity to allow for parental auditing, and restrictions on the amount of time allowed online. All of these technologies may be expected to develop further in response to consumer demand, and additional technologies developed in future in response to emerging needs.

Technological solutions are not without their imperfections, however. Some may lie beyond the capacity of the technologically unsophisticated (recall the difficulty experienced by some in programming a VCR). Screening software may be insufficiently refined; it is said that one should never underestimate the resourcefulness of an inquisitive 15-year-old. Alternatively, it may be overbroad, or incapable of subtle differentiation between subjects. Exclusion of specific terms such as "sex" may block access to information on safe sex or Sussex. Legend has it that excluding content containing the term "couples" had the effect of blocking access to the White House home page, and that prohibition of the term "breast" disrupted an electronic discussion group for survivors of breast cancer.

Caller ID technology is something of a double-edged sword. One the one hand, it is available to individuals and can enhance their privacy. On the other hand, it is equally available to commercial interests, who may record an individual's number and store it for subsequent use.

In the People's Republic of China and the Kingdom of Jordan, authorities have requested the assistance of software providers to develop what would essentially be national "Net Nanny"-type systems to confine Internet access to appropriate sites. This would, for example, permit users to access some materials, but presumably not those containing erotica or advocating Tibetan independence. In September 1996, authorities in China appear to have used some type of filtering system to block access to some 100 websites dealing with such diverse matters as sex, economics, Taiwan and Tibet (Human Rights Watch 1996).

Self-help would no doubt be facilitated by a system of classification. This would enable informed choice on the part of the consumer of telecommunications content. In Australia, a Senate Committee has called upon the Federal Government to pursue at appropriate international forums the concept of classification at source of all material placed online, based on an agreed set of classification standards (Commonwealth of Australia 1995). This would appear to be easier said than done. Taken literally, this would seem as unrealistic as requiring classification of telephone conversations. Indeed, the Internet is already being used for voice communications.

But partial solutions are beginning to emerge. Development of an international ratings system to assist users in identifying Internet content began in 1995. The Platform for Internet Content Selection (PICS) involved collaboration of nearly 40 companies, including America OnLine, Compuserve, Netscape and Microsoft. The classification system will provide parents even greater capacity to block sites which they find offensive. Such a system may well be complemented by specialised classification systems adapted to the standards of certain groups. Whilst it might not be logistically feasible to label every product, consumers of online services will be in a better position to exercise informed choice.

Law enforcement

Those areas of cyberspace which are public are as accessible to law enforcement as they are to any net or web surfer. Not only may they be subject to monitoring, and possibly, to prosecution; so too can they be targeted for investigation using "sting" techniques bordering on entrapment (Weinstock 1996).

In mid-1995, the FBI charged an adult male who had arranged over the Internet to meet someone at a motel whom he thought was a 14-year-old girl. The Internet contact was in fact an FBI agent. The accused was targeted because of his history of sex offences involving minors. Similar tactics have been directed at those who would traffic in pornographic material. Law enforcement officers can easily pose online as prospective consumers of pornography. Laws will vary across jurisdictions with regard to the defence of entrapment, and the extent to which an offence was created by police (Chandrasekaran 1996).

Toward the end of 1995, the FBI's Operation Innocent Images sought to identify purveyors of child pornography on the Internet. Concentrating on America OnLine, the nation's largest online service provider, the investigation led to the seizure of materials from over 125 homes and offices (Lewis 1995).

It would not strain credulity to suggest that law enforcement agencies are in a position to use the Internet to gather tactical intelligence about illegal activity, in addition to obtaining information for use as evidence in criminal prosecutions.

Meanwhile, law enforcement agencies in some jurisdictions have begun to exert pressure on service providers to assist in limiting the availability of objectionable content. In the United Kingdom, the Internet Service Providers Association, representing 60 of an estimated 140 providers, has encouraged members to block access to certain sites. The denial of access was requested by the Metropolitan Police in a letter to service providers which specified 134 sites (*Financial Times* 10 August 96; *Computer Underground Digest* 25 August 1996). The letter concluded with the words "We trust that with your co-operation and self regulation it will not be necessary for us to move to an enforcement policy".[24]

Co-production

Private individuals and organisations may engage in activity that has regulatory consequences. More generally, the complementary activity of private interests in furtherance of public policy has been referred to as "co-production".

Citizen concern about the availability of undesirable content has taken the form of monitoring and surveillance of cyberspace. Two of the more

---

24   Letter from Chief Inspector Stephen French, Metropolitan Police, to Internet service providers 9 August 1996. Published in *Computer Underground Digest*, 25 August 1996.

prominent organisations involved in such surveillance are the Simon Wiesenthal Center, whose CyberWatch Hotline (http://www.wiesenthal.com/watch/whot line.htm) invites notification of anti-semitic and racist material, and the Guardian Angels, whose Cyber Angels division recruits volunteers to "patrol" cyberspace in search of a range of illegal and objectionable content, including images of child pornography; vilification and harassment; fraud schemes; software piracy; computer virus developments; and content pertaining to terrorism and to the manufacture of explosives. In the United Kingdom, the Internet Watch Foundation Hotline invites Internet users to report to the Foundation material considered to be illegal. In the case of most such hotlines, information gathered from volunteers is forwarded to law enforcement authorities, in the case of criminal activity, and to service providers.

Public interest groups also encourage Websites registering as "Child Safe" or "Child Friendly", to enable parents to employ commercially available software to guide children's access.

Governments may actively encourage the individuals who identify illegal material or activity to report the illegality to law enforcement authorities. The United States Customs Service advertises on the World Wide Web, inviting reports of information relating to child pornography. The Customs Service offers rewards for citizen assistance, guarantees anonymity to the informer, and provides a toll-free telephone number to assist in reporting.[25]

An example of collaborative public-private effort in furtherance of controlling objectionable content is the Netherlands Hotline for Child Pornography on Internet, an initiative of the Foundation for Dutch Internet Providers (NLIP), the Dutch National Criminal Intelligence Service (CRI), Internet users, and the National Bureau against Racism (LBR). Users who encounter child pornography originating in The Netherlands, identifiable by a domain name address ending in "nl" are encouraged to report the site to meldpunt@xs4all.nl

The originator is warned about the posting, and asked to desist from further such activity. If the warning is ignored, then the hotline will forward any available information to the vice-squad of the local police.[26]

The very presence of "cyber watchdogs" may themselves be offensive to libertarians. Indeed, the spectre of "cyber vigilantes" intruding upon the privacy of individuals would be disturbing to many. But such intrusiveness would not appear to be the object of the Cyber Angels and similar organisations. Rather, their effect would appear to be to enhance the civility of those areas of cyberspace which are more publicly accessible. To this end, they may well enjoy some success; whether they threaten privacy or inhibit legitimate expression is open to question.

---

25   http://www.customs.ustreas.gov/enforce/index.htm
26   More information about the Netherlands hotline against child pornography on Internet can be found at: http://www.xs4all.nl/~meldpunt

Unintended consequences of regulatory intervention

Actions on the part of government, industry or the general public designed to control objectionable telecommunications may succeed in part, but may produce unintended consequences which are not always beneficial. These unintended consequences may entail over-reaction on the part of authorities, or adaptation by the targets of regulatory intervention.

Prohibitions may be overbroad. "Burning the house to roast the pig" is a common consequence of regulation in various areas of human endeavour. Thus, to prohibit or to impose extraordinary regulatory burdens on commercial advertising over the telephone or the Internet, simply because some people find such communications objectionable, inhibits legitimate expression and commerce. The breadth and vagueness of prohibitions under the Communications Decency Act in the United States attracted constitutional challenge almost immediately, challenges which were upheld by the US Supreme Court in *Reno v ACLU*.[27]

Late in 1995, German authorities prevailed upon the online service provider Compuserve to block access to some 200 sexually explicit newsgroups which were accessible from Bavaria. At the time, it was not technically possible to restrict access only in Germany; access to the newsgroups was denied to four million Compuserve subscribers around the world. This apparently had the additional effect of blocking material with references to Vatican pronouncements on sex education, and to commentary on censorship of pornography in the People's Republic of China.

It is also suggested, particularly by advocates of free expression, that censorship will have a chilling effect on expression. That is, it will generate inhibitions along the chain of communications from originator to recipient which will limit experimentation in the expression and communication of content.

Circumvention/subversion of censorship

Regulation may also backfire by aggravating the very problem it is designed to address. The continuing development of telecommunications technology renders content regulation extremely difficult. The nature of the Internet and its supporting technology, and the ethos of many of its users, are such that great energy and resourcefulness are devoted to circumvention of attempts at censorship.

No one should labour under the illusion that the elimination of objectionable material from cyberspace is completely achievable. Given the origins of the Internet as a military communications system designed to withstand massive attack, it has become a cliché to suggest that the Internet interprets censorship as damage and routes around it.

---

27 In *Reno v ACLU* (op cit) the Supreme Court observed that under the Communications Decency Act, a parent could be liable to imprisonment for allowing a child access to material which the parent deemed appropriate. Indeed, the Court observed that a parent could be liable for e-mailing birth control information to a child away at school, if the community in which the school was situated found the information to be "indecent" or "patently offensive".

In some jurisdictions, such as Germany and France, attempted censorship of online information has proven to be counterproductive. Some users regard it as a sport, if not an obligation, to publish censored materials. Opponents of censorship establish "mirror sites" in more permissive regulatory jurisdictions, and thus increase the number of sources from which the offensive content in question is accessible. This proliferation of access points, combined with the enhanced notoriety accorded the material by the very prominent act of prohibition, may serve ultimately to increase actual exposure to the offensive material in question. This, combined with the notoriety which accompanies the original attempt at censorship, can significantly enhance visibility and accessibility.

In addition to the use of "mirrors" other devices can compound the problems which regulatory interventions are intended to alleviate. The content of a particular UseNet group can be posted to other, unrelated groups. This would increase the volume of undesirable material available on the Internet, and increase the likelihood of Internet users being involuntarily exposed to it.

There are fewer inhibitions on the use of telecommunications to disseminate objectionable content when the originator's identity is disguised. The threat of regulatory enforcement may thus compel a search for technologies to "cover one's tracks". It is currently relatively easy to achieve anonymity; often with the assistance of market forces. Anonymous Internet access providers have begun to emerge in jurisdictions characterised by regulatory permissiveness. For example, one service provider offers privacy-protected accounts from tax-haven island Anguilla for US$50 per month.

Alternatively, web sites exist which can provide a false identity. One site in Canada allows users to enter the address of a page whose identity one wishes to conceal. The Canadian site then enters some insignificant changes, and displays the page with a Canadian address. Blocking mechanisms based on the original address are thus circumvented.

In addition, an informal group of programmers has developed a double-blind pseudonym scheme which allows a site to hide behind a chain of http servers which "proxy" for it. Neither the user requesting the document, nor the ultimate address of the destination web site is identifiable.[28]

Despite their application to avoid detection and investigation, anonymity mechanisms in telecommunications can be functional. They can, for example, disguise the identity and address of victims of sex crimes who may wish to participate in electronic support groups; they can also serve to facilitate the anonymous reporting of illegality, and to protect whistleblowers. Encryption and other technologies to achieve anonymity are a boon to human rights organisations and their supporters in states which are hostile to human rights activity.

Spillover

The rush to introduce policies aimed at enforcing civility in cyberspace has resulted in many paradoxes. Censorship has inspired defiant responses which

---

28   *Computer Underground Digest*, 14 February 1996, vol 8, issue 15.

replicate the objectionable material and disseminate it more widely. Attempted prohibition brings offensive material to the attention of a broader public, including curiosity seekers and those attracted by the "forbidden fruit effect". The Communications Decency Act in the United States was designed to prevent use of the Internet for offensive communications, but materials which are legally available in bookstores and libraries in the United States are defined as illegal if posted on the Web or the Internet. It would appear that censorship can at times be self-defeating.

Conclusion

Absolute control over telecommunications content seems destined to remain an elusive goal. The sheer volume of traffic would seem to preclude systematic oversight. The costs of total surveillance are prohibitive; the considerable effort required to ensure complete compliance with regulations is not feasible in democratic societies and would impede economic development and education.

Thus, the control of objectionable material seems destined to remain high on the policy agenda of many nations for some time to come. The most authoritarian regimes, more concerned with control than with commercial, artistic or political development, seem inclined to deal with the problem by severely limiting access to telecommunications services. Others will seek the national equivalent of "net nannies" to enable wider access to a narrower range of content.

Authorities in more democratic societies will continue to preside over clashes between libertarians and moral entrepreneurs, the most likely outcome of which will entail the imposition of regulations, the primary function of which will be symbolic: enforceable at best selectively and occasionally. These will operate on the margins to reduce offensive content, or at least passive exposure to such content. The most determined producers and consumers of objectionable material will continue, by means of the technologies of encryption, anonymity and pseudonymity, to circumvent those restrictions which are imposed; this, combined with a degree of self-regulation by major industry players and the growing computer literacy of parents concerned about their children's explorations of cyberspace will serve largely to shield the vulnerable and the mildly curious from the most objectionable material.

The limited resources available to law enforcement will probably be reserved for the suppression of those materials widely defined as heinous. The likelihood of international cooperation in the control of objectionable material is limited by the vast differences in standards and tolerance noted above. In this regard, the path to globalisation would seem a rocky one indeed.

At the same time, many would find it reassuring to learn that it is very difficult to be taken by surprise by sexually explicit images. There is a good deal of abhorrent material in cyberspace, but for the most part, one has to go looking for it.

7

TELEMARKETING FRAUD

Telecommunications technology has been a great facilitator of commerce, providing opportunities for contact between buyer and seller, and convenience to both parties. New developments in telecommunications are enhancing these opportunities for better, and for worse: along with their considerable benefits for those engaged in legitimate commerce, they provide opportunities for the unscrupulous.

Direct marketing, by post or telecommunications, is increasing as a medium of commerce in Australia. In 1995, telemarketing comprised 25 per cent less of the volume of the A$4.5 billion Australian direct marketing industry, and nearly half of adult Australians have received a telephone call relating to telemarketing activities (AUSTEL 1995). In recent years, the use of the telephone for selling goods, services, and investment products, as well as for soliciting charitable contributions, has been significantly enhanced by innovations in information technology. The more familiar of these innovations are ones which permit the storage and retrieval of telephone numbers, automatic high-speed dialling, and the transmission of recorded solicitations. Telemarketing has become much more efficient than direct mailing or door-to-door sales.

As we approach the 21st century, the telephone is being complemented as a medium of electronic commerce by the Internet and by commercial online services (Brien 1996; Buckeridge and Cutler 1995). Commercial sites and advertisements have begun to proliferate on the World Wide Web. Anyone exposed to the Web will note the increasing number of commercial advertisements for a vast range of products. The visual impact and allure of these messages is already formidable. Unfortunately, not all of these advertisements are legitimate. Moreover, cyber-frauds may originate from and be accessible to nearly anywhere in the world. In certain respects, this is similar to transnational fraudulent solicitations by telephone or fax. The fundamental difference is that web solicitations tend to be less targeted than telephone or fax solicitations, and less personal. Their reach, however, is vastly wider.

Whether these emerging telecommunications media, or indeed, new media as yet unforeseen, will replace the telephone as we know it as a medium of marketing remains to be seen. While projections at this stage are risky, estimates of the magnitude of Internet commerce by the year 2001 range between six and 600 billion Australian dollars. Ultimately, the actual amount will depend on the timely introduction and security capabilities of user-friendly payment systems.

While most electronic commerce, whether over the telephone, fax or Internet is entirely legitimate, some of it is not. For present purposes, we shall define telemarketing fraud as deceptive or misleading use of telecommunications services for commercial, investment or charitable solicitation. This can embrace activities, as diverse as advertising and selling consumer goods or investment products which turn out to be inferior or nonexistent; soliciting contributions to a bogus charity; manipulating share prices in companies traded on the stock exchange; and the creation of chain letters and pyramid selling schemes.

Although relatively infrequent in Australia to date, frauds using telephone or fax are commonplace overseas, particularly in the United States. Evidence has begun to emerge of questionable sales or investment offerings communicated over computer networks and bulletin boards. As early as mid-1994, state securities regulators in the United States began to address issues of consumer fraud and abuse in cyberspace (Consumer Scam Alert Network 1996). Since then, a number of US state securities agencies have launched investigations into questionable activities on the Internet relating to investments.

While the use of telecommunications services as marketing media in Australia is less common than in the United States, one may predict that electronic marketing will become more common in future. The proliferation of user-friendly technology, combined with its increasing power and decreasing cost, means wider accessibility, to legitimate sellers, as well as to perpetrators and victims of fraud. Moreover, telecommunications technology will become more accessible to the more vulnerable members of society. If this is the case, there will be a commensurate increase in fraud risk.

In March 1996, the Federal Trade Commission (FTC) in the United States announced that it had charged nine companies with making false or unsubstantiated advertising claims on the Internet. Four of the cases involved advertisements for work-at-home businesses online. The charges related to unsubstantiated earnings claims, which stated that participants could make up to US$38,000 a year. Five of the cases involved false claims about repairing consumers' credit records. Most of the cases resulted in negotiated settlements, with the defendants agreeing to discontinue the scams.[1] In at least one case, the settlement followed an order freezing the defendant's assets, and was accompanied by an undertaking to refund the purchase price to those who had bought the product.[2]

The costs of telemarketing fraud

Fraudulent commerce, through whatever medium, is injurious. Telemarketing fraud, in both its contemporary and emerging manifestations, poses substantial risks to society. The very existence of fraud, in whatever form, or perpetrated by means of whatever technology, tends to erode the general fabric of trust within society. Trust is important for social relations generally, and for commercial relations in particular. For commerce to flourish, currently prevailing levels of trust must be maintained.

Fraud poses risks to the individual as well, beyond any monetary loss which might be borne. Those who have suffered a betrayal of trust may endure lasting psychological damage. They may withdraw from social relations, and

---

1   http://netday.iworld.com/textonly/96Mar/0315-ftc.html
2   *FTC v Brian Corzine*, No CIV-S-94-1446 (E D Cal filed 12 September 1994). The defendant was also required under the settlement to cooperate with the FTC in investigating similar credit repair frauds.

remain chronically suspicious of all social contacts. And the financial loss itself can be catastrophic. The annals of fraud are replete with cases of elderly people having been bilked of their life savings.

In addition to consumers, legitimate telemarketers are victimised by fraudulent telemarketing. Their business suffers when consumer confidence is eroded. The increasing use of telephones for charitable solicitations means that legitimate charities will suffer from the taint of mistrust generated by fraudulent solicitations.

Moreover, credit card companies and lending institutions can also sustain significant losses as a result of telemarketing fraud. To the extent that payment for fraudulent goods and services is made by credit card, lending institutions may be forced to absorb a significant proportion of the resulting losses. In 1990, major retail banks in the United Kingdom lost approximately £150 million through plastic card fraud (Levi Bissell and Richardson 1991), while in 1991 credit card fraud was estimated to amount to US$712 million in the United States (Holland 1995).

The occurrence of telemarketing fraud is conventionally explained in terms of greed and callousness on the part of the fraudster, and greed and gullibility on the part of the victim. Common to all successful frauds is an extremely convincing message delivered by the perpetrator. The charm, persuasiveness, and interpersonal skills which make for good selling can be put to more sinister ends. Frauds arising from transactions based on face-to-face contact between parties often require a greater degree of psychological detachment on the part of the fraudster. To take a proverbial "little old lady" into one's confidence, only to plunder her life savings, requires a degree of heartlessness, which is fortunately relatively rare. By contrast, fraudulent transactions which are mediated only by voice, or by electronic mail, require a less callous, and less charismatic, perpetrator.

One hesitates to use the word "fool", but there are many examples of successful telemarketing fraud in which the degree of trust on the part of the victim strains credulity. Not all forms of telemarketing fraud, however, are based on a prospective victim's greed. Charity scams, in which the fraudster solicits contributions for a fictitious "worthy cause", are based on a combination of the victim's gullibility and altruism. While some victims of telemarketing fraud must bear a degree of responsibility for their own misfortune, not all victims are blameworthy. Skilled confidence tricksters are particularly adept at applying psychological pressure on their victims, and many ordinary people are eager to please those who make contact with them. Moreover, there are people in the community who may lack the intellectual and social skills appropriate to the identification of a fraudulent scheme. Telemarketing aimed at children, for example, can entail practices which are unconscionable, if not fraudulent. In the United States, pay-per-call services (the equivalent of 0055 in Australia) inviting children to ring Santa Claus at Christmastime have been documented.

Another example occurred in New York where an offender engaged a service with the telephone company which provided that anyone calling his premium 540 number would be charged the equivalent of A$70 for the call. A tape-recorded message greeted callers but failed to mention the charge. The offender then used a computer to dial large blocks of pager service numbers. When the owner of the pager answered the call, the computer entered the 540 number. Done at night, this caught many pager owners off guard as they called the number and listened to worthless information about real estate, without realising that they were incurring the large fee. During one month, the equivalent of more than A$115,000 had been accrued by the offender. Fortunately, the fraud was discovered before pager subscribers were obliged to pay their accounts (Delaney 1993).

A related type of fraud, recently uncovered in the United States, entails offenders dialling pager numbers and leaving messages requiring the owner of the pager to call a premium service number costing US$25. Because the call is diverted to the Caribbean without the recognisable pay-per-call prefix number, the caller is unaware that the call attracts a substantial fee which is then charged to the caller's account (Cookes 1996). This type of fraud has proliferated recently owing to Caribbean countries adopting a range of area codes, thus making callers less likely to know that they are incurring long-distance charges. In addition, some fraudsters are using a technique by which calls are "rolled-over" from a local call to a long-distance pay-per-call without the caller being aware of the change in billing which is taking place (Lanford and Lanford 1996). Similarly, victims may receive an unsolicited call advising that they have received a prize, instructing them to call a pay-per-call number for further information, or to claim the prize. The "prize", if one exists, may be worth less than the cost of the call.

More recently, an Internet fraud came to light which lured users to a site in Canada which purported to offer free adult entertainment, available by downloading a special "viewer". The act of downloading the software not only enabled the images to be seen, but, unbeknown to the user, disconnected the user's modem from their local Internet Service Provider and re-routed the connection through a provider in Moldova. The connection continued even after the user had left the site, and remained on until the computer was turned off; only later did their telephone bills indicate that they had incurred international calling charges in excess of A$2 per minute. Some thousands of consumers were alleged to have been defrauded in the scheme, which is being investigated by the Royal Canadian Mounted Police (*Corporate Crime Reporter*, 24 February 1997, *Internet Australia*, April 1997).

Despite its contemporary manifestations, consumer fraud is hardly a uniquely modern phenomenon. The number of variations on the basic fraud (colloquially referred to as "scams") is limited only by the human imagination. But the emergence of new technologies for the commission of fraud will require new institutional arrangements for prevention and control. These will include closer cooperation between law enforcement and related regulatory agencies, and contributions from non-government institutions. These new arrangements have the potential significantly to enhance the capacities of traditional law enforcement agencies.

The logistics of traditional telemarketing fraud are basic. Organised telemarketing fraudsters establish temporary telephone banks, commonly termed "boiler room" operations. From these locations, they contact individuals at random, or in specifically targeted groups. Fraudulent schemes are very diverse.

The basic fraud entails an offer which appears to be (and is) too good to be true, accompanied by a request for an "up front" payment. The fundamental strategy of the fraudster is to persuade the victim to pay in advance by cheque or credit card for the product or service in question. The fraudster then either provides a grossly inferior product, or fails to deliver altogether. Fraudsters may operate a particular scam for a short period of time, then close down and move locations before they can be identified.

Fraudsters may request payment in readily negotiable form such as money orders, sent by overnight courier, and immediately convert the instrument to cash upon receipt. A note of urgency can be introduced in order to convey the impression that "supplies are limited", or that "the offer is about to expire". Thus are telemarketing fraudsters able to move quickly, and to "cover their tracks" only too well.

There are two basic forms of telemarketing fraud. The first targets a small number of individuals, often drawn from specific backgrounds, such as professionals, or the affluent elderly, with a view to scoring a few big hits. The second type targets a large number of individuals, and aims at a relatively low return from a large number of victims.

The offer of investment products promising astronomical returns is a familiar example of the first type of fraud. Investment frauds can be based on an endless variety of products, including "rare" coins, ostrich chicks, health cures, gemstones, art, oil and gas leases, interests in oil wells, cellular telephone licences, precious metals, and more.

A common type of fraud in recent years, originating in Nigeria, has entailed the offer of a commission for assistance in transferring a large volume of funds offshore. Contact is made with prospective victims overseas in which they are informed of huge contracts for purchase of vehicles, computers, agricultural machinery, and so on at Ministries of Defence, Transport and Aviation, Agricultural and other State Ministries or that a vast sum of money from fictitious or allegedly existing and unclaimed estates of deceased individuals is available.

Complexities in the scheme are introduced by implicating the Central Bank of Nigeria, Federal Ministry of Finance, and Federal Inland Revenue, which are allegedly involved in the releasing and transferring of funds, approving remittance of funds, and collecting contracts taxes respectively. Investigations conducted so far have revealed that the documents forwarded to victims emanating from the above Federal institutions are forgeries.

The proposals require the use of a bank account outside Nigeria to which many millions of dollars will be credited in the expectation that the assistance given will be rewarded by retention of a proportion of the funds, usually 10 per cent. The proposals also require the initial transfer of an establishment fee to enable the transaction to proceed which is then stolen and the rest of the transaction not completed (Main and Stretton 1994; Anonymous 1995b, Osimiri 1997).

Among the more widely targeted frauds are those based on contests or lotteries. These entail notification that one has just been selected at random as the winner of an automobile or other valuable prize, which will be delivered upon receipt of shipping charges and registration fees. The victim pays the fees, and is thereafter ignored. Otherwise, victims may be selected as winners of "valuable" awards. In order to obtain their awards, however, the victims have to purchase products, such as pen and pencil sets, which are grossly overpriced. At best, the "valuable" awards may be of less value than the payments made by the victim.

Another form of questionable telemarketing entails the solicitation of advertisements in marginal or non-existent publications. Public and private sector organisations are among the favoured targets of this technique. Spurious trade union or charitable affiliations are often invoked to lend an aura of legitimacy to the publication; persistent calls for continuing payments may succeed in inflicting significant losses (Thomas 1993).

Developments in telecommunications have begun to provide the basis for, as well as the medium of, fraudulent pitches. High-pressure telemarketing promotion of paging licences and pay-per-call investment schemes began to proliferate in the United States during 1995.

As noted above, approaches to prospective victims can be random, or targeted. Advances in telecommunications technology have for some time permitted random automatic dialling. Alternatively, fraudsters may focus on a particular target group, such as senior citizens, medical practitioners or wine enthusiasts. Machine readable mailing lists of periodicals with a specialised readership or associations with a defined membership are often obtainable, as are the "electronic white pages". A system called Automatic Number Identification (ANI) automatically identifies and stores the number from which one is calling. By matching these phone numbers with other computerised lists and street directories, one's name and address can often be identified. Professional fraudsters in the United States compile special phone lists according to demographic characteristics of residents, and even trade "sucker" phone lists containing the names of victims who have fallen for previous scams. Currently available information technology permits very sophisticated matching and refinement of lists, to enable increasingly precise targeting of prospective victims.

The move to electronic commerce will be accompanied by even greater threats to personal privacy, as a great deal of activity on the Internet is transparent. Substantial volumes of personal information are thus easily accessible to those who would exploit it for purposes legitimate or otherwise. This accumulation of personal information in private hands is without precedent.

Although many fraudulent "pitches" are quite direct, the Internet provides a vehicle for more insidious marketing. "Disguised advertising" is difficult to recognise because it is not always apparent that a product is being advertised. Bulletin boards and chat forums may contain comments or statements about the quality or the performance of products or services. These may in fact be advertisements. But unless the identity and affiliation of the participants is transparent, the consumer may remain unaware.

In the words of a United States regulator:

> One of the concerns that we have is when you go into a chat room or into various places on a web site, you don't always know whether or not you're talking to an advertiser or whether or not you're talking to an individual who has a good experience with a product . . . When you enter a chat room and somebody is telling you that this wonderful tree bark in Mexico will cure any

kind of fatal cancer, and the person that is making these claims is in fact the owner of the tree bark, and the owner of the airplane that takes you there, and the owner of the place you have to stay while you are there, and you don't know that. That's out-and-out deception (Varney 1996).

The development of telecommunications technology now enables telemarketing fraud to be perpetrated from across the world. Cost considerations, which in the past tended to confine telemarketing fraud to a relatively proximate location, are no longer prohibitive. Telephone calls can originate anywhere, and verification of the bona fides of the caller is that much more difficult. The recent emergence of Internet commerce dramatically extends the reach of marketing, for legitimate or illegitimate purposes. Literally millions of prospective victims are contactable with great speed, little effort, negligible cost, and complete anonymity. Among the misconduct which has been greatly facilitated by the Internet is the so called "pump and dump" scheme, in which a person communicates false or misleading information regarding publicly traded shares. The object is to stimulate buying of the shares and thereby raise their price so that the originator of the rumour can sell his or her own shares at a profit. The Internet is attractive to would-be market manipulators because it offers very inexpensive access to vast numbers of persons (Weiss 1996).

So too is the classic "chain letter" facilitated by electronic mail. The standard message will promise windfall returns to those who send a specified amount to each of a list of specified addresses. Participants not only risk losing their investment, but also are identifiable for purposes of subsequent fraudulent exploitation. Chain letters, and related "pyramid" schemes, tend to collapse when a sufficient number of new recruits cannot be enlisted (Da Silva 1996a; Daly 1997).

Problems in detection and enforcement

It is currently impossible to estimate the magnitude and cost of telemarketing fraud in Australia. Thus far, it does not appear endemic, as it is in the United States. Estimates by the Attorney-General of the United States and the Chairman of the Federal Trade Commission suggest that the cost of telemarketing fraud in the United States is about US$40 billion per year. Lesser estimates are as high as US$15 billion (Kertz and Burnette 1992).

Estimating the cost of telemarketing fraud may be as fruitful as estimating the number of angels which can fit on the head of a pin, because the most effective frauds are never detected. In the case of charitable contribution fraud, the victim is left with good feelings, unaware that he or she has contributed to an unworthy cause. Some investment frauds are structured in such a manner that the victim perceives the loss as resulting from bad luck rather than venality.

Even when victims of fraud are all too aware of their misfortune, they are often loath to report their misfortunes to law enforcement authorities. To reveal one's gullibility can be extremely embarrassing, if not humiliating. Those victims of the occasional scam which itself has a motif of illegality (for example, one which promises a commission for assistance in money laundering) may be reluctant to disclose their inclination to criminal activity. Shame and guilt can trump indignation, and thereby contribute to a substantial "dark figure" of unreported fraud.

Even when telemarketing frauds are reported, identification of the perpetrators is by no means assured. The tools of telemarketing fraud can be dismantled, transported and reassembled easily. Skilled fraudsters close down their operations and move to another location, often under the jurisdiction of a different law enforcement agency. Methods of solicitation, products on offer, and other identifiable characteristics can change from one day to the next. These frequent changes of location and modus operandi hinder the collection of data which might reveal patterns of offending. The legal and financial impediments imposed by trans-jurisdictional investigations, not to mention extradition proceedings, can be prohibitively expensive, particularly in an environment of resource scarcity and competing enforcement priorities. To the extent that there is a lack of communication between agencies, the problem becomes even more difficult. Internet fraud enhances these advantages still further. Routing and anonymous remailing may permit a cyber-fraudster to cover his or her tracks. One can work from one's home, or from any remote connection, without the need for rented space. And one can change or relocate advertisements with great speed.

The control of traditional telemarketing fraud is difficult; responding to telemarketing fraud in its emerging global manifestation will be even more challenging. The globalisation of telephone sales methods and the emerging use of the Internet in marketing raise several questions. Does a person resident in the Caribbean who advertises a bogus investment product through a server in Switzerland, but visible in Australia via the Internet, avoid Australian jurisdiction? In the event that a gullible Australian posts a bank cheque to the Caribbean address, where is the transaction consummated?

Frauds perpetrated from outside Australia may in fact be offences under Australian law. Nevertheless, overseas jurisdictions have their own law enforcement priorities; frauds perpetrated by their nationals or by other foreign nationals against victims on the other side of the globe may not rank highly among them. By operating from a particularly permissive jurisdiction, one can arguably remain beyond the reach of the law. At the very least, distance may effectively place one beyond the reach of law enforcement. Costs of investigation and extradition may be beyond the capacity of Australian agencies. Identification of international telemarketing fraudsters, and their successful prosecution, becomes that much more difficult. By way of illustration, both the Australian Securities Commission and the US Securities and Exchange Commission (SEC) suggest that online investment opportunities originating offshore be approached with great caution, for the understated reason that it may be more difficult for the agency to be of assistance in the event of a mishap. In the words of the SEC: "When you send your money abroad, and something goes wrong, it's more difficult to find out what happened and to locate your money" (http://www.sec. gov/consumer/b-alert.htm). Bringing an overseas offender to justice is another, more difficult matter altogether.

Combating telemarketing fraud

There exists no one safeguard for the effective prevention and control of telemarketing fraud. The challenge is to identify a set of measures which will contain the risks of criminality, without inhibiting legitimate commerce. As in most areas of public policy, any viable solution will entail a balance of competing interests.

Regulatory safeguards

A variety of restrictions can be imposed on telemarketers to minimise the likelihood of unwanted contacts. These were seen in previous chapters on offensive, obscene, and intrusive communications. Among these basic safeguards are restricted hours for calling, silent telephone numbers, caller ID, and various blocking devices.[3]

Although the prospect of international marketing standards may seem remote, individual nations can take steps to prohibit false or deceptive electronic commerce originating from within their borders. The growth in international franchise transactions, due in part to a significant increase in advertisements for American franchise systems on the Internet, has inspired discussion on the desirability of a pre-purchase disclosure rule being made applicable to American franchisors selling territories and franchises in overseas locations, regardless of the laws of the host nation. These principles could be extended to other forms of commercial transaction. In the modern world, however, the likelihood of international cooperation and global uniformity would appear remote.

Enforcement

Given the substantial dark figure of telemarketing fraud, it is important to gather as much information on patterns and trends as can be made available. Encouraging victims to come forward with details of their experience is the obvious first step. Systematic sharing of information across jurisdictions is important, given the mobility of telemarketing fraud. Communication and coordination between agencies is essential, especially when matters may be of interest to a variety of agencies, including police fraud investigators, companies and securities regulators, and consumer affairs agencies. The necessity for coordination becomes particularly important in a federal system, where there are even more opportunities for matters to fall "between the cracks".

In the United States, the National Fraud Information Centre maintains a data base dedicated to telemarketing fraud which allows law enforcement officials desktop access to information about consumer complaints, ongoing investigations, and active or recent cases against alleged perpetrators of telemarketing fraud. Consumers can add their own complaints to this database, which is now

---

3 Caller ID technology, and its Internet variant, is something of a double-edged sword. When a consumer telephones a company equipped with caller ID, the consumer's number can be captured and sold or used for subsequent marketing purposes. Similarly, the originating address of any visitor to a website can be systematically recorded. See Kertz and Burnette (1992); Oates (1992).

available to nearly 100 law enforcement agencies. The NFIC has a website accessible to the general public (http://nfic.inter.net/nfio/alerts.htm).

The difficulty of identifying and investigating telemarketing fraud has invited the use of more intrusive investigative methods. One recent FBI investigation imitated the techniques of telemarketing fraudsters by having agents pose as salespersons for automatic dialling equipment. As part of their "trial service offer" the agents prevailed upon the fraudulent telemarketers in question to record their sales pitch. Subsequent "field tests" of the pre-recorded message elicited calls from other FBI agents posing as consumers interested in the advertised product. These "victim"-agents, upon receipt of the products, were then able to testify about the false or deceptive representations recorded by the telemarketers. The operation, code named "Disconnect", was a coast-to-coast operation involving eighteen field offices. It led to over 200 arrests.[4]

Another investigation, "Operation Senior Sentinel", was initiated and coordinated by the FBI with the cooperation of state authorities. Volunteer retired persons secretly recorded calls from fraudulent telemarketers, and forwarded them to an operations centre for collection, analysis, and investigation. The telephone lines in question were obtained from previous telemarketing fraud victims. The operation resulted in over 400 arrests in more than twelve states.[5]

At least in the United States, initial enforcement responses to online fraud have tended to be relatively lenient. Undertakings to discontinue the offending practice were given by the targets of the FTC actions noted above. Recent actions by the US Securities and Exchange Commission resulted in similar outcomes:

- A Company soliciting investments in an ethanol plant in the Dominican Republic, which promised returns of 50 per cent or more; accompanying literature contained false statements about contractual arrangements.

- A person seeking investors in Costa Rican companies producing coconut chips falsely claimed that a major supermarket chain had contracted to purchase all the chips they could produce.

- Another individual soliciting investors for a proposed eel farm promised "low risk" and a "whopping 20 per cent return." (http://www.sec.gov /consumer/cyberfr.htm).

In terms of domestic arrangements in Western industrial societies, laws appear adequate to cope with most forms of marketing fraud. In Australia, the use of the Internet to communicate misleading or deceptive information may incur civil as well as criminal liability. This can even extend to repeating (without bothering to confirm it) information such as a rumour originating with some other person. Australian law applies generally to investment products or advice

---

4   Federal Bureau of Investigation c 1993, *Telemarketing Fraud*, US Government Printing Office, Washington, http://www.socxfbi.org/socxfbi_html/majorcase.html and see also Gembrowski and Dahlberg (1995).

5   *Corporate Crime Reporter*, 11 December 1995, 8-9. For additional details on telemarketing fraud investigations in general, and Operation Senior Sentinel in particular, see http://199. 170.0.150/majcases/telefrad/telfrad.htm

originating overseas and offered to investors in Australia. The key once again is not the adequacy of the law, but rather the capacity of authorities to enforce it, especially against offshore offenders.

Public information

The best safeguard against telemarketing fraud would appear to be self-defence. Citizens who are aware of typical frauds are less likely to be "taken". Therefore, perhaps the most important means of controlling telemarketing fraud is the provision of information to prospective victims. Basic information to encourage wariness about overinflated claims (risk-free investments with guaranteed gains or guaranteed weight loss) should be widely available. As far as possible, such information should be packaged in a manner which educates the unwary without inspiring the predatory. Crime prevention information should prevent crime, not facilitate it.

Government agencies themselves may be the source of basic consumer information. For example the US Federal Trade Commission produces an abundance of literature for general public consumption about consumer risks, rights and remedies. The FTC also has a web site. FTC ConsumerLine is located on the Internet at CONSUMER.FTC.GOV or through the World Wide Web at http://www.ftc.gov. There is also a growing abundance of cautionary material on the Internet warning of online investment fraud.[6]

Third party co-production

Non-governmental organisations, alone or in partnership with government agencies, may contribute to raising fraud awareness among the general public.[7] Law enforcement and regulatory agencies, working with and through these intermediaries, may be able to communicate much more effectively than they can independently. Senior citizens' organisations, for example, are strategically situated to reach their members with words of caution, without causing undue anxiety. So too can they educate their members about fraud risks, and provide advice regarding the legitimacy of a particular investment or product. This is particularly important given the fact that senior citizens are often the specific targets of telephone scams.

Online services carry great potential for alerting the community in general, and individual consumers in particular, to the risks of fraudulent

---

6   For the Australian Securities Commission, see http://www.asc.gov.au; for various US sites, see http://www.state.ct.us/dob/pages/cyberblt.htm; http://www.sec.gov/consumer/b-alert.htm; http://www.state.pa.us/PA_Exec/Securities/sfap/hightech.html; http://www.nasdr.com

7   Organisations in the United States include the Alliance Against Fraud in Telemarketing, the American Association of Retired Persons, the Commodity Futures Trading Commission, the Communications Fraud Control Association, the Council of Better Business Bureaus, the Direct Marketing Association, the Federal Communications Commission, and the Federal Trade Commission, the High Technology Crime Investigation Association, the Industry Council for Tangible Assets, the National Association of Bunco Investigators, the National Association of Consumer Agency Administrators, the National Charities Information Bureau, the National Council Against Health Fraud, the National Futures Association, the National Insurance Crime Bureau, and Professionals Against Confidence Crime.

commerce. Web sites which alert prospective consumers and investors to possible scams are just as accessible as the sites which house fraudulent offerings. Where successful investigations and/or prosecutions are achieved, Web publicity can also be used for deterrent effect.

Public-private partnerships can also provide information on fraud prevention generally. The National Fraud Information Center (NFIC) noted above, is a partnership of National Consumers League, America's oldest consumer organisation, the National Association of Attorneys-General, and the Federal Trade Commission, with financial assistance from a variety of corporate sponsors, including major credit card companies. NFIC maintains a toll-free Consumer Assistance Service to answer questions regarding telephone or mail solicitations and online scams. They also provide information about how and where to report fraud, and can assist in filing complaints, as well as referring reports directly to the Federal Trade Commission or to the appropriate Attorney-General. The NFIC Internet Fraud Watch facilitates online reporting of suspected fraud.[8]

There are even private citizens who purport to assist in the investigation of telemarketing fraud. One web site in Iceland (http://www.islandia.is/~njall/nig/nigeria) is collating information on the numerous advance fee frauds originating in Nigeria.

The nature of the "Internet community" is such that individuals may close ranks against fraud coming to their attention. In addition to reporting inappropriate conduct to the relevant authorities, they may see fit to "spam" an offender, overloading their mailbox in retaliation for having engaged in questionable marketing behaviour (Brien 1996).

Self-help: individual prevention

In the end, the best line of defence against telemarketing fraud is individual prudence. Individual citizens are in a position to take basic steps to protect themselves against telemarketing fraud. A degree of healthy scepticism is also probably in order. As the saying goes, "if an offer seems too good to be true, it probably is."

One should be wary of buying from telephone callers whom one doesn't know. A simple request for a written description of the product in question and the terms of sale will help screen out fraudulent propositions. Consumers should withstand the seller's pressure for an immediate purchase or investment. Research on the background of the caller can be useful. A number of organisations can assist in this regard. In case of investments or large purchases, it is wise to ask questions and seek information from a variety of sources. If solid information about the company and the investment are not available, one should think twice about the purchase.

One should also take extreme care in disclosing one's credit card or PIN number. There is some risk attached in divulging this information to any person

---

8   http://www.nfic.inter.net/nfic2.htm. See also Royal Canadian Mounted Police 1997, "Economic Crime Prevention Web Page", http://www.rcmp-grc.gc.ca/html/ecbweb.htm

or institution whose integrity may be in question. At present, communication over the telephone is relatively secure. The Internet, however, is much more vulnerable, although presumably encryption technology can soon be expected to improve security (see Chapter 8).

It is also possible to screen one's incoming calls with an answering machine, accepting those which one wants, and ignoring the remainder. This will provide some safeguard against high-pressure sales tactics. Silent telephone numbers provide some protection against unwanted callers, but do not protect against random dialling technology. Similarly, the disclosure of a silent number to a commercial organisation may lead to its wider circulation. When one divulges one's telephone number in response to a newspaper advertisement or fills out a card asking for more information about an investment, or when one signs up for a contest or drawing, a phone number is usually requested.

Self-defence against online investment fraud is based on simple principles. As is the case with earlier technologies, one should be wary of promises of quick profits, and "inside" information. One should undertake some preliminary investigation, particularly when dealing with an unknown individual or institution. Typical red flags include such sales terminology as "guaranteed", "high return", "limited offer", or "risk free". In cyberspace, promoters who use "aliases", or pseudonyms are particularly suspect, as honest sales people have no interest in concealing their identity.

Conclusion

There seems to be no end of people willing and able to apply their considerable talents to the challenge of separating fools (and others who may be more trusting and vulnerable, than foolish) from their money. In this respect, the frontiers of cyberspace are not unlike terrestrial frontiers. But recent developments in electronic commerce will provide them with more refined tools with which to do so. Law enforcement agencies and consumer/investor protection authorities cannot eliminate predatory telemarketing, but they can contain it within reasonable limits. Their initial approach will be to encourage a degree of self-regulation on the part of marketers and a degree of self-help on the part of the general public. A more coercive regulatory posture, absent persistent wilful misconduct, will run the risk of stifling commercial and technological development.

8

ELECTRONIC FUNDS TRANSFER CRIME

The primary motivation which underlies most property crime is the desire to enhance one's wealth without engaging in legitimate wealth-creating activity. Traditionally, thieves directed their attentions at currency in the form of banknotes. Banknotes, however, have no intrinsic value in themselves but only in the information printed on them by the issuing authority. In recent times, money exists in a wide variety of forms, many of which are recorded electronically. Modern thieves are discovering that crime can be carried out with fewer risks by the use of a computer than by employing the traditional implements used to perpetrate bank robberies or burglary.

This chapter considers the various ways in which offences of dishonesty may be committed when funds are transferred between individuals and organisations through the use of electronic telecommunications systems.

After describing the various systems which exist to record and to transfer funds electronically, we explore the nature and extent of the problem of electronic funds transfer crime. The chapter will conclude with an appraisal of the most effective ways in which such crimes may be prevented through a variety of regulatory strategies.

The nature of money and banking

Prior to 1900, it was common for ordinary banks to issue banknotes. To enhance trust in currency and to facilitate commerce, governments then began to exercise control over currencies. In 1893, for example, Australian legislation proclaimed that only certain banknotes could be legal tender. The first Commonwealth note was issued in 1910 and in 1959, Australia's central bank, the Reserve Bank of Australia, was created (Tyree 1990).

Although only the Reserve Bank may now issue currency in Australia, a wide variety of financial institutions may issue plastic cards for use in carrying out various financial transactions. Plastic cards, however, derive their value and legality from the fact that banks guarantee the value placed on them and enable merchants to obtain access to money held by the customer's bank.

As at June 1996, currency issued by the Reserve Bank of Australia totalled A\$20.479 billion, of which nearly A\$2 billion was held by banks. For everyday, low-value transactions, cash remains the most convenient and popular form of payment. Harper and Leslie (1995) estimate that between 85 and 90 per cent of *transactions* in Australia are cash based, between 5 and 7.5 per cent are electronic, while between 2.5 and 10 per cent are cheque or paper-based.

When one considers the *value* of money involved in these transactions, however, it is apparent that only 10 per cent are cash-based with the vast bulk of transactions being carried out with paper. There is, however, a recent trend away from using paper-based systems in favour of payment using plastic cards.

The Australian Payments System Council *Annual Report 1994-95* (1995), for example, reports that goods and services purchased with transaction cards account for almost one-third of retail trade.

When a central bank issues currency, seigniorage is earned. This is defined as the change in the face value of the note issue plus interest earned on assets purchased by the Reserve Bank of Australia from the proceeds of its note issue less the annual cost of printing and maintaining the note issue. Harper and Leslie (1995) estimate this to be around 3.5 per cent of total government outlays. The advent of cashless payments mechanisms erodes the monopoly position of the central bank as the sole supplier of currency; this represents a return to privately-issued currency, something not observed in Australia since the early years of this century. This problem, known as disintermediation, is currently being examined by various financial institutions and regulators as part of a strategic assessment of the introduction of electronic funds transfer systems.

Electronic funds transfers of the future

In the society of the not-too-distant-future, nearly all transactions may be carried out electronically using cards or computers. In such a scenario, most large purchases will be made by means of electronic funds transfer at point of sale (EFTPOS) and credit cards, while small purchases will be made using a stored value card. Many other transactions, including electronic bill-paying, dealings with financial institutions and even withdrawal of funds, may be carried out from home, although in a recent survey of 3258 households in Australia, less than one-third of those surveyed indicated a willingness to use online home banking facilities (Australian Bureau of Statistics 1996).

In the United States at present, more than 60 per cent of banking transactions are carried out electronically. By the year 2000, this is expected to increase to 80 per cent. Already, more than 30 per cent of all utility bills, motor vehicle loans and mortgages are paid electronically (Internet Inc http://www. efunds.com:/efstats22.html).

Stored value or "smart" cards are already being used in many novel ways throughout the world. Smart cards are, for example being used by P & O Holidays to enable ocean liner passengers to conduct transactions in order to prevent theft of cash while on board ship; in Melbourne, where the "smartpark" system, enables car parking fees to be paid by smart cards which have been used to make purchases in the central-city district; in the Hong Kong public transport ticketing system; on Singapore tollways; in Shanghai, where China's first stored value card, the "East Card" is being used for paying taxi fares and supermarket purchases; by Telstra Mobilenet Digital Access System for mobile telephones; and in Quebec where the Health Card employs smart card technology (Commonwealth of Australia, Human Rights and Equal Opportunity Commission 1995).

One of the reasons for the development of electronic alternatives to currency was the desire to reduce the security risks associated with having large amounts of cash deposited with banks, merchants and individuals. Unfortunately, as with other areas of regulation a novel crime prevention strategy has created new risks which may have far worse consequences than the problem which was sought to be avoided (Grabosky 1995b). As Levy (1994) observes:

> Depending on how they work, the various systems of electronic money will prove to be boons or disasters, bastions of individual privacy or violators of individual freedom. At the worst, a faulty or crackable system of electronic money could lead to an economic Chernobyl.

How, then, are funds transferred electronically and what security risks do such systems possess?

Electronic funds transfer systems

International electronic transfers

Telegraphic transfers of funds first took place in 1860 and are now used widely to transfer funds between banks internationally.

There are several systems which operate internationally for clearing wholesale or large value transfers and settling transactions between banks electronically (which in Australian terms means more than A\$10,000). In Australia in 1995, A\$50 billion per day was transferred electronically using these systems (Australian Payments System Council 1996, Table 14).

The Society for Worldwide Interbank Financial Telecommunications (SWIFT), is a Belgian cooperative that connects over 5000 financial institutions in over 80 countries. By the early 1990s it carried over one million messages a day (Mackrell 1996).

In the United States, electronic funds transfers are carried out by Fedwire, a system controlled by the United States Federal Reserve and CHIPS, the Clearing House Interbank Payments System. In London, the Clearing House Automated Payments System (CHAPS) operates for large transactions in a way similar to CHIPS in New York.

In Australia, the Bank Interchange and Transfer System (BITS) carries a large proportion of the Australian dollar leg of foreign exchange settlements as well as customer-to-customer payments. Austraclear is a system (FINTRACS) for the settlement of private sector and semi-government debt securities, and the Reserve Bank Information and Transfer System (RITS) settles trade in Commonwealth Government Securities. Both Austraclear and RITS also allow cash transfers unrelated to security trades (Australian Payments System Council 1996, *Annual Report 1995-96*).

Around the end of 1997, the Australian financial system will be introducing a Real Time Gross Settlement (RTGS) system, in which large payments between banks will be settled through accounts at the Reserve Bank as they occur. All banks (and indirectly credit unions and building societies) will be connected directly to the system, and all transfers will be for credit funds (that is, real dollars) and completed in real time (that is, virtually instantly). Once completed, transfers will be irrevocable. Access to the system will be widespread and the banks have agreed to use SWIFT to access the system instead of BITS (Australian Payments System Council 1996; Mackrell 1996).

As a potential target for fraud on a large scale, these systems hold great attraction by reason of the large sums of money they carry. The expertise needed to infiltrate such systems is, however, highly technical and closely guarded and unlikely to be present without the assistance of confederates within the institutions in question. It is, however, possible to compromise the security of financial institutions as we have seen in Chapter 2 (Nicholson 1989).

Electronic payment orders

While individuals are able to make use of international payments systems to transfer small sums of money, most small value transfers that are carried out by individuals involve domestic banks. Payments may be made by way of direct debit, in which payments are made directly from the payee's account to the recipient's bank, or by way of credit transfer in which a payer advises his or her bank to debit his or her account with a sum which is electronically credited to another account. Small transaction fees often apply in respect of such transactions.

Various other electronic funds transfer systems operate throughout the world as substitutes for paper-based cheque transactions. The United Kingdom GIRO system, for example, has benefits in preventing cheque fraud because the payment order is directed to the banker directly rather than through the payee. In the GIRO system, the person wishing to make a payment, the payer, instructs his or her bank concerning the details of the payment and the funds are electronically transferred from the payer's account to the payee's account.

All such systems create a security risk if procedures are not in place to verify the availability of funds which are to be transferred or if account access controls are not in place. It is usual for plastic cards to be used to initiate such transactions which creates a potential for fraud if counterfeit or stolen cards are used.

Home banking

Home banking is carried out either by using a telephone or a computer terminal in the customer's home which is connected to the bank via telephone wires and a modem, enabling the customer to carry out various banking transactions electronically. Such transactions include obtaining general information such as locations of branches and ATMs, interest and exchange rates; various transaction services such as obtaining account balances and details of past transactions, transferring funds between accounts, using electronic chequebooks to pay bills; and other services including ordering statements, and chequebooks, reporting lost or stolen cards, notifying changes of address, stopping payment of cheques, obtaining loans, investment information or share dealing brokerage, and seeking share portfolio management services (Australian Payments System Council 1996).

Protection against fraud is obtained through the use of PIN authentication, transaction codes, and encryption of data in much the same way as an ATM system operates. The possibility exists, however, that passwords and PINs could be intercepted where these are communicated via telephone lines. To limit the financial consequences of this, banks issue a PIN for home banking which is different from the customer's ordinary ATM PIN.

The terms and conditions of home banking generally reflect those which govern EFT card transactions, although banks are not responsible for losses which result from communication systems malfunctions (Australian Payments System Council 1996).

Both telephone and computer home banking are now being offered in Australia, such as Advance Bank's "QuickPhone" system which is being used by over 4500 customers with approximately two hundred transactions being carried out daily (Da Silva 1996b).

Online (Internet) transactions

At present, most commercial transactions which take place on the Internet are undertaken by customers purchasing goods and services by disclosing their credit card details (see Cavazos and Morin 1994 for a discussion of online business transactions generally). It has been estimated that approximately US$500 million worth of transactions took place on the Internet in 1995. By 2005 global online commerce is expected to reach between US$76 billion and US$186 billion (Lewis 1996). Transmitting credit card information in an unprotected electronic environment such as the Internet is perceived as a significant security risk by many and has led to new encryption systems being devised to protect the transmission of account numbers.

First Virtual in the United States, for example, allows customers and merchants to transact business over the Internet by being registered with First Virtual and then being given a password used to authorise credit card transactions. First Virtual then reconciles passwords and card details on behalf of merchants enabling merchants to submit transaction details to their bank.

Cybercash uses an algorithm to encrypt card details while they are travelling over the Internet. Encryption software is downloaded from the Internet and merchants and customers are required to register with Cybercash before secure purchases may be made.

Microsoft and Visa have developed a payment protocol called "SET" (Secure Electronic Transactions) which uses public key encryption to protect data from being compromised. Digital signatures are also used to authenticate all the parties involved. Credit card details are transmitted only once online to a Certificate Authority. Merchants received payment by passing to their bank an encrypted message which originated with the card holder permitting funds to be transferred from the credit card account to the merchant's account. It is anticipated that SET will be introduced in September 1997 and fully operational by October 1998 (Australian Payments System Council 1996; Lewis 1996; McCrae 1996; Visa International 1997).

Electronic money

Electronic funds can now be stored on computers as well as on cards, thus enabling funds to be transferred through telecommunications networks such as the Internet.

Various companies have started electronic cash systems, including Digicash in The Netherlands (http://digicash.com:80/home.html) and CyberCash Inc. in the United States (http://www.cybercash .com/). Digicash has since opened an office in Australia (McCrae 1996).

The Digicash system, uses a form of electronic money known as "E-cash". Before purchases can be made, both the merchant and the customer need to establish banking arrangements and Internet links with the bank issuing the E-cash. The customer first requests a transfer of funds from his or her bank account into the E-cash system. This is similar to withdrawing cash from an ATM. The E-cash system then generates and validates E-cash coins which the customer is able to use on the Internet. The coins are data streams digitally signed by the issuing bank using its private key (see the discussion of public key encryption in the introductory chapter). The customer is then able to send E-cash to any merchant who will accept this form of payment using the software provided by the E-cash service provider. The customer encrypts the message and endorses the coins using the merchant's public key. The merchant then decrypts the message with its private key and verifies the validity of the coin using the issuing bank's public key. The merchant is then able to turn E-cash into real funds by presenting the E-cash to the issuing bank with a request for an equivalent amount of real funds to be credited to the merchant's bank account (Australian Payments System Council 1996).

An alternative approach is being used by an Australian company "Cybank" (http://www.cybank.net/index.html). Cybank has patented a scheme in which value is created online through the use of telephone accounts. By selecting a cash amount on the Cybank Internet site, the software dials a Telstra 1900 number and the sum requested is debited to the customer's telephone account. The customer is then able to use the credit to purchase goods and services over the Internet (Bowes 1996; Carter 1996).

A central problem with electronic cash is the possibility of electronic funds being able to circulate independently of the banking system. In view of the problem of disintermediation or banks losing seigniorage, noted above, some have suggested that the digital banknote should be issued and verified by a central bank in order to enable central banks to control the amount of currency in the banking world (Wrightson and Furche forthcoming). This may help to guard against money laundering which, as we will see in Chapter 9, could become rife in such an unregulated system (see Wahlert 1996).

Card transactions

The first bank card containing a magnetic stripe was issued by Frankin National Bank of Long Island, New York in 1951 (Masuda 1996) while in Britain, plastic cards were first issued in 1965 (Webb 1996). In Australia, the first bank card was issued in 1974, followed shortly thereafter by MasterCard and Visacard. In 1992, there were almost ten million major credit cards in use in Australia (Bonney 1992), while in Britain there are now 86 million plastic cards on issue (Webb 1996).

Plastic cards contain between one and three magnetised tracks which permit the identification of the user and enable the user to conduct a transaction from a location distant from the central data base, such as a bank. Some allow information to be stored for passive use (read-only) while others enable information to be introduced (read and write).

Plastic card transactions are carried out as follows. Initially a plastic card is inserted into a reader or passed near a target at a terminal in the case of contactless cards. The reader then authenticates that the card is valid and checks the card against "black lists" of lost and stolen cards and card holders whose authority to use the card has been restricted or withdrawn. The card holder's cash withdrawal limit will also be noted before any cash is dispensed. In appropriate circumstances transactions may be terminated at this point and the card confiscated. The reader then authenticates the identity of the user as a person authorised to use the card. For a card with multiple applications (that is, cards which may be used for a range of transactions), the card holder selects the application desired. The security requirements for that card and application are then selected and the card holder inserts a PIN, password or biometric data (fingerprints, retinal scan, signature dynamics) for verification. The card holder is then able to carry out the transaction and the transaction is recorded and transmitted to the reader, to the system provider, and to any third parties who may be involved. A hard copy or paper record of the transaction is printed for the user and the card holder removes the card prior to leaving (Commonwealth of Australia, Human Rights and Equal Opportunity Commission 1995).

Perhaps the most critical step in the transaction from a security point of view is the manner in which the bank's computer verifies that the customer is authorised to make the transaction. This is commonly carried out by the card holder keying-in to the terminal a four or six-number PIN which is able to be verified against information contained in the card's magnetic stripe or chip and the host computer.

In order to enhance the security of the system, the user's PIN never travels through the network in unencoded form. Instead it is replaced by an irreversible string of numbers or an authentication parameter which processes the PIN and card information through a set of equations called an algorithm which calculates the parameter. If the system is tapped, only the parameter is intercepted (Sullivan 1987). There is, as a result, little opportunity for the PIN to be discovered by teeing-into the network.

A more substantial security risk arises from the manner in which the PIN is communicated to the card holder, recorded and remembered by the card holder, and used by the card holder at a terminal during a transaction.

Although card holders are clearly warned of the dangers associated with disclosing their PIN, writing it on the card, or keeping it in the same place as the card, a considerable proportion of card holders refuse to heed such advice and thereby place themselves at risk of loss for which they will be personally responsible (see the Electronic Funds Transfer Code of Conduct ss. 5.6 and 5.7; Sneddon 1995).

Often, however, card holders may disclose their PINs unwittingly or through understandable exploitation by confidence tricks. We have already seen in Chapter 4 how fraudsters may use the techniques of "shoulder surfing", "cracking", "scanning", and "social engineering" to learn a card holder's PIN. It is in combating such strategies that user education and risk awareness have been most helpful in preventing fraud.

Harper and Leslie (1995) group electronic payments systems which use plastic cards into three categories:

- pay later (credit cards);
- pay now (debit cards used with ATMs and EFTPOS); and
- pay before (stored value or smart cards which are pre-charged with value electronically and which may be re-charged).

Pay later cards (Credit Cards)

Credit cards permit card holders to obtain goods and services immediately with the card issuer providing funds to the merchant from the card holder's account which may be held in credit or debit. Transaction fees are paid by the card holder and merchant, and interest accrues on accounts with a debit balance.

In the United States, over 50 per cent of all retail purchases are made using credit cards, and customers are willing to pay up to 20 per cent interest rates for the convenience of having immediate access to credit facilities (Masuda 1996).

If the card is stolen or a counterfeit made, it is possible dishonestly to obtain goods and services, including cash, on credit up to a specified transaction ceiling amount until such time as the fraud is detected and authorisation to use the card is withdrawn.

Pay now cards (Debit Cards)

Magnetic stripe debit cards permit transactions to be conducted and bank accounts debited immediately through the use of online connections between the terminal being used and the bank. Two types of debit card terminals are commonly used: Automated Teller Machines (ATMs) and terminals which permit Electronic Funds Transfer at Point of Sale (EFTPOS).

Automated teller machines. ATMs are electronic vaults which enable users to withdraw or deposit money or obtain other banking services. They contain a supply of cash money and other products such as cheque books, a Personal Identification Code reader, and disk drives for recording transactions when the machine is offline or not connected to the host-computer at the bank's head office.

The main security risks associated with the use of ATMs relate to unauthorised transactions, that is, individuals gaining access to accounts and receiving cash from accounts other than their own or obtaining greater sums than their credit balance permits.

It is essential for data travelling between the ATM terminal and the bank to be resistant to external interference and, accordingly, the Electronic Funds Transfer Code of Conduct requires that Message Authentication Codes (MACs) which satisfy the Australian Standard AS2805 be used for transactions. Compliance with this standard has not yet been achieved throughout Australia (Australian Payments System Council 1995, *Annual Report 1994-95*).

Since 1989, there has been a 78 per cent increase in the number of ATM terminals in Australia, with over 7000 ATMs being present in Australia on 30 June 1996 (Australian Payments System Council 1993-96).

Electronic funds transfer at point of sale. EFTPOS transactions are carried out using terminals connected to a merchant's cash register which enable customers to pay for goods or to withdraw cash electronically via their bank's computer. Transactions are carried out by the customer keying in a PIN to a terminal which then communicates details of the credit or debit through the EFTPOS network to the customer's bank. Similar security checks are conducted as for an ATM transaction in order to verify the card, the card user and the credit balance available in the customer's account when the transaction is made.

Since 1989, there has been a much greater increase in the number of EFTPOS terminals in Australia (919 per cent) than the number of ATM terminals, while the number of EFTPOS transactions has also shown a substantial increase (390 per cent). At 30 June 1996, there were 116,704 EFTPOS Terminals in Australia which were used to conduct some 470 million transactions (Australian Payments System Council 1996).

Pay before cards (Stored Value Cards)

The final category of cards which may be used to transfer funds electronically, is stored value cards. These have value recorded on them electronically prior to customers using them to conduct transactions. A variety of systems have been devised with increasingly complex technology and capabilities.

Memory only stored value cards. Plastic magnetic stripe cards which can be loaded with value and then used to purchase goods and services have been in use for many years now. They were initially used to buy telephone calls, transport services or other small purchases such as photocopies. Early stored value cards were single purpose in that they replaced cash for one purpose only, they were disposed of once the initial value had been used, and were completely anonymous with no way of connecting the purchase to any individual (Australia, Bureau of Consumer Affairs 1995).

The security risks associated with such cards are very similar to those of currency in that cards may be stolen and used immediately, although often only for a single type of transaction. They were originally devised to combat theft of cash from vending machines and public telephones and have been highly effective in reducing vandalism caused to such machines and loss of cash associated with this (Challinger 1992).

Smart cards

A smart card is a plastic card that has electronic logic to store data and in some cases a microprocessor which can process data. The first smart card was developed in France and patented by Roland Moreno in 1974. Smart cards can be contact (which are activated when terminals touch a smart card reader) or contactless (which are activated by radio waves when passed near a transmitter).

They may be memory only cards or processor cards depending on the extent of function given to the chip. In Australia at present, there are between 1.5 and 2 million smart cards in use (Atkinson 1996), while worldwide there are over 420 million in use (McGauran 1996).

Smart card payments systems may take a variety of forms. The system which most closely resembles the early forms of stored value cards involves a scheme operator which administers a central pool of funds. When a card holder transfers value to the card, the funds are actually transferred to a pool controlled by the scheme operator. A merchant who is paid from the card takes evidence of the receipt to the scheme operator, which pays the relevant amount from the pool (Commonwealth of Australia, Bureau of Consumer Affairs 1995).

Other proposals, such as those operated by MasterCard and Visa International, envisage a number of brands of cards being accepted. In such schemes there is then no central pool of funds, but rather each cardissuer is responsible for reimbursing merchants which accept their cards (Australian Payments System Council 1995, *Annual Report 1994-95*).

The Swiss PTT Card (Postal and Telecommunications Commission) conducted a trial in Biel of 15,000 smart cards with an electronic purse function between March 1989 and July 1993. The cards could hold the equivalent of up to A$125 and value could be reloaded onto the cards at PTT offices and public telephones. The cards could be used to pay for a variety of goods and services with merchants transferring the accrued value of smart card sales to their account by taking their cards to the local post office. Although the trial was a technical success, the scheme was not popular with consumers (Harper and Leslie 1994).

Various other European countries have introduced, or are conducting trials of, smart cards. Trials are also being conducted in Johannesburg. In the United States approximately two million Visa Cash Cards were distributed at the Atlanta Olympic Games (Deogun 1996).

In the United Kingdom, the Mondex system developed by the National Westminster and Midland Banks does not involve scheme operators. Funds are loaded onto the card which can then be used without reference to any other person. Funds are transferred from one card to another as well as to merchants but because funds loaded onto the card do not exist anywhere other than on the card, there is no audit trail of transactions or reconciliation of payments. This means that forgery can occur without trace and the scheme can be used for money laundering. The Mondex card can be recharged from a mobile telephone link and can be used in EFTPOS terminals. The system is at present on trial in Swindon in England. Four Australian banks (National Australia, ANZ, Westpac and Commonwealth) have bought the franchise for the Mondex system and a pilot of the Mondex Australia system will be conducted in 1997 (Flint 1996). In the United States, a modified version of the Mondex system is being trialed which will enable banks to trace card use. It will also be possible for money held on cards to be downloaded into computers, thus enabling Internet purchases to be paid for electronically from the card (Hansell 1996).

In Australia, at present, five trials are being conducted of smart card technology.[1] These systems use System Operators who pay merchants who send in transaction reports from cards which have been used. The systems being trialed are as follows:

Visa has had a reloadable card, Visa Cash, on trial on the Gold Coast in Queensland since September 1995. Unlike Visa's earlier disposable card, however, the reloadable card has the potential security risk of permitting thieves to gain access to bank accounts through use of the card.

Quicklink commenced a trial in Newcastle, New South Wales, in November 1995 which extended to 500 merchants and 20,000 cards. Cards are reloadable with funds withdrawn from bank accounts by using specially equipped public telephones. Cards have been issued to University students for use in campus shops and the trial has been extended to the Newcastle public transport system.

MasterCard began a trial of its stored value reloadable card, MasterCard Cash, in Canberra in March 1996. Modified versions of normal debit and credit cards issued by three major banks have been used. More than 150 merchants and 2200 card holders are involved in the trial and the results of the first three months of the Canberra trial indicate that average purchases were approximately A$7.00, the average load of value approximately A$40.00. Some people used their card between five and ten times per week. MasterCard proposes to sell cards publicly in South Africa and New York in 1997 (MasterCard 1996).

Transcard started a trial in Western Sydney in March 1995 which was linked with Cabcharge, enabling the card to be used for taxi fares. The Transcard system employs a reloadable contactless card which is scanned by a reader for use primarily on public transport. The initial maximum balance of the card is A$200. An extended trial is now under way in Western Sydney.

The main security risk associated with smart cards lies in the way in which data are encrypted. Levy (1994), for example, describes the potential for fraud using Mondex smart cards in England if the card's code encryption system fails, in which case the whole system will fail. Bellcore, a United States computer and communications security company, has recently identified a number of design flaws in computer chip cards which may permit data to be leaked or information contained in the card to be tampered with (Bellcore 1996; Spinks 1996).

Super Smart Cards. The latest generation of smart cards, known as super smart cards, contain a microprocessor, a keyboard, a liquid crystal display and a power source which enables the card to be used independently of a card reader (Australia, Human Rights and Equal Opportunity Commission 1995). A simplified version of this is being used by MasterCard in its Canberra trial with a "Pocket Teller" being used in which cards may be read, the latest credit balance displayed and the last ten transactions recalled (MasterCard 1996).

Optical Memory Cards. Finally, Optical Memory Cards have been developed which can store optical images using laser light technology. These cards can store large amounts of data, up to 200 megabytes or 80,000 pages.

---

1   See *Smart Card Bulletin* (reproduced in Commonwealth of Australia, Bureau of Consumer Affairs 1995: 30-3); Privacy Committee of New South Wales 1995; Australian Commission for the Future 1996: 33; Kavanagh 1996: 26; and Australian Payments System Council 1996: 60-5.

Stored information cannot, however, be altered as it is kept in a ROM (Read Only Memory) (Australia, Human Rights and Equal Opportunity Commission 1995).

The nature and extent of the problem

Having considered the range of electronic funds transfer systems which operate throughout the world, we now consider the vulnerabilities of such systems and the extent to which fraudulent abuse has occurred. The following discussion will concentrate on the two principal areas of electronic funds transfer fraud, namely illegally or improperly obtaining access to systems (hacking) and frauds arising from plastic card misuse or counterfeiting.

Other situations in which electronic funds transfer systems have been subjected to criminal abuse, such as threatening to commit fraud on a wide scale in order to extort money or coerce governments or for purposes of international terrorism, will not be examined (see Parker 1983 and Chapters 3 and 10 elsewhere in this book).

Estimating the extent of any increase in electronic funds transfer fraud is highly problematic for a variety of reasons. First, account has to be taken of the substantial increase in the extent to which electronic funds transfer systems are used in the community, as this clearly extends the opportunities for fraud to take place.

Secondly, we have already noted the problems associated with reporting such crimes due to victims being unaware that they have suffered a loss, problems in locating offenders, and a general reluctance to admit that fraud has occurred for commercial reasons. Comparisons over time are further hampered by improved security procedures and crime prevention strategies to reduce losses (Kaspersen 1988). Finally, some incidents which appear to be the work of criminals may in fact be due to system defects and failures or may be transactions made legally by family members of customers, but without express authority.

A number of writers have attempted to provide general estimates of the various types of electronic funds transfer fraud (see OECD 1986; Kaspersen 1988; and Denning 1995). In 1991, the American Bankers' Association *Bankers' Hotline* published the following estimates of annual losses due to financial fraud in the United States (see Holland 1995):

Cheque fraud	US$10 billion
Credit card fraud	US$712 million
ATM fraud	US$18 million
Online fraud	US$5 million

Neumann (1995) recounts numerous incidents of financial fraud carried out using online technologies including ATM frauds perpetrated by the use of counterfeit plastic cards, interception of funds transmitted electronically and diversion of funds. A full understanding of the size of the problem is best provided by considering some specific examples relating to each of the various types of funds transfer.

Illegally or improperly obtaining access to systems

Most of the large scale electronic funds transfer frauds which have been committed have involved the interception or alteration of electronic data messages transmitted from bank computers (see Meijboom 1988).

One of the leading cases of electronic funds transfer fraud involved Stanley Mark Rifkin (see: Anonymous 1978; Rawitch 1979; Sullivan 1987 and Tyree 1990). Rifkin conducted a computer consulting business which allowed him access to the Security Pacific National Bank in Los Angeles. He obtained access to the bank's international wire transfer security codes which changed daily and used these to arrange a transfer of US$10.2 million to a New York Trust company. The transfer was not noticed by the Bank because it was one of 1500 transfers carried out daily totalling US$4 billion. US$8.1 million of the transferred money was then used to purchase diamonds from a dealer in Geneva. Rifkin smuggled the diamonds back into the United States and was able to sell US$12,000 worth before he was arrested and charged with transporting stolen property over state lines. He was sentenced to eight years' imprisonment on two counts of wire fraud.

In the English case of *R v Thompson* [1984] 1 WLR 962 see also [1984] Criminal Law Review 427, the defendant, Thompson, a computer programmer employed by the Commercial Bank of Kuwait, opened a savings account at five local branches of the bank in Kuwait and then programmed the bank's computer to debit various dormant accounts of customers and credit the five accounts he had opened. He then left Kuwait for England where he opened five new accounts with an English bank. He then requested the Kuwaiti bank to transfer the sums in his five Kuwaiti accounts to his English accounts. The Kuwaiti bank transferred about £45,000 in full which he then withdrew.

Thompson was charged with six counts of obtaining property by deception. The Court of Appeal held that he had obtained control of the funds in England rather than Kuwait and so was triable in England. The deception occurred in England when Thompson requested that the funds be transferred from the Kuwaiti bank to the English bank (see Lanham et al 1987; Griew 1986).

An Australian bank has also been the target of illegal hacking. In the early 1990s, a computer programmer employed by the State Bank of Victoria in its Information Systems Department, started working in the Network Operations Section which controlled the bank's Automatic Teller Machine network. He had two accounts with the bank: account no 8831 which was a Visa account and account no 2455 which was operated by a debit card used on ATMs.

The offender, Murdoch, entered instructions into the bank's computer system to take an ATM "off host" which meant that it could dispense up to A$200 even if the account drawn against contained less than this amount. He also altered the computer to permit his debit card to be used on his Visa account.

In 1991, Murdoch was charged with 12 charges of obtaining property by deception (s 81(1) of the *Crimes Act* 1958), 29 charges of computer trespass (s 9A of the *Summary Offences Act* 1966), 2 charges of making a false document (s 83A(1) of the *Crimes Act* 1958), and 20 charges of using a false document (s 83A(2) of the *Crimes Act* 1958).

Both the offences of obtaining property by deception and, on appeal, the offence of computer trespass were proved by reason of the fact that Murdoch gained access to the computer system "without lawful authority", even though he had some authority to gain access to the system for some lawful purposes.

With respect to the offences of making and using a false document, the court held that his conduct amounted to making and using a false document (the bank's computer data base) but because the account was not overdrawn the bank had not suffered any prejudice and so the Director of Public Prosecution's appeal in respect of these offences was dismissed (*Director of Public Prosecutions v Murdoch* [1993] 1 VR 406, see Leader-Elliott and Goode 1993).

In 1994, a group of Russian computer hackers allegedly attempted to steal more than US$10 million from Citibank's electronic money transfer system. In May 1995, Vladimir Levin, a 34-year-old Russian computer expert, was arrested in London and on 17 August 1995 he appeared in a London court charged with electronically robbing Citibank's cash management system from St Petersburg of US$400,000. The prosecution believes that Levin was working in the Russian firm AO Saturn where he manipulated the computers at Citibank to transfer funds to accounts in Finland, Israel and Bank of America (Anonymous 1995c; Holland 1995). United States officials applied to have him extradited to the United States to stand trial.

In January 1996, another Russian involved in the alleged fraud, 28-year-old Alexei Lachmanov pleaded guilty to offences relating to his role in a scheme to penetrate Citibank's computers, steal millions from corporate accounts and transfer the funds to bank accounts he controlled in Israel. The charges against Lachmanov allege that in August 1994 he told co-conspirators in Russia about his personal accounts in Tel Aviv, Israel. The co-conspirators had gained unauthorised access to the Citibank Cash Management System, which allows Citibank customers to gain access to a computer network and transfer funds from their Citibank accounts to accounts at other financial institutions. Lachmanov admitted to transferring funds from accounts to five Tel Aviv banks, and attempting to withdraw US$940,000 from those accounts. Three other members of the gang have pleaded guilty to a variety of offences (Kennedy 1996).

None of the bank's depositors lost money and since the fraud was discovered, Citibank has required customers to use an electronic password generator for every transfer.

Protection against fraud in home banking systems is based on PIN authentication, transaction codes, and encryption of data in much the same way as an ATM system operates. Sexton (1995) describes the potential risk of home banking for fraud because of the fact that some forms of home banking do not encrypt messages. This means that a PIN or password goes down the line in clear text which is capable of interception.

Although home banking has only recently begun in Australia, the police have already been called upon to investigate two individuals who claimed that they could illegally obtain access into Advance Bank's Internet banking system. The two individuals concerned offered to solve flaws which allegedly existed in the bank's security system in return for a payment of A$2 million, thus amounting to a form of extortion. No prosecution occurred, however (Da Silva 1996).

In Sydney recently, the Australian Federal Police arrested a man who had allegedly gained access to an Internet service provider's computerised customer accounts and published details of client credit card and account records, resulting in the service provider losing in excess of A$2 million in trade (Commonwealth of Australia, Australian Federal Police 1996).

In Chapter 7, we saw a fraudulent scheme which has recently come to light involving dubious Nigerians requesting assistance from gullible foreigners in moving non-existent funds out of Nigeria in order to avoid government confiscation of the funds.

Nigeria has developed a comprehensive and effective response to the fraud in which the main objectives are to create awareness and increase prosecution and recoveries in cases where funds are lost, reducing losses and intercepting various attempts. One organisation in Iceland has also undertaken a comprehensive investigation of the frauds using the Internet (see International Investigation Services Home Page http://www .islandia.is/~njall/nig/nigeria.html).

Card misuse and counterfeiting

Ever since plastic cards were introduced, attempts have been made to steal them, counterfeit them or otherwise misuse them in order to obtain funds illegally. Much of the current illegality committed with or by the use of plastic cards involves organised crime, principally emanating from the Far East. Newton (1995) for example, describes the involvement of organised Asian groups who have made an industry out of theft and counterfeiting of plastic cards which is estimated to cost business in excess of US$1000 million per annum.

Fraud may occur when counterfeit copies of cards are created or when other means of access are obtained. As has already been noted, PINs may be obtained by deceiving or coercing customers into disclosing their PIN through the use of deception or violence, and telephoto lenses may be used to observe customers when they key in their PIN in a public place. In 1987, for example, a group of schoolboys in Perth were apprehended after manufacturing cards and obtaining PINs by observing card holders through binoculars (Tyree 1990).

"Card skimming" is a procedure in which possession of a legitimate card is obtained for a few seconds in order to enable it to be passed over a magnetic tape reader so that a counterfeit copy can be made (Sullivan 1987). The technique of "buffering" consists of modifying the information stored in the magnetic strip of the card or obtaining security codes electronically (Meijboom 1988).

Although magnetic stripe cards are relatively easy to forge, smart cards are more difficult to counterfeit, although not absolutely tamper-proof (see Bellcore 1996). Most frauds, however, are committed by cards and PINs being stolen rather than through forgery (Commonwealth of Australia, Bureau of Consumer Affairs 1995). A variety of techniques are used to perpetrate ATM fraud, a number of which are summarised by Sullivan (1987).

Terminal attacks. The most blatant attacks on ATMs involve physical assaults in which machines are reprogrammed, damaged, stolen or destroyed. In Victoria in 1986, for example, an ATM containing between A$42,000 and A$60,000 was stolen with damage to the terminal estimated at A$50,000.

Offline ATMs. When an ATM is not online to its host computer, it is particularly vulnerable to abuse, although this no longer occurs frequently. As long as the PIN on the card matches the PIN used, the terminal will dispense cash to the limit permitted (usually A$500 per day) regardless of the amount in the account or whether an overdraft facility exists.

Online ATMs. Data transmitted from an ATM, including the PIN, are encrypted. The threat of encryption keys being compromised is the major security risk associated with using ATMs. Anyone with a personal computer and a modem may be able to gain access to national and international EFT systems.

System defects

Occasionally, financial institutions have allowed errors to enter ATM systems which enable customers to perpetrate frauds. In one case in Adelaide, in January 1986, a man allegedly stole A$2640 by making forty-four withdrawals on three visits to an ATM which occurred because an employee had entered incorrect data which meant that transactions were not properly recorded (Sullivan 1987). In another incident in July 1987, the Westpac Bank system failed due to a software problem in a way that allowed card holders apparently unlimited access to funds. In 1988, the Commonwealth Bank system failed in a way that confiscated all customers' cards (Tyree 1990).

In the United States it has been estimated that 40 per cent of ATMs have been subjected to fraud, with losses ranging from between US$10,000 and US$63,000 (Sullivan 1987). On occasions, substantial sums have been lost in individual incidents. In Italy, for example, one fraud which involved three ATM transactions resulted in the bank losing US$4 million. Diana Sharpe (1996) refers to the 1988 attempted US$70 million dollar raid on the First National Bank in Chicago by EFT embezzlement where the recipient computer assumed that the message was valid without verifying it.

An indication of the extent to which ATM systems in Australia fail to operate correctly is provided in the statistics of transaction complaints given in the Australian Payments System Council *Annual Reports 1992-96* (1993-96). Some of the more important trends in recent times include the continued increase in the number of complaints concerning system malfunctions and unauthorised transactions over the last four years, the large increase in the number of complaints by employees of institutions or merchants over the last twelve months where fraud was evident, the very large increase in the number of complaints over the last two years where employees and agents of merchants were negligent, and a substantial increase in the number of complaints where neither the card holder not the card issuer contributed to the loss.

In the year 1995-96, for example, there were 579 complaints made to the Australian Payments System Council where the customer was found to have engaged in fraudulent or criminal conduct, while there were 48 instances of fraudulent conduct by employees and agents of financial institutions or merchants, which represents a substantial increase on previous years (Australian Payments System Council 1996).

In Australia, criminal liability may be imposed for improper use of either credit or debit cards under Federal criminal law.[2] This was used to convict a card holder who had used a Commonwealth Bankcard fraudulently.

In that case, the Queensland Court of Criminal Appeal confirmed the conviction of the defendant who had withdrawn A$150 from his Commonwealth Banking Corporation Keycard Savings Account using an ATM when it was off-line and programmed to allow withdrawals of up to A$500 even though this would place his account in debit. He had previously paid certain forged cheques into the account. The bank did not consent to his taking the money and he was rightly convicted of imposing by an untrue representation to obtain money. It did not matter that the representation was made by using the card in a machine rather than to a person.

Various Australian state laws have also been relied upon to convict offenders of property offences arising out of the fraudulent use of ATMs. In *Kennison v Daire* (1986) 160 CLR 129 the High Court dismissed an appeal against conviction for larceny of A$200 at the Court of Summary Jurisdiction in Adelaide. The appellant, Kennison, was the holder of an Easybank card which enabled him to use the automatic teller machine of the Savings Bank of South Australia to withdraw money from his account with that Bank. It was a condition of the use of the card that his account was in sufficient credit to accommodate a withdrawal. Kennison closed his account and withdrew the balance but did not return the card to the Bank. He then used the card to withdraw A$200 from the ATM. The ATM was programmed in such a way that up to A$200 could be withdrawn by any person who placed the card in the machine and entered the correct PIN. It could not tell whether the person had an account that remained current or whether the account was in credit because the machine was off-line.

The High Court upheld the conviction because the appellant acted fraudulently with intent permanently to deprive the Bank of A$200 and rejected the appellant's argument that the bank had consented to the withdrawal of the money by providing a machine which permitted the transaction to take place.[3]

In *R v Evenett; ex parte Attorney-General* [1987] 2 Qd R 753, the Queensland Court of Criminal Appeal confirmed the conviction of the defendant who had withdrawn A$778.97 from his account with the National Australia Bank in excess of the credit of A$181.03 in his account by using his Flexicard in an ATM which was off-line and programmed to permit withdrawals of up to A$500. The court held that the bank did not give its consent to the withdrawal of the

---

2   S 29B of the *Crimes Act* 1914 (Cth) *R v Baxter* [1988] 1 Qd R 537 provides penalties for offences relating to imposing or endeavouring to impose upon the Commonwealth or any public authority under the Commonwealth by any untrue representation made in any manner whatsoever, with a view to obtain money or any other benefit or advantage (see: Tyree 1990: 255-6).

3   In discussing this case, Fisse (1990) argues that the law of theft should not be used to protect organisations such as banks against errors which expose consumers to high temptation and which can readily be avoided by technological means. Similarly, Goode (1986: 60) is critical of the Full Court of South Australia decision, which was affirmed on appeal, on a number of grounds, principally because the Bank created a system which enabled funds to be taken and Kennison should not be guilty of larceny merely for availing himself of that opportunity.

amount despite having programmed the ATM to permit the withdrawal to take place.

Although Electronic Funds Transfers at Point of Sale have only relatively recently been in operation throughout the world, some indications have been given that their security systems have been breached. Clough and Mungo (1992), for example, describe an example of EFT frauds using Telenet in the United States in 1990, an instance denied by the various banks involved.

In Australia, the Australian Payments System Council statistics of EFT system malfunctions have shown a rapid increase over the last four years. In 1995-96, for example, there were 43,817 system malfunctions reported, a 27 per cent increase on previous years. There has also been a particularly sharp increase in the number of unauthorised transactions reported. In 1995-96, these numbered 22,530 which represents almost a 70 per cent increase on the previous year. There were, however, 1.4 billion transactions carried out in the year 1995-96 (Australian Payments System Council 1993-96).

A number of writers have attempted to estimate the security risks which the introduction of smart cards and electronic cash may have for society. Harper and Leslie (1994), for example, refer to the fact that smart cards may be used to carry out all of the traditional functions of cash including illegal transactions in the black economy. The anonymity required for such transactions also exists with smart cards as the owner of the smart card is not identified at the point of sale when the card value is discharged. The recipient of the value merely obtains a credit against the system operator which is eventually cleared through bank ledger adjustments.

The Australian Commission for the Future (1996) has also identified a number of ways in which frauds may be carried out through the use of smart cards. Concerns were expressed that card readers could be programmed to deduct greater value from the card than that authorised by the user, or sales staff intentionally deducting greater sums than they are authorised to deduct. Sums which are rounded off to the nearest 5 cents could then be skimmed to the terminal owner's advantage. Finally, stored value cards may be stolen and if unprotected by a PIN or if the PIN is able to be compromised, the value may then be removed from the card. Other potential threats include the use of smart cards for money laundering and tax evasion as well as for fraud carried out with counterfeit cards (Australian Commission for the Future 1996).

Legal and law enforcement issues

Electronic funds transfer technologies create both problems and benefits for law enforcement agencies. One of the primary difficulties which law enforcement agencies experience in investigating electronic funds transfer crime is that there is no longer a "paper trail" of transactions to follow, but instead, transactions have to be examined through the analysis of computer databases. This creates both technical and logistic difficulties, especially where information is encrypted and the encryption keys are not available to police.

In addition, there are the traditional problems associated with the reluctance of individuals to report commercial fraud to the police. Credit card frauds, for example, are first reported to Cardlink Services Limited in Australia which conducts a preliminary investigation. Only if a definite offender has been located and sufficient evidence is available will the matter be referred to the police (Van Rhoda 1991).

Kaspersen (1988) discusses some of the evidentiary problems in prosecuting ATM fraud and in proving deception. The evidence of fraudulently made cards will be satisfactory but where access is obtained by codes only, it will be very difficult to prove fraud.

Newton (1995) also describes some of the problems of law enforcement agencies not investigating counterfeit plastic payment card frauds because they have limited resources and crimes of violence are seen as being more urgent priorities.

On the other hand, electronic transactions generate computer records which generally identify the individuals who are involved in the transaction as well as information about the amount, nature and the physical location of the individual at the time the payment was made. These could be used by law enforcement agencies to follow money trails and locate individuals suspected of illegality.

Every time an offender passes a stolen credit card to obtain goods or services, a voucher is made out and signed in the presence of a witness. This provides evidence identifying the offender, identifiable property which is stolen, samples of handwriting, and fingerprints on sales vouchers (Van Rhoda 1991). Unfortunately, because the number of transactions is so great, police are often inundated with data which may be beyond their capacity to analyse.

Types of offences

Throughout the world, legislatures have attempted to deal with the problem of electronic funds transfer crime by enacting laws which govern each of the new technologies individually (see Kaspersen 1988 for a review of the law in the United States and Europe). Some specific examples include the *Prepaid Card Act* 1989 (Japan), the *Payments Cards Act* 1984 (Denmark) and Federal Reserve Regulation E and the *Electronic Funds Transfer Act* 1978 of the United States.

In Australia, a wide variety of Federal and State laws govern electronic funds transfers. In mounting a prosecution, care needs to be exercised in choosing appropriate offences with which to charge the offender as often the conduct in question involves both Federal and State offences. Where the same conduct gives rise to offences against various different statutes, it has recently been held that the only charge which most appropriately reflects the gravamen of the conduct should be charged (*R v Liang and Li* (1995) 82 A Crim R 39).

Federal offences

Sections 29A to 29D of the *Crimes Act* 1914 (Cth) may be used in the prosecution of electronic funds transfer fraud. Criminal liability may be imposed for improper and fraudulent use of both credit and debit cards under these provisions which provide penalties of fines of up to A$10,000 or imprisonment for up to ten years for offences of false pretences and untrue representations involving the Commonwealth. As we have seen, these provisions were used to convict the card holder who used a Commonwealth Bankcard fraudulently in the case of *R v Baxter* [1988] 1 Qd R 537.

Various offences relating to telecommunications networks may be committed by offenders who unlawfully obtain or attempt to obtain access to systems and or interfere with messages passing over telecommunications networks such as those used to transmit and receive funds electronically (*Crimes Act* 1914 (Cth) ss 85ZG, 85ZJ, 85ZK and 85ZKB).

In addition, s 253 of the *Telecommunications Act* 1991 (Cth) creates an offence of knowingly or recklessly connecting unauthorised equipment to a network and s 7 of the *Telecommunications (Interception) Act* 1979 (Cth) creates an offence of improperly intercepting a communication passing over a telecommunications system.

Sections 76A to 76F of the *Crimes Act* 1914 (Cth) create various offences to do with computers, such as unauthorised use and damage and these may be relevant where telecommunications equipment is used to facilitate the commission of the offences relating to the electronic transfer of funds. Where, for example, offenders use computers to interfere with banking systems, such as occurred in *Director of Public Prosecutions v Murdoch* [1993] 1 VR 406 (discussed above), it may be possible to mount a prosecution based on acts of computer hacking.

Making or uttering counterfeit money is regulated by the *Crimes (Currency) Act* 1981 (Cth) to the exclusion of State law. Because electronic money and value stored on a smart card may not come within the definition of currency issued by the Reserve Bank of Australia, it may not always be possible to obtain a conviction under this legislation where electronically recorded funds are counterfeited.

Making and possessing devices for use in committing forgery or counterfeiting is an offence dealt with in s 19.6 of the *Model Criminal Code* and this could extend to computer software created for the purpose of counterfeiting plastic cards and electronic money (see: Commonwealth of Australia, Standing Committee of Attorneys-General, Model Criminal Code Officers Committee 1995).

State and Territory offences

The Australian Capital Territory and Victoria have various statutory property offences modelled on the provisions of the *Theft Act* 1968 (Eng), while the other States and the Northern Territory have their own legislative enactments governing property crime.

Where funds are stolen electronically, prosecutions will usually allege that the offender has obtained property or a financial advantage by deception. The conduct may, however, involve a number of additional offences. In *Director of Public Prosecutions v Murdoch* [1993] 1 VR 406, for example, Murdoch was charged with obtaining property by deception (s 81(1) of the *Crimes Act* 1958), computer trespass (s 9A of the *Summary Offences Act* 1966), making a false document (s 83A(1) of the *Crimes Act* 1958), and using a false document (s 83A(2) of the *Crimes Act* 1958).

Clearly there is a wide variety of criminal offences which may be used to prosecute electronic funds transfer fraud, in all its many forms. Some laws require clarification while others are unable to deal with some of the newer forms of fraud which have emerged. The provisions of chapter 3 of the *Model Criminal Code*, which will eventually apply in all Australian jurisdictions, deal with offences of theft, fraud, bribery and related offences and should go some way to improve the operation of the law in the present context (see: Commonwealth of Australia, Standing Committee of Attorneys-General, Model Criminal Code Officers Committee 1995).

Some of the provisions which have particular relevance to the electronic transfer of funds include s 17.1 which defines "deception" in such as way as to deal with the problem which arose in *Kennison v Daire* in which an ATM, rather than a person, was deceived. In addition, ss 17.2 and 17.3 create offences of obtaining property by deception and obtaining financial advantage by deception, respectively. New forgery offences are set out in ss 19.1 to 19.6 which deal with the problem of electronic forgery.

Regulatory issues

User education

In the field of electronic banking, one of the most effective strategies used to control crime is education of the public as to the nature of the security risks which they face, and how they may protect themselves. Sneddon (1995), for example, stresses the need for members of the banking public to realise that their plastic card and PIN represent their electronic signature. Sneddon goes on to recommend that financial institutions use audio and visual electronic media to publicise the need for security such as by community service announcements on radio or television.

In the United Kingdom, one particularly effective plastic card fraud prevention strategy called "Cardwatch" involved a high profile publicity and education campaign by the Association for Payment Clearing Service including posters, leaflets, and television and radio coverage to raise public awareness of the problem and to encourage card holders to take more care of their cards (Webb 1996).

Self-help by financial institutions, merchants and users

Financial institutions. Financial institutions are able to adopt a wide variety of self-help strategies which may reduce the risk of electronic funds transfer fraud. First, they need to adopt in-house security procedures and to ensure that staff are checked for security breaches, as electronic fraud often requires the involvement of confederates with inside knowledge of the institution's security and computer procedures.

Various procedures can also be adopted to ensure that plastic cards are not stolen and that PINs are communicated securely to customers. In Britain, for example, independent couriers were introduced to prevent mail interception of cards and it is now common to ask customers to collect their cards from a branch

(Webb 1996). Where the postal service is used, cards and PINs are sent separately.

Banks are also able to assist merchants by notifying them of stolen cards and PINs. Again in Britain, a National Hot Card File was created by which details of lost and stolen cards were quickly transmitted to retail outlets.

One of the main strategies used to prevent EFTPOS fraud has been to lower floor limits (the transaction value at which authorisation is required from banks before the card can be accepted). This means that many more transactions now require bank approval. By 1996, 45 per cent of transactions required bank approval.

Banks and card issuers protect themselves against plastic card fraud in a variety of ways. Banks, for example, now have a centralised fraud reporting and investigation agency for plastic cards, Cardlink Services Limited, which has close liaison with the police. Cardlink Services investigate cases of fraudulent use of cards in each State and Territory of Australia and gather evidence which is then forwarded to police (Van Rhoda 1991).

Merchants. Frauds in which merchants are involved constitutes a large problem for financial institutions as merchants or their employees are ideally placed to permit access to computer networks and to alter transaction details. Bonney (1992) discusses various ways in which merchants can help to prevent credit card fraud including the conduct of random authorisation checks by merchants of bank account details, merchant advertising of the fact that steps are being taken to prevent credit card fraud and closer examination of cards by sales staff when they are being used. Newton (1995) also discusses various strategies to prevent merchant abuse in relation to plastic card fraud.

Users. Most electronic payments systems require the use of a PIN or password in order for users to gain access. Protection of security numbers is, therefore, the primary crime prevention strategy. Plastic card holders are best placed to protect themselves by taking basic security precautions to ensure that cards are not stolen. This includes not leaving them in public places and ensuring that they are reclaimed after use. Consumers are also advised not to compromise their security by disclosing PINs, keeping them with cards, or writing them on cards. Studies reveal, nonetheless, that between 20 and 70 per cent of people write their PIN on the card or on a piece of paper carried with the card (Sullivan 1987).

Where such strategies have been consistently implemented, substantial reductions in fraud can occur. In Britain, for example, the use of a variety of strategies designed to prevent plastic card fraud resulted in a 41 per cent reduction in such fraud overall between 1991 and 1994, while losses occurring at retail points of sale were reduced by 49 per cent during the same period. Losses from cards lost or stolen in the post were reduced by 62 per cent between 1991 and 1994 (Webb 1996).

Codes of practice

As an alternative to the use of legislative regulatory controls, the banking and credit industries have relied on the use of codes of conduct to prevent fraud and to resolve disputes between institutions and customers. Codes have the dual function of acting as a form of education and publicity for both institutions and customers, as well as providing a statement of recommended practice which may be relied upon to resolve individual disputes.

Codes of practice are, however, only going to be an appropriate regulatory mechanism where financial institutions or system operators are involved. If electronic money or stored value cards are used, then only the consumer and the merchant will be involved.

In Australia, the *Electronic Funds Transfer Code of Conduct* was introduced in December 1989 and revised in 1990. All Australian suppliers of EFT have agreed to comply with the code which is limited to transactions involving an EFT plastic card and a PIN only (para 1.1), thus excluding home banking.

The code exempts the card holder from liability in respect of fraudulent or negligent conduct on the part of card issuers' employees or agents; forged, fault, expired or cancelled cards; losses occurring prior to receipt of the card or PIN; unauthorised transactions occurring after notification; and losses resulting from unauthorised transactions where it is clear that the card holder has not contributed to the losses.[4]

The card holder's liability is limited to A$50 or the balance of the account or the loss at the time of notification of loss or theft of the card.[5]

The code, therefore, provides a wide range of rules which both institutions and users are required to follow in order to ensure that fraud is minimised and that disputes are fairly resolved.

Another code which has relevance to electronic transactions involving banks is the *Code of Banking Practice* of November 1993. This code sets out the privacy requirements which banks are obliged to adhere to in dealing with customers, and also specifies the various rights and duties of banks and customers.

Most recently, Australian building societies and credit unions have established codes of practice which regulate, amongst other things, transactions conducted electronically. Adoption of these Codes of Practice will take place in conjunction with the introduction of Australia's Uniform Consumer Credit Legislation (Australian Payments System Council 1996). A draft Code of Conduct for the Smart Card Industry has also been prepared which deals with issues of privacy, confidentiality, disclosure and dispute resolution (reproduced in *Privacy Law and Policy Reporter*, 1996).

Technological solutions

A wide range of technological solutions have been devised in order to reduce the security risks associated with electronic funds transfer systems. They have been used at all stages of electronic transactions involving both transfers of funds and plastic card transactions.

---

4   Paragraphs 5.2 to 5.4.
5   Paragraph 5.5.

Terminal safeguards. Crime prevention needs to be focussed on areas of particular weakness in electronic systems and the most obvious target for electronic funds transfer systems is the computer terminal at which transactions are carried out.

As is the case with telephone kiosks, ATM and EFTPOS terminals need to be manufactured in such a way as to ensure that access cannot be gained to cables and reserves of cash cannot be stolen, in the case of ATMs (Tyree 1990). Machines should also be located in secure places where users are protected both physically, as well as against shoulder surfing, to obtain PINs.

Sullivan (1987) describes the various ways in which ATMs can be better designed. ATMs can be enclosed and fitted with surveillance equipment. Some have been placed under armed guard. They may be placed in lobbies with card access. Systems which monitor vital points of an ATM for signs of physical attack have also been installed. Barriers can be fitted and horizontal key pads used to prevent shoulder surfing. Standardised requirements for ATMs should be created.

Sneddon (1995) notes the need for ATM and EFTPOS terminals to have shields or hoods which ensure that no-one is able to see a PIN being keyed in. Australian Standard AS 3769 governs the positioning of ATM and EFTPOS devices where PIN entry is required. Another strategy adopted by the First National Bank of South Africa in Johannesburg involves the use of voice-activated ATMs, although these present problems for individuals who are unable to hear messages clearly (due to hearing loss, traffic noise or language difficulties (Sneddon 1995).

Protections against card counterfeiting. Newton (1995) describes various crime prevention strategies which have been used to prevent plastic card counterfeiting. These include the use of security printing; micro-printing; holograms; embossed characters; tamper-evident signature panels; magnetic stripes with improved card validation technologies and indent printing. Smart cards, of course, are much more difficult to copy than ordinary magnetic stripe cards.

Unfortunately, all of these card authentication devices have been overcome by organised criminals except for computer chip circuitry in smart cards, which has yet to be fully counterfeited successfully.

Card restrictions. As an alternative to target hardening, a number of writers have suggested that the risk of large-scale fraud and money laundering using smart cards could be restricted by placing limits on the amounts of money that can be stored on cards. Mackrell (1996), for example, suggests that stored value cards should have a modest limit placed on the maximum value that can be stored on them, especially if they are to be used for card-to-card transfers. There could also be a limit on the life of the cards which would restrict their usefulness for hoarding and money laundering.

In addition, it has been suggested that floor limits which apply to cards be reduced in order for transactions other than those involving very small sums to be checked with a bank online prior to completion.

Card holder verification. One of the greatest areas of risk associated with the use of plastic cards relates to the manner in which card holders' identities are verified. Some of the most recent suggestions for improving security in this area include the use of cards which have a photograph of the user; laser engraved signatures; larger PINs; various biometric means of verifying identity such as signature, fingerprint, palm, lip, ear or retina scanning (Sullivan 1987).

Masuda (1996) provides an examination of a credit card crime prevention strategy employed since 1993 by Tops Appliance City Inc. in New York called "Cardwatch". This involves a computer network in a chain of retail stores in which credit card applications are checked by photographing the applicant digitally, recording the applicant's signature and other identifying information such as driver's licence, telephone and social security numbers, present address and current or last place of employment. This information is then used for future purchases and also when the customer collects merchandise.

Such an approach employs two fundamental checks on identity: something an account holder possesses (the card) and something that an account holder is (photograph etc). Because information is recorded about the individual, offenders are reluctant to take out accounts fraudulently. Cardwatch resulted in a 89.6 per cent reduction in credit card fraud losses over a seventeen-month period following introduction of the scheme, with a 57 per cent reduction in per fraud loss.

Fraud detection software. A number of organisations are now providing software for use in the prevention of electronic funds transfer fraud. The success of such an approach depends upon the extent to which the software cannot be interfered with or modified.

Software has also been devised to analyse plastic card holder spending patterns in order to alert individuals to the presence of unauthorised transactions and also merchant deposit monitoring techniques to detect claiming patterns of corrupt merchants.

Nestor Inc., for example, provides software called PRISM (Proactive Fraud Risk Management) which is used to detect credit card fraud such as lost cards, stolen cards, counterfeit cards, fraudulent applications, cards never received, mail order, phone order and catalogue sales and merchant fraud. It is designed for use by credit card issuers, credit card processors, credit card acquirers, Merchant Banks, and anyone who has over 500,000 card holder accounts. The cost is between A$300,000 and A$1,500,000 depending on system requirements and configuration (see Nestor Inc. 1996).

Improved cryptography. Cryptography is a double-edged sword in the field of electronic commerce as it is able to protect data from unlawful interference while at the same time concealing illegal activities from lawful investigation (Denning 1995). Nonetheless, cryptography is still employed as a mainstay of electronic banking security systems. Sullivan (1987), for example, cites some of the recent developments in cryptography designed to improve bank security for ATMs. New algorithms have been devised which are buried in computer chips, such that any attempt to read the code will destroy the chip.

Conclusions

This chapter has detailed a wide variety of ways in which funds may be stolen through exploiting security flaws in electronic funds transfer systems. The range of electronic systems used to conduct commercial transactions is increasing rapidly and considerable effort is being directed at ensuring the security of digital transmissions which represent monetary value. The opportunities for fraud are, however, substantial, particularly in view of the enormous sums being transferred electronically between financial institutions each day. But these are not the only targets. Security flaws in ATMs, for example, have been used by offenders to obtain sums as small as A$100. These small-scale thefts, however, must be treated seriously by banks as they represent flaws in exactly the same systems which are used to transfer substantially larger amounts.

The solution to electronic funds transfer crime will ultimately depend upon the adoption of a range of strategies both technological and strategic in which close cooperation will exist between all those involved in providing and using systems. This includes telecommunications carriers and service providers, financial institutions, retail merchants, and individual users.

One area of particular importance relates to the need for systems to be put in place which will enable the emergence of weaknesses in systems to be quickly identified. Once recognised, there should be a strategic response to the problem (Webb 1996).

In ensuring that particular weak points in security systems are identified and weaknesses solved, it is likely that technology will provide the most effective response. Biometric user identification techniques, for example, are likely to be the only really secure system for use with ATM and EFTPOS technologies (Newton 1995).

Speaking of ways in which to prevent plastic card fraud, Newton (1995, p 136) argues as follows:

> The key to reducing plastic counterfeiting and disrupting organised criminal enterprises is the establishment of a meaningful partnership between the industry, merchants and law enforcement agencies. Card payment systems and their affiliated financial institutions must be prepared to exchange pertinent, sensitive and timely information with law enforcement agencies to enable them to target corrupt merchants and other organised criminals involved in plastic counterfeiting productively.

Policymakers should recognise that the payment card industry is being deliberately targeted by organised criminal enterprises from around the globe. The perception that it is only an industry problem is no longer sustainable. Subject to resource limitations, law enforcement agencies should be prepared to investigate plastic counterfeiting in partnership with the industry.

The financial industry itself may also have to change. Some of the innovative new funds transfer systems being devised for use on the Internet, for example, challenge the basis of banking itself in that control is being divested from central banks. Without such controls over the issue of currency, the opportunities for fraud may increase substantially. All that we will then be left with is the security which technology provides, which as we have seen, throughout history, has been compromised by technologically competent offenders.

9

ELECTRONIC MONEY LAUNDERING

The term "money laundering" is used to describe the process by which the proceeds of crime ("dirty money") are put through a series of transactions which disguise their illicit origins, and make them appear to have come from a legitimate source ("clean money").

The process in essence entails three stages. The first, termed *placement*, involves introducing the tainted proceeds into a legitimate context (such as a bank account), without revealing the source of funds. The second, referred to as *layering*, involves moving the assets in a series of transactions to conceal their ownership and location. The third stage, called *integration*, involves blending the funds into the mainstream economy, eliminating any indication of tainted origins (Robinson 1994; United States, General Accounting Office 1996b).

Money laundering is of great concern to law enforcement agencies, and for very good reason. A common strategy for concealing the proceeds of crime entails their investment in and commingling with the assets of legitimate business. The infiltration of legitimate enterprise by sophisticated criminals is a significant threat. Not only can legitimate business provide a convenient cloak or cover for further criminal activity, but the enterprise itself can be exploited and its assets stripped for personal gain, at the expense of investors and creditors. A nation's reputation for commercial honesty could be tarnished by criminal infiltration of legitimate business, with attending consequence for its overall economic well-being. At the extreme, smaller economies can be seriously distorted by the infiltration of criminal assets, to the extent that the political stability of a smaller state may be threatened.

Of even greater importance is the fact that the complex criminal activity which generates "dirty money", whether drug trafficking, arms smuggling, corruption, or other offences, is often extremely difficult to detect. Accordingly, finding and following the "money trail" has been a basic strategy to combat these forms of sophisticated crime. Success in money laundering means that detection of the predicate offence, and the identification of the offender, become that much more difficult.

Comparable financial transactions are also undertaken for the purpose of concealing legitimately derived income from taxation authorities, creditors, or estranged spouses. Our primary concern here, however, is with "dirty" money, and how developments in telecommunications have influenced the means by which it is laundered. As is the case with a number of other forms of telecommunications-related crime, the underlying technology is something of a double-edged sword, which can in turn, facilitate both the commission of the offence and its detection.

Until relatively recently money laundering per se was not defined as criminal behaviour, although knowing involvement in concealing the proceeds of crime could render one potentially liable to the charge of being an accessory after the fact. Recognising the importance of money laundering in sustaining criminal enterprise, and concerned with an apparent resurgence in drug trafficking and organised crime, authorities in the United States introduced legislation in the 1970s to enhance the visibility of all financial transactions, with a view towards identifying those which derived from illegal activities.

In the ensuing two decades, a number of other jurisdictions have followed, more or less willingly. Some were more reluctant, especially those whose banking industries thrived precisely because they were favoured for the secrecy provisions which allowed them to maintain client anonymity. There were others who, almost as a matter of principle, were disinclined slavishly to follow examples set by the United States. There exists also a general concern that undue constraints on financial institutions will impede legitimate, as well as illegitimate financial activity, and thereby inhibit economic growth. But over the past quarter-century, most industrial nations have established some mechanism to identify suspicious transactions occurring in their financial systems. Australia enacted the *Cash Transactions Reports Act* in 1988, requiring financial institutions and other cash dealers to report specified transactions to a national monitoring agency.

Techniques of money laundering — past, present, and future

From a wider historical perspective, coins and paper currency are playing but a temporary role as media of exchange and stores of value. After barter, there came commodities, such as salt. In due course, precious metals were favoured because of their portability and universality. With the growth of commerce, coins, then paper currency became more convenient to use. The intensification of commercial activity during the industrial revolution saw the increasing use of cheques.

The use of telecommunications for the transfer of funds is hardly a recent phenomenon. Telegraphic transfer of funds by Western Union dates to 1860, and the US Federal Reserve System began using wire transfers in 1918. Since the 1970s, financial institutions and individuals rely increasingly on telecommunications to move money. Indeed, telecommunications have become an integral part of banking. Payment between banks occurs through the exchange of electronic messages. Electronic transfers now move immense amounts of money around the world at the speed of light. Given the sheer volume and size of interbank transactions, non-automated payment mechanisms have become historical relics. The most prominent mechanism for international financial transactions is the Society for Worldwide Interbank Financial Telecommunication (SWIFT — see discussion in Chapter 8, above).

In the United States, systems such as Fedwire (the electronic network of the US Federal Reserve System) and CHIPS the Clearing House Interbank Payments System) are the major vehicles for funds transfer. Fedwire links 11,000 institutions; in the early 1990s it supported over 250,000 transfers each day, the average value of which was US$3 million. In 1995, some 76 million funds transfers with a total value of US$223 trillion were made over the Fedwire system

(Federal Reserve Bank of New York 1996). In 1991, the CHIPS system, a consortium of private banks, moved US$866 billion on an average day.

Electronic funds transfer is not solely the province of government. There exist numerous other public and private networks which operate under regulatory supervision. Western Union, for example, transfers over $US5 billion dollars annually through some 24,000 agents around the world. It is anticipated that the daily number of electronic financial transactions will exceed 100 billion by the year 2000.

The growing application of telecommunications technology to the banking industry has greatly facilitated the task of money laundering. Constructing a chain of transactions electronically can greatly facilitate layering, and thus more effectively obscure the money trail. So too can integration be facilitated by electronic transfer: dirty funds speedily deposited in a cooperating financial institution can be used as collateral for a loan, which can be speedily repatriated and invested in a legitimate business. As if to add insult to injury, the interest on such loans is tax deductible.

Given the volume and speed with which money is moved around the world, one can readily appreciate the difficulty of detecting ill-gotten gains and tracking their movement through the world's banking systems. By way of illustration, Carroll (1995b) has observed that in Australia, there has been a decline in reports of suspect cash transactions, because advances in automation have been accompanied by a decline in face-to-face banking.

The process of cash transactions reporting is itself becoming increasingly automated (Coad and Richardson 1994). In Australia, over 90 per cent of Significant Cash Transaction Reports (SCTRs) are received in some electronic format, much of it online. An Electronic Data Delivery System (EDDS) facilitates collection of International Funds Transfer Instructions (IFTIs) which accompany a transfer of funds into or out of Australia electronically. Thus, transferring large amounts of money around or out of Australia through conventional channels is likely to attract official attention.

Even so, money laundering is not dependent on telecommunications. Traditionally, the currency of drug deals and many other illicit transactions has been cash. While minor offenders, then as now, were inclined to "spend as they go", successful criminal entrepreneurs often amassed cash in quantities so large that it was very difficult to spend or to safeguard unobtrusively. Some of the earlier forms of money laundering involved transporting large volumes of cash to another jurisdiction, usually one which protected the secrecy of financial transactions, where it could be deposited beyond the gaze of law enforcement. Where bulk export was too risky or logistically cumbersome, quantities of cash were divided up into amounts small enough to avoid suspicion or threshold reporting requirements, and converted to bank cheques or other negotiable instruments. For the time being, there appears to be a growth in the use of non-bank financial institutions, such as check cashing services and exchange houses and the use of bearer instruments such as money orders and bank checks.

Another means of laundering money involves the use of informal or "underground" banking systems, which bypass conventional financial institutions and operate outside the purview of law enforcement and regulatory authorities.

These systems, originating centuries ago in the Middle East and Asia, and based on trust rather than technology, exist in Chinese and Pakistani communities around the world.[1] Under such arrangements, a person wishing to transfer money would deposit it with the "banker" who may be an ordinary merchant, and be given a distinctive receipt or chit redeemable at another specified location, often the business premises of a relative or close associate of the banker. Thus, a person could leave US$10,000 with a shopkeeper in San Francisco, travel to Hong Kong, and receive the cash equivalent (less an agreed-upon commission) in Hong Kong dollars upon presentation of the receipt. Malhotra (1995) estimates that between US$100 billion and US$300 billion pass through underground banks each year. Some informal banking transactions are based on a firm verbal commitment, rather than a receipt. The initial banker will send a coded message to his agent at the agreed destination containing the name of the designated recipient's name and the date, time and location for the payment. Commissions charged may be up to 15 per cent of the value of the transaction.[2]

The technology of money laundering has evolved dramatically from the labour intensive "smurfing"[3] of the 1970s and the underground banking systems which have endured for centuries. The revolution in information technology which we are currently experiencing is having profound implications for the concealment and movement of criminally derived assets. The future is even more daunting, given the rapid move to a cashless society; it has been suggested that within a decade, coin and paper currency will be replaced by various forms of "electronic money", at least in industrial nations (Levy 1994).

The precise nature of electronic money, and the institutional arrangements which will provide the context for its use, are still being developed. Their ultimate configuration will have profound effects on the ability to launder money (Tyree 1997).

As noted in the previous chapter, stored value technology is likely to become a dominant feature of 21st century commerce. Implications of cashless commerce for money laundering arise because electronic access to bank accounts need not be confined within national boundaries. One could access one's account in the Antilles as easily as one could make an electronic withdrawal from a bank in one's own suburb. Not all cyberspace "banks" operate under government charter, nor are they all subject to government regulation.

With the emergence and proliferation of various technologies of electronic commerce, one can easily envisage how traditional countermeasures against money laundering may soon be of limited value. A could sell B a quantity of heroin, in return for a transfer of stored value to A's card, which A then downloads to her account in a financial institution situated in an overseas

---

1 Alternative banking systems provide facilities for the transfer of money or value. Depending upon the communities which they serve, they are termed Fei Ch'ien or "Flying Money" (Chinese); Hawala (Indian); Hundi (Pakistani); or Chiti banking (South Asia generally). For a discussion of underground banking and its application to money laundering, see Carroll 1995a; Cassidy 1994; Malhotra, 1995; Lambert, nd.

2 Underground banking, because of its informality and vulnerability to illicit exploitation, requires an exceptional degree of trust.

3 The term "smurfing" referred to the use of cash couriers who were employed to convert unobtrusive amounts of cash into bank cheques.

jurisdiction which protects the anonymity of banking clients. A can discreetly draw upon these funds as and when she may require, downloading them back to her stored value card. Alternatively, as Tyree (1996b) has observed, it is considerably easier to transport a fully-loaded stored value card across an international boundary than it is a suitcase full of cash.

Today, even the traditional underground or informal banks can exploit new technologies. Communication between "branches" of an underground bank can occur via telephone, facsimile, or presumably electronic mail, although security and the desirability of minimising records of accounts or transactions might still militate against the latter.[4] The advent of encryption facilities could provide a combination of trust and technology which could enable the anonymous and untraceable movement of funds around the world.

The use of the Internet for "conventional" as well as for underground banking may prove to be a boon to money launderers. As we have seen, technologies may well facilitate the process of placement, by enabling the direct transfer of funds to offshore institutions, or to "cyberspace", or underground banks, beyond the purview of a nation's law enforcement agencies. The rapidity of electronic transactions is such that the process of layering can be accomplished with unprecedented speed. Electronic mail and encryption technologies will permit the unobtrusive transfer of assets around the world many times in one 24-hour period. The velocity of transactions, combined with the lack of physical movement of the assets in question, will assist in masking their origins. Integration will be assisted by the development of stored value cards, to which funds can be downloaded from institutional sources.

The deregulation of financial systems around the world has introduced an unprecedented competitiveness in the banking industry. This in turn has introduced a degree of occupational insecurity for bank executives and employees alike. The extent to which this might enhance the risk of corruption in furtherance of money laundering, electronic or otherwise, remains to be seen. Complicity of bank officials in the more traditional forms of money laundering is not uncommon. Criminal organisations have also succeeded in gaining control of traditional financial institutions and using them to their advantage. One may expect that emerging electronic financial institutions will be no less vulnerable to criminal exploitation.

Investigative responses to money laundering

The traditional response to money laundering entailed the systematic monitoring of transactions, with a view towards identifying those of a suspect nature. By analysing the size, timing, origin and destination of cash transactions, authorities are able to detect anomalous movements. A series of large transfers from a small suburban branch bank to an account in a small island nation renowned for its lack of concern about the origin of deposits would, for example, invite further scrutiny.

Recent years have seen law enforcement agencies in Canada and the United States employ more aggressive investigative methods to combat money

---

4   Encryption technology will minimise this risk.

laundering, including covert facilitation or "sting" type operations (Aranson, Bouker and Hannan 1994). These entail law enforcement agencies covertly setting up a cash dealership, or even a small bank, and offering to launder proceeds of crime. Used with great success to date by the Royal Canadian Mounted Police and the US Customs Service, these techniques would seem likely to be accorded greater use in future. The use of such methods by Australian law enforcement agencies poses significant problems of accountability, as well as raising significant ethical and legal questions. The decision of the High Court of Australia in *Ridgeway v R* (1995) 129 ALR 41 is illustrative.

Traditional money laundering investigations are extremely resource intensive. Given the sheer volume of transactions occurring, it would appear that a significant countermeasure to money laundering today entails the design of automated systems for the detection of suspect money movements. Emerging technologies of artificial intelligence and neural networking may well hold the key to the future. For example, the Financial Crimes Enforcement Network (FinCEN), the agency within the US Treasury Department which monitors cash transactions in the United States, is investing heavily in the development of artificial intelligence programs to identify anomalous money flows. FinCEN has also proposed a tracking system which would monitor deposits to, or withdrawals from, United States bank accounts in real time (Kimery 1996).

Interventions to identify and to prevent money laundering were based initially on unilateral action by individual governments. Requirements were imposed on financial institutions to report transactions over a certain value, and all transactions of a suspicious nature, to regulatory authorities. The transnational nature of much money laundering activity soon prompted efforts at international cooperation. Initially, this took the form of bilateral agreements between the United States, where concern over money laundering first arose, and other nations sympathetic to the goal of interdicting organised crime and tax evasion. Gradually, this network of bilateral relationships was complemented by multilateral cooperation, typified by the creation of the Financial Action Task Force (FATF) in 1989. FATF consists primarily of OECD member nations, plus Hong Kong, Singapore, Japan and New Zealand.

During 1990, FATF adopted forty recommendations in response to money laundering (Australian Transaction Reports and Analysis Centre 1995).[5] These included the creation of a global currency tracking system, the requirement that financial institutions report suspicious transactions to law enforcement authorities, that covert facilitation or "sting" operations be used against launderers, and that international electronic funds transfers be monitored. Interventions to identify and to prevent money laundering were based initially on unilateral action. Requirements were imposed on financial institutions to report transactions over a certain value, and all transactions of a suspicious nature, to regulatory authorities. The transnational nature of much money laundering activity soon prompted efforts at international cooperation.

Given the globalisation of finance, the challenge of international cooperation has become increasingly important. The development of the

---

5   See also http://www.ustreas.gov/treasury/bureaus/fincen/border.html

Financial Action Task Force represents a significant achievement on the part of the industrialised world. There remain, nevertheless smaller, more peripheral nations which may serve as money laundering havens. Not all states regard money laundering with the same concern as do the United States and Australia. Some of these may well be "broken" states where sovereignty is contested; in others, political corruption may result in leadership having been "bought off" and regulatory supervision effectively neutralised. Precisely how much pressure can be exerted upon a state without encroaching upon its sovereignty is a matter of some interest. One may well ask at what point do exhortations to assist in combating money laundering constitute interference in the internal affairs of a recalcitrant state?

Just as international cooperation to combat money laundering began to crystallise, emerging developments in technology and financial services are beginning to pose new problems. The possibility of untraceable person-to-person financial transactions without third party contact is a growing source of concern to those whose law enforcement strategies are based on tracking the proceeds of crime, not to mention taxation authorities.

The "simple" solutions to money laundering in the coming age of electronic commerce, are for governments to monopolise payment systems and to monitor all financial transactions. One may question whether such solutions are even achievable. We noted above how time-honoured institutions of underground banking may be enhanced by the application of new technologies, and how developments in telecommunications may facilitate the emergence of parallel payment systems beyond regulatory purview.

Any system of monitoring commercial transactions would be seen as a gross violation of privacy. Even the most law abiding citizens would be disinclined to leave an electronic trail of all their financial transactions. Few would welcome a financial system becoming an instrument of surveillance. Moreover, intensive surveillance of legitimate financial institutions may be partly counterproductive. Within a given jurisdiction, unrestricted access by law enforcement agencies to electronic transfer data could arguably encourage flight of legitimate, as well as illegitimate capital, to financial institutions in more permissive jurisdictions (Jacobs 1995; Froomkin, forthcoming). In the absence of effective international cooperation, this could significantly constrain the capacity of law enforcement.

Exponents of the libertarian ethos which exists in some Western nations have become increasingly enthusiastic about the prospect of alternative monetary systems. This enthusiasm can only be strengthened by the development of technologies which ensure privacy and anonymity. The stage is set for a policy struggle of profound significance.

Regulatory alternatives

Without seeking to appear overly dramatic, one might suggest that the years ahead will be marked as a defining moment in economic history. The precise configuration of electronic money will be hotly contested. On the one hand, there may be those governments which will resist the advent of electronic money, regarding the attendant regulatory problems as intractable.

Other governments may seek to monopolise electronic money, and impose a system which would be fully traceable. This would enable law enforcement agencies to track the use of money with an omniscience which has heretofore been unimaginable. The extent to which this could entail a chilling effect on legitimate commerce, as well as illicit commerce, remains to be seen. It could spell the end of financial privacy.

Yet another scenario would see private monetary systems develop, beyond the regulatory purview of the state. Private corporations, large and small, would compete for "market share", with security, integrity, and perhaps total anonymity being among their selling points. Fundamentally, this is not new. Governments have not always been the exclusive issuers of currency.[6] As recently as the mid-19th century, individual financial institutions issued their own currencies in the form of banknotes. Negotiability varied, depending upon the perceived integrity of the issuing institutions in question. One may speculate about the future of private electronic currencies: some would thrive and eventually dominate, others would wither and die. But unlike the 19th century, national boundaries may become less relevant to money flows, and the global economy may become truly global.

Between these polar extremes lie hybrid systems of electronic commerce, combining some elements of governmental oversight, and some elements of private sector involvement. One such hybrid might, for example, look like existing credit card arrangements, which involve a diversity of participants ranging from major international cards, to specialised credit cards issued by a particular merchant.

As technologies and institutional forms continue to emerge, the issues which governments have begun to confront include the following:

- At what point, if any, will regulatory intervention be appropriate?
- If some degree of regulatory intervention is to occur, what institutional configuration might this entail?
- To what extent should electronic payments be traceable?
- To what extent will there be a limit or cap on the size of a transaction?

Current wisdom, in this as in other areas of telecommunications-related crime, is inclined against what might be referred to as premature regulation. Untimely regulatory intervention runs the risk of stifling innovation and product development. Rather than "jump the gun", governments will be inclined to intervene only when they perceive a clear and imminent threat to the public interest. For the time being, governments seem to be proceeding with caution, so as not to inhibit technological innovation.

---

6   Confidence in private monetary systems would not be inevitably less than confidence in money guaranteed by governments, as the recent experience of the peso, and the behaviour of international bond markets would suggest.

Having said that, however, it seems likely that in the fullness of time, some degree of state intervention will be inevitable. This intervention will be guided less by the need to surmount any general impediments to law enforcement arising from money laundering, than from the need to maintain the integrity of the money supply and the financial system. These are, after all, important foundation stones of commerce. For electronic commerce to flourish, individuals must be confident that their digital cash will not evaporate, or become diluted in some "meltdown scenario" arising from electronic counterfeiting (Tyree 1997). One need only look at the collapse of numerous small savings and loan institutions in the United States during the 1980s and the subsequent failure of the Bank of Credit and Commerce International (BCCI) to appreciate the importance of prudential supervision.[7] A completely unregulated market for electronic banking could see some institutions vulnerable to predation by unscrupulous employees, or the collapse of entire institutions because of deceit or negligence. The potential for industry-wide crisis, with attending loss of faith in all Internet-based financial institutions, is a most undesirable scenario.

This then raises the question of what type of regulatory structure will be created, or which existing ones modified, in order to achieve public confidence in electronic money. One convenient option available to governments would be to restrict the ability to issue electronic cash to banks or other financial institutions already subject to regulatory supervision. This need not "freeze" circumstances as they are at this moment; the definition of eligible institution can be widened to accommodate newly emerging institutional forms as they enter the market.

For the time being, banks and credit card companies, because of their status and legitimacy, have already begun to play a major role as sponsors of electronic money. In some nations, one is beginning to see the emergence of hybrid forms of public-private partnerships to provide the infrastructure for electronic money. For example, a retail bank owned by the Swedish Post Office is using software licensed by DigiCash. A corporate subsidiary of the Bank of Finland is developing a cashcard system for that country (Froomkin 1996a).

One would be naive to suggest that a modification of existing systems of prudential regulation would solve all problems, however. The risk that unauthorised individuals and organisations might offer electronic financial services is a real one. Electronic informal banking may become a no less enduring institution than the centuries old informal banking based on chits and chops. Basic legal definitions of banking — which institutions they include and which they exclude — may require periodic modification. One must be realistic and suggest that strategies for the prevention of underground banking are likely to warrant attention sooner or later.

Whatever regulatory structures begin to emerge, the key question for authorities will be the degree of traceability and anonymity which will attach to electronic money. There are numerous permutations and combinations which any given form of electronic cash might entail (Tanaka 1996; Froomkin 1996b). These may vary within and between cash systems; some might offer buyer (payer)

---

7   These cases also illustrate that regulatory regimes themselves are subject to failure.

anonymity, but seller (payee) identification. Anonymity may attach to one party, or the other, or both, or neither.

The most problematic situation for law enforcement would be the latter case: one in which direct person-to-person fund transfers can occur without the intermediation of a bank (or functional equivalent thereof — see the discussion of the Mondex system in Chapter 8). But such configurations are by no means inevitable. For example, DigiCash Inc. maintains that under its system, all digital cash must be given to a bank for confirmation, and any customer would be able to prove that a given payment occurred (DigiCash 1996).

Thus, the criminal risks arising from the emergence of electronic money would be minimised if there were a requirement that all funds clear through a bank (or other authorised institution) and that the payee remain identifiable.[8]

The basic question is whether those systems which are developed will be required to establish and maintain an audit trail, whether confined to the specific transaction or to prior and subsequent events in a chain of transactions. The question of which, and under what circumstances, third parties may obtain access to such an audit trail is an issue of considerable importance. Concerns need not be limited to the spectre of "Big Brother", but will also extend to private interests who might wish to exploit the details of one's spending history for marketing purposes.

Another consideration is whether authorised transactions would be limited so as not to exceed a specified amount. Just as small cash transactions today tend to occur beyond the gaze of regulators and law enforcement, so too might a system of electronic cash be designed so that small denomination electronic payments be invisible.

Of additional concern is the traceability of sequential transactions, and the ability of authorities to identify repeated transactions designed to circumvent reporting requirements.

All of these plausible alternatives are likely to be contested in due course. At the time of writing, governments have begun to recognise emerging risks and benefits of electronic money, and to anticipate technological and institutional developments. Should a natural monopoly emerge, regulatory intervention would be easier.

Depending upon the ability of nations to achieve a degree of international consensus, centralisation — if not globalisation — of currencies, would be a real prospect; the unification of European currency may be hastened by such developments. But internationalisation of electronic money may pose additional problems. Assume, for example, that a resident of Australia is able to open an account in Australian dollars with a bank in Pakistan. In the absence of close cooperation between Pakistani and Australian authorities, telecommunications may deliver considerable potential for concealing legitimate or ill-gotten gains from Australian authorities.

The precise configuration of anonymity and traceability would have corresponding implications for commerce and crime control. The fundamental

---

8   In Hong Kong, for example, the proposed legal framework would limit the authority to issue
      multi-purpose stored value cards to licensed banks. See Australia (1996, p 139).

challenge facing financial regulatory authorities and commercial interests alike is to develop systems for the prevention and control of money laundering, without unduly restraining commercial activity. A similar balancing act will be necessary in order to achieve a compromise between the competing values of financial privacy and traceability. Crede (1996) suggests that, assuming a degree of traceability, the development of electronic money is a potential boon to law enforcement. Money laundering and the financial exchange which sustains black markets will be more transparent than ever.

Traceability is hardly without precedent. Most credit card transactions, not to mention cheques and other negotiable instruments and wire transfers, are already quite transparent. In a sense, it is not the accountability of those who pay and receive electronic money which will matter most, but rather the accountability of those who would have access to the records of these transactions.

When governments see a need to act, they are increasingly coming to the realisation that they should work with, not against, market forces. Governments should articulate their goals, and to the maximum feasible extent, allow the private sector to develop solutions. Governments are, of course, able to exert quite significant influence over market forces. Given the vital role played by the governments of many advanced democracies in income support and the provision of other welfare benefits, they are well placed to dictate standards for electronic payments systems. By specifying systems which are not fully anonymous, they may well give the competitive edge to a preferred system.

One might speculate on what the broad contours of a regulatory framework for electronic money might look like. Governments would appear unlikely to allow the introduction of systems based on totally anonymous digital cash, at least in excess of a specified threshold. Essentially, this would entail a continuation of the status quo, in which small cash transactions remain anonymous, but larger transactions, whether through cash or electronic media, are traceable (Froomkin 1996). It seems likely that large institutions with established reputations will have a significant competitive advantage over smaller, newer organisations. This would not necessarily preclude the emergence of a "rising star"; Microsoft itself rose from humble beginnings.

Governments may also be expected to embark on other institutional rearrangements which, without chilling emerging technologies and entrepreneurial developments, will reduce the risk of their abuse.

Taxation systems, for example, are likely to become increasingly reliant upon consumption or value added taxes, to compensate for any increased risk that taxable income might be concealed. The state which waits, and then adapts to emerging markets, may well achieve more than the state which seeks to hold back the tide of technological innovation.

10

TELECOMMUNICATIONS IN FURTHERANCE OF CRIMINAL CONSPIRACIES

In previous chapters, we have seen a variety of ways in which telecommunications technology has provided new methods of committing crime and new targets for illegality. New technology can also be applied to organised criminal activity. Contemporary public discussion of organised criminal activity (or of simpler criminal conspiracies) barely touches upon the application of telecommunications. In its fundamental form, such application is not new; the criminal exploitation of telecommunications has existed for over a century. Criminals use voice or data telecommunications because they offer prompt acknowledgment and authentication of the message, and a high degree of transmission reliability. Other methods of communication, such as messenger or postal services, are slower and much more vulnerable. Moreover, until recently, there was a relatively low likelihood of their adversaries eavesdropping upon telecommunications (see, however, the instances discussed in Chapter 2). Thus, telecommunications contributed to an overall reduction in the risk of doing business of a criminal nature.

The growth and pervasiveness of telecommunications technology, and the scope of the illegality to which it may be applied, have increased markedly in the past two decades. This chapter explores some of the ways in which telecommunications technology may be applied in furtherance of organised criminal activity. We hope to demonstrate how new technology has increased the capability of criminal offenders, while at the same time posing new challenges for law enforcement. In countless instances, telecommunication facilities are merely incidental to the commission of a crime. In other cases, however, telecommunications may be instrumental. In any event, telecommunications permit criminal activities to occur with a degree of efficiency and on a scale which is unprecedented.

The discussion will range from the use of telecommunications to support complex criminal organisations, to their use in furtherance of the smallest criminal conspiracies — those involving interaction between two people. We first present a small selection of incidents to illustrate the changes in applications which have occurred since the advent of telecommunications. We then discuss some of the basic functions performed by telecommunications technology in furtherance of traditional criminal enterprise, and identify some of the problems that the new developments in technology have begun to pose for law enforcement agencies. Then, we discuss the means by which criminal communications may be controlled, or at least intercepted for the purpose of detecting impending criminal activity, or to facilitate the investigation and prosecution of an offence. Noting that emerging technologies of information security will serve both criminals and law-abiding citizens, we conclude with a discussion which seeks to identify how the balance of interests might be struck between the imperatives of law enforcement on the one hand, and the rights of the individual on the other.

Organised crime involving telecommunications was reported as early as 1867. We noted in Chapter 2 how a Wall Street broker collaborated with Western Union operators to intercept financial news telegraphs to the New York Stock exchange, and used the new technology to mislead financial markets (O'Toole 1978). The legendary Al Capone relied upon the telephone to manage his 1920s criminal rackets and protection business along with the rest of his criminal organisation. The telephone kept him, and his activities, out of sight of the authorities. Use of the telephone and available telecommunications technology to facilitate criminal enterprises were common during the American Prohibition era (Balsamo and Carpozi 1988).

Between 1985 and 1986, an individual involved in drug trafficking arranged for the hire of aircraft for transporting two 700 kilogram shipments of cocaine between Colombia and Mexico. Each flight cost US$80,000. The individual was later arrested in Arizona, where he had not only continued to broker the aircraft hire but had also facilitated the laundering of the drug monies. A legitimate gold dealer would daily receive millions of dollars in small denomination cash, derived largely from cocaine sales. He would purchase gold at above market rates, and then exchange it — at below market rates — for cheques and wire transfers to Latin American banks. These banks then wired the hiring expenses to the aircraft hire broker in Arizona. Telecommunications services between the United States, Mexico and Latin America played a key role in the furtherance of these drug shipments (United States, 1994a).

In a more modest scenario, one played out countless times around the world, drug dealers conspired together to supply heroin. Many buyers telephoned to arrange to collect the product. As the supply of heroin at the street dealer's house ran low, or when it ran out, they made contact with the person who supplied them by telephoning a Telecom pager operator who was requested to transmit a message to the pager.[1]

As will become apparent in more detail below, electronic communications in furtherance of crime are not always inaccessible to law enforcement agencies. Indeed, interception of criminal communications has become a useful (if somewhat costly)[2] tool of law enforcement agencies, not only for learning about crimes before they occur, and then preventing them, but also for acquiring information for use in investigating and prosecuting criminal cases (Reno 1996). For example:

- Evidence derived from pagers and wire transfers were a vital element in convicting 28 participants of a Boston heroin ring on

---

1 *Vaso Davidovic v R* (1990) 51 A Crim R 197. See also *R v Padman* (1979) 25 ALR 36, *R v Migliorini* (1981) 38 ALR 356, and *R v Campbell* (1994) 78 A Crim R 1, discussed above in Chapter 2.

2 Other forms of surveillance may be even more costly. Barrett (1994) published the following comparison of surveillance costs prepared by the Victoria Police: telecommunications interception (A$570 per day), video surveillance (A$1376 per day), listening devices (A$1630 per day), physical surveillance (A$1895 per day) and vehicle tracking (A$2772 per day). We are indebted to Simon Bronitt for calling this to our attention.

charges including conspiracy, heroin distribution and money laundering (PR Newswire 1996).

- A street gang in Chicago, acting on behalf of the Libyan Government, allegedly planned to shoot down a commercial airliner with a stolen military weapon. The plan was foiled when it was discovered in advance by means of telephone wiretaps (Denning 1994).[3]
- The "Ill Wind" investigation of fraud by US defence contractors relied extensively on wiretaps. It resulted in the conviction of 65 persons and the recovery of over US$250 million.
- In 1992, police in San Jose, California infiltrated an electronic bulletin board that operated for paedophiles. On the board, the police discovered a plot to lure a boy for purposes of sexual exploitation. The suspects were charged before the planned abduction could occur.[4]

Today, satellite telecommunications services and other wireless technologies have overcome many of the problems — such as laying cables in remote areas — associated with land-based services. Telecommunications services are now available everywhere on the earth's surface, from the opium-growing regions of Burma, to illegal fishing boats operating in another nation's territorial waters; they are accessible on aeroplanes, on boats, and on foot. Recent advances in telephony include viable voice-mail services, corporate centralised attendant telephone services that join callers from many locations, and personal computer/telephone integration that maximises use of telecommunications channel capacity. The scope of their application to criminal activity appears without limit.

The function of telecommunications in furtherance of criminal conspiracies

Telecommunications facilitate organised criminal activity in four basic ways. First, they enhance the capacity to plan and coordinate criminal activity. Secondly, they are instrumental in the marketing and distribution of illegal services. Thirdly, they sustain the organisational structure which supports the above functions. The nature of the technology is such that it allows these functions to occur unobtrusively, reducing the need for face-to-face contact or visible interaction in public. Fourthly, they can be used to obstruct law enforcement and criminal investigation.

---

3   The investigation was called RUKBOM. See http://www.eff.org/pub/Privacy/Clipper/denning_crypto_law.paper; Newsday, 22 February 1994.

4   See also Ford 1997; Akdeniz 1996; Australia 1995. For extensive materials relating to prosecutions concerning child pornography and the Internet, see Akdeniz (1996).

Coordination of small-scale crime

Telecommunications technologies are often employed to coordinate criminal activities and to avoid detection.

A group of thieves in one city used mobile telephones to facilitate thefts from delivery trucks in the central business district. One accomplice followed the truck's driver when he left the vehicle, while the other accomplices plundered the truck's cargo. The first accomplice warned the others by mobile phone when the driver was about to return to the truck, thus assuring them of an undetected getaway (Cooke 1994).

In another case in November 1994, a group of kidnappers used a small transmitter, concealed in his car, to signal to three accomplices in another vehicle when best to abduct the victim.

Devices are said to exist which can record and play back the signals transmitted by the remote control devices commonly fitted to garage doors. Such instruments would be of more than passing interest to prospective burglars.[5]

Criminals also use telecommunications for expressive as well as instrumental purposes. Offenders customarily discuss their past crimes and future plans with accomplices or other parties.

Planning and coordinating large-scale criminal activity

Large-scale criminal activity almost always requires complex organisation and communications. One can imagine the logistical challenges confronting those who would engage in the clandestine transportation of contraband, often in bulk quantities, across international frontiers. Following successful importation, new challenges exist in the form of marketing and distribution. To be sure, this activity is rarely if ever the province of one monolithic organisation, but rather entails a number of collectivities operating sequentially or overlapping to some extent. Nevertheless, the activity as a whole may involve the coordination of thousands of individuals. It is simply impossible to conduct operations on such a scale without telecommunications. Even such mundane matters as payroll records are maintained on electronic databases. One cocaine trafficking organisation was reported as having a management information system designed to monitor expenses and thereby enhance profitability (Ramo 1996). It has been suggested that the Cali cartel use satellite communications for global positioning (Freeh 1996a).

Many criminals maintain detailed records of their activities; the most sophisticated organised crime often produces records in complex detail, which can be crucial to an investigation or prosecution. Large-scale drug trafficking, for example, may generate revenues of hundreds of millions of dollars, which are not usually buried in someone's garden. As noted above in our chapter on electronic money laundering, the proceeds of crime are often moved and reinvested in a manner designed to conceal their origins. In any event, records of illicit enterprise are often kept in electronic form.

---

5   As noted above in Chapter 2, there is a thriving trade in surveillance technology.

Consider, for example, the activity which was interdicted by an operation of the US Drug Enforcement agency, codenamed "Green Ice". In the initial stage of the operation, directed at the financial infrastructure of the Cali drug cartel, seven of the cartel's top money managers and almost 200 other individuals were arrested in an operation involving law enforcement agencies of eight different nations. Among the evidence seized were computer hard drives and disks containing information relating to bank accounts and financial transactions (Wankel 1996).

Among the advanced communications devices seized from the Cali cartel in 1995 were radios that distort voices, videophones which provide visual authentication of the caller's identity, and instruments for scrambling transmissions from computer modems. It has been suggested that the technological competence of the Cali cartel in 1995 was comparable to that of the KGB at the time of the Soviet Union's collapse just six years earlier (Brooke 1995).

In Russia today, the technology gap between state and offender may now be closed. Russian organised criminals have attracted notice for their use of high technology communications equipment, including facsimile machines and mobile telephones (and occasionally encryption) far more sophisticated than anything used by beleaguered Russian law enforcement officials (Hersch 1994).

Marketing illicit goods and services

Just as developments in telecommunications have led us to the threshold of a new era in legitimate commerce, they greatly facilitate the marketing of illicit goods and services. Telephony and paging systems facilitate the distribution of drugs no less than pizzas. They can summon a medical practitioner to an emergency, or a receiver of stolen goods to a source of supply. Criminal organisations are at least as dependent upon telecommunications resources as is any similarly sized legitimate organisation.

Paging receivers (pagers) have evolved from the simple tone devices of the 1970s, which beeped when the telephone subscriber's number was rung, to terminals which can receive and acknowledge many alphanumeric messages: 330,000 Australians subscribed to paging services by 1995, while the United States had 20 million users. The ability of the new generation of two-way pagers to acknowledge receipt of the transmitted message offers the sender additional confidence that the receiver will reliably act upon the message. However, these transmitted acknowledgments also offer a new opportunity to physically locate the pager holder — an aspect that invites attention of both the criminal and the investigator.

In one case, cocaine dealers minimised the risk of detection through their ability to separate the physical exchange of the drugs from the physical exchange of monies. Hence they used fixed telephone services in five separate locations (shops), and a mobile telephone. The illegal deals were negotiated and money changed hands at one of the shops. The cocaine delivery was then arranged at another location by the remote "invisible" mobile telephone user, enabling a quick and relatively safe, transfer of the illegal goods (United States 1994). Mobile telecommunications services facilitated these crimes.

One of the most time-honoured forms of criminal activity involving telecommunications technology has been illegal gambling. The efficiency and unobtrusiveness of illegal bookmaking has been, and remains, greatly facilitated by the telephone (Reuter and Rubenstein 1982). The use of information technology also facilitates the management of high-volume transactions which larger gambling operations entail. Bookmakers have been known to exploit other basic telecommunications resources such as telephone diverters, and exchange enhancement features (for example Telstra's Easycall and Centel) (Queensland Criminal Justice Commission 1991). If law enforcement appears ill-equipped to combat this exploitation of telecommunications facilities, it would seem all but powerless in the advent of online gambling. Numerous online betting operations now operate from offshore havens, beyond the purview of local law enforcement. While citizens in some jurisdictions are occasionally reminded that online gambling is illegal, enforcement would appear unachievable.

On a much more mundane level, maintaining a record of one's client base, whether one be in the sex industry or a drug dealer, is a common business practice. The address book is giving way to personal digital assistants and online databases.

Other illegal payments

Froomkin (1996) discusses how other offences, such as extortion,[6] can be facilitated by anonymous electronic payment systems.

> Alice commits an act of extortion (e.g., blackmail or kidnapping). Instead of demanding small unmarked bills, Alice demands that Bob force a bank to issue blinded digital cash based on numbers contained in Alice's ransom note, and publish the result. Because the payoff occurs via publication in a broadcast medium such as a newspaper, Alice faces no danger of being captured while attempting to pick up the ransom. If Alice used the right blinding protocol only she can unblind and spend the coins. (Or for extra security, Alice can demand that the blinded coins be encrypted with a public key generated for the occasion.) And because the blinded digital cash is anonymous and untraceable, Alice is able to spend it without fear of marked bills, recorded serial numbers, or other forms of detection (Froomkin 1996).

One can easily see how the same technology may be applied to structure and disguise other questionable payments, such as bribes.

Telecommunications as infrastructure for criminal organisations

Telecommunication services have become more important to criminal organisations as they expand their activities across national boundaries, with the consequent need to communicate more effectively over longer distances. Reliable communications are no less critical to business of a criminal nature, as it is in the law abiding community. Increasing transnational activity of such groups as the Japanese Yakuza and the Hong Kong-based triads, as well as Russian criminal organisations, is supported by telecommunications. So too are loose confeder-

---

6   For further discussion of extortion, see Schwartau (1996).

ations of crime groups. Particularly vulnerable are those nations in which the sophistication of telecommunications technology coexists with undeveloped law enforcement and regulatory agencies. Criminal organisations in the emerging democracies of Eastern Europe are taking advantage of newly relaxed borders and improved telecommunications systems to extend their sphere of operations (Freeh 1996b). Such technology also greatly facilitates the formation and maintenance of coalitions and informal collaborative arrangements between criminal organisations across long distances. Indeed, it has become increasingly common to refer to the globalisation of organised crime (Raine and Cilluffo 1994).

Obstructing criminal investigations and other law enforcement activity

Telecommunications technology can also be used to impede law enforcement activity. Gorelick (1996) revealed that a man in California gained access to computers running local telephone switches, discovered information concerning US Government wiretaps, and warned at least one target. Radio scanners, which have long been generally available at retail electronics stores, can be used to monitor police wireless communications. These can provide a general indication of enforcement strategies, as well as early warning of police detection of and response to a crime which one may be in the process of committing.

Another type of device which has proven useful to drug smugglers is a small transmitter which may be concealed in a consignment of contraband. These may be designed and set to emit a transmission in the event the shipment had been intercepted (Associated Press 1995).

Offenders have their own intelligence systems, which lend themselves to automated storage and retrieval no less than those of law enforcement. It has been suggested that information on law enforcement personnel involved in vice and narcotics enforcement has been marketed amongst criminal and criminal organisations (Icove, Seger and VonStorch 1995). One Colombian cocaine organisation was able to identify originating numbers of calls made to the US Embassy in order to determine which citizens might be cooperating with drug interdiction efforts (Ramo 1996).

Police information systems would also seem attractive targets for intrusion by criminals; one imagines that information security in law enforcement agencies is accorded an appropriate degree of priority. Disruption of tactical law enforcement communications can conceivably provide offenders time to effect a getaway; damage to or destruction of law enforcement information systems could hinder intelligence or impede investigations.

Concealing criminal communications

As noted above, various applications of telecommunications help conceal criminal communications from law enforcement authorities. Unobtrusive criminal contacts, all else equal, are less likely to attract the attention of bystanders or police.

Innovative application of network services and products, such as telephone diverters and calling number display (CND or "caller ID") allow call screening. CND enables illegal gambling operations, for example, to screen out calls from non-punters and so avoid investigators. Mobile telephones, paging services and electronic mail services have features which may conceal the origin and/or the destination of the communications. Techniques of telecommunications service theft, discussed above in Chapter 4, are applied in furtherance of other criminal activity. Cellular "cloning" enables criminals to communicate by using a series of phone numbers unconnected to one's identity, and thereby avoid systematic monitoring, if not detection (Ramo 1996).

Encryption

Despite the long history of cryptography (as noted in our introductory chapter), it remained largely the province of governments, valued for its military and national security application, until only recently. In about 1970, the FBI intercepted a communication between a murder suspect and another inmate. The crude numerical message was successfully decrypted to reveal a conversation about pills changing hands. In a separate instance, the FBI decrypted a prisoner's messages that revealed attempts at smuggling and prison escape. The FBI noted that at that time it had provided cryptanalytic assistance to local law enforcement agencies "on numerous occasions" (FBI 1970) implying that encryption was already well used throughout the US criminal community. However, at that stage the encryption technologies described were computationally weak.

One of the most significant technological developments of the past decade has been the growing public accessibility of cryptography. The telecommunications revolution, with its dramatic increases in capacity and commensurate decreases in cost, have made cryptographic technology generally available, initially to industry, and recently to a wider public. In 1992, AT&T announced its intention to market a small portable telephone with voice encryption capabilities. Previously, voice scramblers had been used to limit access to the content of telephone conversations. In contrast to encryption, voice scramblers transform a voice's analog waveform in a manner which is unintelligible to those without a receiver especially designed to reverse the transformation.

The current easy access to consumer and professional encryption services is readily apparent from product information published on the Internet. A variety of free and subscription encryption packages is offered for e-mail, voice products, files, communications and financial transactions. A number of these are provided on resource lists such as: http://www.cs.hut.fi/ssh/crypto/software.html #crypto-libraries.[7] Even cryptanalysis products and working groups are advertised. Many of these cryptographic packages are user friendly; for those which are not, there are numerous interest groups that operate electronic mail and bulletin services. The digitisation of the telecommunications network is providing easier access to faster transmission speeds, such as the 2 x 64 kilobits/second

---

7   E-mail encryption — such as PGP (Pretty Good Privacy), PEM (Privacy Enhanced Mail), voice encryption — such as Speak Freely, Nautilus, and PGPFone.

basic rate ISDN services. Complementing this is the increased computational speed of computers. Together they offer near-real-time encryption services that are accessible to the ordinary user. By the year 2005, when many national telecommunications digitisation programs and information infrastructure programs should be nearly completed, it is likely that encryption of voice and data services will become a regular subscription service.

These regular subscribers, of course will include persons engaged in illegal activity who would avail themselves of cryptography to minimise the possibility that their communications might be intercepted by law enforcement agents. It will also include those who wish to conceal incriminating records or other evidence of wrongdoing. Seizure of stored records is much more common in criminal investigations than is the use of interception.

Criminal applications of encryption technology have begun to pose significant problems for law enforcement (Denning and Baugh 1997). In the United States, the Director of the FBI acknowledged the potential of cryptography to prevent investigators from understanding the content of seized computer files and intercepted criminal communications. He identified a number of prominent investigations where the subjects used encryption to impede detection and investigation, including the Aldrich Ames espionage case, where Soviet handlers requested that Ames encrypt his computer files. Other examples included a terrorist plot to bomb US commercial aircraft in Asia, the use of encryption in transmitting child pornography, and a major drug trafficking case in which telephone surveillance through court-ordered wiretaps was hindered by means of a encryption device. The FBI Director also observed that the Cali cartel engage the services of software engineers to encrypt communications, and that some anti-government militia groups in the US are advocating the use of encryption to inhibit surveillance and investigation.[8]

Criminal exploitation of encryption technology may be used to penetrate secure communications by potential victims. We observed above in Chapter 2 how English blackmailers successfully decrypted electronic transaction information and used it to extort a significant sum from a bank and several of its customers (Nicholson 1989). Concern over the use and availability of robust encryption technology is hardly limited to the United States. Some nations, including France, Israel and Russia restrict the importation, manufacture, sale and use of encryption products. On the other hand, Scandinavian states have elected not to regulate encryption at all, in the belief that personal privacy is more important than criminal intervention capabilities (Baker and Barth 1996). Similarly, the OECD has recently confirmed in its Guidelines for Cryptography Policy (OECD 1997), that cryptography should be freely available in order to enhance the security and confidentiality of digital communications. Only under strict legal controls should law enforcement and national security agencies be able to gain access to encrypted data.

---

8   Freeh 1996a; 1996c; Shenon 1995b; Swisher 1995, for another example of the use of cryptography to conceal sexually explicit depictions of children, see Ford, 1997.

Legitimate commerce in the 21st century will become increasingly dependent upon telecommunications. Even today, companies communicate vast amounts of business information by electronic means. In the increasingly competitive global economy, the economic performance of individual companies, not to mention national economies, can hinge on access to economic intelligence. Such information can be an attractive target for foreign governments and business competitors. In addition to trade secrets and proprietary information discussed in Chapter 5 above, industrial espionage may target strategic information such as contract, pricing and bidding information, project and merger proposals, marketing strategies, and product specifications (Schweizer 1993; Venzke 1996). In mid-1996, the Director of the FBI states that the Bureau had 800 cases involving 23 foreign state-sponsored economic espionage operations (Freeh 1996a).

In the United States, the recently established National Counter-intelligence Center concluded that:

> ... specialized technical operations (including computer intrusions, telecommunications targeting and intercept, and private-sector encryption weaknesses) account for the largest portion of economic and industrial information lost by U.S. corporations.

It was further noted that:

> [b]ecause they are so easily accessed and intercepted, corporate telecom-munications — particularly international telecommunications — provide a highly vulnerable and lucrative source for anyone interested in obtaining trade secrets or competitive information. Because of the increased usage of these links for bulk computer data transmission and electronic mail, intelligence collectors find telecommunications intercepts cost-effective. For example, foreign intelligence collectors intercept facsimile transmissions through government-owned telephone companies. The stakes are large — approximately half of all overseas telecommunications are facsimile transmissions. Innovative "hackers" connected to computers containing competitive information are able to evade security controls and to access companies' information. In addition, many American companies have begun using electronic data interchange, a system of transferring corporate bidding, invoice, and pricing data electronically overseas. Many foreign government and corporate intelligence collectors find this information invaluable (National Counterintelligence Center 1995; see also Tripp 1995).

Infiltration of legitimate telecommunications business

Complicity of telephone company insiders with organised criminals can and does occur. Australian bookmakers have been the beneficiaries of assistance from telecommunications carriers (Australia 1963; Vincent 1984). Opportunities for the criminal exploitation of telecommunications services are likely to proliferate in an environment of privatisation.

The global move toward deregulation of telecommunications also facilitates the entry of organised criminals as either service providers or users of telecommunications services and products. Shelf companies are a feature of the service provider industry in the Australian market at present. With the expectation that service providers will operate under an even more flexible voluntary code of conduct following full deregulation in Australia in 1997,[9] Australian law enforcement and telecommunications regulators have signalled concern for the integrity of the service provider industry. American service resellers are vulnerable to exceptionally high levels of industry fraud. These telecommunications industry characteristics — the potential profits, the inelastic demand for telecommunications services, the regulatory environment, and the service provider industry profile — identify an industry that can invite the infiltration of organised crime.

Just as a number of banks in the former Soviet Union are reputed to be owned or controlled by criminal groups, so too could telecommunications systems in a deregulated environment be acquired and exploited for illicit purposes by criminal enterprises. There is evidence that criminal organisations are making substantial investments in the telecommunications infrastructure of some African states.

Control of criminal communications

The initial response by law enforcement agencies to the criminal misuse of telecommunications systems has been interception. If successful, interception can produce evidence to sustain a criminal prosecution.[10] When it occurs early enough, it may even enable law enforcement agencies to prevent a crime from happening. The classic means of intercepting criminal communications has been wiretapping.

The current legal principles which govern the interception of telecommunications had their foundation in Britain in the *Birkett Report* (United Kingdom 1957). This report arose out of an incident in 1956 in which the Metropolitan Police had intercepted the telephone of a gangster, Billy Hill, known at the time as the "King of the Underworld". The interception of Hill's telephone was authorised by the Home Secretary but not disclosed in his subsequent trial. During the course of the trial, allegations were made that Hill's barrister, Patrick Marrinan, had obstructed the course of justice. The transcripts of the intercepted conversations between Hill and his barrister were subsequently shown to the Bar Council and Marrinan was disbarred from practising as a barrister by Lincoln's Inn. Questions were then raised in the House of Commons and a Committee of Privy Councillors under the Chairmanship of Sir Norman Birkett was appointed to consider the law of interception (Fitzgerald and Leopold 1987).

The Birkett Report was delivered in September 1957 and affirmed the need for the regulated availability of telephone interception to aid law enforcement. The police and security agencies in Britain continued to employ

---

9   Better Communications, see: http://www.liberal.org.au/ POLICY/COMM/cpart6.html, March 1996.

10   Assuming, of course that it was lawfully accomplished. Even then, Bronitt (1997) argues that electronic interception threatens not just privacy interests, but also the fair trial principle, a view which may be questionable on pragmatic grounds.

interception authorised by the Secretary of State in detecting and prosecuting a wide range of serious crimes which included the Great Train Robbery. Between the 1950s and the 1980s, the number of warrants for telecommunications interception increased steadily from 129 in 1958 to 352 in 1985.

In a 1979 case (*Malone v Metropolitan Police Commissioner* [1979] Ch 344) the police admitted having intercepted the telephone conversations of one James Malone, a London antique dealer, suspected of handling stolen property. Although eventually acquitted, Malone challenged the legality of the telephone interception. Sir Robert Megarry held in the High Court that the interception did not infringe any law but that legislation was called for to clarify the practice. On 2 August 1984, the European Court of Human Rights ruled that the police interceptions in Malone's case, while in accordance with English law, infringed Article 8 of the European Convention for the Protection of Human Rights and Fundamental Freedoms[11] (*Malone v United Kingdom* (1985) 7 EHRR 14).

Following a number of government reports which identified a growing need for interception in dealing with organised drug trafficking and other serious criminal activities, and which recognised the lack of clarity of existing practices, the current English legislation was passed (see United Kingdom 1980, 1981, 1985 and Fitzgerald and Leopold 1987).

In Australia, the first piece of legislation to govern the physical protection of the telephone system was the *Post and Telegraph Act* 1901 (Cth), although this largely failed to deal with interception of communications unless the telephone system was damaged in some way. The first Australian Federal Act to deal specifically with interception was the *Telephonic Communications (Interception) Act* 1960 (Cth) which provided clear protection for the privacy of telephone communications. Under that Act, it was illegal to intercept telephonic communications except for technical reasons connected with the operation of the system, to trace calls made in contravention of the legislation such as nuisance calls, or where interception was authorised pursuant to a warrant.

Between 1960 and 1979, interceptions under a warrant could only be issued to the Australian Security Intelligence Organization (ASIO) for national security purposes. In 1977, the Hope Royal Commission on Intelligence and Security examined, inter alia, the use of interception by ASIO, but found that the Act was being complied with. It was found that although only a modest number of warrants had been issued, the intelligence yield derived from interception was extremely valuable (Hope 1977).

The *Telecommunications (Interception) Act* 1979 (Cth) was the first Act to permit interceptions for law enforcement purposes, initially limited to narcotic offences such as drug importation. The 1979 Act also extended protections from voice systems to data transfer systems.

---

11   Article 8 provides: (1) Everyone has the right to respect for his private and family life, his home and his correspondence. (2) There shall be no interference by a public authority with the exercise of this right except such as is in accordance with the law and is necessary in a democratic society in the interests of national security, public safety or the economic well-being of the country, for the prevention of disorder or crime, for the protection of health or morals, or for the protection of the rights and freedoms of others.

Since the 1980s, in Australia, there have been a number of inquiries which have investigated the use of interception for law enforcement purposes. These include the Royal Commission of Inquiry into Drugs conducted by the Honourable Mr Justice E. S. Williams (1980); the investigation into the activities of the "Mr Asia Crime Syndicate" (Stewart 1983); The Australian Law Reform Commission's Report No 22 on Privacy (1983); Mr Justice Stewart's further Royal Commission Report (1986) into the so-called "*Age* Tapes"; a Parliamentary Joint Select Committee under the Chairmanship of Mr S P Martin MP, to examine the recommendations made by Mr Justice Stewart in the 1986 Royal Commission Report; a further review of the Act in 1991 to extend interception to various State law enforcement agencies (Commonwealth of Australia, Attorney-General's Department 1991); and, most recently, a review of the long-term cost-effectiveness of Australia's telecommunications interception capability in the light of rapid changes in telecommunications technology, the introduction of new services, and the need to safeguard individual privacy (Barrett 1994).

The current legislation only permits interceptions to take place in connection with the operation or maintenance of the system or under the authority of a warrant for the investigation by a specified law enforcement agency of serious offences or by ASIO for national security purposes.[12] The Criminal Justice Commission of Queensland has recently called for an extension of interception powers to law enforcement agencies in Queensland (Queensland, Criminal Justice Commission 1995), although the Australian Council for Civil Liberties has opposed any such extension (Callinan 1996).

The *Telecommunications (Interception) Amendment Act* 1993 also now permits some interceptions to take place without warrants in cases of emergencies and where kidnapping and extortion demands are being made where the victim consents.

In *Grollo v Palmer* (1995) 184 CLR 348, the High Court of Australia held that the *Telecommunications (Interception) Act* 1979 (Cth) was constitutionally valid in so far as it provided for warrants to be obtained from a judge permitting the interception of telephone conversations. Such a law did not infringe the doctrine of the separation of powers because the power to authorise the issue of an interception warrant was not part of the judicial powers of the Commonwealth.

The wiretapping laws of the United States evolved in a piecemeal fashion from prohibitions under individual state laws, to the *Federal Communications Act* 1934, which applied to state and federal officers as well as to private persons. More recent legislation introduced in 1968 (the *Omnibus Crime Control and Safe Streets Act* (18 USC §§ 2510-20)) is similar in approach to the laws in Australia in that the law makes it an offence to intercept or attempt to intercept, without judicial authorisation, any oral or wire communication through the use of any electronic, mechanical or other device. It also forbids the

---

12   The law enforcement agencies which are able to obtain warrants are the Australian Federal Police, the National Crime Authority, the Victoria Police, New South Wales Police Service, South Australia Police Service, the New South Wales Independent Commission Against Corruption, the New South Wales Crime Commission and the Royal Commission into the NSW Police Service.

manufacture, distribution, possession or advertisement of such devices when done in the course of interstate or foreign commerce, other than when carried out by Federal officials. The *Foreign Intelligence Surveillance Act* introduced in 1978 (50 USC §§ 1801-11) permits the monitoring of communications for foreign intelligence purposes (see Fitzgerald and Leopold 1987 and Schwartz 1995), while the *Electronic Communications Privacy Act* 1986 (18 USC §§ 2510-20) prohibits unauthorised interception of computer communications and creates the offence of obtaining, altering, or preventing unauthorised access to data stored electronically in a facility through intentional unauthorised access to the facility (see Carroll and Schrader 1995 and Schwartz 1995). Recent amendments to the legislation in 1994, known as the *Digital Telephony Act* (18 USC § 2602) require carriers and service providers to assist law enforcement agencies in intercepting digital communications which pass over telecommunications systems (see below).

The interception laws of various other countries are summarised in the Report of the Royal Commission of Inquiry into Alleged Telephone Interceptions (Stewart 1986).

Statistics on interception

Prior to the introduction of legislation which authorised and monitored the use of interception by law enforcement and security agencies, little statistical information existed of the number of interceptions which took place. In Britain, for example, prior to the *Interception of Communications Act* 1985, relatively few authorised interceptions were undertaken.

Table 3
Authorised Interceptions in England and Wales 1960-84

Year	Number
1960	195
1965	299
1970	395
1975	468
1980	414
1984	352

Source: United Kingdom (1980, 1985)

Details of the types of cases in which interception is used are rarely disclosed and in cases of national security such information is highly classified. An early Home Office Report said obliquely, for example, that warrants for the security service were directed to countering terrorism, subversion, and espionage:

> For obvious reasons of security, it would not be appropriate to give any examples of the successful use of such warrants, but over the years a number of serious terrorist attacks and threats to national security would not have been countered had it not been for interception (United Kingdom 1980: 6).

Only rarely do challenges to lawfully undertaken interception come before the courts. One such case was *R v Preston* [1993] 4 All ER 638 in which five individuals had been apprehended as a result of lawfully undertaken telephone interceptions and charged with conspiring to import prohibited drugs from Holland into England. It was argued on behalf of the defence that it was unfair for the content of the intercepted conversations to be withheld as disclosure in this case could have assisted in establishing the defence of duress. The relevant law in England, however, was that evidence of intercepted telephone conversations was not required to be disclosed and that, as a result, the defendants had not been treated unfairly.[13]

In Australia, since 1979, the *Telecommunications (Interception) Act 1979 Annual Reports*, have recorded the following statistics on the number of warrants applied for, issued and rejected.

Table 4
Interception Warrants in Australia 1989-96

Year	Applications made	Refused/ withdrawn	Issued
1989	249	3	246
1990	341	1	340
1991	381	1	380
1992	466	1	465
1993	533	6	527
1994	669	1	668
1995	698	6	692
1996	758	11	747

The steady increase in the number of warrants applied for is in part due to the reliance which is placed on such evidence in recent court proceedings, and in part due to the extended range of agencies which are now able to apply for warrants.

Most warrants relate to the investigation of narcotic offences and drug trafficking (see, for example, the popular account of the success of such investigations by Bottom 1989). One recently reported case is illustrative of the size of some lawful police interception operations. The operation involved a number of individuals who had been charged with conspiracy to import commercial quantities of cannabis resin, corruption, and conspiring to pervert the course of justice. After May 1993, the Australian Federal Police undertook the electronic and physical surveillance of one of the accused. This resulted in more than 4000 hours of recorded conversations on 149 cassette tapes being obtained, in which some 80,000 telephone calls were lawfully intercepted. The surveillance led to the investigation of further allegations of bribing jockeys to fix horse races in Sydney and using substantial betting activities to launder moneys procured

---

13 See also the Australian cases of *R v McHardie and Danielson* [1983] 2 NSWLR 733 "Woolworths bombing extortion case"; *R v Oliver* (1985) 57 ALR 543 "conspiracy to import cocaine from Peru into Australia"; and *Carroll v Attorney-General (NSW)* (1993) 70 A Crim R 162 in which Gerard Carroll and former Magistrate Murray Farquhar were charged with conspiracy to commit offences against the *Passports Act* 1938.

from the drug importation business (see *John Fairfax Publications Pty Ltd v Doe* (1995) 37 NSWLR 81 at 91-3).

In recent years, in addition to warrants issued for the investigation of narcotics offences, there has been an increased use of interception in cases of serious fraud and special investigations conducted by the National Crime Authority. The National Crime Authority (1996), *Annual Report 1994-95* (Table 2) reports that 103 warrants were issued during the year 1995-96 authorising communications interceptions by the National Crime Authority. Since 1985, the number of such warrants has shown a steady increase, apart from last year:

Table 5
National Crime Authority Interception Warrants 1985-96

Year	Number
1985-86	15
1986-87	15
1987-88	21
1988-89	33
1989-90	44
1990-91	28
1991-92	30
1992-93	72
1993-94	78
1994-95	105
1995-96	103

Each year, a few warrants are issued in urgent circumstances by telephone pursuant to ss 100 (1)(b) and (2)(b) of the *Telecommunications (Interception) Act* 1979. In 1995, for example, nine such warrants were issued in urgent circumstances (*Telecommunications (Interception) Act 1979 Annual Report 1995-96*).

Most interceptions last for a little over one month. In 1995, for example, the average duration of original warrants was forty-one days (*Telecommunications (Interception) Act 1979 Annual Report 1995-96*).

Table 6 presents data on authorised electronic surveillance for law enforcement in the United States from 1968 through 1995.

Delaney et al. (1993) summarise US data on electronic surveillance authorisations in 1992, including wiretaps. During the period 1983-93 the average number of authorised intercepts per year throughout the United States was about 780. Of the 919 intercepts authorised in 1992, 340 (37 per cent) were federal, the remainder involving state and local agencies.[14]

- Interceptions authorised (919); denied (0); installed (846)

- Average duration of original authorisation (28 days); of extensions (30 days)

---

14 Between 1980 and 1985 the number of federal wiretaps authorised increased from 79 to 243 (Marx 1988, 54). The 1992 total represents a fourfold increase since 1980.

Table 6
United States, Title III Electronic Surveillance 1968-95

Year	Federal	State	Total
1968	0	174	174
1969	33	268	301
1970	182	414	596
1971	285	531	816
1972	206	649	855
1973	130	734	864
1974	121	607	728
1975	108	593	701
1976	137	549	686
1977	77	549	626
1978	81	489	570
1979	87	466	553
1980	81	483	564
1981	106	483	589
1982	130	448	578
1983	208	440	648
1984	289	512	801
1985	243	541	784
1986	250	504	754
1987	236	437	673
1988	293	445	738
1989	310	453	763
1990	324	548	872
1991	356	500	856
1992	340	579	919
1993	450	526	976
1994	554	600	1154
1995	532	526	1058

(Source: Administrative Office of the US Courts)
(http://www.epic.org/privacy/wiretap/wiretap_stats.html)

- Location of surveillance (303 single family dwelling; 135 apartment; 3 multi-dwelling; 119 business; 4 roving; 66 combination; 289 other)
- Major offences involved (634 narcotics; 90 racketeering; 66 gambling; 35 homicide/assault; 16 larceny/theft; 9 kidnapping; 8 bribery; 7 loan-sharking/usury/extortion; 54 other)
- Where interception devices were installed, average number of:
    - (a) interceptions (1861),
    - (b) persons intercepted (117),
    - (c) incriminating intercepts (347)

- Type of surveillance used for the 846 interceptions installed (632 telephone, 38 microphone, 113 electronic, 63 combination)
- Number of persons arrested (2685) and convicted (607) as the result of 1992 intercepts

(Source: Delaney et al. 1993)

Table 7 presents data on intercepts in the United States for counter-intelligence purposes from 1979 through 1995.

Table 7
United States: Data on Intercepts 1979-95

Foreign Intelligence Surveillance Act Orders 1979-95	
Year	Number
1979	199
1980	319
1981	431
1982	473
1983	549
1984	635
1985	587
1986	573
1987	512
1988	534
1989	546
1990	595
1991	593
1992	484
1993	509
1994	576
1995	697

Source: Electronic Privacy Information Center
(http://www.epic.org/privacy/wiretap/fisa_stats.html)

The costs of legal interception

Each year in Australia, substantial sums of money are expended on telecommunications interception. In the year 1995-96, for example, the total cost of interceptions in Australia was A$12,092,252 (*Telecommunications (Interception) Act 1979 Annual Report 1995-96*). Depending upon the manner in which interceptions are costed, estimates for individual warrants range from under A$1000 to more than A$7000, while in the United States it has been estimated that each telephone interception costs the equivalent of A75,000 (Barrett 1994; Australia, Attorney-General's Department 1991).

Such costs may, however, be justified in terms of increasing the number of convictions obtained and assets recovered for the government. The Victoria Police have estimated, for example, that in five operations where the interception costs were about A$150,000, an early guilty plea saved the government over A$800,000 in court costs (Barrett 1994).

The costs of telecommunications interception facilities are escalating primarily due to the introduction of a wider range of digital services that are more difficult to intercept than analogue services, and due to an increasing number of telecommunications suppliers (and networks) in respect of which capabilities need to be developed (Barrett 1994). Separate interception facilities are needed for each telecommunications supplier with its own directly connected customers and switching facilities (p 42). Since 30 June 1997, when the industry was deregulated, and the number of carriers and providers may be expected to expand, this is likely to result in interception costs further increasing.

The role of carriers and service providers in controlling criminal communications

Legislation is now in force which requires telecommunications carriers to assist law enforcement agencies in conducting legal interceptions of communications. Carrier networks must now be interceptible by law enforcement agencies unless exempted by the Minister. Carriers are also required to consult with law enforcement agencies on proposed new technology and offer reasonable assistance to law enforcement agencies in the enforcement of the criminal law.[15]

Such consultation is now provided by the Australian Telecommunications Authority's (AUSTEL) Law Enforcement Advisory Committee (LEAC) which was established in 1990. LEAC comprises representatives from the Australian Federal Police, National Crime Authority, Commonwealth Law Enforcement Board, state police services, security agencies, the three carriers, the Service Providers' Action Network, Department of Communications and the Arts, the Attorney-General's Department and is chaired by AUSTEL. The Committee deals with emerging issues of a general nature such as encryption and other new technology, as well as such specific matters as negotiation of contacts for interception facilities and call tracing. One of LEAC's Sub-Committees specifically deals with interception. The obligations of carriers and service providers to assist law enforcement agencies is explained in detail in the Law Enforcement Advisory Committee document *Telecommunications and Law Enforcement* (1995).

In the United States, legislation requires carriers to design their telecommunications systems to permit law enforcement agencies to intercept digital communications as well as provide traffic data. However, the legislation does not cover private networks, private branch exchanges, automated teller machine networks, electronic mail services, electronic bulletin boards, Internet service providers, and commercial online information services thus severely limiting the extent to which law enforcement agencies will be able to intercept digital communications provided by such services (Schwartz 1995).

---

15   Clause 3 of the *Telecommunications (General Telecommunications Licences) Declaration (No 2)* 1991 and clause 8 of the *Telecommunications (Public Mobile Licences) Declaration (No 2)* 1991.

Australia's *Telecommunications Act* 1991 provides that carriers and service providers, as well as the regulatory authority AUSTEL, must "do their best" to prevent the use of their facilities for the commission of crime (s 47(1)).

They are also required to render such assistance "as is reasonably necessary" to federal and state authorities for:

- enforcing the criminal law and laws imposing pecuniary penalties;
- protecting the public revenue;
- safeguarding national security (s 47(2)).

Section 88 of the Act permits the disclosure of information to law enforcement agencies of information about customers and services supplied, if the disclosure is required or authorised under law, or is reasonably necessary for the enforcement of the criminal law. Compliance with these provisions requiring cooperation is reinforced by subordinate regulations and licensing conditions.[16]

Implementation of these provisions has been not without difficulty, however. Only in the most unusual circumstances are telecommunications carriers and service providers likely to become aware that their facilities are being used in furtherance of criminal activity. In years past, a request for the installation of multiple lines might have aroused suspicion that the client was involved in SP bookmaking. But the advent and proliferation of market survey research, telemarketing, and electronic bulletin board systems has been accompanied by requests for multiple connections. Moreover, increasing concern for the privacy of subscribers has significantly limited the ability of carriers to scrutinise customer traffic. Even so, the massive volume of communications does not lend itself to cost-effective screening by a carrier.

In one case, Telstra was advised by the Queensland police that a certain telephone connection was being used in furtherance of prostitution, and was requested to disconnect the services (*Telstra Corporation Limited v Kendall* (1994) 55 FCR 221). On each occasion, the courts denied Telstra power to use s 47 to disconnect the customer's service. Telstra submitted to the court that if disconnection is not sanctioned by s 47, there is little it will be able to do in most situations to prevent its network and facilities being used to commit crimes (Watts 1995).

In the post-1997 deregulated Australian telecommunications industry, carriers and service providers will not all be of the scale or integrity of Telstra. And the responsibility of participants in the industry to prevent, detect and disclose subscriber illegality may continue to defy clarification. These new players will regularly face the question of when and to what extent they should inquire into subscriber behaviour, and what action they should take when confronted with indicia of illegality, which may well be ambiguous. As commercial actors, they may understandably ask what commercial purpose will be served by seeking to apply this law, or its successor, to subscribers suspected of criminal activity. They may be expected to consider the risk of lost business or revenue, or indeed, damage to commercial reputation attached to an unproductive judgment. The issue of s 47 and similar provisions is also important to Internet service providers who become aware of arguably illegal material passing through

---

16   *Telecommunications (General Telecommunications Licenses) Declaration (No 2) of 1991.*

their servers. Similarly, service providers need to be cautious in suspending or interfering with paging services used by suspected illegal drug dealers. The interpretation of the courts leaves the current industry perplexed as to what real purpose s 47 is able to serve, and how much of the corporate effort should be channelled into coping with an obsolescent law. This Australian law makes it difficult for the industry to impose lawful restrictions on the use of telecommunications for criminal purposes.

Until recently, law enforcement agencies seeking to intercept telecommunications traffic were confronted with simple analog technology, maintained by a public or private monopoly. Enlisting the cooperation of a single, large organisation was a relatively routine matter. But dramatic changes in telecommunications technology and regulation are creating an entirely new environment. As we have noted, the advent of digital communications, combined with global trends towards privatisation and deregulation of the telecommunications industry, have posed new challenges for law enforcement. A proliferation of carriers and service providers may make it difficult to discern which one to approach for assistance in undertaking surveillance of a particular target. Moreover, telecommunications systems can be designed to be more or less accessible to interception. The issues of whether design configurations should provide for access by law enforcement, whether such design should be specified by government, or made a condition of licence (assuming some vestige of regulation remains), and who should bear the costs of industry assistance with law enforcement have become contested issues wherever telecommunications deregulation occurs (Barrett 1994). In the United States, for example, legislation has been enacted which will require telecommunications carriers to facilitate law enforcement access for purposes of interception pursuant to lawful authorisation. The *Communications Assistance for Law Enforcement Act* (CALEA) (47 USC 1001-1010), sometimes called the "Digital Telephony" Act, contains procedures by which telecommunications carriers can recover costs incurred in complying with the Act, whether by means of design solutions or direct assistance on a case by case basis. In late 1996, considerable controversy arose from the question of whether this legislation might serve as the basis for configuring cellular phone services in a manner which would facilitate real time tracking of the physical location of the phone.

As if the above challenges were not formidable enough, they in turn are compounded by the increasing accessibility of encryption technology. Requirements imposed upon carriers and service providers cannot be open-ended, lest they be prohibitively burdensome. Exemptions are available which relieve the carrier from the responsibility for decrypting a subscriber's communications, unless the encryption facilities were themselves provided by the carrier, and the carrier possesses requisite information to permit decryption.

In addition to encryption, law enforcement agencies are concerned about the development and convergence of other technologies such as digital compression, high speed data links, multiplex cables, and asynchronistic transfer mode technology. These all contribute to reducing law enforcement access to voice and data transmissions. The democratisation of telecommunications technology, that is, its widespread accessibility to ordinary citizens, has begun to make many traditional law enforcement techniques obsolete.

Recent years have seen developments which significantly increase the challenges to law enforcement. The development and democratisation of encryption technology, once available only to military and intelligence authorities, has enhanced the ordinary citizen's access to secure communications. The use of encryption as a means of concealing criminal communications was discussed above. So threatening was the potential democratisation of cryptography that the export of cryptographic materials from the United States was for many years prohibited under the same legislation restricting the export of munitions. Yet worldwide commercial demand for secure communications is greater than ever, and software entrepreneurs are concerned about losing competitive advantage in an over-regulated environment.

The proliferation of new telecommunications media in a rapidly deregulating environment has further complicated the task of law enforcement agencies. So too has a resurgence of concern for values of personal privacy, and a greater degree of mistrust in government in a number of western democracies. In consequence, a great deal of thought has been given to solutions which might balance law enforcement interests with privacy rights and commercial interests.

One of the earlier proposals advanced in the United States, referred to as the "Clipper" initiative, was based on what is termed key escrow encryption (Denning 1995; National Research Council 1996). This would permit the use of cryptographic products, subject to the user depositing the encryption algorithm or key with the government. The Clipper proposal envisaged that custody of the key was to have been the joint responsibility of the Commerce and Treasury Departments. Access to the key would have been subject to judicial warrant.

Subsequent developments in the United States have tended to focus on a variety of methods of key recovery, with keys held by designated third parties. By the end of 1996, the US Government was seeking to use export control policy to encourage the development of cryptographic technology with key recovery capabilities.

Although export policies differ, a somewhat similar key management infrastructure is under consideration by members of the European Union. This plan allows for encryption keys to be held in escrow by a "Trusted Third Party", an independent, non-governmental party (Denning 1996b; Denning and Baugh 1997). Government access would only be obtained pursuant to proper legal authority.

Those who would require some form of key escrow encryption have been locked in controversy with privacy advocates and with industry entrepreneurs. Meanwhile, their debate may have been overtaken by events.

It would appear that law enforcement responses in the face of these changes will head in two directions. It seems doubtful that law enforcement will simply "give up" and concede defeat to those who would apply increasingly sophisticated telecommunications technology to criminal ends. Therefore, one may expect a game of technological "leap frog" where the more sophisticated criminals continue to refine their telecommunications capabilities to adapt to law enforcement developments. In response, law enforcement agencies will develop increasingly sophisticated applications for investigative use. And so it will go.

Law enforcement may also be expected to rely on other investigative methods, particularly covert facilitation or undercover methods.[17] Some of these may themselves involve telecommunications technology, while others will entail more traditional "low-tech" approaches.[18] New forms of surveillance are likely to be more intrusive than those currently in use. Regardless of whether they require legislative authorisation, their introduction heralds considerable conflict between law enforcement agencies and privacy advocates in Australia, as in most democratic societies (OECD 1997).

Conclusions

The electronic transfer of information is a primary key to success of modern enterprise — legitimate and illegitimate. Telecommunications is the medium for achieving this transfer and it is not generally structured to discriminate between its users. Whether locally or globally, from the exchange of child pornography[19] to real-time planning and execution of terrorist operations, organised criminal activity depends increasingly upon telecommunications.

The increasing sophistication of telecommunications technology will provide new and greater opportunities for criminal activity. Yet the same technology also will provide law enforcement with greater potential as well.

In 1996, a panel convened by the National Research Council in the United States concluded that non-government use of cryptography was increasing around the world, and had become very difficult for governments to control. It concluded that not only is widespread non-government use inevitable, but that cryptography was soon likely to become an integral feature of standard telecommunications services (National Research Council 1996). Large industry players are already preparing for the time when they will be able to launch a strong encryption product as an add-on to their existing product range.

Short of a laissez-faire approach to the use of encryption technology, it has been suggested that the intentional use of encryption in the concealment of criminal activity be made an offence. This could extend to those who knowingly provide the technology for criminal application. At the present time, such restrictions seem reasonable. In the United States, for example, the use of a firearm in the commission of an offence constitutes an additional crime. But in the event that the use of cryptography becomes more widespread, and integrated into more general telecommunications applications, its use in communications may become automatic, and special provisions may be gratuitous.

The risk attached to the wide availability of encryption technology — that it will be applied in furtherance of criminal activity — will be weighed

---

17 For a discussion of undercover methods, their strengths and limitations, see Marx (1988; 1992) Fijnaut and Marx (1995) and Levinger (1987).

18 Not all interception involves the use of expensive high tech equipment: the police can use an ordinary radio receiver with tape machine to record a cordless phone conversation. (Personal Communication, Simon Bronitt, January 1997).

19 Bernstein (1996).

against the potential benefits flowing from secure personal and commercial communication of an entirely legitimate nature, as well as the economic potential flowing from relatively unrestrained technological development. In addition to the risks which it would pose to privacy, excessive restriction on the development and distribution of encryption technology may exert a chilling effect on innovation. Nations such as the United States and Australia would risk sacrificing a degree of competitive advantage by restricting commercial innovations in cryptography.

We noted in earlier chapters how secure communications are essential for the full development of electronic commerce. Individuals must feel confident that their credit card details, not to mention other sensitive financial information, are not accessible to the world. Companies, from the small firm to the major multinational, also depend on secure communications in an increasingly competitive environment. One may infer from our brief excursus into the realm of industrial espionage and from our earlier chapters relating to electronic commerce that cryptography can be an important tool of crime prevention. An environment in which multinational companies can conduct their business free from risks of espionage and intrusion is an attractive prospect. Combined with user authentication, cryptography can help safeguard data against unauthorised alteration, such as changing the value of an electronic payment.

Whatever their utility to criminals, telecommunications are regarded as a key to social and economic development. Current conventional wisdom holds that full development of the technology will be best achieved by minimising regulatory burdens.

It would appear, at least in the United States and Australia, and perhaps in the European Community, that the advantages which can flow from something approaching a free market in encryption technology and a deregulated telecommunications environment will triumph over law enforcement imperatives. Should this come to pass, law enforcement in the 21st century will be required to demonstrate a degree of resourcefulness significantly greater than that of its criminal adversaries.

11

TOWARDS SECURITY AND PROSPERITY IN CYBERSPACE

The preceding nine chapters have provided a graphic demonstration of how developments in telecommunications have enhanced the possibilities for those less honest members of the community to engage in criminal or otherwise deviant conduct. One may confidently assert that the future will see a substantial increase in the number of potential targets and potential perpetrators of digital crime. The capacity of governments, singly or collectively, to control some forms of telecommunications and cyberspace illegality is, and seems destined to remain, limited. The fundamental question, therefore, is in what situations will self-help suffice, and when does the "mobilisation of law" (Black 1973) become appropriate?

Often, technological changes have enabled new forms of conduct to emerge which were not previously considered to be illegal, and these have resulted in legislative action to proscribe the conduct in question. The interception of telecommunications is a good example of conduct which has only recently been the subject of legislative controls throughout the world, and even these controls are not considered to be adequate to regulate the problem effectively.

If we consider the nine forms of illegality examined in this book, it is apparent that developments in computing and communications technology have not so much enabled new types of crime to emerge, but rather have enabled existing forms of deviance to be carried out more extensively, more efficiently, more quickly, with greater ease of concealment, and thus with greater difficulty of detection. Not to mention with more profound impact in terms of the harm caused.

Telephone communications have, for example, been intercepted since telecommunications systems were first developed but now they may be intercepted more easily through the use of digital scanners rather than through having to affix alligator clips to wires. The wilful destruction of property has always been a problem, and online facilities have merely enabled such vandalism to occur against electronic targets rather than physical ones. Devices to obtain telephone calls without payment have been used since the early 1960s, but their newest models now enable millions of dollars to be taken from international telecommunications networks. People have copied works in breach of copyright since the first monopolies were granted over publication, but now copying may be carried out almost instantaneously through electronic means. People have been tricked into buying worthless or non-existent goods through telephone advertising for many years, but now such conduct may be carried on from home with connections to millions of potential victims throughout the world. Telephone wires have been used to carry out business transactions and to transfer funds for the past century, but now the sums of money being carried have increased substantially, and the speed and complexity of transactions have made the opportunities for illegal gain more rewarding. Finally, the activities of criminal organisations have been made easier and more anonymous through the use of digital communications systems.

It may be concluded, therefore, that digitisation has greatly facilitated the ease with which crime may be committed. It has occasionally given rise to forms of conduct which the community has determined should be proscribed. The motivations for such offending, however, have changed little. Greed, need, mischief-making, voyeurism, envy, and vengeance still remain the primary reasons behind crime in the digital age and it is to these motivations that regulatory controls need to be directed. However, history has taught us that conventional legal channels do not always meet with success in bringing about positive changes in human motivation. Accordingly, the technology of crime prevention may be enlisted to help control future offending.

Technology thus provides both a tool to enable further offending to take place, as well as a possible control mechanism for use in prevention, detection, and prosecution. Gone are the days, however, when crime control could be achieved without the assistance of telecommunications and computer technicians.

Technological changes of the future

As we move into the 21st century, the forms of telecommunications-related crime will alter. Some may disappear while others will expand; some may diversify, while still others may be created. The speed, capacity, accessibility, and commercialisation of information technology are all likely to increase. Dramatically enhanced searching and surveillance capabilities will be confronted by greater access to crypto-graphic technologies.

Digital technology will undoubtedly enhance the speed and efficiency with which the nine forms of illegality, discussed above, may be carried out, and the profits to be realised from telecommunications crime will grow substantially. The increasing demand for telecommunications services will lead to an expansion and improvement in the types and quality of services which will be available. Digitisation will be the primary factor in enhancing the quality of voice, data, and image-based services while improved delivery technologies will ensure that services are provided across the globe. As existing copper coaxial and unshielded twisted pair (UTP) cables are replaced by hybrid fibre coaxial cable (HFC), the range of services available will be greatly improved. Broadband interactive television services, for example, will be capable of wide-scale delivery and satellite technologies will greatly expand the regions throughout the world from which people will be able to gain access to these services. Such technological improvements will, however, greatly expand the range of opportunities for unlawful conduct. Not only will offenders of the future try to gain access to these services at little or no cost to themselves, but the telecommunications infrastructure itself may be the object of theft or vandalism. One can imagine the gratification which members of a terrorist organisation would derive from destroying a communications satellite.

Just as the Internet has provided an hospitable environment in which organised paedophiles may operate, groups of individuals will be able to coordinate their activities in relation to each of the nine forms of illegality which previous chapters have considered. This will result in law enforcement agencies being faced with a considerable challenge in terms of the technological expertise required to engage in effective policing in the future. Traditional law enforcement strategies will, however, also be required in conjunction with high-technology approaches. Often the most sophisticated offender will make mistakes and leave a trail of evidence which may be followed by means of conventional policing skills. At other times, methods of undercover investigation may be appropriate.

It is also likely that the social importance which is attached to various human activities will change with the evolution of technology. Because technology will permit individuals to record and analyse much greater amounts of personal data, including health information and information about an individual's daily activities such as spending patterns, privacy will become a significant issue. Governments may be compelled to expand existing privacy protections to ensure that technology is not used for unnecessarily intrusive record-keeping by private sector organisations or by agencies of the state.

Technology will also enable people to communicate more freely throughout the globe and this will result in new forms of interjurisdictional offending such as moving information or funds between countries electronically in breach of the rules of individual nation states. The export of encryption software, gambling services, offensive materials, and large amounts of money are good examples of this.

Finally, technological changes will enhance the number of offences which may be perpetrated in the digital age. It is just as easy to steal one work in breach of copyright on the Internet as it is to steal a thousand, while a computer chip embedded in a smart card may be used to record ten thousand pages of unlawful material just as easily as ten.

Chronology of changes

In considering the relationship between the introduction of telecommunications technology and the commission of offences which make use of such technology, it is helpful to employ a chronological framework.

Table 8 presents a diagram of such a framework in which each of the nine forms of illegality considered in this book is arranged according to the period of time during which it first achieved significance. The moment of emergence of each form of offending cannot be specified with great precision, but an indication can be given of which forms of illegality achieved significance earlier rather than later in the twentieth century, and which are of most recent origin. Each of the forms of illegality continues to exist, although not in exactly the same form as it started life (telegraphic interception, for example, now may be carried out through the airwaves).

Table 8
A Chronology of Telecommunications Crime

<1900	1960	1970	1980	1990	2000
Illegal Interception ———————————————————————————————————→					
Conspiracies ———————————————————————————————————→					
Theft of Services ———————————————————————————→					
		Telemarketing Fraud ————————————————→			
		Money Laundering —————————————→			
		Hacking ————————————————→			
		Pornography—————————→			
		EFT Fraud —————————→			
		Piracy —————————→			

Table 8 also permits a comparison between the various forms of illegality and the introduction of new technologies. Telecommunications technology was first created in 1837, while the earliest example of illegal interception occurred in 1867. The 1960s saw a rapid expansion in the use of telephony services which corresponded with attempts at obtaining services for nothing through "phreaking". The introduction of electronic funds transfer technologies such as ATM and EFTPOS led to the use of such facilities to transfer funds illegally in the 1970s, which was followed by the widespread use of computer networks which corresponded with the commission of money laundering and hacking offences. Most recently, the introduction of the Internet in the late 1980s has created an environment in which copyright may be infringed and offensive materials disseminated across international networks.

Part of the challenge for law enforcement is dealing with the speed at which new technological advances may be exploited for illegitimate purposes. This problem may be exacerbated by those with the necessary expertise leaving employment in the telecommunications industry for more lucrative pursuits in the underworld. In this respect, there is evidence of telecommunications employees either being involved in the commission of offences or, at least, lending their expertise to others to do so, for many years now (see Vincent 1984).

What is of particular interest is the phenomenon of displacement in telecommunications crime. As one avenue of offending is closed by developments within the industry, another is created by those seeking to make use of new technology for unlawful activity. This is clearly apparent in the case of theft of telecommunications services. As each new way of obtaining services without payment was closed off from within the industry, new techniques were devised to achieve the same result only through the use of different technological means. In the jargon of the time, the "Blue Box" (switching system by-pass) gave way to the "Black Box" (meter inhibition), which gave way to the "Red Box" (coin drop simulation), all within the space of ten years or so (see Clough and Mungo 1992)).

Detection and reporting

Detection of offending

In few other areas of law enforcement is the detection of crime as difficult as in the digital world. Although human actors are present in the commission of crime, their activities and identities are often concealed by a technological veil making the results of their conduct undetectable to all but the most determined agencies.

Unlike analogue transmissions, the process of digitisation makes electro-magnetic impulses difficult to decipher without the use of appropriate equipment. Where communications have been encrypted, the transmission may be impossible to decipher by all but those who possess the relevant decryption keys. This has created the profound problem for law enforcement, discussed in a number of previous chapters, of whether government law enforcement agencies should always be provided with the means of access to encrypted messages.

The speed with which messages may be transmitted also creates problems of detection. Funds may be transferred internationally in seconds, leaving little or no trail with which to detect infringements of cash transaction and money laundering laws. Obscene images may appear on a computer screen for seconds only, with no record being maintained or copy kept of what was displayed. We have seen, for example, that instead of computer line interception, this problem can be solved through the use of video cameras installed in a suspect's computer designed to record the image rather than the electronic information which gives rise to the image. Unfortunately, existing interception laws do not extend to video computer surveillance in most jurisdictions through-out the world. It is, in any event, an extremely cumbersome means of investigation.

Some crimes may also be committed without any form of physical contact or without leaving any physical trace. Scanning radio communications and computer screen electromagnetic radiation are cases in point. The offender is able to obtain information without the victim being made aware of the inter-ception until such time as some loss has been suffered or other disadvantageous result ensues. Many copyright infringements which take place on the Internet may also be carried out without leaving any trace; the owner's work is left unscathed, but identical copies made which may destroy the commercial market for the work.

In other cases, an offence may be carried out but the adverse consequences not brought into effect for some considerable time. Time and logic bombs planted in computer networks may be undetectable until they "explode", sometimes years after they were installed.

Finally, there are the situations in which individuals simply do not know that they have been victimised, such as where bogus charitable solicitations on the Internet result in members of the public giving funds to non-existent charities.

Technology may, however, assist in the detection of offending. Computer Anomaly Detection Systems (CADS), for example, are computer programs which use the power of the computer to identify suspicious activity. A simple example is a program that monitors when individuals log onto a computer system. Assuming a certain user logs on every day between 8 and 9 am, the computer can notify a system administrator whenever that user's password is entered at any other time. Thus, an intruder who uses that password at 3 am will be detected by the computer and investigative action may then be taken (Charney 1996).

Although technology may be able to detect some crimes in years to come, substantial resources will be needed by law enforcement agencies to keep pace with the technological developments which are occurring.

Reporting of offences

Even if telecommunications crime is detected, it is by no means certain that it will be reported to the authorities. A wide range of factors may make reporting personally unattractive or commercially unviable, leading to a substantial "dark figure" of unreported crime which detracts from the utility of official police statistics. Despite the following impediments, more thorough reporting of incidents is a necessary step to the better understanding and control of telecommunications-related crime. A regime of mandatory reporting to law enforcement authorities may be unrealistic, although perhaps less so for military and other public sector organisations. At the very least, however, measures to encourage and facilitate voluntary disclosure of victimisation should be developed. These could include anonymous third-party clearinghouses, CERTs, or other private information systems.[1]

To be victimised in the digital age may be an obvious demonstration of one's foolishness, stupidity, or lack of care. Telemarketing fraud victims will often, for example, be humiliated by the experience and unwilling to make their experience public. Some victims may also be implicated in present or past criminal activity, and obviously not want law enforcement agencies examining their own conduct as part of a wider investigation into the reasons for their victimisation. The situation which arose with the Nigerian scam letters is a good example of how victims would be unlikely to report having suffered a loss through their own avarice by being willing to defraud a national government.

Other victims, particularly commercial organisations, may be commercially embarrassed by their having suffered a security breach and willing to suffer the loss privately in order not to lose custom in a highly competitive environment. The reasons why businesses may be reluctant to report crime range from the time wasted by employees in attending court, to dissatisfaction with the penalties imposed. It is much simpler and cheaper, either to claim the losses on insurance or merely pass on the costs to the customers. The reluctance of telecommunications carriers to report security breaches is a clear example of this, as is the reluctance of banks to declare that their funds transfer systems are less than secure.

In a recent survey of hacking conducted by the Computer Security Institute in the United States, less than 17 per cent of respondents had reported incidents to law enforcement agencies, with 70 per cent citing fear of negative

---

1   Staff Statement, United States Senate Permanent Subcommittee on Investigations (Minority Staff) Hearings on Security in Cyberspace, 5 June 1996. http://www.senate.gov/~gov_affairs/ dem/psi/hearings/960605/staffsta.htm

publicity as the primary reason for non-reporting (Computer Security Institute 1996b).

There is also the perceived futility of reporting incidents where nothing can be done to recover the loss sustained, and where the chances of obtaining a conviction are remote. Once a copyright protected work appears on the Internet, for example, a market for its sale may be lost and if the work has been re-routed through various remailing sites, the chances of finding the offender may be impossible. It is in such situations that a commercial solution may be desirable, such as by regularly up-dating information in a work, making each version useful for a limited period of time.

Finally, there is the perception that law enforcement may be incapable or reluctant to investigate digital crimes and that even if a prosecution were to be successful, the sanctions meted out would most likely be inadequate. It is to these issues that we now shall turn.

Law enforcement

Expanded data collection and analysis procedures

Given the substantial dark figure of telecommunications crime, it is important to gather as much information on patterns and trends of offending as can be made available. Encouraging victims to come forward with details of their experience is the obvious first step. Law enforcement and research agencies across the various jurisdictions need to collect and collate data in a consistent, detailed, and uniform manner. In particular, the use of a national database including all forms of high technology crime would be an invaluable tool in describing patterns of offending and in predicting the likely course which offending in the future will follow.

Already steps are being taken to conduct systematic surveys of crime in the digital age. In the United States, for example, the Computer Security Institute conducts regular computer crime and security surveys which give an indication of the extent to which various forms of online and computer crime take place, and what security procedures are being used to prevent it (see Computer Security Institute 1996a).

The need for coordination

Systematic sharing of information across jurisdictions is also important as many offences take place internationally. Communication and coordination between law enforcement agencies is essential. The necessity for coordination becomes particularly important in a federal system, where a variety of law enforcement and court systems exist. In addition, because many telecommunications offences involve offenders and victims in a variety of countries, it is important to have international coordination and cooperation.

Already such cooperation is emerging in the realm of computer crime, with the Australian Federal Police establishing cooperative liaison with various agencies including the Australian Security Emergency Response Team, the Australian Academic and Research Network and the Defence Research Program in the United States. Such liaison has been important in achieving a number of successful outcomes in international computer hacking investigations in recent times (Australian Federal Police 1995).

In the United States, the National Fraud Information Centre maintains a data base dedicated to telemarketing fraud which allows law enforcement officials desktop access to information about consumer complaints, ongoing investigations, and active or recent cases against alleged perpetrators of telemarketing fraud. Consumers can add their own complaints to this database, which is now available to nearly one hundred law enforcement agencies as well as being on the Internet. The United States Securities and Exchange Commission also maintains a Web site (http://www.sec.gov/enforce/comctr.htm) and invites online reporting of incidents of suspected securities fraud.

The Federal Bureau of Investigation has established computer crime squads in selected offices throughout the United States which are charged with investigating a wide range of infringements of telecommunications and computer laws. These include intrusions to public switched networks, major computer intrusions, privacy violations, industrial espionage, pirated computer software and other crimes where the computer is a major factor in committing the criminal offence (see Computer Security Institute 1996a).

Barnes (1994) provides a useful summary of doctrines or interventions which have been used to support international law enforcement. One may easily see that given the financial cost and political risks which they may entail, such interventions are likely to be employed in only the most extreme cases.

Some jurisdictions seek to prosecute offences committed abroad by foreign nationals against their own citizens. The United States, for example, can seek extradition of alleged terrorists who have offended against citizens of the United States while abroad.

The abduction of suspects from foreign soil and subsequent prosecution is an old, if controversial, practice. The most prominent example in recent times involved the kidnapping of Adolf Eichmann by Israeli agents; a more recent example entailed the abduction in Mexico at the behest of authorities in the United States of a suspect implicated in the murder of a DEA agent (*United States v Alvarez-Machain*, 112 S Ct 2188 (1992)). Other forms of intervention may entail the opportunistic seizure of passengers in transit, or apprehension through military invasion, as was the case with General Noriega of Panama, and assassination, as employed against the publishers and translators of the works of Salman Rushdie.

Even the domestic policing of digital illegality may require measures which go beyond traditional law enforcement tactics. The technologies of encryption and anonymity noted above are invoked to justify aggressive investigative methods such as covert facilitation, more commonly referred to as "stings". We have already seen how in mid-1995, the FBI charged an adult male who had arranged over the Internet to meet someone at a motel whom he thought was a 14-year-old girl. The Internet contact was in fact an FBI agent. Similar tactics have been directed at those who traffic in pornographic material. We have also seen how law enforcement officers in the United States intercepted electronic mail replies to advertisements which agents had placed in which they pretended to be prospective purchasers of cloned mobile telephones (Chapter 4 above). Laws will vary across jurisdictions with regard to the defence of entrapment, and the extent to which an offence was encouraged or suggested by police (Chandrasekaran 1996).

To the extent that international telecommunications-related crime is amenable to international enforcement, it will require concerted international cooperation. Past performance in the context of other forms of criminality would suggest that this cooperation is unlikely to be forthcoming except in the relatively infrequent types of illegality where there is widespread international consensus about the activity in question, and about the desirability of suppressing it. In many instances, extradition is likely to be more cumbersome, the greater the cultural and ideological distance between the nations involved.

Need for specialist units and improved training

Achieving inter-jurisdictional cooperation is, however, only part of the challenge facing law enforcement agencies.[2] We have seen throughout the preceding discussion, the need for law enforcement agencies to be better resourced and for officers to be trained in telecommunications and computer technology. Such training does not come cheaply, but governments would be well advised to devote just as many resources to preventing and detecting crime as are being expended by criminal organisations in availing themselves of the opportunities for crime which exist in the digital age.

Use of technological consultancies

Where the available resources within agencies are lacking, it may be preferable for governments to engage consultants trained in security management and computer forensic science to undertake the necessary investigations. As down-sizing of telecommunications organisations continues to occur, there will be a ready supply of trained technicians with the skills needed by law enforcement and security agencies. Governments should seek to make full use of the expertise they have to offer. The engagement of such individuals needs, of course, to be conducted with adequate security checks in place in order to ensure that confidential technical information is not made available to the criminal world.

Increased funding and staffing

At a more general level, governments may need to allocate much greater resources to combat telecommunications crime. Although industry often builds into budgets the estimated losses to be expected from such offending, the losses in terms of overall expansion of business may be of such a magnitude that they can no longer be ignored. Already we have seen the computer software industry take decisive steps in order to prevent copyright infringement and it is to be expected that similar campaigns will be taken to deal with various other forms of digital crime. Business may even be willing to devote resources to assisting government law enforcement agencies to take action in pursuing digital criminals

---

2   For a discussion of the challenges to the detection and investigation of crime in cyberspace, see Australia 1996, Chapter 5.

(Marx 1987). Government spending should, however, be done in a manner which encourages the market to devise preventive technologies.

Legal system

Harmonisation of laws

Part of the difficulty in conducting effective prosecution of telecommunications crime, lies in the wide variety of potential charges which may be brought. Within each jurisdiction, telecommunications crime may entail various offences which apply both to telecommunications and to computer systems. There are also the many traditional laws relating to property offences which may be used to prosecute various online crimes.

Within Australia, attempts at codification of the criminal law uniformly across all jurisdictions are progressing with the *Model Criminal Code* being drafted by the Commonwealth's Standing Committee of Attorneys-General, Model Criminal Code Officers Committee. Although the enactment of laws based on this code in each jurisdiction may solve the problems associated with the general provisions of the criminal law, reform may also be needed to deal with specific telecommunications and computer offences. One possibility would be for all such criminal offence provisions which relate to Federal jurisdiction to be contained within the *Crimes Act* 1914 (Cth), rather than having the criminal provisions scattered across many other statutes such as those regulating telecommunications, copyright, and banking. This may help to focus the attentions of federal law enforcement agencies when mounting prosecutions.

In addition, there is the problem that telecommunications offences may involve a number of jurisdictions internationally, with the offender, the victim, and the technology necessary to carry out the offence all being present in different countries. This, of course, can lead to the anomalous situation of the same conduct giving rise to criminal liability in one jurisdiction, but not in another.

Although most countries have laws which enable prosecutions to take place where illegal conduct has only some limited connection with the jurisdiction in question, such as the offender being within the jurisdiction when the offence takes place or causing a result which occurs within the jurisdiction in question, telecommunications crime raises various problems of interpretation in this regard. We have already seen that the defendant in the case of *R v Jones* (3 June 1993, County Court of Victoria, Smith J) who hacked into the computers of NASA using a computer in Melbourne, was prosecuted for offences against the Victorian *Crimes Act* 1958 following a direction of the court that the relevant provisions had extra-territorial application. What may be needed is clearer more specific legislation clarifying this matter such as exists in Minnesota's general criminal jurisdiction statute (1994 §609.025) which has been interpreted to apply to illegal activities conducted on the Internet (see: http://www.state.mn.us/ebranch/ag/memo.txt).

Expanded extradition capabilities

Traditionally, the jurisdiction of courts was local. That is, courts could only entertain prosecutions in respect of offences committed against local laws where there existed a sufficient link between the offence and the jurisdiction in question. There is, however, always the possibility that parliament will specifically grant extraterritorial jurisdiction. Some common examples include offences committed on the high seas, counterfeiting offences, crimes committed by members of the defence forces, and, recently, underage sexual offences committed by Australians travelling overseas.

In rare circumstances, a nation's laws may apply to acts committed overseas by foreign nationals. General Noriega, currently imprisoned in the United States, was convicted for activities which he undertook in Panama. Iranian authorities found the writings of Salman Rushdie so repugnant that he remains under a death sentence for a book which he wrote far from Iran, and which has not been published there. Recent war crimes prosecutions in Australia involved defendants resident elsewhere at the times the alleged offences were committed. But these circumstances are, to say the least, most unusual.

One need only look at how it has taken a quarter century to achieve a modicum of international cooperation regarding drug trafficking, money laundering, and other manifestations of organised crime, to imagine the difficulties inherent in achieving meaningful international consensus about anything other than perhaps child pornography (Friman 1994).

Even so, this would assume a seamless world system of stable sovereign states. Such a system does not exist today, nor is it likely to exist in our lifetime. Law enforcement and regulatory vacuums exist in some parts of the world, certainly in those settings where the state has effectively collapsed. Even where state power does exist in full force, the corruption of individual regimes can impede international cooperation.

Where serious offences have been carried out by individuals residing in various countries, the need for functional and clear extradition laws arises. In the absence of an international criminal court, individual nation states will still be required to pursue criminals who commit crimes beyond their own borders by prosecuting them locally, and extradition is one way in which this may be achieved. There is, accordingly, an ongoing need for extradition capabilities to be expanded to all countries which make use of telecommunications systems, especially the 177 or so which at present use the Internet.[3]

Reliance on international treaties

One of the clearest ways in which to ensure that uniform laws apply to telecommunications crime throughout the globe is for international treaties to be developed, and those which already exist, to be expanded to deal with the range of crimes which may be carried out using telecommunications facilities. Already, international treaties regulate intellectual property, and it would be appropriate to

---

3   Technology, of course can facilitate the identification of international fugitives. The United States Justice Department has an international fugitive lookout website: http://www.usdoj .gov/criminal/oiafug/page1.htm

create other treaties which will ensure that telecommunications criminal laws are uniform and capable of coordinated application throughout the world. Organisations such as the Organisation for Economic Cooperation and Development (OECD), are well-placed to facilitate such reform.

Ongoing review of laws to deal with technological changes

As we have seen, technological developments over the last century have provided a wide range of new criminal opportunities. These developments have also resulted in some existing laws becoming outmoded and incapable of effective use against the new forms of digital crime. Even developments such as the introduction of uniform criminal laws throughout the various States and Territories of Australia in the form of the Model Criminal Code will need ongoing monitoring and review to keep pace with technological changes. In the future, for example, the widespread use of broadband interactive services may make certain laws inappropriate while new technological capabilities of interception of communications may require new legislative controls. Emerging technologies may present new regulatory opportunities as well. In her separate opinion in *Reno v ACLU*, Justice O'Connor suggested that developments in gateway technology might permit more effective "zoning" of cyberspace in due course.[4]

The continual downsizing of government and contracting out of government services, however, may result in the situation in which no agency will be charged with the responsibility of monitoring the effectiveness and applicability of the laws which apply throughout the country.

Evidentiary reforms

One particular area of the law which will need reform to deal with the expansion in digital crime is that which regulates the use of evidence in criminal proceedings. Although the Australian Federal Government has reformed its laws of evidence with the enactment of the *Evidence Act* 1995 (Cth), other jurisdictions will need to consider the changes which are required to accommodate the new technologies.

As we have already seen, an OECD report some time ago identified various evidentiary problems associated with prosecuting computer crime including those which relate to search and seizure, service of documents, and the taking of testimony (OECD 1986).

Sanctioning reforms

The final area of legal reform relates to the range and use of sanctions available for digital crime. Those rare cases of telecommunications crime which result in a conviction, seem not to attract severe sentences, a problem common to other areas of white collar and high technology crime. Offenders may be seen as not inflicting serious harm or not being motivated by entirely antisocial values when carrying

---

4   26 June 1997, Supreme Court of the United States.

out such crime, and thus not deserving of the most severe sanctions traditionally reserved for offences which result in personal injury.

We have seen many examples of instances in which telecommunications offenders have received seemingly less than adequate punishments. In one recent case in Victoria, for example, an offender received an eight-month term of imprisonment, four months of which was suspended, for stealing 100 mobile telephones from motor cars in the inner city region of East Melbourne (Adams 1996). Assuming the value of these goods totalled A$20,000, one wonders if a court would have imposed a similarly lenient sentence on an individual who stole such a sum in cash.

In the computer hacking case involving three individuals in Melbourne who obtained unauthorised access to computers at the CSIRO, University of Melbourne, and NASA, suspended sentences and community-based orders were imposed, despite the fact that their activities caused considerable disruption to these organisations (Australia, Director of Public Prosecutions 1994).

Telecommunications crime may, however, entail substantial financial losses which may destroy small businesses or result in severely adverse personal consequences for individuals. "Stalking" the Internet is a case in point. As community attitudes to computer crime change, so will its perceived seriousness. Eventually, such attitudes will be reflected in the sentencing remarks of the judiciary. In a celebrated American case in which the offender had introduced a "worm" into a computer system causing tens of thousands of dollars in rectification costs, a sentence of three years' probation, 400 hours of community service and a fine of US$10,050 and costs of supervision were imposed (*United States v Morris* 928 F 2d 504 (1991)). In the first conviction obtained in respect of the transmission of material involving images of bestiality and sexual fetishes over the Internet, a Californian couple were sentenced respectively to thirty-seven months' and thirty months' imprisonment, the sentence being upheld on appeal (*United States v Thomas* Fed App. 0032P (6th Cir) (1996).

Sentencing a telecommunications offender may, however, require imagination and innovation. Often a prison term will be inappropriate and a fine ineffective in terms of specific and general deterrence. More effective sanctions may involve community service by requiring offenders to teach computer skills to disadvantaged groups or to repair computers damaged through viral infections. Publicity sanctions may also be highly effective for Internet offenders and courts may require convicted offenders to be clearly identified on a Internet "Prison Home Page", thus constituting a form of digital shaming.

Offenders may also be ordered to refrain from using online services for specified periods or have their online activities monitored electronically. In recent times when electronic tagging by way of wristlets and anklets is popular in some countries, an extension to online monitoring is not implausible. The United States Parole Commission has recently approved the discretionary use of special conditions of parole which would restrict parolees' use of online services. For example, they may be required to obtain prior written permission before using the Internet; refrain from possessing or using data encryption programmes; permit the monitoring of their computer usage; or maintain a daily log of computer usage (Anonymous 1997b).

Caution may, however, be needed in imposing overly severe conditional requirements on offenders and parolees. The case of Kevin Lee Poulsen is illustrative. Poulsen was convicted in the United States of various computer hacking offences for which he received a five-year term of imprisonment. On release from prison in July 1996, conditions were imposed as part of his parole that he pay restitution of US$57,925.69 and refrain from possessing computer equipment or working with computer equipment without the permission of his probation officer, for a three-year period. Such conditions may prove to be unworkable as Poulsen's principal skill lay in computing, and without access to computers he may be unable to find employment and be unable to make restitution. Arguably, strict supervision of his use of computers may have been a better condition to impose than one which required complete inability to work with computers (Morello 1996).

Finally, confiscation of assets and profits may be a powerful tool in the hands of the courts, especially where expensive computer hardware and software has been used in the commission of offences. Where large organisations such as online service providers have been convicted of an offence, seizure of their computer equipment may be a substantial deterrent as well as a considerable revenue enhancement strategy for the State. Law enforcement agencies may also have the satisfaction of being able to use confiscated computers to conduct their own investigations into other crimes, such as occurred in Sydney recently where a convicted computer hacker's equipment was given to the computer crime office of the Australian Federal Police (Australian Federal Police 1995).

In Australia, we have seen how legal reforms have facilitated the prosecution of transnational crimes and the confiscation of profits derived from such illegality. The challenge for governments is to make sure that those agencies which are charged with the administration of such schemes, such as the Australian Transaction Reports and Analysis Centre, are adequately funded and provided with the facilities necessary to support such international crime prevention activities.

Preventive countermeasures

Turning now to preventive countermeasures, it seems appropriate to think in terms of a variety of institutions and instruments which can be brought to bear on the illegalities in question. The varied nature of telecommunications-related illegality defies a single policy solution. Indeed, each of the basic forms of illegality described above is sufficiently complex, that if a solution exists at all, it is likely to be both context specific, and to entail a combination of instruments. In general, this combination will include elements of self-protection by prospective victims of digital crime; market-based commercial solutions; self-regulatory initiatives by the targets of regulation; traditional law enforcement or regulatory intervention by the state; and third party "co-production" of surveillance by private individuals and citizens' groups.

Moreover, the pace of technological change will almost certainly necessitate frequent adaptation of law enforcement and regulatory solutions in response to new challenges. Recognising the inevitability and rapidity of change, one is inclined to risk sounding equivocal rather than attempt to enunciate solutions which might soon appear outmoded.

It goes almost without saying that the most potentially fruitful focus for the control of digital crime is prevention. While this should not be taken as suggesting that the detection, investigation and prosecution of "digital offending" is beyond the capacity of governments, the preceding chapters have illustrated the considerable difficulty and expense which reactive response usually entails. Issues of prosecution and deterrence aside, the information to be gained from such activity can be extremely valuable. Accordingly, the most productive investments are to be made in prevention. In cyberspace, as in health policy, prevention is better than cure.

Given the rich variety of digital crime described in the chapters above (not to mention the diverse motives of those who would perpetrate such offences), it should be apparent that there will be no single best strategy for control or prevention. Indeed, any single policy instrument is likely to have its shortcomings or limitations. We have just seen how conventional law enforcement, for example, has but a limited capacity to patrol cyberspace, to identify telecommunications criminals, and to provide the evidentiary basis for a successful prosecution. It would thus seem appropriate that scarce and valuable law enforcement resources be reserved for the most serious forms of telecommunications-related illegality, rather than be spread too thin in the pursuit of relatively minor matters. Individual citizens may be able to protect themselves to some extent. Market solutions will have some applicability. Inextricably bound with these are emerging technologies themselves. The following pages discuss these basic forms of preventive mechanism.

Self-help

As the story goes, a former Governor of California was asked at his inaugural press conference what he proposed to do about the State's rising crime rate. "Stay low, move fast, and not carry a lot of cash" he is said to have replied.

With telecommunications-related crime, as with more conventional forms of criminality, the first line of defence lies in the exercise of prudent behaviour by prospective victims. Just as the first step in the control of burglary is to lock one's doors and windows, so too the basic principles of information security should be honoured by any individual or institution at risk. Whether the risk in question entails becoming the victim of hacking, fraud, or unwilling exposure to objectionable content, individuals and organisations can take positive steps to protect themselves. The exercise of simple prudence based on an understanding of systems will suffice in many cases. While standards of simple prudence have already improved substantially from those which prevailed when Clifford Stoll (1991) confronted his intruder, they nevertheless remain inadequate.

Many organisations have no written policy on how to deal with network intrusions, or on how to preserve evidence for criminal or civil proceedings. Many do not even know if they have been attacked, and of those which do know, the threat of adverse publicity inhibits them from reporting the incident.

Changes which most of the world's economies are currently experiencing have been accompanied by pain as well as by benefit. Both are accompanied by risk. Those who regard themselves as the victims of economic change may well seek to extract revenge upon their former employers or upon "the system" generally. Disgruntled former employees with expertise in information technology are in a position to inflict significant damage. We have already seen massive downsizing in the North American telecommunications industry. In the years to come when telecommunications and information technology organisations expand and contract, the number of displaced individuals with the skills necessary to engage in unlawful practices may present a significant threat. This calls for great care in the management of human resources and heightened attentiveness to issues of security. Indeed, the results of a survey fielded by the Computer Security Institute (1996a) revealed that over 50 per cent of institutions which experienced intrusions, or attempted probes of their internal systems, traced them to *current* employees.

Individuals, too, can act to protect themselves against all but the most persistent attacks. The exercise of simple prudence can help safeguard Personal Identification Numbers, account passwords and credit card details. It is as easy to avoid objectionable content on the Internet as it is to find it. Proper parental supervision can protect children from inappropriate images, as well as from the "electronic lurking stranger".

After the event, the first line of redress may lie with victims too. The usual avenue of recourse in cases of intellectual property infringement is the civil courts in an action for damages. In Australia, the vast majority of actions taken in respect of infringements of the *Trade Practices Act* are by private parties. In both Australia and the United States, companies and securities regulators allow private actions on the part of aggrieved parties.

Successful private litigation may result in awards of damages that exceed criminal penalties available to the state; the deterrent effect posed by many potential private enforcers should not be underestimated. This can extend to libel. We noted above how a university lecturer in Western Australia was awarded substantial damages after having been the subject of unflattering comment on the Internet (*Rindos v Hardwick*, 31 March 1994, Supreme Court of Western Australia; unreported decision 1994/1993, SCLN #940164).

These private legal solutions are likely to be more effective within jurisdictions than across them. One would not expect Microsoft, for example, to receive a great deal of comfort from the legal process of the People's Republic of China. Organisations with access to considerable resources may, however, pursue telecommunications offenders across the globe. A recent example involves the protracted litigation being taken by the Church of Scientology (The Religious Technology Centre) in respect of alleged copyright infringements on the Internet. Such remedies do not come cheaply, however, and one of the problems of private remedies is that they are only available to those who are able to afford them.

In those instances where service providers may be aware of the injurious nature of the content, they too may be liable. In these circumstances, legal risk helps to leverage an extra degree of scrutiny which might not otherwise occur.

Self-help is least relevant to those circumstances involving the use of telecommunications systems in furtherance of money laundering and other organised criminal activity. By their nature clandestine, and intended specifically to avoid the attention of third parties, these forms of illegality will require other countermeasures.

As we now will observe, technologies to assist in self-defence are being provided in abundance and sophistication by one of the world's growth industries of today — the computer security industry. Corporations in the United States, for example, are said to have spent US$6 billion on network security in 1996 (Behar 1997).

Commercial solutions

An additional avenue of prevention exists in the market itself, which may deliver products and services to assist individuals to defend themselves against digital illegality. This avenue entails technological and commercial solutions in furtherance of self-help, as it were.

First and foremost is the design of systems. Neumann (1995) has compiled a litany of computer mishaps, many of which occurred not as a result of malicious intervention, but simply because of software malfunctions. Good design can greatly reduce the risk of systems crashing unaided; they can also reduce their vulnerability to unauthorised penetration.

Computer security is a thriving industry. Enormous profits will fall to those who successfully develop various technologies for protecting telecommunications systems against intrusions. Intrusion detection systems and anomaly detection devices will be essential for managing risks of digital crime in years ahead.

In addition to more rigorous management practices and the introduction of more sophisticated password and verification procedures, new technologies such as biometric security devices and anomaly detection computer software, which identify unusual patterns of computer use, help alert organisations to system weaknesses and enhance the security of computer systems themselves (Russell and Gangemi 1991; Price 1996). Other security tools record keystrokes of individuals accessing a computer system and automatically match them against the keystroke patterns of known hackers. The system then makes an analysis of the threat and assesses its seriousness. This technology discovered over 2000 attempted intrusions at US Air Force installations in 1995 (US Senate 1996).[5] Similarly, sophisticated technologies based on artificial intelligence and neural networking may be used to detect suspicious financial transactions. Security systems do not rely exclusively on technology, and can involve what are colloquially termed "tiger teams". IBM has a team of "ethical hackers" who are themselves immersed in the hacker culture, and who are available to conduct integrity tests of a client's system at the client's request (Butler Group 1996).

In addition, there is likely to be an increasing market for damage control services in the aftermath of an attack on telecommunications systems. Victimised

---

5   It should be noted that automated intrusion technologies leave much less of a "signature" than do manual intrusion attempts.

organisations may well be more concerned about enhancing system security and restoring normal operations than about mobilising the law. The latter course of action may, inevitably, attract public attention to their vulnerability. The development of computer emergency response teams (CERTs), industry-funded and arms length from law enforcement, helps meet this need.[6] IBM has a 24-hour emergency response service which delivers incident management assistance and damage control to clients who have experienced intrusions (Butler Group 1996).

Ideally, telecommunications emergency services, whether organised under private sector auspices or under those of government, will develop in a manner which permits an organised accumulation of wisdom. Effective control of telecommunications-related crime will be enhanced by systematic information on patterns and trends. One sees the beginnings of such an approach with catalogues and typologies of viruses, the alerts publicised by various CERTs around the world (Telstra 1996), and the technologies which identify keystroke patterns and other idiosyncrasies of known intruders (Price 1996). Such systematic knowledge can assist in short-term damage control, and may also be useful in identifying offenders. It can also serve as the basis for public information and education.

In another area of risk, consider the problem of restricting access to offensive materials on the Internet. A rich variety of commercial software now exists with which to block access to certain sites.[7] In addition, a market is currently emerging for service providers specialising in content suitable for family consumption, guaranteed to be free of sex, violence, and vilification.

The commercial potential of the Internet, which may well become the dominant medium of commerce in our lifetime, has not been lost on entrepreneurs around the world. No individual or institution has a greater vested interest in the security of (and public confidence in) electronic payment systems than major financial institutions and credit card companies. Commercially developed technologies will seek to safeguard the trust which is required as a basis for commerce, and minimise the risk of abuse. At the end of the day, no-one has more to gain by reducing theft of telecommunications services, than service providers themselves. The imperative will become that much greater in the forth-coming environment of deregulation. One imagines that service providers, if they are to survive, will focus even more intently on introducing technologies to reduce theft of their services. The demand created for security products will be communicated upstream to entrepreneurial engineers.

Sometimes, problems themselves can be converted into solutions. Consider the computer virus, the bane of systems operators worldwide. As a countermeasure against software piracy, a "logic bomb" could be incorporated in a commercial software product, designed to be activated when copied for the second time. A less drastic technological solution would be to develop software capable of preventing certain digital works from being reproduced without payment to a copyright collecting society.

---

6   For an Australian example, see http://www.auscert.org.au

7   An impressive catalogue of blocking software is listed in the judgment arising from challenges to the United States Communications Decency Act. See *ACLU v Reno*; Adjudication on motions for preliminary injunction (Unreported decision of the United States District Court for the Eastern District of Pennsylvania, No 96-963, 11 June 1996).

At other times, however, solutions may pose problems of their own. Consider Caller ID or Calling Number Display CND. Such technology can be useful in combating unwanted or intrusive calls. It can also threaten privacy, as when it is used by commercial interests to capture the origin of incoming calls for subsequent exploitation, including integration with existing personal information which the company might hold, or may obtain from other commercial organisations.

Market forces may also generate second-order controlling influences. As large organisations begin to appreciate their vulnerability to electronic theft or vandalism, they may be expected to insure against potential losses. It is very much in the interests of insurance companies to require appropriate security precautions on the part of their policyholders. These may well be specified in insurance contracts. Indeed, decisions to set and to price insurance may well depend upon security practices of prospective insureds.

Indeed, there would appear to be at least a partial commercial solution or technological fix for most of the forms of illegality discussed in previous chapters.

Self-regulation

A degree of self-regulation may also be exercised by telecommunications carriers and service providers. Indeed, with regard to the control of communications content, this seems to be the basic direction in which major industrial democracies are heading. While the sheer volume of traffic may preclude scrutiny of all content, many service providers now require signed undertakings as a condition of service that the user refrain from illegal activity, as well as from a range of lesser breaches of protocol. Breaches of these undertakings may result in termination of services. Faced with the threat of heavy-handed attempts by government to impose regulation on Internet communications, various industry groups are developing codes of practice, to reduce the likelihood of some of the more egregious abuses of cyberspace. For example, America OnLine specifies detailed terms of service and rules of the road for subscribers.[8]

Such specified undertakings, while laudable in their intent, may be insufficiently strong to satisfy copyright owners, or fundamentalists with strong objections to particular types of content, such as sexually explicit material or that entailing racial vilification. Codes of conduct also have limited enforceability in an unregulated system.

Citizen co-production of regulatory services

Citizen concern about the availability of undesirable content has given rise to the private monitoring and surveillance of cyberspace. We saw in Chapter 6 how two of the more prominent organisations involved in such surveillance, the Simon Wiesenthal Center and the Cyber Angels division of the Guardian Angels, keep alert for questionable conduct, and contact authorities in the event that they

---

8   See also the code proposed by the Western Australian Internet Association cited in Jones 1995, 22.

encounter illegality. So too has the Software Publishers Association established mechanisms for citizen reporting of suspected cases of piracy: SPA invites reports to their telephone Anti-Piracy Hotline, or by e-mail to piracy@spa.org.

Public interest groups also encourage Websites registering as "Child Safe" or "Child Friendly", to enable parents to employ commercially available software to guide children's access. To some extent, this might be regarded as the informal surveillance and peer pressure of a small-town culture projected into cyberspace. No doubt there are those who find it comforting, and others who find it suffocating.

For their part, governments also invite members of the public to report suspected illegality. We have seen how the United States Customs Service Web page invites citizens to report child pornography or high-tech smuggling coming to their attention.[9]

One also observes within at least some sub-communities of cyberspace the development of norms which serve at least to inhibit some low-level incivilities. As we shall observe, ethical standards can make an important contribution to the security of cyberspace. The term "netiquette" describes the phenomenon which, while not directly relevant to the control of more predatory forms of telecommunications-related crime, contributes to a degree of order (Ciolek 1996). Consider, for example, the following:

The Ten Commandments for Computer Ethics

1. Thou shalt not use a computer to harm other people.
2. Thou shalt not interfere with other people's computer work.
3. Thou shalt not snoop around in other people's files.
4. Thou shalt not use a computer to steal.
5. Thou shalt not use a computer to bear false witness.
6. Thou shalt not use or copy software for which you have not paid.
7. Thou shalt not use other people's computer resources without authorisation.
8. Thou shalt not appropriate other people's intellectual output.
9. Thou shalt think about the social consequences of the program you write.
10. Thou shalt use a computer in ways that show consideration and respect.
(Source: Rinaldi 1996)

These could, at the very least, be distributed along with a new computer at the point of sale.

Information and education

Key to many of the above types of countermeasure is the provision of basic information. In these early years of the digital age, one is still able to say that a substantial degree of both vulnerability and threat are born of ignorance. Lack of understanding about new technologies, their capabilities and limitations, can give rise to gaping lapses in security, as well as to regulatory interventions which, while well intended, are ill-conceived.

---

9   http://www.customs.ustreas.gov/enforce/index.htm

The nature of telecommunications media are such that offenders rarely, if ever, see their victims face to face. When technology mediates human contact in this manner, the reality of an offence, and of the harm which it inflicts, may be lost on the perpetrator. Ethics awareness should impress upon users of telecommunications technology from an early age the very real and very human impact of the technology and its use. Telecommunications is more than a videogame.

Many prospective victims remain unaware, or dimly aware of the dangers which they face. It is a common human tendency to overestimate some risks and to underestimate others. Users of telecommunications services would benefit from greater knowledge of the risks which their use of the technology can entail.

The extreme dependence and vulnerability of telecommunications systems require a heightened security consciousness on the part of individuals and institutions. At the end of 1996, one could assert with confidence that most government agencies in the United States lacked the expertise to detect an intrusion or an attempted intrusion (US Senate 1996).

The status of information security as a profession, and within organisations generally, is destined to increase as a result of the heightening awareness of risk. A major disaster, should one occur, will escalate this trend. Those organisations which do not develop a culture of security will find themselves at much greater risk (Carter and Katz 1996).

Unintended consequences of regulatory intervention

The terrain of telecommunications-related illegality includes many conflicts and contradictions: many apparent solutions turn out to be double-edged swords. Regulation of the Internet has proven a formidable challenge. One of its creators has been quoted as saying "we built it to be Russian-proof, but it turned out to be regulator-proof".[10] Regulatory initiatives can, and do, become unstuck. They may backfire, or produce unintended consequences which in some cases are worse than the underlying problem. As in other areas of regulation and public policy, one must take care that a particular defence against telecommunications-related illegality does not create more harm than it is intended to address.[11] The US Supreme Court noted the chilling effect which the *Communications Decency Act* could have on legitimate expression (*Reno v ACLU*, 26 June 1997, Supreme Court of the United States, 96-511 June 26, 1997).

Restricting access to telecommunications may reduce the opportunity for criminal exploitation, and/or the risk of becoming the victim of harm which such exploitation might occasion. At the same time, however, it can limit opportunities for constructive use of the technology.

---

10   Craig I Fields, quoted in Sterngold (1996).

11   Unintended consequences may arise from commercial activities and citizen intervention as well as from state regulatory initiatives. We have seen above in Chapter 6 how filtering software can be overinclusive; citizen cyberpatrols posing as child decoys for pedophiles may risk impeding police investigations *The Independent* (UK) 27 January 1997, p 13; http://www.infowar.com/class_1/class1_zd.html-ssi

Consider efforts to regulate content of communications on the Internet. Keywords with suggestive connotations are often used to block access to particular Internet sites. It has recently been suggested that some blocking software is over-inclusive, thus preventing access to many sites of educational value.

There also exists what might be termed the "forbidden fruit effect". Official attempts to block access to a given site can inspire the emergence of so-called "mirror sites" in more permissive jurisdictions, which serve to proliferate points of access to the material in question. Indeed, some "cyberlibertarians" regard it as a moral obligation to respond in this manner to attempted censorship. The metaphor of Hydra, the monster which grew two new heads to replace each one which was severed, is not inapposite. Moreover, the publicity surrounding an act of censorship often serves to attract a much wider audience than would be the case if the offending content were ignored by authorities. Attempts in recent years to suppress Canadian sites which promulgated neo-nazi propaganda, and arguably prejudicial information about an ongoing criminal trial, were singularly unsuccessful in this regard.

Regulatory tensions

There is a fundamental tension between the desire to control the less pleasant consequences of telecommunications, and the deregulatory imperative which characterises the world's advanced economies. Some may take pleasure in the ambiguities and contradictions which this will entail. Nonetheless, it does appear that the deregulatory ethos will prevail, at least in western democracies for the time being. If this results in significant harm, then one may expect to see the emergence of adaptive strategies.

One can understand how public officials may be inclined to join the "rush to regulate". Faced as they are in some jurisdictions with vocal minorities demanding the end to a particular evil, whether it be online gambling, money laundering, information on fertility control, or electronic nudity, politicians are often attracted to a "quick fix". In striking down the *Communications Decency Act*, the US Supreme Court noted in passing that the two statutory provisions in question were the subject of almost no congressional deliberation. In footnote 24 to its opinion, the Court quoted Senator Leahy, who observed at a one-day hearing held *after* the Senate adopted the provisions:

> It really struck me in your opening statement when you mentioned, Mr Chairman, that it is the first ever hearing, and you are absolutely right. And yet we had a major debate on the floor, passed legislation overwhelmingly on a subject involving the Internet, legislation that could dramatically change — some would say even wreak havoc — on the Internet. The Senate went in willy nilly, passed legislation, and never once had a hearing, never once had a discussion other than an hour or so on the floor. (Quoted in *Reno v ACLU* 26 June 1997, Supreme Court of the United States 96-511, n 24).

Even when hasty legislation passes judicial muster, it may prove to be unenforceable; the sheer volume of content on the Internet defies comprehension, much less careful monitoring and control.

The pace of technological change is such that some policies begin to appear outmoded while still on the drawing board. Recall how prohibitions on the export of cryptographic technology appear to have been overtaken by events, given the proliferation of cryptographic software and its widespread dissemination over the Internet.

Unfortunately, even while some fixes amount to, "too little, too late," others might be characterised as "too much, too soon". As we have noted, there is a significant danger that premature regulatory interventions may not only fail to achieve their desired effect, but may also have a negative impact on the development of technology for the benefit of all. Over-regulation, or premature regulatory intervention may run the risk of chilling investment and innovation. Copyright restrictions are introduced at the expense of information availability; prohibitions on the export of cryptographic technology placed growing markets beyond the reach of creative software developers.

Given the increasingly competitive nature of the global marketplace, governments may be forced to choose between paternalistic imperatives and those of commercial development and economic growth. The challenge facing those who would minimise digital crime is to seek a balance which would allow a tolerable degree of illegality in return for creative exploitation of the technology. At this early stage of the technological revolution, it may be useful for individuals, interest groups and governments to articulate their preferences and let these serve as signals to the market. Markets may be able to provide more efficient solutions than direct state interventions.

The sending of market signals may well rival direct government command as a means of influencing behaviour in cyberspace. In October of 1996, the US Government suggested that it might relax restrictions on the export of cryptographic products if the products in question were designed in a manner to facilitate key escrow. Governments have also encouraged the development of blocking and filtering software to permit users to decide for themselves what content they are to avoid. Of course, governments are significant consumers of goods and services in their own right, and their specifications can be very influential indeed.

Cynics could perhaps be forgiven for suggesting that premature regulation, regardless of its futility, serves at least a symbolic purpose. In a democratic society where values often clash, the enactment of unenforceable law may serve to appease the uncomfortable minority.

Regulatory dilemmas

Like most new technologies, telecommunications has its advantages and its disadvantages. The double-edged nature of telecommunications technology presents modern society with an entire menu of dilemmas, each of which provides an arena for conflict. It is unlikely that anyone of these arenas will be marked by total victory, as the following brief review may illustrate.

Privacy v accountability

A great deal of activity which is essential for the maintenance of a healthy democratic society, and for a flourishing economy, requires a degree of privacy (Froomkin 1995). From matters as lofty as human rights discussions occurring in a repressive state, to things as mundane as the secure transmission of credit card details and PINs, secrecy is essential. Whistleblowing often requires an environment of anonymity, and freedom from retaliation. Other forums such as electronic support groups for vulnerable people may also benefit from a modicum of privacy. Privacy becomes an increasingly important consideration as developments in information technology permit tracing and matching of identities and transactions to an extent heretofore unimaginable. At the same time, transparency and accountability are also important democratic values. While it would certainly assist law enforcement and taxation agencies if all electronic financial transactions were traceable, and the respective parties identifiable, the violation of privacy which this entails would strike many as repugnant.

The transparency of communications which law enforcement regards as highly desirable, would inhibit the secure communication of proprietary and other commercial information upon which global business increasingly depends.

It is not surprising that the information technology industry does not see itself as an adjunct of law enforcement. Indeed, some industry participants, while not necessarily regarding themselves as enemies of law enforcement, embrace a liberal if not a libertarian world view.

The development of technologies in a manner where law enforcement interests are at least given some consideration is embraced by some; it would nevertheless appear that the tension between preferences for privacy and transparency will persist.

National sovereignty v globalism

The assertion of national sovereignty can be difficult in a world without borders (Froomkin 1996). One can understand the German government's desire that its citizens not be exposed to neo-nazi propaganda, but such content is readily accessible in Germany from sites located in more permissive jurisdictions. One can also appreciate the desire of some nations to preserve their cultural heritage from eclipse by North American influences, or of any jurisdiction to prohibit activities such as gambling. Such aspirations, however, appear increasingly elusive. Perhaps the most significant examples of the diffusion of sovereignty in cyberspace are the dominance of the English language and the potential for electronic currency to dissolve international monetary barriers. Some states will continue attempts to erect and bolster electronic barricades, at the risk of impeding educational and economic development. Others such as Singapore will attempt to have their cake and eat it too, by making symbolic affirmations and establishing a regulatory regime which will discourage opportunistic access to some of the more unsavoury reaches of cyberspace. But for the most part, the metaphor of the global village is more real than ever.

One advantage of this trend is the opportunity which it provides various minority groups to share their cultures with a wider world. Indigenous communities which were once invisible, and indeed, literally endangered, are now able to reach an audience of hundreds of millions. Rather than bemoan the risk of one's culture's eclipse by the Chicago Bulls and Coca-Cola, one might regard new technologies as a boon to cultural preservation.

User-friendliness v security

Although children of today, at least in technologically advanced societies, embrace new technologies with little effort, the same cannot always be said of their grandparents. As more and more aspects of life become dependent upon telecommunications, tremendous profits await those who can design and market systems which are accessible to the ordinary individual. At the same time, accessibility and user-friendliness usually imply vulnerability to illicit penetration. What is accessible to the honest person is just as accessible to the dishonest one. The challenge faced by the information industry is to enhance legitimate access, while limiting access for illicit purposes. The solution would appear to lie in the development of "smart" technologies such as those based on biometric, temporal, or locational data which ask little of the honest user, but demand the impossible of the cyber criminal.

Trust v efficiency in law enforcement

Interpersonal trust is, in a real sense, the cement of our society, particularly in commercial dealings and where fiduciary relationships exist. Systematic surveillance, not to mention the use of telecommunications for purposes of covert facilitation of crime, poses substantial risks. When one can never be sure about the identity of the person with whom one is dealing, interpersonal relations inevitably suffer. But again, the inviolability or impenetrability of interpersonal communications may defeat law enforcement. Law enforcement no longer has exclusive access to superior telecommunications technology. Tools which were once solely available to governments or to such large private institutions as banks, are now available to ordinary citizens. Technology has begun to eclipse conventional methods of law enforcement.

The ability to disclose one's credit card details in complete confidence that they will not be captured and misused requires a degree of impenetrability. There are those who would favour the introduction of blinded digital signatures, which do not disclose the identity of the sender, not even to a financial institution or a merchant.

On the other hand, private citizens are just as capable of abusing trust as are agents of law enforcement. Indeed, the law enforcement advocates would argue that their very selective, and accountable, abuse of trust is essential in order to prevent the most serious forms of abuse of trust by private parties.

Security v creativity

Measures necessary to protect humankind from all of life's misfortunes would be suffocating. Worthy activities require freedom no less than do illicit activities. One could hardly hope to state the general metaphor better than James Madison in Federalist 10:

234

Liberty is to faction what air is to fire, an aliment without which it instantly expires. But it could not be less folly to abolish liberty, which is essential to political life, because it nourishes faction, than it would be to wish the annihilation of air, which is essential to animal life, because it imparts to fire its destructive agency.[12]

In order to realise the full educational, artistic and economic potential of telecommunications, a degree of liberty is necessary. Liberty, however, entails respect for other people's rights. The risk, or indeed, the fact, that such liberty will be abused by some, is insufficient justification for "pulling the plug" on telecommunications. Excessive constraints on freedom of expression and communication may inhibit the realisation of competitive advantage. This particular dilemma is shared by those nations, from the People's Republic of China to Syria, which seek the fruits of economic development without the distraction of challenges to their culture or political authority.

The interests of the individual v the interests of the state

The distinction between what is public and what is private is currently contested terrain. The traditional assumptions which served as the basis for the regulation of broadcasting and for justifying the interception of telephone communications have, to a significant extent been overtaken by technology. At no time in human history has the ordinary individual had the capacity to communicate to an audience of tens of millions, at negligible cost. Entire new areas of commerce and public policy are being contested. The emergence of networked environments, the multi-directional flow of information, and multimedia telecommunications have blurred distinctions considerably, to the extent that private communications may at times be more public than in the past. Consider the domain of expression. Two consenting adults exchange thoughts which you and I might find objectionable in the course of a quiet evening stroll or over the telephone. Unless these thoughts entail a criminal conspiracy, it is entirely their business. What if they exchange the same thoughts by means of electronic mail? What if they share these thoughts with a few invited guests on an exclusive electronic bulletin board? What if they make their thoughts available on a web site, accompanied by a warning that some consumers might regard it as objectionable? Such possibilities have changed the nature of communications and altered the scope of public broadcasting with the result that users of online services may be circumspect in communicating questionable information.

As we write this, titanic struggles are being waged in western democracies between privacy and consumer advocates on the one hand, and law enforcement officials on the other. The former show remarkable tenacity and considerable persuasiveness; the latter invoke a future fraught with risk which calls out for enhanced state power as the key to individual security. These struggles will continue, their outcomes by no means certain. Meanwhile, private, commercial interests have begun to pose threats to individual privacy which rival those of government. Massive amounts of personal information, amenable to collation and matching for commercial, or indeed, criminal purposes, now reside

---

12   http://grid.let.rug.nl/~welling/usa/fed/fed10.html

in private hands. As the distinction between public and private spheres becomes increasingly blurred, it may be more appropriate to speak in terms of the interests of the individual in conflict with the interests of large institutions generally.

Conclusion: countermeasures in combination

The varied nature of telecommunications-related illegality defies a single policy solution. Those who would deny widespread access risk missing out on the most significant social, artistic, and economic developments of the 21st century. Given the absence of a panacea for problems of telecommunications-related crime, it seems appropriate to think in terms of a variety of institutions and instruments which can be brought to bear on the illegalities in question.

The appropriate response to crime in the digital age will thus depend on the precise nature of the threat, and in the capacity of available measures to confront it. This capacity will vary over time and by location.

International crime of a more conventional nature has proven to be a very difficult challenge for law enforcement. Digital crime poses even greater challenges. There may be a lack of agreement about whether or not the activity in question is criminal at all; about who has committed it; about whether in fact it has been committed; about who has been victimised because of it; about who should investigate it; and about and who should adjudicate and punish it. We have hardly begun to address the many gripping questions of law and policy touched on above. We do not promise definitive solutions. The directions in which we point may soon be eclipsed by still newer technologies.

As we have seen, the criminal opportunities presented by emerging telecommunications technologies are formidable. The current realities and potential risks posed by telecommunications crime are never-the-less surpassed by the tremendous opportunities for the constructive application of telecommunications technology in so many areas of human endeavour. For this reason, the design and deployment of countermeasures against digital illegality should be undertaken with care, so as not unduly to limit the potential advantages inherent in the new technology. Given the rich variety of telecommunications-related crime described in the chapters above (not to mention the motives of those who would perpetrate such offences), it should be apparent that there will be no single best strategy for control or prevention. Indeed, any single policy instrument is likely to have its shortcomings or limitations.

It might be instructive to envisage three different forms of digital crime, to identify what these control configurations might look like. Telemarketing fraud, and its Internet equivalents, are best defeated by self-help on the part of an informed public. The requisite information can be provided by public or private sources. Commercial technologies will be of assistance in deflecting uninvited overtures. Recognising that there will still be those whose gullibility (and greed) will prevail, government intervention may be appropriate. In the most extreme cases, where perpetrators remain accessible within one's own jurisdiction, traditional law enforcement strategies might be applied.

Electronic money laundering, by contrast, will require more direct governmental intervention for its control. As electronic commerce continues to

236

expand, governments will ultimately determine what types of institutions can issue electronic money, and where that money can flow. One imagines that what we call banks will be very different organisations from the banks which our grandparents knew; these institutions will nevertheless continue to play a central role in the economies of industrial nations. The monitoring of electronic money movements will continue, one imagines with no greater success than has been the case to date, for as the capability of monitoring technology improves, so too will the technologies available to those who would conceal their ill-gotten gains.

Illegal interceptions, and theft of services, would seem most amenable to control by interventions primarily technological in nature. Passwords, PINs, biometrics and encryption would appear the most reliable means of securing tele-communications services. Recognising that the services in question are designed for use by humans, a species whose members are far from infallible, a degree of self-help will also be required. In an age of mobile telephony it will be important to warn people to avoid the telephonic equivalent of leaving one's car unlocked with the keys in the ignition. Organisations will be well advised to ensure that their employees are recruited and managed with care.

Conventional law enforcement agencies, have but a limited capacity to patrol cyberspace, to identify telecommunications criminals, and to provide the evidentiary basis for a successful prosecution. It would thus seem appropriate that scarce and valuable law enforcement resources be reserved for the most serious forms of telecommunications-related illegality, rather than be spread too thinly in the pursuit of relatively minor matters. Individual citizens may be able to protect themselves to some extent. Market solutions will have some applicability.

As a general principle, measures for the prevention and control of telecommunications-related crime should minimise coercion, maximise privacy, and minimise impediments to future technological development.

Of course, a technological breakthrough could occur at any time, and change the contours of the playing field entirely. There will then be an opportunity for another book on crime in the post-digital age.

References

Adams, D, 1996, "Thieves Answer Call for Mobile Phones", *The Age*, 25 May: A3.

Adler, M, 1996, "Cyberspace, General Searches, and Digital Contraband: The Fourth Amendment and the Net-Wide Search", *Yale Law Journal*, 105: 1093-120.

Akdeniz, Y, 1996, Regulation of Child Pornography on the Internet, http://www.leeds.ac.uk/law/pgs/yaman/child.htm.

Albanese, J, 1988, "Tomorrow's Thieves", *The Futurist*, 22: 25-8.

Amos, T, 1995, "Net Benefits", *Australian Communications*, October: 60.

Anderson, K, 1994, "International Intrusions: Motives and Patterns. Proceedings of the 1994 Bellcore/Bell South Security Symposium", May 1994, http://www.aracnet.com/~kea/Papers/paper.shtml.

Annotation, 1977, "Criminal Prosecutions for Use of 'Blue Box' or Similar Device Permitting User to Make Long-Distance Telephone Calls Without Incurring Charges", 78 ALR3d 449-60.

Anonymous, 1978, "The Ultimate Heist", *Time*, 20 November: 48.

Anonymous, 1993, "Phone Fraud Crack-Down Not Enough", *Mobile Asia-Pacific*, December: 15.

Anonymous, 1994, "MCI Worker is Charged in Huge Phone-Card Theft", *Chicago Tribune*, 4 October: 4.

Anonymous, 1995a, "Software Piracy Case in Los Angeles Leads to Felony Charges", *Wall Street Journal*, 15 November.

Anonymous, 1995b, "Australians Fleeced by World Wide Investment Scam", *Canberra Times*, 22 May.

Anonymous, 1995c, "Russians Score Electronic Heist", *St Petersburg Times*, 19 August: E1.

Anonymous, 1996a, *The West Australian*, 8 August, p. 36.

Anonymous, 1996b, "Police 'Illegally Tapped Phones' ", *Daily Telegraph*, 16 August: 16.

Anonymous, 1996c, "Vodac's Database Latches on to Stolen Mobile Telephones", *Canberra Times*, 29 April: 15.

Anonymous, 1996d, "Industry Attacks Pirates", *The Age*, 1 October: D4.

Anonymous, 1996e, "Two on Phone Scam Counts", *West Australian*, July 9: 47.

Anonymous, 1997a, "Spy Shop Gets Death Penalty After Pleading Guilty to Money Laundering", *Corporate Crime Reporter*, 11: 3-4.

Anonymous, 1997b, "In Brief: December 16, 1996", *Corporate Crime Reporter*, 11: 10.

Aranson, J, Bouker, J, and Hannan, D, 1994, "Money Laundering", *American Criminal Law Review*, 31: 721-46.

Associated Press, 1995, The Spy Shop Busts: Customs Sting Targets Illegal Listening Devices, http://www.thecodex.com/c_spyshp.html.

Atkinson, J, 1996, "The Future of Smart Cards", paper presented at the Policy Network Conference, Smart Cards: The Issues, Sydney, 18 October.

Austen, J, 1996, "Computer Crime", *Proceedings of the IEE Colloquium on Information Security: Is it Safe?*, 27 June, Institute of Electrical Engineers.

Australia, 1996, *Report of the Electronic Commerce Task Force to the Commonwealth Law Enforcement Board*, Australian Transaction Reports and Analysis Centre (AUSTRAC).

Australia, 1963, *Royal Commission on Alleged Improper Practices and Improper Refusals to Cooperate with the Victoria Police Force on the Part of Persons Employed in the Postmaster General's Department in Victoria in Relation to Illegal Gambling*, (Mr Justice R.L. Taylor, Royal Commissioner), Government Printer.

REFERENCES

Australia, Attorney-General's Department, 1991, *Review of Telecommunications (Interception) Act 1979*, AGPS.

Australia, Parliamentary Joint Committee on the National Crime Authority, 1995, *Organised Criminal Paedophile Activity*, AGPS.

Australian Broadcasting Authority, 1995, *Investigation into the Content of On-Line Services: Issues Paper*, Australian Broadcasting Authority.

Australian Broadcasting Authority, 1996, *Investigation into the Content of On-Line Services: Report to the Minister for Communications and the Arts*, 30 June, http://www.dca.gov.au/aba/olsrprt1.htm.

Australian Bureau of Statistics, 1996, *Household Use of Information Technology: Australia, February 1996*, AGPS.

Australian Commission for the Future, 1996, *Smart Cards and the Future of Your Money*, Australian Commission for the Future Ltd.

Australian Copyright Council, 1996, *Fair Dealing in the Digital Age*, Australian Copyright Council.

Australian Federal Police, *Annual Reports*, 1992-93, 1993-94, 1994-95, AGPS.

Australian Law Reform Commission, 1983, *Report No 22, Privacy*, 3 vols, Australian Law Reform Commission.

Australian Law Reform Commission, 1996, *Legal Risk in International Transactions*, (ALRC 80), AGPS.

Australian Payments System Council, 1996, *Annual Report 1992-93, 1993-94, 1994-95, 1995-96*, Reserve Bank of Australia.

Australian Telecommunications Authority, 1995, Telemarketing and the Protection of the Privacy of Individuals, AGPS.

Australian Telecommunications Authority, Law Enforcement Advisory Committee, 1995, *Telecommunications and Law Enforcement For Organisations Providing Telecommunications Services*, Austel.

Australian Transaction Reports and Analysis Centre, 1995, *Money Laundering and Financial Industry Regulators*, AGPS.

B D Software, 1997, "Hot IMEI: A Tracking System for Stolen Mobile Phones", unpublished proposal.

Baker, S, and Barth, R, 1996, "The International Market for Encryption", paper presented at the Symposium of Information, National Policies and International Infrastructure, Harvard University, 30 January.

Balsamo, W, and Carpozi, G, 1988, *Under the Clock: The Inside Story of the Mafia's First Hundred Years*, New Horizon Press.

Barlow, J, 1994, "Selling Wine Without Bottles: The Economy of Mind on the Global Net", http://www.eff.org/pub/Publications/John_Perry_Barlow/HTML/idea_economy_article.html.

Barnes, D, 1994, "The Coming Jurisdictional Swamp of Global Internetworking", http://www.replay.com/cpunk/cptext.html.

Barrett, P, 1994, *Review of the Long Term Cost Effectiveness of Telecommunications Interception*, Australian Department of Finance.

Beaumont, P, 1994, "Bargain Basement Bugging", *Police Review*, 102: 26-7.

Behar, R, 1997, "Who's Reading Your E-Mail?", *Time*, 3 February: 64-7.

Bell Atlantic, 1996, "Outfox Phone Fraud!!", http://www.bell-atl.com/security/fraud/index.htm.

Bellcore, 1996, "New Crypto-Attack Weakens Seeming Strength in Smart Cards, Secure ID Cards, or Vale Cards", http://www.infowar.com/sample/infosec4.html-ssi.

Bequai, A, 1987, *Technocrimes*, Lexington Books.

Bernstein, N, 1996, "On Prison Computer, Files to Make Parents Shiver", *New York Times*, 18 November 1996: A1.

Black, D, 1973, "The Mobilisation of Law", *Journal of Legal Studies*, 2: 125-49.

Blakeney, M, 1995, "Electronic Infringement: The New Piracy", *Copyright Reporter*, 12: 17-31.

Blau, J, 1994, "GSM Immobilized: Germany, France may Block Roaming", *Communications Week International*, 14 March: 1.

Bonney, R, 1992, *Preventing Credit Card Fraud*, New South Wales Bureau of Crime Statistics and Research Crime and Justice Bulletin No 17, New South Wales Bureau of Crime Statistics and Research.

Bottom, B, 1989, *Bugged: Legal Police Telephone Taps Expose the Mr Bigs of Australia's Drug Trade*, Sun Books.

Bowes, C, 1996, "Digital Dollars", *Bulletin*, 20 August: 50.

Bradley, M, 1997, "Security Slip on MI5 Hotline", *Press Association*, 23 May.

Brien, C, 1996, "Internet: The New Trade in Goods, Services and Ideas", *Journal of Law and Information Science*, 7: 69-86.

Bronitt, S, 1996, "Contemporary Comment: Electronic Surveillance and Informers: Infringing the Rights to Silence and Privacy", *Criminal Law Journal*, 20: 144-52.

Bronitt, S, 1997, "Electronic Surveillance, Human Rights and Criminal Justice", *Australian Journal of Human Rights*, 3: 183-207.

Brooke, J, 1995, "Crackdown Has Cali Drug Cartel on the Run," *The New York Times*, 27 June: A-1.

Brookes, P, 1996, *Electronic Surveillance Devices*, Butterworth-Heinemann.

Brooks, T, and Davis, M, 1994, "Are Your Phone Bills Fraud Free?", *Security Management*, 38: 67-8.

Brown, A, 1996, *Reform and Regulation of Australian Telecommunications*, Working Paper No 5, Griffith University, School of Economics.

Brown, M, 1996, "Police Chief 'Knew of Illegal Phone Tapping' ", *Sydney Morning Herald*, 13 November: 8.

Buckeridge, R, and Cutler, T, 1995, *The Online Economy: Maximising Australia's Opportunities from Networked Commerce*, Cutler and Co.

Burton, T, 1996, "Copycats on the Net", *Financial Review*, 15 October: 14.

Butcher, S, 1996, "Woman Convicted on Phone Stalking Count", *Sunday Age*, 28 January: 5a.

Butler Group, 1996, *The Corporate Intranet/Internet: Strategies and Technologies*, Butler Publishing Ltd, Hessle.

Butler, A, 1996, "Regulation of Content of On-Line Information Services: Can Technology Itself Solve the Problem it Has Created?", *University of New South Wales Law Journal*, 19: 193-221.

Callinan, I, 1996, "Police Left on Hold in Request for Phone Taps", *Courier Mail*, 21 August: 9.

Carroll, M, and Schrader, R, 1995, "Computer-Related Crimes", *American Criminal Law Review*, 32: 183-211.

Carroll, S, (ed), 1995a, "Anti-Money Laundering Laws and the Quasi-Banker: A Report on Alternative Banking in Australia", Appendix to Australian Transaction Reports and Analysis Centre *Money Laundering and Financial Industry Regulators*, AGPS.

Carroll, S, 1995b, *Money Laundering Triggering Mechanisms: The Australian Experience*, Australian Transaction Reports and Analysis Centre.

Carter, D, and Katz, A, 1996, "Computer Crime and Security: the Perceptions and Experiences of Corporate Security Directors", *Security Journal*, 7: 101-8.

Carter, S, 1996, "Online 'Bank' Cashes in on Cyber Commerce", *The Australian*, 30 July, Computers: 49.

REFERENCES

Case, L, 1995, "Computer Security", *Security Management,* 39: 60-5.

Cassidy, W, 1994, "Fei-Chien, or Flying Money: A Study of Chinese Underground Banking", http://www.deltanet.com/users/wcassidy/Flyingmoney.html.

Cavazos, E, and Morin, G, 1994, *Cyberspace and the Law: Your Rights and Duties in the Online World,* MIT Press.

Cellular One, 1994, "Cellular Fraud Facts", paper presented at the International Crime Stoppers Conference, Hawaii, September, http://www.wireless101.com/new/fpf/fraud.htm.

Center for Public Interest Law, 1994, "How to Put an End to Unwanted or Harassing Phone Calls", Privacy Rights Clearinghouse, Fact Sheet, No 3, http://www.cpsr.org/dox/factshts/harassing.calls.html.

Challinger, D, 1992, "Less Telephone Vandalism: How Did it Happen?", in Clarke, R, (ed), *Situational Crime Prevention: Successful Case Studies,* Harrow and Heston: 75-8.

Chandrasekaran, R, 1996, "Undercover on the Dark Side of Cyberspace; On-Line FBI Agents Troll for Those Who Prey on Children, but Cybercops' Tactics Chill Critics", *The Washington Post,* 2 January: D1.

Charns, A, 1992, *Cloak and Gavel: FBI Wiretaps, Bugs, Informers, and the Supreme Court,* University of Illinois Press.

Cheng, H, 1995, "Hacking, Computer Viruses, and Software Piracy: The Implications of Modern Computer Fraud for Corporations", in Spencer, M, and Sims, R, (eds), *Corporate Misconduct: The Legal, Societal and Management Issues,* Quorum Books: 125-47.

Chester, R, 1996, "Piracy Worst in Western World", *Brisbane Courier Mail,* 16 April: 5.

Cheswick, B, and Bellovin, S, 1994, *Firewalls and Internet Security: Repelling the Wily Hacker,* Addison Wesley.

Ciolek, M, 1996, "Ethics and Etiquette of Internet Resources", Research School of Social Sciences, Australian National University, http://coombs.anu.edu.au/SpecialProj/QLTY/QltyEtiq.html.

Clarke, R, 1995, "Situational Crime Prevention", in Tonry, M, and Farrington, D, (eds), *Building a Safer Society: Strategic Approaches to Crime Prevention,* University of Chicago Press: 91-150.

Clarke, R, (ed), 1992, *Situational Crime Prevention: Successful Case Studies,* Harrow and Heston.

Clarke, R, 1990, "Deterring Obscene Phone Callers: Preliminary Results of the New Jersey Experience", *Security Journal,* 1: 143-8.

Clough, B, and Mungo, P, 1992, *Approaching Zero: Data Crime and the Computer Underworld,* Faber and Faber.

Coad, B, and Richardson, D, 1994, "Reducing Market Opportunities for Organised Crime" in Australian Transaction Reports and Analysis Centre, *AUSTRAC Papers 2.* AUSTRAC.

Collier, A, 1994, "When Does Unauthorised Listening Become Interception"? *Law Institute Journal,* 68: 58-63.

Commonwealth of Australia, Attorney-General's Department and Department of Communication and the Arts, 1994a, *Report of the Computer Bulletin Board Systems Task Force: Regulation of Computer Bulletin Board Systems,* Attorney-General's Department.

Commonwealth of Australia, Attorney-General's Department and Department of Communication and the Arts, 1994b, *Proposed Moral Rights Legislation for Copyright Creators: Discussion Paper,* AGPS.

Commonwealth of Australia, Attorney-General's Department, Copyright Law Review Committee, 1995, *Computer Software Protection: Final Report,* AGPS.

Commonwealth of Australia, Australian Federal Police, 1996, *Annual Report 1995-96*, AGPS.

Commonwealth of Australia, Bureau of Consumer Affairs, 1995, *A Cashless Society? Electronic Banking and the Consumer: Issues Paper No 1*, AGPS.

Commonwealth of Australia, Bureau of Transport and Communications Economics, 1995, *Communications Futures: Final Report*, AGPS.

Commonwealth of Australia, Copyright Convergence Group, 1994, *Highways to Change: Copyright in the New Communications Environment*, AGPS.

Commonwealth of Australia, Director of Public Prosecutions, 1994, *Annual Report 1993-94*, AGPS.

Commonwealth of Australia, Human Rights and Equal Opportunity Commission, 1995, *Smart Cards: Implications for Privacy*, Information Paper No 4 of the Privacy Commissioner, AGPS.

Commonwealth of Australia, Privacy Commissioner, 1994, *Privacy Implications of New Communications Networks and Services: Information Paper No 1*, AGPS.

Commonwealth of Australia, Privacy Commissioner, 1992, *Submission to the AUSTEL Inquiry into the Privacy Implications of Telecommunications Services*, AGPS.

Commonwealth of Australia, Senate Select Committee on Community Standards Relevant to the Supply of Services Utilising Electronic Technologies, 1995, Report on Regulation of Computer OnLine Services, Part 2, AGPS, http://senate.aph. gov.au/committee/csrssuet_rep/report.html.

Commonwealth of Australia, Standing Committee of Attorneys-General, Model Criminal Code Officers Committee, 1995, *Model Criminal Code: Chapter 3 Theft, Fraud, Bribery and Related Offences*, AGPS.

Computer Security Institute, 1996a, "Computer Security Issues and Trends", http://www. gocsi.com/iss_t.htm#ComputerCrime.

Computer Security Institute, 1996b, "Testimony of Richard G. Power, Editor, Computer Security Institute Before Permanent Sub-Committee of Investigations, United States Senate Committee on Governmental Affairs", http://www.gocsi.com/ testify.htm#ComputerCrime.

Consumer Scam Alert Network, 1996, "Online Investment Schemes: Fraud and Abuse in Cyberspace", http://www.pic.net/microsmarts/invest.htm.

Cook, W, 1991a, "Costly Callers: Prosecuting Voice Mail Fraud", *Security Management*, 35: 41-5.

Cook, W, 1991b, "Paying the Bill for Hostile Technology: PBX Fraud in 1991", *Computer Law and Security Report*, 7: 174-7.

Cooke, J, 1994, "Gang Preyed on Deliveries, Court Told", *Sydney Morning Herald*, 3 March: 5.

Cookes, T, 1996, "Copycat Warning on Use of Caribbean Phone Scam", *The Age*, 14 September: A9.

Cooper, R, 1995, "Grievous Bodily Harm by Telephone", *Journal of Criminal Law*, 59: 401-10.

Coutorie, L, 1995, "The Future of High-Technology Crime: A Parallel Delphi Study", *Journal of Criminal Justice*, 23: 13-27.

Cream, A, 1994, "Ninth Survey of White Collar Crime: Intellectual Property Crimes", *American Criminal Law Review*, 31: 687-702.

Crede, A, 1996, "Electronic Commerce and the Banking Industry: The Requirement and Opportunities for New Payment Systems Using the Internet", *The Journal of Computer-Mediated Communication* (JCMC).

Crowe, D, 1996a, "Wrong Numbers", *Financial Review*, 15 February: 16.

Crowe, D, 1996b, "Computer Games Group Launches Piracy Crusade", *Financial Review*, 10 September: 32.

REFERENCES

Crowell, W, 1995, Statement to the Subcommittee on Domestic and International Monetary Policy of the Committee on Banking and Financial Services, US House of Representatives, *Hearing on the Future of Electronic Forms of Money and Electronic Payment Systems*, 11 October, http://www.house.gov/castle/banking/crowell.htm.

Csonka, P, 1996, "Criminal Procedural Law and Information Technology: The Main Features of the Council of Europe Recommendation No R(95)13", *Computer Law and Security Report*, 12: 37-42.

Cunningham, J, 1996, "Cutting Cell Fraud Frequency", *Security Management*, October: 43-6.

Da Silva, W, 1996a, "Con Artists of the Internet", *The Age*, 10 December, D1.

Da Silva, W, 1996b, " 'Hackers' May Evade Charges", *The Age*, 11 June: C1.

Daly, M, 1997, "The Sting of '96", *The Age*, 4 January: A9.

Dancer, H, 1996, "Totally Mobile is Just a Mindshift Away", *Australian Personal Computer*, 17: 74-6.

Dash, S, 1959, *The Eavesdroppers: The Unknown Story of Wire Tapping Today—Its Victims, Its Practitioners, The Techniques, and What the Law Says About It*, Rutgers University Press.

De Zwart, M, 1996, "Copyright in Cyberspace", *Alternative Law Journal*, 21: 266-70.

Defense Science Board, 1996, *Report of the Defense Science Board Task Force on Information Warfare-Defense* (IW-D).

Delaney, D, 1993, "Investigating Telecommunications Fraud", in Grau, J, (ed), *Criminal and Civil Investigation Handbook*, 2nd edn, McGraw-Hill Inc.

Delaney, D, Denning, D, Kaye, J, and McDonald, A, 1993, "Wiretap Laws and Procedures: What Happens When the U.S. Government Taps a Line", http://guru.cosc.georgetown.edu/~denning/wiretap/Wiretap.txt.

Denning, D, 1994, "Encryption and Law Enforcement", http://www.eff.org/pub/Privacy/Clipper/denning_crypto_law.paper.

Denning, D, 1995, "Crime and Crypto on the Information Superhighway", *Journal of Criminal Justice Education*, 6: 323-36.

Denning, D, 1996a, "Protection and Defense of Intrusion", paper presented at the Conference on National Security in the Information Age, US Air Force Academy, Colorado Springs, 28 February-1 March, http://www.cosc.georgetown.edu/~denning/infosec/USAFA.html.

Denning, D, 1996b, "Encryption Policy and Market Trends", http://guru.cosc.georgetown.edu/~denning/crypto/Trends.html.

Denning, D, and Baugh Jr., W, 1997, *Encryption and Evolving Technologies as Tools of Organised Crime and Terrorism*, National Strategy Information Center, US Working Group on Organised Crime, June.

Denning, D, and MacDoran, P, 1996, "Location-Based System Delivers User Authentication Breakthrough", *Computer Security Alert*, 154: 1, http://all.net/journal/csi/csi-96-01.html.

Deogun, N, 1996, "The Smart Money is on 'Smart Cards', But Electronic Cash Seems Dumb to Some", *Wall Street Journal*, 5 August: B1, B7.

Digicash Inc, 1996, "Ecash and Crime", http://www.digicash.com/ecash/aboutcrime.html.

Donner, F, 1980, *The Age of Surveillance: The Aims and Methods of America's Political Intelligence System*, Knopf.

Dunning, M, 1982, "Some Aspects of Theft of Computer Software", *Auckland University Law Review*, 4: 273-94.

Durie, R, 1988, "Telecommunications and Broadcasting", ch. 151 in *Australian Commentary to Halsbury's Laws of England*, 4th edn, Butterworths.

Edwards, O, 1995, "Hackers from Hell", *Forbes*, 9 October: 182.

Erickson, J, 1996, "CD Pirates Face the Music", *The Age*, 7 May: C12.

Federal Bureau of Investigation (FBI), 1970, "Crime and cryptology", *FBI Law Enforcement Bulletin*, April: 13-14.

Fabrizius, K, 1995, Carnegie-Mellon Censorship, http://www.cs.cmu.edu/afs/cs/usr/kcf/www/censor/index.html.

Faris, P, and Andrews, P, 1995, "Internet Crime", http://www.lawnet.com.au/crime/.

Farr, R, 1975, *The Electronic Criminals*, McGraw-Hill Book Co.

Ferguson, S, 1996, "Telecommunications, Consumers and Social Policy", background paper for the Communications Law Centre Conference, Public Choices: Reforming Australian Telecommunications, 12 April.

Fielding, D, 1993, "Is It Legal? Copyright Issues in the Supply of Electronic Data", *Information On Line and On Disk*: 71-82.

Fisse, B, 1990, *Howard's Criminal Law*, 5th edn, Law Book Co. Ltd.

Fitzgerald, P, and Leopold, M, 1987, *Stranger on the Line: The Secret History of Phone Tapping*, The Bodley Head Ltd.

Flanagan, W, and McMenamin, B, 1992, "For Whom the Bells Toll", *Forbes*, 3 August: 60-4.

Flint, J, 1996, "Banks' Smart Money on Mondex", *The Age*, 19 June: B3d.

Ford, P, 1997, "Operation Cybertrader", *International Journal of Forensic Computing*, Issue 1: 7-9.

Forney, M, 1996, "Piracy: Now We Get It", *Far Eastern Economic Review*, 159: 40-3.

Fox, B, 1995, "Speedy Net Threatens Movie Moguls", *New Scientist*, 16 December: 22.

Freeh, L, 1996a, Speech to the District of Columbia American Bar Association Winter Convention, Washington, DC, 6 March, http://www.fbi.gov/dcbar.htm..

Freeh, L, 1996b, "The International Crime Problem", Statement before the United States House of Representatives, Committee on International Relations, Hearing on Russian Organised Crime, 30 April.

Freeh, L, 1996c, "The Impact of Encryption on Law Enforcement and Public Safety", Statement before the United States Senate Committee on Commerce, Science and Transportation, 25 July.

Friman, H, 1994, "International Pressure and Domestic Bargains: Regulating Money Laundering in Japan", *Crime Law and Social Change*, 21: 253-66.

Froomkin, A, 1995, "Anonymity and its Enmities", *Journal of Online Law*, art. 4.

Froomkin A, 1996a, "Flood Control on the Information Ocean: Living With Anonymity, Digital Cash, and Distributed Databases", *University of Pittsburgh Journal of Law and Commerce*, http://www.law.miami.edu/~froomkin/ocean1-7.htm.

Froomkin, A, 1996b, "The Internet As A Source Of Regulatory Arbitrage", in Kahin, B, and Nesson, C, (eds), *Borders in Cyberspace*, MIT Press, http://www.law.miami.edu/~froomkin/arbitr.htm#ENDBACK1.

Gawenda, M, 1990, "Bond Battles into the '90s", *Time Australia*, 5: 50-1.

Godwin, M, 1996, "Fear of Freedom: The Backlash Against Free Speech on the 'Net' ", paper prepared for delivery to the conference on New Media Technology: True Innovations or Electric Fork?, jointly sponsored by the Freedom Forum Pacific Coast Center and The Freedom Forum, Media Studies Center, 13 February.

Goode, M, 1995, "Stalking: Crime of the 90s?", *Criminal Law Journal*, 19: 21-31.

Gorelick, J, 1996, "Statement Before the United States Senate Committee on Governmental Affairs, Permanent Subcommittee on Investigations, 16 July.

Grabosky, P, 1989, "Telephone Tapping by the New South Wales Police", in Grabosky, P, *Wayward Governance: Illegality and its Control in the Public Sector*, Australian Institute of Criminology.

REFERENCES

Grabosky, P, 1995a, "Fear of Crime, and Fear Reduction Strategies", *Current Issues in Criminal Justice*, 7: 7-19.

Grabosky, P, 1995b, "Counterproductive Regulation", *International Journal of the Sociology of Law*, 23: 347-69.

Grabosky, P, 1996, "Unintended Consequences of Crime Prevention", in Homel, R, (ed), *Crime Prevention Studies*, 5: 25-56.

Grant, R, 1984, "Theft of Information", *Law Quarterly Review*, 100: 252-64.

Great Britain, 1957, *Report of the Committee of Privy Councillors appointed to inquire in the Interception of Communications* (Birkett Report), HMSO, London.

Greenleaf, G, 1996a, "Interception on the Internet: The Risks for ISPs", *Privacy Law and Policy Reporter*, 3: 93-4.

Greenleaf, G, 1996b, "Law in Cyberspace: Censoring Cyberspace", *Australian Law Journal*, 70: 33-6.

Griew, E, 1986, "Stealing and Obtaining Bank Credits", *Criminal Law Review*: 356-66.

Hafner, K, and Markoff, J, 1991, *Cyberpunk: Outlaws and Hackers on the Computer Frontier*, Simon and Schuster.

Hansell, S, 1996, "AT&T and Wells Fargo Investing in an Electronic Cash Card", *New York Times*, 19 July: C2.

Hardy, I, 1994, "The Proper Legal Regime for 'Cyberspace' ", *University of Pittsburgh Law Review*, 55: 993-1055.

Harper, I, and Leslie, P, 1994, *Electronic Payments Systems and their Economic Implications*, Working Paper No 7, University of Melbourne, Melbourne Business School.

Harper, I, and Leslie, P, 1995, "Electronic Payments Systems and their Economic Implications", *Policy*, 11: 23-8.

Harris, D, 1995, Interview with General Manager, Telstra Corporate Security, at Melbourne Head Office of Telstra, 12 December.

Hawkins, W, 1716, *A Treatise of the Pleas of the Crown*, 8th edn, 1824, J, Curwood.

Heffernan, R, and Swartwood, D, 1996, *Trends in Intellectual Property Loss Survey*, American Society for Industrial Security: 4, 17.

Hersch, S, 1994, "The Wild East", *The Atlantic Monthly*, 273: 6.

Hiber, N, and Christy, J, 1994, "Understanding the Computer Criminal", *Security Awareness Bulletin*: 13-16.

Higgins, K, 1996, "How Vulnerable is Your Network? A Distributed Network is not Necessarily Safer for Business", *Communications Week*, Issue 599: 43.

Holland, K, 1995, "Bank Fraud, The Old-Fashioned Way", *Business Week*, 4 September: 88.

Hope, The Hon. Mr Justice R, 1977, *Royal Commission on Intelligence and Security: Fourth Report*, 1, AGPS.

Hughes, G, 1990, "Computers, Crime and the Concept of 'Property' ", *Intellectual Property Journal*, 1: 154-63.

Hughes, G, 1991, *Data Protection in Australia*, Law Book Co. Ltd.

Human Rights Watch, 1996, "Silencing the Net: The Threat to Freedom of Expression", *Online Human Rights Watch*, 8: 2 (G).

Hundley, R, and Anderson, R, 1995, "Emerging Challenge: Security and Safety in Cyberspace", *IEEE Technology and Society Magazine*, 14: 19-28.

ICAC (Independent Commission Against Corruption), 1992, *Report on Unauthorised Release of Government Information*, ICAC.

Icove, D, Seger, K, and VonStorch, W, 1995, *Computer Crime: A Crimefighter's Handbook*, O'Reilly and Associates.

Jacobs, M, 1995, "Software May Dry Up Money Laundering", *The Wall Street Journal*, 13 September: B2.

Johnston, C, 1997, "AOL Users In Britain Warned of Surveillance", *International Herald Tribune*, Saturday, 26 April, reprinted in *Computer Underground Digest*, No 9.35, Wednesday, 7 May 1997.

Jones, F, 1996, "No Where to Run . . . No Where to Hide: The Vulnerability of CRTs, CPUs and Peripherals to Tempest Monitoring in the Real World", http://www.thecodex.com/c_tempest.htm.

Jones, M, 1995, "A Code of Conduct", *Internet Australasia*, 1: 22-3.

Kaneshige, T, 1996, "ID Tag Unravels Copyright Puzzle", *Australian*, 20 February: 27.

Kaspersen, H, 1988, "Fraud in Relation to EFT and Telebanking/Teleshopping Systems and Applicability of Criminal Law", in Poullet, Y, and Vandenberghe, G, *Telebanking, Teleshopping and the Law*, Kluwer Law and Taxation Publishers: 133-58.

Kassel, M, and Kassel, J, 1995, "Don't Get Caught in the Net: An Intellectual Property Practitioner's Guide to Using the Internet", *John Marshall Journal of Computer and Information Law*, 13: 373-89.

Kavanagh, J, 1996, "Smart Cards Limber Up as Race to Secure Outlets Begins", *Australian*, 3 July: 26.

Kearney, M, and Papadopoulos, N, 1997, "Anger as Police Track Mobile Phones", *Sydney Morning Herald*, 10 February: 1.

Kelcey, W, 1995, "The Offence Provisions of the Copyright Act 1968: Do They Protect or Punish?", *Australian Intellectual Property Journal*, 6: 229-45.

Kennedy, D, 1996, "Russian Pleads Guilty to Stealing from Citibank Accounts", http://catless.ncl.ac.uk/Risks/17.61.html#subj.

Kertz, C, and Burnette, L, 1992, "Telemarketing Tug-of-War: Balancing Telephone Information Technology and the First Amendment with Consumer Protection and Privacy", *Syracuse Law Review*, 43: 1029-72.

Kessler, R, 1993, *The FBI*, Pocket Books.

Keyes, R, 1993, *Nice Guys Finish Seventh: False Phrases, Spurious Sayings and Familiar Misquotations*, Harper Collins.

Kimery, A, 1996, "Big Brother Want to Look into Your Bank Account (Any Time it Pleases)", http://www.hotwiredcom/wired/1.6/features/big.brother.html.

Kling, R, 1996, "Beyond Outlaws, Hackers and Pirates: Ethical Issues in the Work of Information and Computer Science Professionals", *Computers and Society*, June: 5-15.

La-Vey, D, 1996, "Telephone Encryption: The Neglected Countermeasure", *Intersec*, 6: 395-6.

Lambert, L, (n.d.), "South Asian Underground Banking", http://www.deltanet.com/users/llambert/underground_banking.html.

Lanford, A, and Lanford, J, 1996, "Internet Scam Busters", http://www.infowar.com/class_2/class2_6.html-ssi.

Lanham, D, Weinberg, M, Brown, K, and Ryan, G, 1987, *Criminal Fraud*, Law Book Co. Ltd.

Law Commission, 1988, *Computer Misuse*, Working Paper No 110, HMSO.

Law Reform Commission of Tasmania, 1986, *Computer Misuse*, Government Printer.

Leader-Elliott, I, and Goode, M, 1993, "Trespass, Fraud and the Automated Teller", *Annual Survey of Australian Law*: 221-6.

Leonard, P, 1995, "Should the Law Make Content Providers Content?", *Australian Communications*, July: 57-8.

Levi, M, Bissell, P, and Richardson, T, 1991, *The Prevention of Cheque and Credit Card Fraud*, Home Office Crime Prevention Unit Paper No 26, HMSO.

Levy, S, 1994, "E-Money (That's What I Want)", *Wired*, December: 174-9, 213.

Levy, S, 1996, "Wise Crackers", *Wired*, 4: 128-202.

REFERENCES

Lewis, P, 1995, "The F.B.I. Sting Operation on Child Pornography Raises Questions about Encryption", *The New York Times*, 25 September: D5.

Lewis, T, 1996, "Secure Electronic Transactions", paper presented at Standards Australia, 25 November.

Lieberman, J, 1973, *How the Government Breaks the Law*, Penguin Books Inc.

Long, C, 1995, *Telecommunications Law and Practice*, 2nd edn, Sweet and Maxwell Ltd.

Lyman, S, 1992, "Civil Remedies for the Victims of Computer Viruses" *Computer Law Journal*, 11: 607-35.

Mackrell, N, 1996, "Economic Consequences of Money Laundering", in Graycar, A, and Grabosky, P, (eds), *Money Laundering in the 21st Century: Risks and Counter-measures*, Australian Institute of Criminology: 29-35.

MacLean, R, 1994, "Boeing Hacker Incident", *Security Awareness Bulletin*, 2-94 August: 19-22.

Main, A, and Stretton, R, 1994, "Nigeria Calling", *Australian Financial Review*, 1 August: 47.

Malhotra, A, 1995, "India's Underground Bankers, Asia, Inc." (August), http://www.asia-inc.com/archive/0895bankers.html.

Markoff, J, 1997, "Code Set Up to Shield Privacy of Cellular Calls Is Breached", *New York Times*, 20 March: A1, D2.

Martin, S, 1996, "Controlling Computer Crime in Germany", *Information and Communications Technology Law*, 5: 5-28.

Marx, G, 1987, "The Interweaving of Public and Private Police in Undercover Work", in Shearing, C, and Stenning, P, (eds), *Private Policing*, Sage Publications: 172-93.

Marx, G, 1988, *Undercover: Police Surveillance in America*, University of California Press.

Marx, G, 1992, "Some Reflections on 'Undercover': Recent Developments and Enduring Issues", *Crime, Law and Social Change*, 18: 193-217.

MasterCard, 1996, "MasterCard Cash: A Canberra Success", *Canberra Times*, 24 July: 32.

Masuda, B, 1993, "Credit Card Fraud Prevention: A Successful Retail Strategy", in Clarke, R, (ed), *Crime Prevention Studies*, vol 1, Criminal Justice Press: 121-34.

Masuda, B, 1996, "An Alternative Approach to the Credit Card Fraud Problem", *Security Journal*, 7: 15-21.

McCrae, P, 1996, "The Agony and the Ecstasy of E-Cash", *Australian*, 28 May, Computers: 39.

McGauran, P, 1996, "The Smart Card Industry: Opportunities and Threats", Keynote Address presented at the Policy Network Conference, Smart Cards: The Issues, 18 October.

McIntosh, T, 1996a, "Hollywood to Untangle On-Line Copyright Maze", *The Australian*, 30 April: 49.

McIntosh, T, 1996b, "Software Piracy Costs Industry $200m a year", *The Australian*, 4 June: 43.

McIntosh, T, 1997, "Dial F for Fraud-Busters", *Australian*, 4 February: 48.

McKenzie, H, 1995, "Attack of the Hackers", *Banking Technology*, 12: 20.

McKinley, J, 1995, "US Agents raid Stores in 24 Cities to seize Spy Gear", *New York Times*, 6 April: 1.

Meijboom, A, 1988, "Problems Related to the Use of EFT and Teleshopping Systems by the Consumer", in Poullet, Y, and Vandenberghe, G, *Telebanking, Teleshopping and the Law*, Kluwer Law and Taxation Publishers: 23-32.

Meijboom, A, and Stuurman, C, 1988, "Description of Telebanking Systems", in Poullet, Y, and Vandenberghe, G, *Telebanking, Teleshopping and the Law*, Kluwer Law and Taxation Publishers: 7-16.

Meredith, H, 1996, "E-Mail Messages Total 95 Billion", *Financial Review*, 28 November: 2.

Meyer, M, and Underwood, A, 1994, "Crimes of the Net", *Bulletin/Newsweek*, 15 November: 68-9.

Morello, C, 1996, "Computers Forbidden Fruit for Paroled Hacker", *Salt Lake Tribune*, 15 September, http://www.sltrib.com/96/SEP/15/twr/01254824.htm.

Morfesse, L, 1996, "Telstra Widens Probe", *West Australian*, 12 December: 3.

Morrison, D, 1995, "Cell-Phone Scam: First Court-Approved Tap of E:mail Breaks Up Ring", *Newsday*, 30 December: A03.

Morton, A, 1994, *Diana: Her New Life*, Michael O'Mara Books Ltd.

Nadelmann, E, 1993, *Cops across Borders: The Internationalization of U.S. Criminal Law Enforcement*, Pennsylvania State University Press.

Natarajan, M, Clarke, R, and Belanger, M, 1996, "Drug Dealing and pay Phones: The Scope for Intervention", *Security Journal*, 7: 245-51.

National Counterintelligence Center, 1995, *Annual Report to Congress on Foreign Economic Collection and Industrial Espionage*, July, National Counter-intelligence Center.

National Research Council, 1996, *Cryptography's Role in Securing the Information Society*, National Research Council.

Negroponte, N, 1995, *Being Digital*, Hodder and Stoughton.

Neiger, D, 1996, "Software Theft Can Occur in Many Ways", *Engineers Australia*, May: 22-3.

Nestor Inc, 1996, "Proactive Fraud Risk Management: Neural Network Based Credit Card Fraud Detection from Nestor Inc.", http://www.nestor.com/rmd.htm.

Netlaw, 1996, "FAST Cracking Down on Piracy", http://www.ftech.net/~netlaw/0396e.htm.

Neumann, P, 1995, *Computer-Related Risks*, Addison-Wesley Publishing Company.

New South Wales Police Service, 1996, Planning and Performance Section Statistics, unpublished paper.

Newton, J, 1995, *Organised Plastic Counterfeiting*, HMSO.

Nicholson, E, 1989, "Hacking Away at Liberty", *Times (London)*, 18 April.

O'Neill, J, 1996, "The Great Mobile Phone Rip-Off", *Independent Monthly*, April: 20-5.

O'Toole, G, 1978, *The Private Sector: Private Spies, Rent-A-Cops, and the Police-Industrial Complex*, W. W. Norton and Company Inc.

Oates, S, 1992, "Caller ID: Privacy Protector or Privacy Invader?", *University of Illinois Law Review*: 219.

OECD (Organisation for Economic Co-operation and Development), 1986, *Computer-Related Crime: Analysis of Legal Policy*, OECD.

OECD (Organisation for Economic Co-operation and Development), 1997, *Guidelines for Cryptography Policy*, OECD.

Olson, B, 1994, "Phone Hacking", *Your Computer*, December: 12-13.

Osimiri, U, 1997, "Appraisal of Nigerian Advance Fee Fraud Legislation", *Journal of Financial Crime*, 4: 271-77.

Pacific Bell, 1996, "Pacific Bell LockOn: Toll Fraud Protection Services", http://www.pacbell.com/products/LOCKON/lockon-3.htm.

Paik, H, and Comstock, G, 1994, "The Effects of Television Violence on Antisocial Behaviour: A Meta-Analysis", *Communication Research*, 231: 516-46.

Parker, D, 1983, *Fighting Computer Crime*, Charles Scribner's Sons.

REFERENCES

Peachey, D, and Blau, J, 1995, "Fraud Spreading in Corporate Nets", *Communications Week International*, 16 January: 1.

Pianin, E, and Merida, K, 1997, "Agreement Was Violated, Counsel Says", *Washington Post.Com*, 18 January: A01 http://www.washingtonpost.com/wp-srv/digest/daily/jan/18/agree.htm.

Platt, C, 1996, *Anarchy Online*, Harper Collins.

Post, D, 1995, "Anarchy, State, and the Internet: an Essay on Law-making in Cyberspace", *Journal of ONLINE Law*, art. 3.

PR Newswire, 1996, "Two Ring Leaders of Large Scale Boston Heroin Ring Sentenced on Federal Charges", *Newspage*, Individuals Inc, 13 May.

Price, K, 1996, "Intrusion Detection Pages", http://www.cs.purdue.edu/coast/intrusion-detection/.

Privacy Committee of New South Wales, 1995, *Smart Cards: Big Brother's Little Helpers*, Privacy Committee of New South Wales.

Purton, P, 1994, "Fraudsters Check Card Revolution", *The European*, 8-14 July: 24.

Queensland, Criminal Justice Commission, 1991, *Report on SP Bookmaking and Related Criminal Activities in Queensland*, Criminal Justice Commission.

Queensland, Criminal Justice Commission, 1995, *Telecommunications Interception and Criminal Investigation in Queensland: A Report*, Criminal Justice Commission.

Raine, L, and Cilluffo, F, (eds), 1994, *Global Organised Crime: The New Empire of Evil*, Center for Strategic and International Studies.

Ramirez, A, 1992, "Theft Through Cellular 'Clone' Calls", *New York Times*, 7 April: D1, D27.

Ramo, J, 1996, "Crime Online", *Time Digital*, 23 September: 28-32.

Rawitch, R, 1979, "Expected Bank Plot to Fail", *Los Angeles Times*, 23 February: 1, 27.

Re, D, 1995, "Aspects of Criminal Investigation: Arrest, Search and Seizure, Listening Devices and Telephone Taps", paper presented at a Young Lawyers Section Continuing Legal Education Seminar, 16 August.

Reilhac, G, 1995, "Copyright Clamp-Down", *Forum*, December: 18-19.

Reno, J, 1996, "Law Enforcement in Cyberspace", Address to the Commonwealth Club of California, San Francisco Hilton Hotel, 14 June.

Reserve Bank of New York, 1996, "Fedpoint 43: Fedwire", http://www.ny.frb.org/pihome/fedpoint/fed43.html.

Reuter, P, and Rubenstein, J, 1982, *Illegal Gambling in New York: A Case Study in the Operation, Sructure, and Regulation of an Illegal Market*, National Institute of Justice.

Review Committee, 1996, *Copyright Reform: A Consideration of Rationales, Interests and Objectives*, AGPS.

Ricketson, S, 1996, "The Challenge to Copyright Protection in the Digital Age: An Australian Perspective", paper presented at the Joint Australian/OECD Conference, Security, Privacy and Intellectual Property Protection in the Global Information Infrastructure, 7-8 February.

Ricketson, S, 1984, *The Law of Intellectual Property*, Law Book Co. Ltd.

Ries, I, 1996, "The Telecom Consumer Case", *Financial Review*, 17 September: 52.

Rimm, M, 1995, "Marketing Pornography on the Information Superhighway: A Survey of 917,410 Images, Descriptions, Short Stories, and Animations Downloaded 8.5 Million Times by Consumers in Over 2000 Cities in Forty Countries, Provinces, and Territories", *Georgetown Law Journal*: 1849-935.

Rinaldi, A, 1996, "The Ten Commandments for Computer Ethic from the Computer Ethics Institute", http://www.fau.edu/rinaldi/net/ten.html.

Robinson, J, 1994, *The Laundrymen*, Simon and Schuster.

Russell, D, and Gangemi, G, 1991, *Computer Security Basics*, O'Reilly and Associates.

Samuelson, P, 1996, "The Copyright Grab", *Wired*, 4: 134-8, 188-91.

Schieck, M, 1995, "Combating Fraud in Cable and Telecommunications", *IIC Communications Topics* No 13, International Institute of Communications.

Schwartz, D, 1995, "The Digital Telephony Legislation of 1994: Law Enforcement Hitches a Ride on the Information Superhighway", *Criminal Law Bulletin*, 3: 195-210.

Schweizer, P, 1993, *Friendly Spies*, The Atlantic Monthly Press.

Seline, C, 1990, "Eavesdropping on the Electromagnetic Emanations of Digital Equipment: The Laws of Canada, England and the United States", http://news.janet.ac.uk/newsfiles/janinfo/cert/Seline/tempest.txt.

Sexton, E, 1995, "Fraud Alert", *Bulletin*, 4 July: 76-7.

Sharpe, A, 1989, "Unauthorised Importation of High-Tech Products: Some Recent Developments", *Law Institute Journal*, 63: 496-8.

Sharpe, D, 1996, "Telephony and Computer Crime and Misuse: The Need for Protection and Legislation", paper presented at the Joint Australian/OECD Conference on Security, Privacy and Intellectual Property Protection in the Global Information Infrastructure, 7-8 February, Canberra.

Shenon P, 1995a, "2-Edged Sword: Asian Regimes On the Internet", *New York Times*, 29 May: 1.

Shenon P, 1995b, "World Trade Center Suspect Linked to Plan to Blow Up 2 Planes", *New York Times*, 26 March: 37.

Shiver, J, 1996, "Few Get Smart on the Phone", *The Australian*, 10 December: 44.

Simpson, M, 1995, "Colonising CyberSpace: Life and Law on the Electronic Frontier", *Commonwealth Judicial Journal*, 11: 26-30.

Sims, S, and Sims, R, 1995, "Countering Corporate Misconduct: The Role of Human Resource Management", in Spencer, M, and Sims, R, (eds), *Corporate Misconduct: The Legal, Societal and Management Issues*, Quorum Books, Westport: 183-208.

Smith, R, 1994, *Medical Discipline: The Professional Conduct Jurisdiction of the General Medical Council, 1858-1990*, Clarendon Press.

Smith, R, 1996, *Stealing Telecommunications Services*, Trends and Issues in Crime and Criminal Justice No. 54, Australian Institute of Criminology.

Sneddon, M, 1995, "A Review of the Electronic Funds Transfer Code of Conduct", *Journal of Banking and Finance Law and Practice*, 6: 29-48.

Spafford, E, 1992, "Are Computer Hacker Break-ins Ethical?", *The Journal of Systems and Software*, 17: 41-48.

Spinks, P, 1996, "Tests Show Up Smart Card Flaws", *The Age*, 6 December.

Steffens, C, 1993, "What You Should Know About PBX Security", *Telecommunications: America's Ed*, 27: 53-4.

Sterling, B, 1993, *The Hacker Crackdown: Law and Disorder on the Electronic Frontier*, Viking.

Stewart, The Hon Mr Justice D, 1983, *Report of the Royal Commission of Inquiry into Drug Trafficking*, AGPS.

Stewart, The Hon. Mr Justice D, 1986, *Report of the Royal Commission of Inquiry into Alleged Telephone Interceptions*, AGPS.

Stix, G, 1995, "Fighting Future Wars", *Scientific American*, 273: 74-80.

Stoll, C, 1991, *The Cuckoo's Egg*, Pan Books.

Sulc, L, 1994, "Communicating Cellular Security Needs", *Security Management*, 38: 63-5.

REFERENCES

Sullivan, C, 1987, "Unauthorised Automatic Teller Machine Transactions: Consequences for Customers of Financial Institutions", *Australian Business Law Review*, 15: 187-214.

Sumner, M, 1996, "Ethics Online", *Educom Review*, 31: 32-5.

Sweeney, D, and Williams, N, 1990, *Commonwealth Criminal Law*, Federation Press.

Swisher, K, 1995, "On-Line Child Pornography Charged As 12 Are Arrested", *Washington Post*, 14 September: 1.

Tanaka, T, 1996, "Possible Economic Consequences of Digital Cash", *First Monday*, 5 August, 1.

Telecommunications Industry Ombudsman, 1994, *Annual Report*, Telecommunications Industry Ombudsman.

Telstra, 1996, "Computer and Network Security Reference Index", http://www.telstra. com.au/info/security.html.

Tendler, S, and Nuttall, N, 1996, "Hackers Leave Red-Faced Yard with $1.29m Bill", *Australian*, 6 August: 37.

Thomas, J, 1995, "Copyright in Australia's 'New Communications Environment': Convergence, Transmission Rights and the Internet", *Journal of Law and Information Science*, 6: 3-18.

Thomas, T, 1983, "How Phone Ad Scam Traps Businesses", *Business Review Weekly*, 19 February: 54-61.

Thompson, D, 1996, "Pablo Escobar, Drug Baron: His Surrender, Imprisonment, and Escape", *Studies in Conflict and Terrorism*, 19: 55-91.

Thorogood, R, 1996, *Law Enforcement and Mobile Communications*, Institution of Electrical Engineers.

Thrasher, R, 1994, "Voice-Mail Fraud", *FBI Law Enforcement Bulletin*, 63: 1-4.

Tripp, B. 1995, *Survey of the Counterintelligence Needs of Private Industry*, National Counterintelligence Center and the US Department of State Overseas Security Advisory Council.

Tyree, A, 1990, *Banking Law in Australia*, Butterworths.

Tyree, A, 1996a, "Virtual Cash: Payments on the Internet: Part 1", *Journal of Banking and Finance Law and Practice*, 7: 35-38.

Tyree, A, 1996b, "Computer Money: Legal Considerations", paper presented at the First Australian Computer Money Day, University of Newcastle, 28 March.

Tyree, A, 1997, *Digital Cash*, Butterworths.

United Kingdom, 1972, *Report of the Committee on Privacy* (Cmnd 5012) (Younger Committee) HMSO.

United Kingdom, 1980, *The Interception of Communications in Great Britain* (Cmnd 7873), HMSO.

United Kingdom, 1981, *The Interception of Communications in Great Britain* (Cmnd 8191), HMSO.

United Kingdom, 1985, *The Interception of Communications in the United Kingdom* (Cmnd 9438), HMSO.

United Kingdom, Industry and Government Study Group on Mobile Phone Fraud, 1995, "Briefing Paper on Threats Posed by Mobile Phone Fraud and the Study Group's Subsidiary Recommendations", unpublished paper.

United Kingdom, Parliamentary Office of Science and Technology, 1995, "Mobile Telephone Crime", *Science in Parliament*, 52: 27-30.

United Nations, 1994, "United Nations Manual on the Prevention and Control of Computer-Related Crime", *International Review of Criminal Policy*, nos. 43 and 44, United Nations.

United States Senate, Permanent Subcommittee on Investigations, 1996, Minority Staff Statement, Hearings on Security in Cyberspace, 5 June.

United States, Department of Justice, Bureau of Justice Statistics, 1994, *Sourcebook of Criminal Justice Statistics*, United States Government Printing Office.

United States, General Accounting Office, 1996a, *Information Security: Computer Attacks at Department of Defense Pose Increasing Risks*, GAO/AIMD-96-84, United States Government Printing Office.

United States, General Accounting Office, 1996b, *Money Laundering: A Framework for Understanding United States Efforts Overseas*, Report to the Ranking Minority Member, Committee on Banking and Financial Services, House of Representatives (GAO/GGD-96-015), United States Government Printing Office.

United States, Information Infrastructure Task Force, 1995, *Intellectual Property and the National Information Infrastructure: Report of the Working Group on Intellectual Property Rights*, (Bruce A. Lehman: Chair), US Patent and Trademark Office.

Van Caenegem, W, 1995, "Copyright, Communication and New Technologies", *Federal Law Review*, 23: 322-47.

Van Eck, W, 1985, "Electromagnetic Radiation from Video Display Units: An Eavesdropping Risk", *Computers and Security*, 4: 269-86.

Van-Rhoda, T, 1991, "Credit Card Fraud", *Journal of the Australasian Society of Victimology*, Special Edition, April: 127-9.

Varney, C, 1996, "Regulating Cyberspace: An Off The Record Interview with FTC Commissioner Christine Varney, 22 February, 1996", reprinted in *Computer Underground Digest*, No 8.24, 25 March 1996.

Venditto, G, 1996, "Safe Computing", *Internet World*, September: 48-58.

Venzke, B, 1996, "Economic/Industrial Espionage", *The Boston Globe*, 16 June, http://www.infowar.com/class_2/class_2.html-ssi.

Victoria Police, Statistical Services Division, 1996, *Crime Statistics 1995-96*, Victoria Police.

Vincent, F, 1984, *Review of Matters Affecting the Australian Telecommunications Commission (TELECOM): Report to the Special Minister of State*, AGPS.

Visa International, 1997, "SET Draft Reference Implementation", http://www.visa. com/cgi-bin/vee/sf/set/intro.html?2+0.

Wahlert, G, 1996, "Implications for Law Enforcement of the Move to a Cashless Society", in Graycar, A, and Grabosky, P, (eds), *Money Laundering in the 21st Century: Risks and Countermeasures*, Australian Institute of Criminology: 22-8.

Walker, K, 1994, "Federal Criminal Remedies for the Theft of Intellectual Property", *Hastings Communications and Entertainment Law Journal*, 16: 681-9.

Waller, D, 1995, "Onward Cyber Soldiers", *Time*, 21 August: 38-46.

Wallman, M, 1994, "Perils of the Dial-Up Generation: Regulating Bulletin Boards", *Australian Communications*, June: 55-6.

Walters, D, and Wilkinson, W, 1994, "Wireless Fraud, Now and in the Future: A View of the Problems, Some Solutions", *Mobile Phone News*, 24 October: 4-7.

Wankel, H, 1996, Testimony to the Banking and Financial Committee, United States House of Representatives Hearings on Money Laundering by Drug Trafficking Organisations, 28 February.

Wasik, M, 1991, *Crime and the Computer*, Clarendon Press.

Watson, A, 1997, "The Case For: The Internet is a Secure Place for Conducting Business", *International Journal of Risk, Security and Crime Prevention*, 2: 51-7.

Watts, K, 1995, "Crime and Carrier Punishment: Power of Disconnection", *Australian Communications*, June: 59-60.

Watts, K, and Gilchrist, S, 1996, "Stop the Music: Carriers and Content", *Australian Communications*, February: 49-50.

Webb, B, 1996, "Preventing plastic card fraud in the UK", *Security Journal*, 7: 23-5.

REFERENCES

Weinstock, J, 1996, "Online Stings: High Tech Entrapment or Innovative Law Enforcement?", http://www.law.miami.edu/%7Efroomkin/seminar/papers/weinstock.htm.

Weiss, G, 1996, "The New Grapevine is Online: Amateur Internet Gurus are Moving Stocks in a Big Way", *Business Week*, 27 May, http://www.businessweek.com/1996/22/b3477101.htm.

Whalley, I, 1996, "Virus Defenses for the Future", *Security Management*, November: 46-54.

Whittle, R, 1995, Submission to the Senate Select Committee on Community Standards Relevant to the Supply of Services Utilising Electronic Technologies, Inquiry into the Regulation of Computer OnLine Services. http://www.ozemail.com.au/~firstpr/contreg/ssub1.htm.

Wilding, E, 1997, "Logic Bomber" *International Journal of Forensic Computing*, 3: 7.

Wilkinson, M, and McClymont, K, 1990, "Operation Deceit: The Truth Behind the Bond Bugging", *Sydney Morning Herald*, 21 April: 65 and 71.

Williams, C, and Weinberg, M, 1986, *Property Offences*, 2nd edn, Law Book Co. Ltd.

Williams, G, 1983, *Textbook of Criminal Law*, 2nd edn, Stevens & Sons.

Williams, The Hon Mr Justice E, S, 1980, *Report of the Royal Commission of Inquiry into Drugs*, AGPS.

Wodetzki, J, 1996, "A Stronger Copyright: Death of the Public Domain?", *National Library of Australia News*, 6: 11-13.

Wolfe, H, 1995, "An Important Reminder (Anti-Surveillance Measures)", *Computer Fraud and Security Bulletin*, April: 16-18.

Wong, K, 1995a, "Fighting Mobile Phone Fraud: Who Is Winning? Part 1", *Computer Fraud and Security Bulletin*, January: 9-16.

Wong, K, 1995b, "Fighting Mobile Phone Fraud: Part 2", *Computer Fraud and Security Bulletin*, February: 10-14.

Wood, The Hon. Justice J, 1996, *Royal Commission into the New South Wales Police Service: Interim Report*, Government Printer.

World Intellectual Property Organization, Diplomatic Conference on Certain Copyright and Neighboring Rights Questions, 1996, "Copyright Treaty", World Intellectual Property Organization, Geneva, http://www.wipo.org/eng/diplconf/distrib/94dc.htm.

Wrightson, G, and Furche, A, (forthcoming), "Central Bank Control of Computer Cash", Department of Computer Science, University of Newcastle.

Young, T, 1995, "Wireless Bandits", *Police*, May: 32-5.

Index